What Does It Mean to 'Make' Love?

What Does It Mean to 'Make' Love? shows how the choice of gender does not conform to anatomy and is based on an often unrecognised psychic bisexuality.

Everyone chooses a gender by repressing another gender, which becomes the site of both an attraction and a conflict, a 'war of the sexes', the contingencies of which animate desire. Gérard Pommier explores phantasy, desire and perversion and their role in 'sexual machinery', before considering the question of orgasm. Pommier's work demonstrates that the analysis of orgasm brings out a political dimension and that aspects of both social and personal life are illuminated by the study of how we think – consciously and unconsciously – about orgasm and the role we ascribe to it.

This book makes valuable contributions to the study of sexuality and will be of interest to all psychoanalysts and students of psychoanalysis, as well as those in the fields of gender studies, anthropology and psychology.

Gérard Pommier (1941–2023) was a psychiatrist and psychoanalyst. He was Professor of Psychopathology at the University of Strasbourg, director of the journal *La clinique lacanienne* and co-founder of the European Foundation for Psychoanalysis.

The Centre for Freudian Analysis and Research Library

Series Editors: Anouchka Grose, Darian Leader, Kristina Valendinova

CFAR was founded in 1985 with the aim of developing Freudian and Lacanian psychoanalysis in the UK. Lacan's rereading and rethinking of Freud had been neglected in the Anglophone world, despite its important implications for the theory and practice of psychoanalysis. Today, this situation is changing, with a lively culture of training groups, seminars, conferences, and publications.

CFAR offers both introductory and advanced courses in psychoanalysis, as well as a clinical training programme in Lacanian psychoanalysis. It can provide access to Lacanian psychoanalysts working in the UK and has links with Lacanian groups across the world. The CFAR Library aims to make classic Lacanian texts available in English for the first time, as well as publishing original research in the Lacanian field.

Treating Autism Today
Lacanian Perspectives
Edited by Laura Tarsia and Kristina Valendinova

Critique of Psychoanalytic Reason
Studies in Lacanian Theory and Practice
Dany Nobus

What Can We Know About Sex?
A Lacanian Study of Sex and Gender
Gisèle Chaboudez

What Does It Mean to 'Make' Love?
A Psychoanalytic Study of Sexuality and Phantasy
Gérard Pommier

www.cfar.org.uk

https://www.routledge.com/The-Centre-for-Freudian-Analysis-and-Research-Library/book-series/KARNACCFARL

What Does It Mean to 'Make' Love?

A Psychoanalytic Study of Sexuality and Phantasy

Gérard Pommier

Translated by Ben Hooson

Routledge
Taylor & Francis Group

LONDON AND NEW YORK

Designed cover image: Getty | 1001nights

First published in English 2025
by Routledge
4 Park Square, Milton Park, Abingdon, Oxon OX14 4RN

and by Routledge
605 Third Avenue, New York, NY 10158

Routledge is an imprint of the Taylor & Francis Group, an informa business

Translated from the French by Ben Hooson. Original title: *Que veut
dire «faire» l'amour?* © Flammarion, Paris, 2010.

British Library Cataloguing-in-Publication Data
A catalogue record for this book is available from the British Library

ISBN: 978-1-032-85659-9 (hbk)
ISBN: 978-1-032-85658-2 (pbk)
ISBN: 978-1-003-51928-7 (ebk)

DOI: 10.4324/9781003519287

Typeset in Times New Roman
by Apex CoVantage, LLC

Contents

Translator's preface

This is a book about human sexuality in a psychoanalytic perspective, from the Oedipus complex to the castration complex, the bisexuality of human beings, choice of gender (distinct from anatomical sex), choice of object, psychosexual saliencies – perversion, frigidity, etc. – and the phenomenon of orgasm.

To dwell for long inside any of these topics would require a book in itself. Instead, Gérard Pommier traces a polemical path through each of them in an ambitious attempt to find an underlying mechanism. He starts from the concept of the drive (German 'Trieb', badly translated as 'instinct' in the *Standard Edition* of Freud's works in English), which Freud described in a dedicated metapsychological paper as 'the psychical representative of the stimuli originating from within the organism'[1] as opposed to those originating from outside.

We might put a motto over the entrance to Pommier's book, taken from the same paper by Freud: 'Every drive is a piece of activity; if we speak loosely of passive drives' – Freud had in mind masochism, exhibitionism and, perhaps, femininity – 'we can only mean drives whose aim is passive'.[2] The author extracts a corollary from this: if the drive is by nature activity, it ought to be *somebody's* activity. His book is about how that somebody keeps their head above the floodwaters of their own drive energy.

Pommier disregards Freud's half-hearted distinction between self-preservative and sexual drives (between hunger and love),[3] following Jacques Lacan, who moored all of the drives to sex via his concept of the object *a*. Pommier, who was in analysis with the best-known French Freudian and was a member of his school until its dissolution, writes in a Lacanian spirit but is very sparing of Lacanian terminology – the object *a* is not mentioned by name, there are no mathemes and occurrences of the word 'signifier' in the pages that follow can be counted on the fingers of one hand. This last omission is striking: whether Pommier can handle his subject matter in a Lacanian spirit without the master's use of linguistics is a question I will return to.

The initial goal of the drive, according to Pommier, is as follows:

the transformation of the psychical body into the maternal phallus, an enterprise so impossible that all of the subject's energy is used to break free from it, with 'escape' the only aim. And what is the best recipe for ceasing to be the phallus if not to have the phallus? That requires the passage from an external erogenisation to a self-erotisation, by applying oneself to one's own body as if to an external object.

So Pommier takes libidinal investment of the penis or clitoris and masturbation to be the child's first expedient against drowning in the drive, which pulls almost irresistibly towards acquiescence in the mother's urge to make her child into the phallus that she lacks.

However, refusal to be the mother's phallus engenders in the child a guilty anxiety that can only be assuaged by punishment, a punishment which is perceived (hopefully only in fantasy) as being inflicted by the father. A further complication then ensues: the 'blows' perceived as directed by the father at the child's genitals (Freud's castration threat) are felt by children of both sexes as arousing, whence, a drift towards passive enjoyment – a fantasy of seduction and feminisation at the hands of the father. Pommier contrasts the traditional account with his own account of what occurs, calling them, respectively, 'nice' and 'not-so-nice' versions of the Oedipus complex:

> The nice version of the Oedipus complex condenses and greatly simplifies this process: it seems as if the father castrates in order to punish the son's desire for the mother. But this loses sight of the genesis of the complex and makes the erectile moment of desire opaque: castration appears to be an emasculation, whereas, in fact, it arouses to the point of erection.

Pommier's first thought is that the mother was never 'genitally' desired: 'She was, is and will be this Thing of the drive, the Thing towards which we gravitate but always eludes us'. This idea, and its casting in terms of the Thing (Freud's *das Ding*), is eminently Lacanian. But the role which he ascribes to the father bears Pommier's own stamp. He writes:

> Desire is not born because the mother has been 'forbidden' by the father. [. . .] The point is that this father himself becomes the hidden cause of arousal, or rather he would be, if he were not immediately doomed to parricide.

The parricide is what makes this account of the Oedipal process 'not so nice', although it is, of course, only a fantasy parricide. Pommier takes it to be the third and last in a series of fundamental fantasies that slip into the unconscious and, from there, define our sexual constitution, the first two being the 'beaten child' (the first step in the not-so-nice Oedipus, referencing a paper by Freud)[4] and seduction by the father (the second step).

Pommier's theory is striking by its double rejection, first of the mother (refusal to be her phallus) and then of the father (the fantasised parricide). We might wonder how these rejections are related to the crucial phenomenon of early childhood that

Freud called 'primal repression'.[5] Is the latter not a single event and, therefore, quite different from what Pommier describes? Perhaps not, at least not in the Lacanian version, which theorises the first repression using two related concepts that he calls 'alienation' and 'separation'.[6] Both concepts are linguistic through and through. As noted earlier, Pommier is remarkably light on linguistics, but if we marry his double rejection with Lacan's two concepts, something interesting emerges.

In alienation, *à la Lacan* language as a system of mutually defining elements (signifiers), each of which exists solely by its difference from all the others (a notion that, he says, the human mind can never fully grasp due to 'a certain incapacity of your thinking'),[7] is acquired from the principal caregiver, usually the mother. For Lacan, this is a 'signifier identification'; the child's emerging subjectivity is identical with the acquired language system, which in a way replaces the maternal-object (the 'Thing'). He calls it 'alienation' because the dependence of each signifier for its being on all the other signifiers entails that the emerging subjectivity is constantly alienated in otherness. Is this not precisely Pommier's 'escape' from being the mother's phallus? The pressure of the drive towards fusion with the mother (offering completeness to the maternal-object by being its phallus) is thwarted, albeit at the cost of a constant flight, which is alienation.

But the escape is by no means conclusive since the child's subjectivity remains within the closed language system that has assumed the role of the maternal object. What Lacan calls 'separation' takes the next step. It is the act by which the emerging subject acknowledges the alienation inherent to the language system (the unthinkable dependence of each element on all the others for its very existence) and thereby rises above it, ceasing to be its plaything. This may sound metaphysical, but Freud's description in the *Project* of the birth of the ego-subject by 'withdrawal' (*Entziehung*) from an association between elements proves at least that separation is not just Lacan's myth.[8]

A good way of understanding separation is as negation of negation – a rejection of the negativity inherent to alienation, where each element *is* solely by *not* being the others.[9] If we then ask where the child finds the strength to carry out separation – this conclusive break with the maternal object – it must be in a perceived limitation on the all-power of the mother, a paternal limitation, therefore, in the broadest sense (coming perhaps from a flesh-and-blood father but just as well from some other relative or perhaps from circumstances).

My idea, then, is to say that Pommier's three fantasies linked to the father (beating, seduction, parricide) are equivalent to Lacanian separation, following on from the proposed equivalence between Lacanian alienation and the child's refusal, which Pommier describes, to be the mother's phallus. Why are these equivalences plausible? After all, the three-to-one equivalence between the three fantasies and separation appears particularly *implausible* – confusing even. But the value we get from reading Lacan through Pommier is precisely a certain 'confusion' because, looked at closely, it is not at all clear how the things he shows us happening between child and mother are distinct from what he shows us between child and father. In particular, how plausible is it that fantasies of punishment and seduction by and reactive murder of the father would not attach equally to the (supposedly earlier) interaction with the mother? Is her urge to make the child into her phallus not a seduction, and is the child's refusal to acquiesce not in some sense a murder?

By 'putting a human face' on the linguistic and rather abstract frameworks of alienation and separation, Pommier implies their probable interpenetration and the misguidedness of trying to keep them separate in time. This is surely true to the spirit of Lacan's approach, as when he speaks approvingly of Melanie Klein's readiness to find Oedipal phenomena already at work in the immediate neonatal phase.[10]

The interpenetration of stages is particularly clear in Pommier's abundant discussion of the role of a person's name in their psychosexual development (as I already mentioned, the text has just five uses of the word 'signifier', but it has 350 uses of the word 'name'). He writes:

A mother who pressures her child to eat, but calls the child by its first name as she does so, gives the child a means of resisting her at the same time as the order to eat seeks the opposite. The subject can oppose the injunctions by identifying with the given name. [. . .] It makes it possible to take advantage of one's own drive body in the same way that the Other takes advantage of it.

The mother's acceptance of the child's refusal to be her phallus, expressed by her use of the child's first name even as she tries to obtain its submission, closely parallels Pommier's much more extensive discussion of how the child obtains the father's surname with all the crucial consequences for subjectivity that Lacan attributes to the 'name of the father'. As Pommier tells us, the child can assume the name and, thereby, obtain a space for its own subjectivity just to the extent that the father acquiesces in the fantasised parricide that is directed against him. Is that not exactly what the mother does when she sets aside the struggle for supremacy (to make the child into her phallus) and lets the child have its name?

Pommier applies the logic I have discussed in order to lead the reader through choice of gender, transgenderism, homosexuality, femininity, perversion and the fundamental fantasies in his first seven chapters before (*sit venia verbo*) reaching orgasm, which takes up the last third of the book, honouring the promise of its title. The 'gift of the name' is the crux of these perhaps most intriguing chapters of the book, where Pommier deals with the phenomenon of orgasm as the perfect instantiation of Lacan's maxim – 'the gift of what one does not have', where what is given with the name is desire (a lack) and the giving itself is love.

My thanks to Darian Leader for editing the translation in the sensitive way that translators always need but very rarely get.

Ben Hooson

Introduction

Popular wisdom tells us to 'make love, not war'. If making war implies an intention and a resolve, why do we say 'make' love, when the truth is rather that love makes us? Love is stronger than our will. We are driven by a force more powerful than ourselves – a bit more or a lot more but always as if we don't have much of a say in the matter. Love imposes itself with or without our body's consent. Modern English is sparing with the expression 'to make love'. It prefers 'to have sex', love being supernumerary to copulation. And 'to have sex' draws attention to a truth: we only have (a) sex (organ) – in a state of excitement – at the moment of desire. This possession is relative, improbable except at these moments. It is perhaps true that we 'have (a) sex (organ)', but we need to somehow own it and in circumstances that largely escape us. We are at the mercy of situations where love makes itself by making – or unmaking – us.

'Make' is one of those modest, abundant, generous words, with an aristocratic pedigree and sovereign lineage we forget: a subject must first be born, a subject that begins by making itself through speech, after which its action seems natural, oblivious of this verbal antecedence. The subject is first master of its cry and later of its speech. Then the person will begin to 'make' like a virtuoso: anger, excrement, toys, tools, children . . . and love. This making is akin to the fetish, the factitious, craftsmanship, business pursuits, etc. And we, all of us, advance along these frontiers: strategists, poets, inventors, fetishists, philosophers, lovers, fathers, mothers, etc. Along this limit, on the edge of being overwhelmed, we make our factitious world that did not exist before. Even a simple perception has to be 'made': it requires an act without which it does not reach consciousness (with all due respect to Kant). To make is to transform, even from nothing. We construct a dream from nothing. We fashion a fetish from whatever was to hand at the empty but crucial hour of dread.

And humans themselves – who made them? God created 'man' in his own image, the Bible tells us. But God has no image. Humans, on the other hand, create things that give them an image. The making of things, similarly, produces the body and gives it its finish: the created thing becomes a mirror of its creator. We are reflected in our objects. Who were we before we saw ourselves in them? We fashion them blind, and sight comes to us as we create.

And we can surely all agree that love makes the lover by growing inside them. Loving is making long before the sexual overflow that relieves it. There is a plurality of possible loves: one can love milk, music or somebody. The verb 'to love' is ubiquitous, and we use it from jam to the passion of lovers who need little beyond love itself to subsist on. The libido is interactive, metamorphosing as it encounters limits and obstacles. A multiplicity of loves coexists. Filial love differs from the loves of childhood, which are already exogamous and embarked on the delights of autoerotism for two. And sexual love establishes yet another regime, magnified by art and literature. Each of these loves has a transitive aim. The love of parents relives through their children their own childhood struggle against incest, so it is a love that represses sexuality rather than a desexualised love. Following this first divorce between love and erotism, sexual love searches endlessly to reconcile them, helped by the swirl of fantasies. Between these two extremes – marked by desexualisation and sexualisation – Eros presents a multiplicity of faces, from platonic love to pornographic obsession, not forgetting the middle way: the resurgence of childhood in neurosis, which doggedly keeps desire and love apart.

Sexual love is 'made' through a subtle modelling, like other human undertakings that involve taking, giving or exchanging. The 'making' of love varies according to the lovers or according to the particular moment between the same lovers, who are always exceeded by what they share. A specific making is crystallised by the particular effects that a lover inspires: erotism, far from being solitary, clearly depends on another making, which can be more or less enterprising, more or less resistant. It opens up a world beyond masturbation. What is specific to love is not specific to any organ. The body only knows pleasure thanks to another body, and without the fantasies in which the body is caught, enjoyment[11] is interrupted. The same bodies know or do not know how to enjoy together, depending on circumstances that may have sexual arousal as their result. And where do those bodies get such knowledge from if not from speech that may come from another place and that finds its echo at that moment?[12]

To make love is, before all else, to say something, and etymology[13] gives a glimpse of this kinship between the sexual act, which aims to possess a body, and speech, which pays court and declares its passion. By the magic of words, the old Provençal expression 'far amor ad alcun' (12th century) meant only 'to court', and that meaning lingered until the 18th century. The carnal meaning of 'to make love' is only found from 1622 and did not become dominant until the 19th century. The history of language tells us even more because it also carries within it the struggle between masculine and feminine, which is both the condition of and what is at stake in the 'making' of love: in modern French, almost uniquely, the noun 'amour' ('love'), although masculine in most uses, can also be feminine. It is transgender, contrary to 'désir' ('desire'), which is masculine only. From the 10th until the 17th century, 'amor' was mainly used in the feminine, so its predominantly masculine use came late. It long retained the same meaning as 'friendship', until the influence of the Occitan language gradually inflected it towards sexual passion, while, by a contrary process, friendship was detached from its erotic connotations. This inflection owes much to medieval conceptions of the courtly universe, the 'fine amor' that was idealised at the same time as sexuality. Men sang of the beloved woman, who was both desired and sublimated.

We might venture a hypothesis on the double gender of 'love' in French based on this enchantment with the feminine, which lasted several centuries and had profound links with the Christian conception of the woman (so virginally embodied by Mary). Love is addressed to the woman, so it bears the gender of its object – it is feminine. A beloved woman is 'une amour' ('a love'). But this idealised woman is loved by a man. He is the subject of an active love, which, following this sense, will be expressed in the masculine. From the end of the 12th century, 'amour' designates the person who is loved primarily in the feminine, which is the gender of the virginal woman, the object of courtly love. The masculine does not appear until later, in 1671, in reference to the act and even to possession, in the expression 'mon amour' ('my love'). Both active and passive, 'amour' acknowledges through this transition the power of bisexuality.

So a love that was initially declined in the feminine follows the path of enjoyment, which is never realised so well as when it coincides with the enjoyment of the partner. The man enjoys by proxy, but in a sense, 'no one 'enjoys in this pure transition due precisely to the depersonalising division created by orgasm. The woman also loves this proxy person: she may experience orgasm as if it happened to someone else. And if love addresses itself in this way to women, it should have kept its feminine gender. But both men and women prefer to be the agents in love. The act of loving is virile. The man feels love for a woman, and the gender of his feeling rubs off on its object. To be loved as a woman, in contrast, is situated almost in another world. Because who is loved in this idealised woman? God alone knows! The masculine gender has thus taken possession of the word 'love'. It has credited[14] the word to its own account.

Notes

1 Freud, *Instincts and Their Vicissitudes* in *Standard Edition 14*, p. 121.
2 *Ibid.*, p. 122.
3 In *Instincts and Vicissitudes* and earlier, in *On Narcissism*, Freud sketches the distinction but leaves the door open to its retraction (*Ibid.*, pp. 78–79, 124–125).
4 Freud, *A Child is Being Beaten* in *Standard Edition 17*, pp. 175–204.
5 See, for example, the description in *Repression* (*Standard Edition 14*, p. 148).
6 Jacques Lacan, *The Four Fundamental Concepts of Psychoanalysis* (J-A. Miller, ed., A. Sheridan, trans.). London: Hogarth Press, 1977, pp. 203–215.
7 *Ibid.*, p. 209 (I amend Sheridan's 'a certain impotence in your thinking').
8 Freud, *Project for a Scientific Enquiry* in *Standard Edition 1*, p. 369, footnote 3.
9 This negation of negation has Hegelian resonances, which are not accidental. Consider the intricacies, which Slavoj Žižek traces as he argues for the Lacanian and linguistic nature of Hegel's thesis-antithesis-synthesis, which is just the negation of a negation (Slavoj Žižek, *The Most Sublime Hysteric*. Cambridge: Polity Press, 2014).
10 Jacques Lacan, *The Object Relation* (J-A. Miller, ed., A. Price, trans.). Cambridge: Polity Press, 2020, pp. 104–105.

11 Here and everywhere, I translate 'jouissance' as 'enjoyment'. See also footnote 4 to Chapter 8, later (translator's note).

12 Virgil's Dido says when she sets eyes on Aeneas: 'Agnosco veteris vestigia flammae' ('I recognise the signs of the old flame' (Virgil, *Aeneid* (R. Fizgerald, trans.). New York: Random House, 1983, Book 4, line 31)).

13 Amour, *Dictionnaire historique de la langue française* (A. Rey, ed.). Paris: Le Robert, 2010.

14 The French word is 'viré' resonating with 'virile' (translator's note).

Chapter 1

On the metamorphic principle of bodies

In Chapter 3 of *The Interpretation of Dreams*, Freud comments on a dream of his 2-year-old daughter, Anna. On the day before the dream, she had not been allowed to eat strawberries due to an upset stomach. At night, in her sleep, she protested: 'Anna Freud: strawberries, big strawberries!'[1] This oneiric wish fulfilment has two surprising grammatical features. Firstly, Anna speaks of herself in the third person, as if objectified by the prohibition that was issued to her. She does not say 'I' but refers to herself by her name. Alienation objectifies her, and she (as subject) maintains a distance from her own manufactured ego. What is more, she does not say, 'Anna Freud wants strawberries' or 'Anna Freud eats strawberries' but 'Anna Freud: strawberries, big strawberries!' By doing so, she identifies with the objects she covets. The subject is first reduced to a third person and is then identified with the strawberries that it desires. The subject is depersonalised in the strawberries, which it devours and which thus come alive in the subject's place. The object here can cancel out the subject, which is dissolved in jam, music or sport – starved to the point of being swallowed by its own teeth. Similarly, young people nowadays often express their tastes by identifying with the object of those tastes. They say, 'I'm really Coca-Cola' instead of 'I like Coca-Cola'. Or even 'I'm more chocolate than coffee for breakfast', etc. So they lose themselves in their chosen object. They fall into what they consume and plunge into a bulimic spiral since what have they become after they have eaten? They are chocolate. The hell of a drive-based devouring of oneself has opened up!

Is this consumption of the body specifically postmodern? Not really. It was already described by Dante. Remember how the gate of hell opens in the first canto onto the mouths of menacing beasts (panther, lion and wolf) and the first sentences that pass between the pilgrim hero and Virgil, his guide, describe a spiral of endless devouring: 'See the beast that forced me to turn back', which 'after she feeds is hungrier than ever'.[2] This reflexive consumption of a body is the infinity of hell. The poet describes here something very characteristic of the relationship we have to the object that we eat and that eats us. Similarly, certain anorexic infants refuse food from the moment they are born, preferring physical death to mental annihilation.

DOI: 10.4324/9781003519287-1

Is there an alternative to this *crash* into the drive object? There is because although every child refuses food at one time or another, they avert mental death when they are acknowledged in their right to say 'No'. This happens when the mother, who initially is nothing but a force-feeding Other, recognises the infant as a subject who refuses. When the infant cries and refuses, its subjectivity is affirmed no matter what is being refused. And this negativist subjectivity is pacified when it is recognised by another subjectivity, notably that of the mother when she speaks to her child. The drive character of crying is subjectivised in speech: love transforms the sound of crying into the meaning of words. This love, which is specific to a mutual recognition between mother and child, tempers the annihilation of self-devouring. By being recognised as a subject – and not simply as an organism with needs – by another subject, the infant escapes its strawberry-being or its chocolate-nothingness. Starved on its own territory, launched on the conquest of another body, the drive wants to seize an object but encounters a subject whose resistance generates love. The subject camps in this fortress where it refuses to simply be the object of the Other. The drive becomes unrecognisable behind the mask of love. It was cannibalistic, but now its bites come back as kisses.

What is the distinguishing mark of the drive? It can never be satisfied, and the principle of the drive is metamorphosis. Under the sway of the drive, the furious body aspires to mutate, to materialise what it initially was, namely, a dream.[3] The body, ever fleeing from itself, refuses to embody maternal demand. Rather than be the mother's incestuous thing, it prefers to engage with things, to manipulate, transform or destroy them. What lightning strike could relieve the body of its excess, as if there was an absolute need to transform this cumbersome mass of flesh, always a burden to itself, an object to be dragged around for its own sake? To 'make' is to leave behind our status of object, to forget the self through action and, in this amnesia, to be project oneself into what is created. The body saves itself by identifying with what it loves; it is transformed and grows thanks to its chosen objects.

Prior to love, the subject of the drive projects itself wherever its sensations go: it is a wanderer, an explorer of the infinite – our first dimension. We still resemble it when we follow our daydreams; when, for example, faced with a beautiful landscape, we are borne far away from ourselves by our perceptions, hobnobbing with the clouds, the mountains, the grass, the leaves – brothers and sisters of the infinite. This subject of the drive projects us towards a loss of the body; it aspires to nothingness. In this shimmering world, the subject is like a chameleon overcome by an infinity of colours, all of which it finds pleasing and which could absorb it.

The love of a particular person puts an end to this infinite expansion of the body in the universe of things. It calls time on this limitless effusion and offers a bodily lodging for subjectivity. The same power, at play in the hell of addiction and the fires of love, undergoes a transformation. It leaves behind this hell of the drive but only to enter at once into its own hell. Because what does this subject resemble now after escaping from its strawberries? It no longer resembles anything; all that it can do is to love the Other subject, the Other which took it out of the strawberry comfort zone that the same Other had initially given it. The person who is loved is loved freely, in empty space, without any why. It is impossible to give a reason for this love because what causes it is what the subject forgets when the subject first emerges, namely, the repression of the drive. Love offers itself 'without a cause'; it erases its footsteps as it advances, *sui generis*, born of itself and without any future other than itself. It tolerates no 'why' or 'because'; it resists both capture and flight and leaves us helpless. So it opens the door to its own hell, as Dante wrote in the same canto of *Inferno*. The poet escapes the devouring monsters only to find Beatrice, his lost love, of whom he will write elsewhere that he loves her only because he is lost. The *amor amandi* of St. Augustine.

No sooner is the flame of love lit than its relation to loss becomes evident since the subject is recognised (loved) at the cost of the drive, which is thereby repressed and effectively lost. Later on, this link between love and loss becomes more complex. The loved person stands for the loss, without the lover knowing what the loss is of. This fatality remains present in the amorous encounter as a suffering that is latent in happiness. It at once sets to work on the subject, which it has freed from the morass that threatened to engulf it in a scent of strawberries or the taste of chocolate. As Virgil says to Beatrice in the *Divine Comedy*: 'O lady of such virtue that by it alone the human race surpasses all that lies within the smallest compass of the heavens!'[4] By the grace of love, the human species goes beyond its reification, its oblivion in objectification; it escapes from 'what Is'. This is the relief that Beatrice brings to Dante by sending Virgil to rescue him from the beast that had 'forced him to turn back'. Love offers separation from objects but it also allows separation from the one who is doing the separating because the beloved could also be a consumable object; they could be another reason to be reduced to that object. But that is exactly what does not happen: love separates, it hollows out the lack of the very person who provokes it. The beloved creates a lack even when they are present.

By the grace of the beloved – as they resist the lover – the subject ceases to soar into the infinity of sensations. The subject, in a way, comes back to itself and gathers itself together again. The world changes direction, suspends its glittering, its call to nothingness. Eros, in its entirety, puts Thanatos under its yoke. So love becomes the field of a confrontation, an arena in which two subjects have come together and look at each other. It is and is not a combat because the drive retains its right to devour. I love you; I eat you. Does love not always create its own dramas, without which it wanes? For so long as it renews its drama, love delimits the menacing space that the subject inhabits.

We might compare this with what happens in a bullfight, when the bull thunders out onto the sand. Certainly, neither of the two lovers is the beast, and the other is not the bullfighter. Each of them confronts their own monster, that of the infinity of the drive. Each lover struggles against their own demons. In like fashion, is it not in the name of its solitude, of its sovereignty, that the bull bears down on the intruding matador? Luis Miguel Dominguin said: 'Death is like a square metre that skates about in the arena. The bullfighter must not step on it when the bull charges him, but no one knows where this square metre is'.[5] By the grace of love, the lover finds their space outside this square metre, and their infinite wandering turns into singular torment. What is this single square metre in love if not the singularity that each lover confronts in a collision that may prove their undoing?

Love invests the loved one's body so entirely that it sucks the lover into it. The multiple, delicate pseudopodia of love construct each psychic body. Each drive balances its impossibility thanks to the reversal of love, which anesthetises the zest of the drive for the infinite. The importance of a particular love may only be recognised when it is mourned, when its drive pseudopodia retract and are desubjectivised. We then realise the extent to which the body of the other was our own.[6] But this magnetisation alone does not trigger sexual excitement; there are loves without erotism, when love only asks for a love that can maintain it. But sexual excitement knows how to use love as a pretext to ignite. Love separates, creates a distance, which desire then seeks to fill. So the lack inherent to love activates the sexual machinery. In reality, love, eroticised or not, never stays still. Based on lack, its position is precarious, and it has to keep moving. Its metamorphic principle advances across the thresholds of age, from child to teenager, then towards what passes for maturity, always already forged by the dreams of childhood. Love forces one's hand and governs the mutations of a body which, without it, would vanish.

This happens because there is a forced choice to be made at each moment. In thrall to the same fire of the drive, the body must grow and make itself by *making*: make itself in its objects, in what it manufactures and make itself in love. There is a double dislocation here: first of all, making the self using objects, then subjectivising this making in love. This double destiny was first described in a Greek myth: the myth of Prometheus, who stole lightning from heaven and used it to begin the conquest of objects, which could be endlessly manufactured and exchanged. He had brought men fire, the symbol of progress. We know what happened next: Zeus took his revenge, and the same fire, the master of forges and factories, underwent another metamorphosis, into Woman. The love of things and the love of women unwrap their destinies from out of the same lightning flash. Every myth exists in several versions. In the best-known version of the Prometheus myth, described by Aeschylus, the fire thief is chained by Zeus to a mountaintop, where an eagle returns daily to peck out his liver,[7] a torture that is offset by the glory of being the rebellious initiator of civilisation. This version of the myth has prospered as each passing age highlights the parts best suited to itself.[8]

But long before Aeschylus, Hesiod, the poet-contemporary of Homer, had recounted the myth of Prometheus in his *Theogony* and *Works and Days*. He was less interested in humanity's progress, made possible by the gift of fire, than in that second transformation of lightning, into love, the flash of which creates the most radical mutation of the body. In Hesiod, the lightning metamorphoses not into a single woman (Pandora in other versions) but into the generality of women, who fall like lightning among men and bring to them desire and the sickness of desire. Zeus wreaks vengeance not on Prometheus alone but on all mankind, beneficiaries of the stolen lightning. In the *Theogony*, Zeus in his fury has a female statue of implacable beauty and infinite charm modelled in clay. The lightning and its civilising blessings are metamorphosed into this maleficent grace:

> But when he had made the beautiful evil to be the price for the blessing, he brought her out, delighting in the finery which the bright-eyed daughter of a mighty father had given her, to the place where the other gods and men were. And wonder took hold of the deathless gods and mortal men when they saw that which was sheer guile, not to be withstood by men. For from her is the race of women and female kind: of her is the deadly race and tribe of women who live amongst mortal men to their great trouble. [. . .] Even so Zeus who thunders on high made women to be an evil to mortal men, with a nature to do evil. [. . .] And as for the man who chooses the lot of marriage and takes a good wife suited to his mind, evil continually contends with good; for whoever happens to have mischievous children, lives always with unceasing grief in his spirit and heart within him.[9]

More expeditious, the version in *Works and Days* makes Zeus say: 'But I will give men as the price for fire an evil thing in which they may all be glad of heart while they embrace their own destruction'.[10] The woman strikes like lightning, and the afflicted body is transformed to the point of forgetting its own pain because the sufferings of love – that innocently created lack – offer refuge from the annihilation threatened by the drive, from ineluctable fragmentation. For Hesiod, it is Woman – rather than the sexual partner, rather than the partner of discourse, rather than the protagonist of love – who embodies this lightning strike. If a man wanted to play this role, he would have to dress up as a woman, to resemble Pandora, 'delighting in finery', made up and sparkling in the jewels of a god.

Notes

1 Freud [1900], *The Interpretation of Dreams* in *Standard Edition 4*, p. 130.
2 Dante, *Inferno* (R. & G. Hollander, trans.). New York: Anchor Books, 2002, Canto I, lines 88, 99.
3 Transplants, genome decoding, cosmetic surgery or the intrusion of metal into the flesh (piercing) colonise the organism with the hardness of a dream body, according to the ideal of a psychical body reconciled with the organism.
4 Dante, *op. cit.*, Canto II, lines 76–78.
5 François Zumbiehl, *Des taureaux dans la tête*. Paris: Autrement, 1987.
6 Freud [1917], *Mourning and Melancholia* in *Standard Edition 14*, pp. 237–258.
7 But he is said to have been finally forgiven by Zeus in the two lost plays by Aeschylus, *Prometheus Delivered* and *Prometheus the Bringer of Fire*.
8 Schlegel, Shelley and Gide shifted the emphasis onto the revolt against fate, the mastery of matter and even denial of the gods (an atheism that has little connection with the Greek spirit).
9 Hesiod, 'Theogony' in *The Homeric Hymns and Homerica* (H. Evelyn-White, trans.). London: William Heinemann, 1914, lines 585–612.
10 Hesiod, 'Works and Days' in *The Homeric Hymns and Homerica* (H. Evelyn-White, trans.). London: William Heinemann, 1914, lines 57–58.

Chapter 2

From autoerotism to autoerotism for two, on the way to . . . erotism

From the drive to phallicism – from Being to Having

In the *Introductory Lectures on Psychoanalysis*, Freud notes that 'in children the first phobias relating to situations are those of darkness and solitude'.[1] The phobia emerges at night in the absence of a reflection or when the echo of speech is lacking because an echo is also a kind of reflection: 'If someone speaks, it gets lighter'.[2] As soon as they no longer have the support of vision, children may fear that their body will be sucked into the darkness and that they will then become what their mother has always asked from them: her own object, her phallus. This is the first consequence of maternal castration anxiety. Solitude and darkness confront the child with the emptiness of the Other, and masturbatory practices stem from this anxiety-provoking context: masturbation defuses the omnipresence of a latent incest.[3] Fear of the dark has this bizarre consequence of provoking erection and masturbation. Everything happens as if the imperious erogeneity of the penis or the clitoris affirms that the body is not the phallus. Masturbation is a movement of resistance and protest. The body says 'no' by playing the part against the whole, by, as it were, initiating a struggle of the penis against the phallus. It is a way of saying, 'No, I'm not your phallus since I have a penis'.

The anxiety-ridden enjoyment that results does not relieve anything because discharge is immediately followed by the threat of a relapse into the nothingness of phallic identification. So masturbation must be resumed almost immediately: solitary, sometimes frantic excitement becomes a means of survival. To masturbate is rather to masturbate one's double, another self caught in a reflection, copulation with which would mean a fall into the abyss. The body struggles against itself in a sort of masturbation of the double, which fights against annihilation. Its excitation strives to resist a fall into the reflection. This frenzy of masturbation sometimes remains a habit into adulthood as masturbation in front of the mirror or masturbation *à deux*, which can pass for love. The power of this masturbatory relief, which no genital need can explain, precedes erotism. It calls for clarification.

This bizarre 'sexuality' comes into play in the first days of life, seemingly innocent, a response to the mother's love. Her demand eroticises a child who is initially passive; with her breast, her caresses and ministrations, her songs, etc., the child's

DOI: 10.4324/9781003519287-2

body is magnified as the beautiful phallus that she lacks. But in this heat, the wondrous child dreams only of anorexia, autism, of a degree zero that could offer a path to recovery of the self. Children constantly reject this suffocating excess. They reject it only to accept it again greedily because how could they do without it? So the drive begins its orbit, describing an endless loop, turning from passive to active. Even when the body is sated, our mouth continues to activate on its own; keeping time, it mimics devouring in order to prevent the body from being devoured. Rather than be instrumentalised, children make themselves enjoy; they save themselves by taking themselves as objects. The spasmodic nature of the drive generates a rhythmic alternation between 'being enjoyed' and 'enjoyment', as what is unbearable in the first triggers the impossible realisation of the second. For if to passively be the maternal phallus has an effect of alienation (the goal of the drive), it is also impossible to achieve it without self-annihilation. A pulsating psychical body is constructed on this infernal tempo, and the organism follows the music as best it can, falling ill when its own speed becomes too much for it. The active moment frees the child from its position of Being the phallus, and it is at that moment that the child can have the phallus by investing a part of its body with a phallic value, the spasmodicity of which is already masturbatory. When, at the limit of its passivity, the drive turns into activity, this rhythmicity, which is already masturbatory, produces erection.

This motor of the drive seems abstract until it is linked to a particular goal.[4] This goal is the transformation of the psychical body into the maternal phallus, an enterprise so impossible that all of the subject's energy is used to break free from it, with 'escape' the only aim. And what is the best recipe for ceasing to be the phallus if not to have the phallus? That requires the passage from an external erogenisation to a self-erotisation by applying oneself to one's own body as if to an external object. Rather than being enjoyed from the outside, the subject makes itself enjoy in rhythmic patterns, which are now oriented from the inside to the outside; one begins by masturbating with the mouth, the anus, with this or that part of the skin.[5]

Only one of these erogenous zones can break the circuit of the drive and open outwards, without returning like a boomerang to the body, namely, the elected zone of penile or clitoral masturbation. Masturbation is freedom. By what wave of a magic wand can drive energy engender excitation of the penis or the clitoris and, ultimately, masturbation? It can do so because the erogeneity of these parts of the body escapes maternal demand. These are not conventional drive bases. They quickly become the locus of a powerful pleasure – witness, for example, the jet of urine, the highly erotised value of which signifies by itself the equivalent of a masturbatory (and lifelong) Having.[6] The flow of urine, we might say, extinguishes the fire of maternal desire and does so all the better because this zone remains relatively free; mothers tend not to play with this part of the child's body, and in any case, they dare not ask anything from it, due specifically to the repression of their own infantile sexuality (although they might ask much of it, if they gave themselves a little more leeway). Even though the penis may be their favourite dream, they touch it as little as possible (as if it did not interest them) and thus mark out themselves the only masturbatory locus that escapes them. Their own repression of 'penis envy' paves the way for autoerotism, thanks to which their child can create a distance from them. This is how repression of the sexual is transmitted from generation to generation.

In this way, enjoyment of the phallic organ (penile or clitoral) offers liberation from the drive enjoyment that it challenges to give an image: the drive connects to an organism that is propelled like a rocket all the way to the limit that gives its meaning to the enjoyment of the phallic organ. Drive fuel powers the launch rocket, and its successive failures (oral, anal, etc.) ignite a new stage, with each of them connected to the phallic terminal.[7] Phallic excitation functions as a retro-thrust to the drive because erection does not result from any particular drive from which it seeks to free itself. Genitality, like a retrorocket designed to decelerate, burns the fuel of the drive rocket to escape from the goal of the drive, and its thrust is achieved thanks to masturbation. The retrorocket of the 'genital' does not go towards the drive goal which gave it its impetus. Solitary erections, without fantasies or thoughts, arise from this kind of counter-discharge of the drives. Masturbatory autoerotism goes against and challenges the drive goal, or rather, it uses the power of the drive to go somewhere else than where it was pushed. It counters identification with being the phallus by having it or, at least, by setting itself this new goal, now compatible with the existence of the subject. This retro-thrust of phallicism ignites an excitation that is ignorant of what could satisfy it. Masturbation liberates without knowing what from. It relieves an unbearable upstream tension that comes from the onrush of the drives. Downstream, the world opens up, abuzz with a single certainty – that of a fault and a punishment to come, which will give meaning to erotism. Having broken the circle of maternal alienation, this sexual subject immediately stumbles upon guilt. The subject encounters anxiety – the anxiety of the mother's castration, which is discovered by leaving her. The subject was to have been her phallus, if he or she had remained faithful to her love. This setting in motion, which pertains to both genders, corresponds to an 'urge to have the phallus'.

The child's excitation goes as far as the autoerotic limit of organ pleasure, which is solitary because it provides freedom from the Other. This bizarre movement falls under the banner of perversion because it does not correspond to anything from the point of view of future sexual enjoyment, nor of the reproduction of the species, nor of any organic or instinctual excitation. Demiurges of identification with the phallus, the drives trigger a perverse enjoyment because they deny the absence of the maternal phallus. They are animated by a latent fetishism.

Can a human body relieve itself of the excess of the drive without the help of love or even without fantasies? Naturally, it can . . . but not naturally. Solitary autoerotism manages to enjoy merely from the liberation of drive excitation. Autoerotism can follow this course for a long time and may even stop there – precarious, perhaps, but no more nor less impracticable than other drive destinies, compared with which its narcissism and its sexual potency, animated by the force of despair, offer undeniable advantages. But its discharge is followed immediately by a low that is sometimes akin to melancholia, a bottomless vertigo that a new excitement seeks to alleviate in an endless loop from Being to Having.[8]

The grip of autoerotism for two

The drive maddens the body and pushes it to the point of masturbatory overflow, but this activity will always leave the drive unsatisfied. How will it be able to attain relief, to deny itself, to do something that brings respite? Its possible destinies include the attempt to possess another body, a movement by which autoerotism will transition to an autoerotism for two. The drive haunts a body that fails to satisfy it, and – at the limit of its impossible realisation – it seizes on another body. Each drive thus generates a drive to possess another body, a *Bemächtigungstrieb*,[9] ready to satiate itself on another person, or at least to try. It finds in the body that it seizes on a new locus and a new place – that of the subject come to replace the object. The drive to possess seizes the body of a fellow being. It pushes towards coupling. This autoerotism for two already actualises the power of a kind of repetition governed by the drive.[10] The aim is to actively repeat on the body of another person what has been passively experienced, in the hope of liberation from this straitjacket. From childhood onwards, autoerotism for two (or more than two) relieves drive tensions, at least temporarily. (But is this 'temporary' not the usual tempo of human sexuality?) Such autoerotism is not merely a displacement of masturbation, which might seem more entertaining in company. It advances towards erotism as such from the moment that the pleasure of giving pleasure to another body emerges – or of imagining giving pleasure.

By putting the subject in the place of the object, this effort to possess creates a lack in the subject. In grasping the other, the subject is separated from its own body, at the same time as it liberates itself in this distance. The other body is ours in so far as that body will (perhaps) enjoy. The result of this pairing is reminiscent of narcissism, but the word 'narcissism' evokes a specular relationship, which is not the case here, because whoever actively seizes the body of the other seeks to rid themselves through their partner of the burden of being the phallus (the goal of the drive). In short, it is a struggle where the stakes are being and nothingness, so it establishes an asymmetry. This philosophical formulation of a 'struggle between being and nothingness' means that the party who seizes puts the party whom they seize in their place (inversion of subject and object). The possession of the other makes the other into the subject (being), while the party who takes possession is impersonalised (nothingness). If the drive is decanted from one body to another, the body that is put in the place of object becomes the subject of enjoyment and the agent of this decanting no longer knows who they are or what they do. Nothingness inhabits them so that the death drive looms on the horizon of the drive for possession; its tempo will become violent, bringing something like a relationship of force into play, which erotism will seek to relieve.

If we consider this relationship of force, the effort to possess involved in autoerotism for two appears in two forms, simple or crossed. 'Simple' means that a subject puts an object in its place – most often by forcing it – in a transgressive way (for example, in exhibitionism). 'Crossed' means that the first 'simple' operation is also performed by the partner (the object) so that two subjects (this time, consenting) perform the same solitary operation together (they may also love each other proportionately). The partner of this autoerotism is created through the movement of the drive. Children already invent this partner in their daydreams; they speak with a double, a secret companion, a play partner, whom subsequent friendships then embody either more or less successfully. Autoerotism quickly finds who to have fun with, experimenting with these fictions and sexual games, which, as children soon learn, it is better to hide because they prolong masturbations so culpable that they are immediately forgotten.

Freud pointed out that these games already involved a repetition. For example, a child will play out with another child a seduction that was enacted on them, whether in fact or in fantasy. They will know how to play at 'making love' if they have seen adults do it. They thus imitate a scene that struck them because it fell opportunely in the already moving train of their fantasies. But when they play it out with other children, they do not know what it represents, and in any case, they do not derive from it the relational enjoyment that will only come later, at the time of the break with infantile sexuality. When children imitate adult sexuality, their enjoyment remains within the frame of infantile drives and their masturbatory outlet. What sets them free, without their knowing what from, is a form of repetition compulsion that offers relief from their personal traumas. They are in thrall to this compulsion, which is not necessarily pleasurable.

This 'make-believe' inherent to infantile sexuality is very important because it functions as a launch pad for sexual arousal towards genitality via a repetition which is already, in itself, a liberation, if not an enjoyment. Children, then teenagers and then, for a while, adults, are haunted by the repetition of gestures or of a scene, without yet knowing where it leads them. They perform these scenarios blindly, pretending if necessary to be aroused or to enjoy (if called for), even though they may feel little else than a bizarre 'forced liberation'. But they persevere all the same; they repeat with or without pleasure, sometimes out of love for their partner. They acquiesce, submitting to a vertigo that is stronger than them.

Any pleasure to be found in this search for enjoyment is that of a persisting autoerotic drive energy. The pleasure of kissing, seeing, being seen, holding, touching, submitting, etc., take centre stage. Repetition brings liberation because it stages actively what was undergone passively. And this relief gives pleasure because the drive finds an outlet. But it leads to consequences that call for further action, either in repetition or in another modality – one that will be, strictly speaking, erotic.

Nothing better demonstrates this power of repetition than the tastes and preferences of autoerotism for two since it never occurs accidentally. Hormones, nerves – the whole panoply of nature – do not respond outside of conditions that are already highly mentalised. As soon as it metamorphoses into possession of another body, the drive chooses what it likes or dislikes; these are our preferences. Depending on the partner, a kiss produces pleasure or disgust. The seemingly mechanical arousal that it involves is by no means an automatic pleasure.[11] Even being beaten can procure pleasure, if a mistress administers it at the right time. At each moment of erotism, both arousal and satisfaction depend on the tastes of the lover, even if they are passive or reticent. The degree of arousal is linked to what we like or what disgusts us, and disgust itself can be highly arousing in some cases.

No one can tickle themselves. Each sensation is invested by the drive and the choices of each person will depend on the vicissitudes of the drive. Being in constant excess, the drive seeks to discharge this 'too much' of enjoyment – which is, therefore, 'bad' – and is rejected at the moment of a traumatic emotion.[12] Excess renders 'bad' what had been good, retaining the memory of what pleased or, on the contrary, displeased. When this rejected part invests something, it immediately reproduces its own split on this object, dividing it between 'good' and 'too good' (i.e., a too good that turns bad). It involves a *judgment* according to these criteria, which give a final fixation of our tastes. This judgment depends on a certain characteristic of the drive which seals an experience in the past under the influence of an emotion. Our aesthetic criteria are last on the scene, but behind them lie these likes or dislikes based on the drive.[13]

The alienation inherent to enjoyment

So the condition for the possibility of human enjoyment is the impossibility of its satisfaction on a person's own body; it is achieved thanks to another body, which protects us from enjoyment and, by so doing, sets it free. Do we ever enjoy except from a distance, thanks to this other body, as if it was our own? To make someone enjoy is already to enjoy, a discharge that gives a basic sense of possession at the very moment that the partner gets off. Enjoyment comes thanks to this other body which enjoys; it is not ours and it is ours. In reality, this sort of crucifixion fixes the pleasure of giving oneself and, therefore, of taking. Our body ravishes us, in every sense of the verb 'ravish', when it has finally flown away from us. The ravishment carries the risk of impersonalisation, towards which enjoyment tends; it frightens and seduces us. It pushes us irremediably towards what we should not do. We must go there without going there, by prohibiting ourselves from going there, even by enjoying the prohibition itself. This necessary distance from what is most intimate is specific to human sexuality from its origin, as distinct from the sexuality of animals which is regulated by reproduction.

Finding one's pleasure thanks to that of another person heralds a harsher pleasure because to enjoy their enjoyment is to approach blindly an impersonality that will impose its own requirements. When the question is asked, 'Where am I, and who am I when the other enjoys?' then demands for exclusivity in love, which are destined to be re-personalised, are already not far away. By the narcissistic requirement that it entails, autoerotism for two has already taken the risk of love, of a declared love that may immediately fail or at least remain on the dramatic threshold of its entry onto the scene, endlessly repeated: 'I love you, me neither', etc.

Love, destiny of the drive

Love is there from the first moment of the drive to possess, when a subject gives up the possession of itself for the benefit of the subject whom it possesses. By this inversion of places, the object is subjectivised, and love can take up residence in its lack. Love, avatar of the libido, first presents itself as a vicissitude of the drive, which seizes the body of another. It sets out, perhaps, in pursuit of an 'object' – as we say in psychoanalytic jargon – but rather than being simply seized, this object is metamorphosed into a subject, according to the very laws of drive transitivism, which decree that the subject surrenders its place to its object. The lover becomes the object, and the beloved becomes the subject who dominates them; the lover is thus manipulated by their own desire, which they cannot resist.

The love of someone combines and transforms our drive attachments to voice, gaze, skin, etc. It is a continuous metamorphosis, distilled drop by drop, redone over time because this subjectivation will never satisfy the drive, which seeks to assuage itself on an object (only pornography interests it). This love seems narcissistic since it seeks to grasp another self which has become the home of a body in exile. Such a beloved makes a strange subject since they resist capture indefinitely, reigning supreme while at a distance. This subject may represent an 'object' for the one who strives to take possession of it, but its resistance subjectivises the drive and thereby opens the door to love. And yet the drive to possess does not abate even for a moment and will continue to animate a love that does not stay put, that is alive and must make its way upwards by degrees or risk falling back into the original savagery of the drive. It must change ceaselessly, abandoning old habits for new or destroying what it possesses in order to take it up again.

Far from being reduced to a beautiful feeling that falls from the sky in the hour of despair, love is what happens to the drive when it encounters the obstacle of a subjectivity. Love cannot but be violent since it results from this very resistance. This violence remains active in all forms of love, endogamous and exogamous, and Thanatos can disengage from Eros at any moment. From the moment it takes hold, even the simplest love carries within it the idea of murder because what is to be done with this body that resists our capture? This dark power always haunts the tenderness of mothers, who counteract their thirst to devour their infant by the ministrations they lavish upon it. And, gradually, the gesture of love sets itself in opposition to Thanatos, its secret precursor. Each lover feels the same violence, which is active right to the heart of the sexual act. From the very beginning and always, the psychical body overflows onto the other's body in an indefinite attempt at conquest. Our neighbour, from whom our drives hope for relief, is dissymmetrical to us; bigger than us, they embody an 'ideal ego'. Bigger, more beautiful, they draw us magnetically and we love them – except when, in an effort to exorcise their domination, we loathe them. A hallucinatory aura lingers around the beloved due to this transit of the drive. Who does not know this unreal dimension of love, so blinding that it transforms the beloved, who becomes unrecognisable, at least for as long as the passion lasts?[14]

To which gender is possession directed?

This coupling, which depends on the appetite of the drive, is in principle transgender. It is magnetised solely by narcissistic sameness and the search for a being like oneself. It would be hasty, therefore, to think that autoerotism for two is, to begin with, homosexual. That would be to believe that anatomical sex corresponds to psychical gender. But this is far from the truth, and the first autoerotic couplings are often heterosexual. The boy who straightway chooses a girl loves in her the feminised subject whom he almost became for his father. He loves what he risked being, and his masculinity gains assurance in proportion to this love. So homosexual autoerotic coupling depends on the way in which a child was desired by their parents. It is a special case and not the rule. Autoerotism for two does not imply a homosexual choice (although it is possible) because this movement is heterosexualised in proportion to paternal seduction; a subject who was feminised by his father may seize upon a feminine *alter ego*, rather than remaining feminine himself. He gains virility in proportion to this, and all the more so if he was masculinised by his mother.

The choice of partner in autoerotism for two aims to satisfy both the drive (for example, large breasts, a certain shape of the hips, etc.) and narcissism, i.e., the sameness of a like-being. It thus happens, in this second case, that lovers resemble each other or that there is a secret correspondence in at least one trait. This resemblance is even more striking when lovers adopt the same style and dress. The narcissistic feature may differ for each of the partners, so it can happen that two lovers do not resemble each other even though they are united under the regime of autoerotism for two. From the point of view of narcissism, an idealised self-image (a certain aesthetic) generates an excitement in taking the other for oneself.

We thus find that two forces, contrary to one another in principle, govern the movement of autoerotism for two: on the one hand, the drive-based path of taste, which is excited by certain part-objects (large breasts, etc.), and, on the other hand, the transitive narcissistic path of the drive to possess, which seeks to capture the other body for want of its own. These movements are in contradiction since one seeks the difference that completes and satiates, while the other is fascinated by sameness (enjoyment of the self thanks to the other since one cannot do it alone). The toboggan of autoerotism for two can take advantage of every detail on its drive side without worrying too much about the person. A few small details suffice to set it alight: an appetising mouth, a sultry look, certain hips, etc. By contrast, narcissism imposes severe, finicky limitations that can prompt sudden discordances; each must duplicate the other in every detail of their existence. These movements are even so contrary that one may require heterosexuality and the other homosexuality. But – despite a decisive choice in favour of one or other – there will always be a 'homoerotic' trait beneath a 'straight' attraction. And in a homosexual pairing, a difference will be found, which duplicates heterosexuality; a distribution of male and female roles is rarely lacking.[15]

When autoerotism changes to autoerotism for two, its tension is relieved with a partner, homo- or heterosexual. The other is not only a playmate and an outlet but they may also be loved and may be the cause of suffering, although they may also be quickly interchangeable. Their absence causes suffering, particularly when a replacement is slow to appear. But once found, the story begins again and is swiftly or slowly exhausted, worn down by the sexual exasperation of autoerotism. The hyper-consumption of autoerotism fights against the sadness, the disgust even, which follows drive discharge. Because so as long as satisfaction depends on drive excess, it risks generating a feeling of annihilation after love, similar to the post-masturbatory low which swings endlessly between being and having; Being signs a 'death warrant', which Having seeks to overturn, etc.

Notes

1 Freud [1916–1917], *Introductory Lectures on Psycho-Analysis* in *Standard Edition 16*, p. 407.
2 *Ibid.*
3 Freud [1926] writes in *Inhibitions, Symptoms and Anxiety*: 'The phobia of being alone is [. . .] an endeavour to avoid the temptation to indulge in solitary masturbation' (*Standard Edition 20*, p. 127).
4 Theories that reduce the drive to its object dimension describe a motor whose direction is unknown.
5 The drive enjoyments accessible to the child are described as 'polymorphous perversion'. They are 'perverse' in the sense that this liberation makes do with what, in adulthood, will be lacking genitality (except for perversion as such).
6 Both boys and girls find relief in this urinary escape, which releases aggression and excitement later and throughout life, by day and by night. The image seems facile, but it is appropriate: the urinary stream functions as a fire hose, well-suited to extinguish the mother's ardour. Can we say that this is still a drive? Yes, because denying the drive is itself a destiny of the drive. Moreover, it is the origin of an 'adult' perversion, that of the pyromaniac, who loves to start fires in order to extinguish them (the curious complex of the pyromaniac fireman).
7 This process sketches the preliminaries that 'adults' will replay before the sexual act: drive excitation (the kiss, the look, the embrace) is followed by a heterogeneous rupture, that of genitality (if the person is lucky).
8 Such are the frenetic masturbations of some psychotic states.
9 See: Freud [1905], *Three Essays on the Theory of Sexuality* in *Standard Edition 7*, particularly pp. 208–218. In the French text 'pulsion d'emprise' is used to translate Freud's 'Bemächtigungstrieb', which indexes the drive to seize hold of, grasp and possess. Strachey often translates the German term as 'drive to master', but this obscures its connotation of physical urgency (translator's note).
10 'It is tempting to pursue to its logical conclusion the hypothesis that all instincts tend towards the restoration of an earlier state of things' (Freud [1920], *Beyond the Pleasure Principle* in *Standard Edition 18*, p. 37).
11 Prostitutes refuse to kiss; it disgusts them much more than the penetration of a cavity, the weak investment of which leaves them cold.
12 This 'emotion' is the effect of a repression.
13 Not that it is unimportant – quite the contrary – but it is variable because it depends on the aesthetic canons of the time, on fashions, etc., and consequently, it enters into a field of comparisons and rivalries that is already Oedipal.
14 The aura of the drive to possess hangs halo-like around the beloved, and we will see that the orgasm can discharge its power in the same way as an epileptic seizure discharges the contradictory tensions of hysteria.
15 This perhaps offers the key to the enigma of the perversions which are sometimes homosexual, sometimes heterosexual or both.

Chapter 3

Invariants and variables of human sexuality

The variables of human sexuality

Sexual life is governed by features that can be counted on the fingers of one hand. Anatomical sex is the first given. It is not the same as sexual gender. A subject can inhabit a man's body and claim to be of feminine gender. The extent to which the choice of psychical gender – masculine or feminine – deviates from anatomy is demonstrated by the number of exceptions: no geneticism seasoned with hormonal weighting will be able to provide the key.[1] This distinction between anatomy and psychical gender is not enough to understand the *choice of object* – the gender of the sexual partner. To be psychically a 'man' does not imply the love of women, and identifying with a 'woman' does not necessarily entail a taste for men. A man can feel like a woman, and a woman can see herself as a man while choosing a man or a woman as object.[2] Could we use these first three givens to construct a table that would exhaust the number of possible 'object relations'? Such a reduction would not take account of narcissistic or aesthetic criteria (as unpredictable as they are decisive) nor, above all, of the symbolic criteria that determine the choices which are made.

A fourth given has to be added to these first three, namely, that of the sexual goal: what shall I do with the chosen partner? This goal includes such a vast range of activities that it would be futile to attempt an exhaustive list. It may be satisfied by the simple play of an impulse (in voyeurism, for example), by walking hand-in-hand, kissing, masturbation, sodomy or the relationship traditionally recommended by the Church. Moreover, the discharge of tension is not always what organises the sexual goal, which may also be achieved through abstinence and vows of chastity.

With these four variables, of which only one (anatomy) is usually clearcut, we could already work out so many configurations that each subject might represent a separate case. This mass of complexities, it will be agreed, does not allow any classification in terms of 'man' on one side and 'woman' on the other. The givens are an obstacle to any explanation of human erotism in terms of anatomical sex, instinct, nature or reproduction, and moreover, their combination is relatively unpredictable. So much so that we cannot guess how a couple is formed or what it will do

DOI: 10.4324/9781003519287-3

or why it will do it; our desire makes each one of us into his or her own sexual minority. If there is a multiplicity of possible figures, they are deduced from these four invariants by progressive complexity. In particular, the masculine/feminine polarisation remains unchanged in its successive presentations. One cannot say, for example, that 'lesbian' is an additional identity.[3]

The combination of these first four terms presents us with one invariant (anatomy) and three variables (psychical gender, choice of object and sexual goal), and it still says nothing about a fifth term, which is desire. This fifth term depends on another problem that comes into perspective when we ask: what is the source of sexual arousal, that is, of desire itself? Its very power might make it seem self-explanatory when it is nevertheless quite mysterious[4] because, as we all know, desire is capricious: it imposes itself when we do not expect it and vanishes when it would be welcome, etc., and it does so when the other givens (gender, choice of object, goal) are all present and in place. Nothing seems to explain how desire can suddenly appear and submerge a subject whose will it subverts and who is left pretty much helpless. Our four variables tell us nothing about the combustion of desire because their simultaneous occurrence does not always entail their proper functioning, at least not without additional conditions.

When we have distinguished anatomical sex from psychical gender and added the choice of the sexual object and of the sexual goal (what to do with the body of the other) and when we have made their combination depend on the cause of desire (which, as we shall see, depends on fantasy), we have not yet taken a sixth term into consideration, namely, what allows orgasm. For there is no predicting how excitement will end and the modalities of its relief. Freud made no mention of this sixth variable in the *Three Essays*, and its sparse appearances elsewhere in his work refer mainly to the removal of a tension, using unpoetic expressions such as 'discharge'[5] or, more often, 'end-pleasure'. None of the six alternatives which we have listed can be considered independently of the others. They are, as it were, vertically stacked, in a deceptive synthesis, as if associated by links of natural causality. Analysis of the six will show that such links are hardly natural and, indeed, may well be absent.

A bizarre psychical bisexuality

The variables just listed present us with facts that are, in reality, problems. For example, 'Why do we choose a psychical gender?' or 'Where does sexual arousal come from?' These 'facts' must be based on certain presuppositions: if the choice between masculine and feminine psychical genders is made, it must be on the basis of a potential bisexuality in all of us, and we might then conjecture that this is then what orients desire. The bisexuality in question has nothing anatomical about it nor is it 'cerebral', as Krafft-Ebing had suggested.[6] It is a kind of mental struggle that goes on inside each subject, a struggle the solution of which is sought in their desire for the other sex – the sex in which they do not recognise themselves.[7] However, that is not to say that desire is just this tension, as if each subject were both masculine and feminine and that, since they only recognise themselves in one gender, they desire in the other gender the part of themselves which they renounce.[8] No doubt, this dream of harmony corresponds to a number of myths about love, but those myths completely elide what is at stake in bisexuality and implicit in the choice of gender.

If we approach the problem of desire from the perspective of this choice, we run into a major contradiction concerning 'bisexuality': How is bisexuality compatible with the idea not so much of the primacy of the phallus as of the phallus as the unique symbol of human erotism?[9] As we already noted, autoerotism as such does not imply any gender distinction but gives each human being access to phallic enjoyment regardless of their anatomical sex. It is not difficult to understand why the phallus alone is the symbol of sexuality: the child who is sure of being the phallus of its mother has the certainty that she has the phallus and that if she has it, everyone has it. So there is no need for jealousy – not for boys and, particularly, not for girls. Boys and girls will both believe in the existence of the maternal phallus, which they themselves embody. They *are* it before they try to *have* it. Being the phallus erogenises the body, but beyond a certain threshold, it threatens the body with annihilation. Good can be too good. How is this unbearable excess to be dialecticised, if not in the passage from Being the phallus to Having it, as materialised in penile or clitoral excitation? Penis and clitoris are both equally erotised. There is an equality of enjoyment here regardless of the size difference,[10] and the belief in a single symbol – the phallus – is thereby established. This remains true for adults, most of whom are in constant doubt regarding the female sex organ. There is a compulsion to investigate its structure or even (and above all) not to look too closely.

This belief gives rise to a problem: if the enjoyment of men and of women is linked to the phallus, is there bisexuality, or is there just a single symbol? The two propositions seem incompatible. How are these two psychical realities, which are unrelated to physiology,[11] to coexist? The existence of a sole sexual symbol, the phallus, contradicts the existence of two genders, masculine and feminine, unless we take the view that there is, in fact, only one gender, namely, 'male', and a non- (non-existent) gender, namely, 'female'. This is the mistake made by those who equate 'man' with 'masculine', on the one hand, and 'woman' with 'feminine', on the other. Of course, we could resolve the matter simply: there would be those who have the phallus (men) and those who lack it (women). But this totally misses the point because we would be deducing from the existence of a single symbol (the phallus) that there is a single gender (masculine), while on the side of the feminine, there would be an absence of gender! A single gender opposed to a non-gender.[12]

The contradiction here might seem insoluble unless considered in terms of historical development. We will describe that development first of all, leaving its explanation until later. What happens once a single erogenous zone has been marked out? For both sexes, the masturbation of this phallic zone is immediately a source of guilt since the child thereby escapes from its mother,[13] who would like it to be her phallus and who is betrayed when the child has the phallus. This guilt corresponds to anxiety regarding the mother's castration, magnified by the fear of losing her love since masturbation betrays her demand. Ceasing to be an angel to become a devil, the discovery of organ enjoyment – the enjoyment of shameful but delightful masturbation – brings guilt and the fear of abandonment.

What brings the subject into the realm of guilt is not external prohibition but the fact that its guilt already structures a pleasure that ought not to occur. The only way to be rid of this guilt is by meriting punishment, which gives hope that the mother's love will subsist despite the fault. And so the myth of a punitive father is invented even before a real father appears. Because how else could the problem be solved? Punishment is needed, but who is to punish? Since the punishment seeks to preserve the love of the mother, it is best administered by someone else. A father is the obvious choice for the role.[14] Punishment both safeguards love and preserves sexual arousal.

Naturally, the punitive 'blows'[15] will have to fall on the object at issue, the penis or clitoris, so the father will also appear as the agent of castration. Masturbatory sexual arousal, anxiety regarding the mother's castration and the demand for punishment come hot on each other's heels, followed, finally, by castration by the father. The appearance of the punitive father preserves the mother's love (now desexualised), and his punishment is equivalent to the sexual arousal that it sanctions. Masturbation being culpable and, therefore, punishable, the punishment assumes the same eroticised meaning as erection. The 'blows' themselves will provoke it, and without the punishment, the excitement would be inhibited by excessive guilt. Indeed, the guilt is so powerful that the idea of punishment (or prohibition) will *precede* arousal and thereby make it seem innocent. The reconstruction of this chain has no better proof than the profound masochism that conditions human sexuality, which is never so voluptuous as when a transgression is added to the mix.[16] The 'blows' administered (in fantasy) by the father produce an erection of the phallus, and this condition of arousal imprints its masochism on human erotism, giving it a taste for, at the least, tears and humiliation, if not for whips and physical torture.[17]

So the father gives the phallus because he excites, in the sense that his punishment provokes erection. The 'blows' administered by the father are a seduction. He is both the agent of castration and of seduction, producing the final version of a sexual trauma that was originally linked to castration anxiety. The result is unexpected and 'immoral': the father, disguised as the agent of castration and chastisement, becomes the first seducer. Boys and girls both receive 'blows' that excite them and are seduced by a father, in relation to whom they are guilty. This seduction is not about manipulation or charm but punishment, which, it is hoped, will bring redemption. Desire is born in fault and thanks to it. Paternal seduction is part and parcel of the passage from Being to Having or, more exactly, to *trying* to have – the pursuit of the phallus, which, for a moment, erection allows the subject to have. This erection gives access to an entirely new state which no other part of the body can exteriorise more conveniently. An incestuous, chastising father imposes his myth when the subject of sex (the subject, period) is born. This is the subject who has come to doubt (to doubt the reality of maternal castration) and who will bear the father's name if successful in escaping the clutches of this terrifying monster. The idea of murder or, more simply, the idea of God underpins the thought of the sexual 'I' which seeks to think in his name.

This is the unbreakable core of an unconscious bisexuality, which is incomprehensible if interpreted through the purely subjective dimension of a sexual trauma which the subject feels guilty about even though they were the victim. Penile or clitoral masturbatory pleasure are immediately marked by shame and prohibition. Under the blows of the father, the fantasy that produces erection in both boy and girl feminises them and gives meaning to *psychic bisexuality: on the one hand, the child is feminised by its father when it receives 'blows', and on the other hand, it is masculinised since this punishment provokes an erection. This psychic bisexuality is, in essence, correlative to castration, which is its synonym.*

Many enigmas are illuminated once we recognise this. The mystery of femininity, which scares or fascinates men,[18] is nothing less than their own femininity, which they want to know nothing about! Woman's so-called 'penis envy', in turn, is usually understood as her awaiting the phallus from the father after being disappointed by the love from the mother. People are sometimes surprised by Freud's declaration that 'girls want the phallus from the father'. Yet they do so because his blows give them an erection, just as for boys, and their clitoral pleasure occurs under the shadow of this violent fantasy. When they masturbate, girls sometimes imagine thrashings administered to the *alter egos* that are boys. In this drama of 'a child is being beaten', the 'father' is no more the keeper of the phallus than men since, on the contrary, he gives it. The phallus given by the father is offered to both genders, and the choice of gender is made at this moment.[19]

Choosing gender from bisexuality

How is the choice of a single gender made for each subject, setting out from the infernal triptych of masculine, feminine and phallus? The choice is the consequences of the fantasy of seduction, experienced by every child. This seduction can operate independently of the material facts, without the slightest punitive action by the father. The father seduces, even if he sleeps. Everyone is seduced by the father, not by his charm or by his acts but because his 'blows' excite.[20] The trauma of sexual seduction by the father feminises both boy and girl who, until then, were certainly different in their anatomy but were equal as regards enjoyment of the phallus.

Starting from this shared position, psychical bisexuality is divided up between those who refuse feminisation and go to war against the father – they will be on the masculine side, even as the refusal acts as the motor of their arousal – and those who accept it, i.e., girls but who accept it either more or less.[21] This choice is what decides between masculine and feminine gender, regardless of anatomy. The consequence is immediate: whoever wants to ensure their masculinity must be violent. With erection, there's war. In the relationship with counterparts, the use of force decides who is on the feminine side and who on the masculine. The struggle against the *alter ego* is the first trait of masculinity, prior to any knowledge of the sexual relationship.[22] Violence establishes dissimilarity on the basis of an apparent similarity. Two boys confront each other to decide who is masculine and who is feminine. Virility is a constant contest, never won in advance.

However, even this division of genders is not symmetrical because those who accept their feminisation cannot submit to it fully without risking incest and madness. They renounce their primary masculinity only in part, keeping a subtle attachment to it (so that the clitoris nearly always remains a necessary element in sexual arousal).[23] No woman fully accepts her feminisation by a father, and the mystics consent to such nuptials only because the father they marry is safely dead (their certainty of this is proportional to the eternalisation of their orgasm).[24] There is no absolute 'woman' to be found in the earthly world but rather, a feminisation relative to a man who (thank God) kills the father. Women are 'not completely' feminised. They remain a little, a lot or passionately masculine.

So the dividing line of psychical gender is established starting from bisexuality: the masculinity of boys is based on a refusal of feminisation, and if they do not want to wait to receive this phallus from the father, they will have to give it if they want to have it thanks to the arousal of desire, which alone can elicit their erection. The femininity of girls depends on their expectation of receiving the same phallus from the father, although they find it more prudent to ask for it from the man who can do away with this impossible father. Girls can wait for the phallus, while boys most certainly do not – for fear of receiving it. Boys are in a rush to give it in order to have it.[25]

So boys no less than girls look to receive the phallus from the father in the sense that his punishment makes the phallus erect – not for later, in the radiant future of copulation, but for now, in the secrecy of masturbation. (What could be easier, when the cup of shame is drunk to the dregs?) Contrary to the expectation that only women hope to receive the father's phallus, the threat of receiving it is there, too, for men but precisely as a threat. Note how boys accumulate so many more transgressions than girls, both in order to be punished and, therefore, to have it (like girls) and in order to refuse it (so as to be boys). So the phallus seems to be the unique symbol from which are established, firstly, a psychical bisexuality and then the choice of gender.

Men become men by fighting against their feminisation. They act and deal blows as cruelly as the father, whose victims they take themselves to be. Is that to say that women are passive and masochistic? To avoid this confusion, we must distinguish 'the Woman' from 'femininity'.[26] Because women also prefer to escape paternal seduction, which they accept only more or less and which they most often oppose thanks to a man. Could this hero be he who defeats the father in their place? Not really. It is enough that they love a man in order for this love to deal a blow to the father, without the man having to engage in any actual fight with her father. Paternal danger itself stirs them to action; as we have said, they are 'not all' feminine, and they become more or less so on the basis of a primary activity.

This becoming feminine often takes time, even the best part of a life. So rather than contrasting active (masculine) and passive (feminine), we would do better to distinguish 'activity with an active goal' (masculine) from 'activity with a passive goal' (feminine).[27] A child orients itself one way or the other from the primacy of the phallus and then from a psychical bisexuality. The choice of sexual gender depends on the response to paternal seduction. To respond to seduction by seduction is to deploy activity with a passive goal and so to be feminine, while going to war in order to put oneself in the place of the father and to seduce in turn gives a parricidal masculinity. Activity is required on both sides, masculine and feminine, and women do not 'receive' what men strive to 'give' them.[28]

So the terms 'active' and 'passive' are not concepts which would define 'man' or 'woman' but qualifiers of a fantasy activity. What is enacted is a fantasy that is either active or passive. We can, therefore, distinguish two instances of the seduction fantasy: 'activity with an active goal' and 'activity with a passive goal', each of them related to the masculine and to the feminine. The activity will be the fixed term in the context of each subject's bisexuality, and its fantasmatic goal will be a variable that depends on partners and circumstances. If we stay at the level of gender generalities, women in some way deploy an 'activity with a passive goal'. They seduce actively by showing themselves (passively), and many men behave in the same way. But women may also be quite simply active; they may 'make' love by treating their lover as if his penis were their own, as if they had it. The field of their 'passivity' is delimited by their having been desired. But their lover has also been desired, even when he does not remain passive. These multiple combinations show that although erotic tension results from a certain relationship between passive and active, this relationship is particular to each subject and varies depending on the lovers and the moment.

To summarise, the two sexes initially take the same path:

1 Separation from the mother but at the cost of entering into paternal seduction.
2 'Killing' this incestuous and seductive father but now in ways that are distinct and that decide the choice of gender:

1 Boys make war (on the father).
2 Girls make love (with a boy who makes war).

The choice of masculine or feminine depends on the attitude towards the father's seduction: frontal or oblique. This choice will then become embodied in surface differences: woman and men are distinguished by their style, the way they speak, the way they dress, etc.

If masculinity assures itself of its gender by denying feminisation by a father, it is a choice that results from the process of identification; it is not a repression, in the sense of a retroactive effect that creates the symptoms, dreams, etc., of a neurosis. Masculinity is not a symptom. But this relativity of virility must be linked to a bisexuality which remains its basic principle at the 'parricide hour' of the assumption of identity. Boys want to seduce as their father sought to seduce them (following their fantasy) and as he seduced their mother. So they make a frontal assault on the father in order to take his place. And if daughters allow themselves to be seduced – up to a certain point – by the father, they do so only for so long as they need to in order to gather the strength, which the seduction gives, so that they can turn it against the seducer who will be caught in his own trap.

As well as determining the choice of a psychical gender, the father's seduction lights the touch paper of desire. The child who has been seduced as if they were feminine wants to seduce in turn but in a manner that is virile: they want to conquer another self, following the tracks of the 'drive to possess',[29] which has been much altered by the blows of the father. It is no longer a question of simple drive discharge induced by the body of the other since erection is now erotised by castration and is at the service of phallic enjoyment which operates for both genders. The other has to be taken, to be caught by the thousand tricks of seduction. The attempt at physical possession is plain for the boy. But it is no different for the girl: whether she possesses a boy or another girl, she does it as a boy. She has not renounced her primary masculinity. Such is the nature of feminine activity, which is always effective even if, at a given moment, it turns into 'activity with a passive aim' – the manoeuvring that is necessary for being possessed.

Finally, in the gender choice between masculine and feminine, the phallus always remains the sole symbol. And that is because neither men nor women have the phallus. A man only has it as an erection when he desires a woman who, therefore, is as much its owner as the man. Neither has it without the other. So the single phallic symbol presides not only over the birth of bisexuality and its separation into two genders but also over the game of seduction between these two genders, which are always obsessed with this same symbol. Each of them only has it thanks to the other, so desire is brought alive through this *alter ego*, which alone can provide it. Seeking to 'have the phallus' is the mainspring of sexual arousal, which is henceforth entrusted for each subject to the good offices of this 'half of themselves' incarnated by the other sex.[30]

How do we choose between one gender and another?

Thinking about the choice of gender from the starting point of bisexuality is illuminating but also poses new problems. For how will a child make the choice between 'activity with an active goal' and 'activity with a passive goal'? All depends on the child's history and the place that the parents make for the child, treating it as a boy or a girl. This determination results from the attitude of two people, the father and the mother, and from the balance of power between them, which is almost impossible to describe accurately. The best approach is to take two relatively clear scenarios as examples.

The father may feel that he is in a rivalry with his son, which is not a confrontation between man and man; he relives through his son his own position as a child vis-à-vis his mother, and this unconscious transitivism engenders a displaced rivalry (most often repressed by paternal tenderness). This father-son confrontation crystallises in details, most often of an educational nature. The confrontation lends virility to the son (provided that he does not always come off worse and is not physically beaten).

The sense of being in rivalry with this same father will disappear if the child in question is a daughter, especially if (despite his repression) he feels an eroticised emotion towards her – the mark of an incestuous desire that has also been displaced. He plays out with his daughter the part he was unable to play with his own mother; all men were sons before being fathers, and they remain so. This repressed seduction ignites the fire of the daughter's feminisation. So the choice of gender may depend on how the father was more or less seductive towards his child. A father who confronts his son pulls him towards virility. And if he is stirred emotionally by his daughter, she will know how to find the weapons she needs and to turn the situation to her own advantage.

From the point of view of his relationship with his mother, a son will be all the more confident in his masculinity if she experiences herself through him as the boy she once partially was.[31] She can feel the same sexual emotion towards him as she felt towards her father through a transgenerational leap of repressed and displaced incestuous desire.

On the other hand, a daughter of the same mother will risk being devalued because the mother cannot re-enact her masculine transitivism or erotisation with the father. This devaluation makes the girl feel guilty and creates an inextricable bond between her and her mother because how can the latter be content with her daughter? The mother can nevertheless take pleasure in her daughter as a daughter but on condition of a transitivist intimacy which is often suffocating or by maintaining a relationship with her where she plays the man's role. In this case, the mother remains phallic in relation to her daughter.[32]

These scenarios give a sense of the complexities that are involved. We have to reckon with the transitivism of both father and mother (not just with that of one or of the other), not to mention other factors that may be at play between them; the parents may be at war over the gender of their child. To add to the complexity, the child him- or herself will have something to say about these determinations, by either rejecting or going along with what pushes them towards mother or father.

So psychical 'gender' ignores anatomy.[33] But since the choice of psychical gender represses the conditions which determined it, once the choice is made, everyone thinks that he or she was always on the masculine or feminine side (independent of anatomy). Considering themselves to be a man or a woman, they will declare that they were born like that through a 'natural' disposition.

Castration, the engine of desire: wanting to have the phallus or wanting to give it

Some of Freud's reflections on castration seem to privilege visual observation of the anatomical difference between the sexes. The simplicity of the 1925 text on the psychical consequences of the anatomical distinction between the sexes gives an important place to this. According to Freud, the boy exits from the Oedipus complex and the girl enters into it because they actually see the difference and are, therefore, affected by castration anxiety. This observation in her disfavour causes the girl to yearn after the phallus of the father. Later on, Freud nuanced this point of view and suggested that what is at stake is not so much entry into or exit from the Oedipus complex, which plays tricks on both sexes throughout their lives, but rather, entering or exiting from feminisation. Boys leave it behind, or at least start to do so, while girls travel in the opposite direction.

Visual observation of the difference between the sexes is certainly important, but its impact comes later; it is secondary to dread of feminisation by the father which preceded it. Little girls can observe their male playmates for a long time without being much impressed by what they see. The anatomical difference only becomes the support of anxiety insofar as it is preceded by a risk of feminisation by the father. The anxiety provoked by seeing the anatomical difference is subsequent, after the fear of castration has had its impact.[34]

Even supposing that anatomy is seen with crystal clarity, it still harbours a mystery, and the female sex remains the object of an anguished fascination, embodying an otherness that is disturbing and yet indispensable because it enables virility to assert itself. Incredulity regarding the female sex infects the whole of psychical life, not laterally or pathologically but foundationally. How long do children need in order to recognise that their mother does not have a penis? All their life because they remain her child to the end, born in the place of this absence. The being of both child and adult depends on this belief; it is their philosophy.

Anatomy remains a reality quite separate from psychical belief, which elevates the female sex to the height of a difference from itself and thereby makes it a cause of unease or even of anxiety. At every encounter, it is the place of an incredible discovery, a mystery over which a veil must be cast. It remains unassimilable, split off from another belief – that of a world where everyone is equal. The nature of the female sex remains an enigma. It is the origin of thought itself and in a way actually creates the universe. The female sex fascinates and generates a constant doubt: is it really as anatomy describes it? Its configuration is forgotten the moment it is seen. Like the time outside time of the phallic mother, is the phallus there, or is it not there? This uncertainty gradually infects the entirety of perceptions and punctures space with its discontinuity. In true Cartesian fashion, if doubt is the origin of thought, this uncertainty is what founds the subject. Doubt is inscribed from this origin, of which Cartesian doubt is but the poor relation, a ratiocinative thought in endless flight from what it owes to sex.

In the famous painting by Gustave Courbet, *The Origin of the World*, a woman generously offers her sex organ to the contemplation of the aesthete. But what is the origin in question? Not so much childbirth as the existence of the subject of sex, which is born to consciousness precisely when it doubts its perceptions. How many adults are comfortable with the configuration of the female sex organ? Probably none. Even after close examination of how it is made, none of us – not even the most level-headed – can really be comfortable with it and ask to see again in order to verify what has become a cause of excitation that organises the visible world, in a space that is always already sexualised.

In his article on the uncanny, commenting on Hoffmann's tale, *The Sandman*,[35] Freud writes that the '*unheimlich*' effect is provoked by a return of the repressed. The hero of the story is as if hypnotised by the gaze of the doll Olympia. What lends strangeness to the gaze is its sexualisation; in Olympia's eye, the man sees the reflection of a lack that he fears for himself. The eyes tell him that she does not have that which (as he hopes) he does still have, and they also tell of their expectation of what he might give her . . . if he can! So the eyes appropriate in advance a phallus, the volatility of which – that of a fragile erection between two subjects – is conveyed in the gaze more than in any other perception. The confrontation of eyes supports (or does not support) what is at stake, namely, having or not having. Fascination, linked in this way to castration, shows in Hoffmann's tale what the appeal of femininity becomes when its demand is eternalised by the eye of a doll, which never lowers its eyelids. He who looks upon Olympia feels ice-cold dread; it is he who must lower his eyes (and not just his eyes).[36] Based on this relation of the erection to the gaze, the female sex might be roughly represented as an eye, in front of which a man experiences his inner truth; neurotic men, Freud writes, say that they find the female sex uncanny. This is a 'familiar' ('*heimlich*') anxiety since it concerns a testing of desire. To call this paradox 'castration' is to say that what fascinates and provokes dread in men is their own repressed femininity returning in the feeling of the uncanny.

The woman embodies a kind of double, but visibly castrated,[37] and to which men, therefore, desire ardently to give the phallus. She must have it, too, they absolutely must give it to her, and their sexual desire is proportionate to their fear of losing it themselves. Because why would men desire women when women are precisely what makes them anxious? Strongly, erectile castration anxiety orients sexual desire here; one must give in order to restore a parity that has become unbalanced. The denial of castration haunts desire; it is the anxiety-engine that drives desire.

Desire long outlives hope.[38] Freud's neat formula emphasises that the observation of difference motivates unconscious desire rather than collapsing it. For is hope really disappointed? Is it renounced? Not really, not for as long as the fantasy of seduction lasts because seduction obtains, by proxy, what nature seems to refuse. Through seduction, a woman has a man's penis as if she owned it. A woman's jealousy arises from regarding his penis as her own. When a woman provokes an erection, this phallus belongs to her, and her lover may experience castration anxiety, which feminises him. And so it happens that a lover makes the slip of putting himself in the feminine when speaking to the woman he desires; this is a virile slip,[39] which anticipates what he wants to give. Conversely, many women (the most 'feminine' of them and precisely because they are so 'feminine') sometimes talk about themselves using the masculine gender. What is really happening in such instances is a reiteration of the making-two, where the parties try to apportion their own bisexuality. The masculine-feminine slips testify to a struggle: they are the slips of desire. After all, as we noted, 'castration' is synonymous with 'bisexuality'.

In this 'wish for equality' that is at work in desire, the feminine interest in the phallus[40] corresponds to a desire on the masculine side to give the phallus. The symmetry is remarkable. This exchange, with the merits of simplicity and fair dealing, emphasises that castration anxiety and its denial activate desire. Men give to women a phallus which is erect thanks only to women's desire. Men give what they do not have, what women have elicited (what, in a way, belongs to women) and of which they are fearful of being robbed.

In sexual relations, the co-ownership of a single phallus re-enacts the apportioning of bisexuality between feminine and masculine, as testified by the frequent misadventures of sexuality. Erection does not always survive the preliminaries of autoerotism for two, even when driven by a strong desire. Pleasant and exciting as they were, such preliminaries may be followed by erectile failure in the man or the impossibility of being penetrated for the woman. The desire on the male side to give the phallus or, on the female side, to take it (which is also a way of having an erect phallus) puts an end to autoerotic pleasure as the partners enter the field of an enjoyment riven by powerful contradictions, most notably that of the co-ownership of a single phallus. Many facts attest to this: for example, that a man may ejaculate as soon as he penetrates, as if he were himself being penetrated. Or that his erection fails to outlast foreplay. Or even that final discharge cannot be achieved because the momentum becomes continuous; excitement is present, there is give and take, perhaps with enthusiasm, but without conclusion, in what might be described as an anonymous pleasure of the phallus. This suspension is often not a problem for men, when they are less interested in their own pleasure than in that of women. But since some women reason in the same way, the encounter may end by fizzling out. These common scenarios illustrate the sharing of a single phallus, which can only be made erect in the context of a community reduced to a community of acquisitions (which penetration actualises). But how then are we to specify who makes love to who? Who is active and who passive? Where is masculine and where is feminine? We find ourselves in a realm of strife,[41] regulated by the fantasy of seduction: who seduces whom?

This 'war of the sexes' seems to have only two combatants, but if it is governed by castration anxiety, the paternal agent can never be far away. The man, in order to be virile, must take the place of the father, and the woman must release her femininity from capture by this same paternal figure. Behind the scenes of this confrontation, the memory of the father is ever present to the lovers. They must take their bearings from his latent presence. If desire is activated by castration, an impersonal father presides over the scene: the paternal function is evoked not just by what the man is to the woman but also through the woman as desired by the man. Distinct from autoerotism, the fantasy of paternal seduction accentuates the drama of this

back to front enjoyment, structured by an ambivalence of opposites triggering one
another, always jostling each other and colliding.

Homosexualities . . . (and their importance for understanding the interactivity of sexual positions and the 'decline' of the father)

Man or woman? From the viewpoint of psychical gender, there is something like
a mythical starting point, that of being an angel without any sex; this transsexual
position, by wanting to identify the body with a pure phallus, separates it off from
its secondary sexual attributes. This aspiration belongs already to the register of
homosexualities. It is the dream of total equality between male and female: *homo*
without the sexual, a self-intersecting *homo*. This initial angelic aspiration sometimes persists for a lifetime as a wish for the future.

But even in this case, the subjective urgency of phallic sexuation is a prerequisite for survival. Why? Because the choice of sex becomes the card that must be
played in order to counter the death drive (transsexual identification with the phallus). The brutality of this mandate explains the great rigidity of gender choices,
so strong that they seem to be an organic destiny, which cannot be gainsaid.[42] It
is a very early and constant given – whether or not it corresponds to anatomical sex – and it emerges against the background of an initial 'masculine' identity,
where 'masculine' means 'activity', organ enjoyment and choice of the mother as
object. This 'masculine' corresponds to the entry into phallic enjoyment, escaping
the enjoyment of the Other. In this sense, boys and girls identify first of all with the
father, insofar as they want to possess their mother, whom they must at all costs
avoid resembling.

So the child goes to war for a masculinity that they will only obtain on the condition of being at the same time feminised (castrated) by the father with whom they
want to identify. In this combat, the desired objective entails rejection of the feminine and the affirmation of phallicism. This repression of the feminine is such that
women must then battle to recover femininity, which will always remain problematic for them. For men, this repression governs the operation of their heterosexuality. A man loves in a woman what he himself almost was for his father, a movement
from which proceeds both love (for what he was) and hate (for the part of himself
which he rejected). Heterosexuality (exogamous) is based on a 'homosexuality'[43]
(endogamous).

This reminder opens up the field of the homosexualities. We already noted a
mythical 'originary' transsexual moment that would precede the entry into phallicism. It was never viable and corresponds to a regressive potentiality; if they want
to live, the child, whether it likes it or not, enters into phallicism by identifying
with a father.[44]

To see how the different orientations towards gender and the choice of object,
including homosexuality, bifurcate, we must suppose a starting position, which

implies in all cases a 'sexual' attraction towards the mother, that is to say 'hetero-sexuality' for boys and 'homosexuality' for girls. The sexual stance that is easiest to understand is what might be called an 'active feminine homosexuality'.[4546] When certain theoreticians of the feminist movement declare that a first relationship with the mother is what governs homosexuality among women, they are stating a fact, although they omit to say that this relationship with the mother starts out from an identification with the father (so perfect that it remains unnoticed). It is a modality of the murder of the father, without which such a close bond between daughter and mother could not have come about.[47]

The heterosexual link between men and their mother is less well defined. On the one hand, their 'heterosexuality' conceals (represses) the potential feminisa-tion of the subject, and on the other hand, the outcome of this heterosexuality will depend on the place occupied in the family by the father. He may oppose any attempt at identification by the son, or the mother may do her best to undermine the paternal figure, who may indeed be far from robust, etc. If this happens for a girl, these ingredients will strengthen her 'homosexuality', but they have the effect of weakening masculine 'heterosexuality'. If this happens, the bond of identifica-tory love with the father will remain prevalent, creating the conditions for a pas-sive 'homosexual' relationship with the father, which may turn to activity through transitivism.

For a boy, identification with the father can play out according to one of three possibilities. The first (already noted) is the transition to heterosexuality. In this case, the 'homosexual' bond is repressed, and this passage will be even more clearcut when the father desires the mother and vice-versa. In this case, castration will take on its meaning for the child to the extent that he imagines, first of all, that his mother desires his father (she has been castrated by him) and then, sub-sequently, that his father desires his mother (desire which, in a way, castrates the father too). These two conditions together push towards heterosexuality, while the homosexual bond is repressed. Or it might be that only one or other of these two scenarios appears to the child (these are the other two of the three possibilities). One cannot measure in advance the extent to which a man desires a woman or vice-versa or both reciprocally. But we can get an idea of it from the result, namely, on the side of the child, either passive or active homosexuality.

The choice of 'passive homosexuality' corresponds to the scenario where the mother desires the father, but the opposite is not true. The man then embodies an overbearing but distant virile figure. The child, terrorised by this too powerful father (who is not castrated by his desire for his wife), will put himself in a position of passive seduction in relation to him. When he grows up, the son will seek to be loved by men as he would have liked to be loved by his father.

'Active homosexuality' occurs in the opposite scenario: the father may desire the mother, but the converse is not true. The mother gives preference to her child over the father. In this case, the child will grow up to love a man as his mother loved him.[48] Such a mother invalidates sexual desire in general and desire for her husband in particular. So her son will actively love a boy who is reminiscent of himself as he was in the eyes of this maternal love but also as he would have wanted to be desired by his father. He must love boys as his mother loved him but with the addition of the erotism of such a father as he would have liked to have had. It is exciting to love a boy because this other of oneself must enjoy the sexual desire that the intense love emanating from the mother left in suspense. 'Active masculine homosexuality' palliates the erotic lack in the mother's love by the addition of sex, so it operates as a denial of maternal castration, a denial that is prolonged by the capture of another body. Its sexual goal is something like a passion for sodomy.

How are these forced choices to be understood? To make the situation clearer to heterosexuals who repress exactly the same forms of homosexuality: a man will be in a position of passive but repressed homosexuality if he arranges for his wife to be seduced by other men. And he will be in a position of active but repressed homosexuality if nothing excites him more than the conquest of other men's wives. These are commonplace positions, easily observable in everyday life.

The urgency of sexual identity and of the selection of a corresponding object determine different choices. We have examined four positions: 'active feminine homosexuality', 'masculine heterosexuality', 'passive masculine homosexuality' and 'active masculine homosexuality'.[49] These descriptions concern the sexual choices (gender identification and choice of object) made in childhood, but they are inscribed only as dotted lines. Not until adolescence can these choices be confirmed in the form of a fixation of the polymorphous perversion of childhood. Heterosexuality or one of the homosexualities may assert itself, but the latter may also turn into more or less firmly established heterosexuality after a certain period of activity during adolescence. Most children and then most adolescents manifest homosexual inclinations at one time or another, which are confirmed or invalidated thereafter.

The logical possibilities so far mark out three types of homosexuality: an 'active feminine homosexuality' and two 'masculine homosexualities', one 'active' and the other 'passive'. The spirit of symmetry calls for the existence of a 'passive feminine homosexuality', but this category is problematic because desire is vectorised only from the agent of castration, i.e., the father. It is easy to see that 'passive homosexuality' in relation to the father can exist for a man, but if a woman is in this position, it is of course called heterosexuality. And yet 'passive feminine homosexuality' does exist. How can such a preference come about? To see how, we need to ask: why would a woman allow herself to be loved by one of her sisters and to be loved by her as a woman? We often notice that when a woman allows herself to be seduced by an active female homosexual, this adventure follows an episode of orthodox heterosexuality. Everything happens as if a disappointment in heterosexual love resulted in an episode of homosexuality, which lasts for some time. A certain number of 'object changes' follow one another in this way, although a fixation may also occur. So we find a general rule: everything suggests that this disillusionment in relation to a man follows an earlier disappointment in relation to the father. The father provoked sexual arousal but did not satisfy it. In particular, the father is experienced as disappointing at the time of the girl's first period (of which he is often not informed). Menstruation signifies the absence of the child expected from him, and here, we have the disappointment, the consequence of which may be homosexuality as the first stage of feminine love life.

The young woman who has been disappointed allows herself to be loved by an active female homosexual who is indeed well-suited to invoke the flawed father since she represents one of the stereotypes of his image; every neurotic has imagined at one time or another that his or her father was absent, homosexual or impotent since he provokes desire in his son or daughter but fails to take action. So the homosexual, whatever their sex, is a worthy representative of the father to the point of becoming worthy of interest for many women, who prove fond of such friends, and active female homosexuals can occupy a place of choice in this incarnation of the father. They signify not only that the father is impotent but that he can be advantageously replaced by a woman, who will always manage things better than him when it comes to enjoyment.

The existence of passive homosexuality alternating with heterosexuality enables a further step – that of qualifying this type of passive feminine homosexuality as 'adult' since to access it, one must first experience love for a father who disappoints. It is a homosexuality which follows a disappointed heterosexuality, as is the rule with the father; this feminine homosexual moment is the exogamous condition of the passage to adulthood. As we have already seen, adult masculine heterosexuality also presupposes an earlier adolescent passage via latent or manifest homosexuality. However, on the masculine side, it is not disappointment that governs the passage to heterosexuality but rather, the anxiety of being feminised.

A passive 'adult' homosexual woman often forms a couple with an active homosexual woman by identification with the father (linked with the polymorphous perversion of the child). But two 'adult' homosexual women may also pair up because this female homosexuality is passive in the same way as femininity: it is 'actively passive'.[50] Each of the partners can exchange with the other her love for the Woman. It should be emphasised that it is a *masculine* identification here that is part of this 'adult' homosexuality, by identification not with the father but with the man (by mourning the man who disappointed). There is a transition to homosexuality by identification with the man in order to mourn him, by putting oneself in his place and behaving with a woman in the same way as he should have done. 'Passive adult feminine homosexuality' can, therefore, be linked with another form that follows disappointment: an 'active adult feminine homosexuality', also situated beyond the framework of childhood. 'Adult' feminine homosexuality is, therefore, divided into two currents: a passive one (seeking to be loved by a woman) and an active one (identifying with the man who loves this woman).

This concept of 'adult' homosexuality may seem bizarre, yet it corresponds to the transition from infantile neurosis to adult neurosis. It is distinct from the first three types of homosexuality described earlier, which are endogamous and extend the endgame of childhood and the polymorphous perversion of those years. Object choices are then direct duplicates of parental figures, usually inverted: for example (as already described), a man loves a boy as his mother loved him or as his father made himself desired, which amount to two very different kinds of homosexual attractions. By contrast, masculine and feminine heterosexuality, as well as the passive and active feminine homosexualities that deserve to be qualified as 'adult', pass through the pangs of adolescence before their choices are settled.

This 'adult' feminine homosexuality is very different from that of militant lesbians, who identify less with the man than with the father. Although it is surely more widespread than masculine homosexuality since it is a basic part of structure ('normal', one might say), and is compatible with heterosexuality, this 'adult' feminine homosexuality is little acknowledged in lesbian subculture. While most male homosexuals are attached to 'gay' culture, to which they look for legitimisation and protection, the majority of female homosexuals take no interest in it.

There is a great difference between the 'adult' character of feminine homosexuality and that part of the homosexuality of men that we have considered so far, where sexual practices are predominantly attached to the polymorphous perversion of childhood. Contrasting attitudes to relationship loyalty are evidence of this. 'Adult' feminine homosexuality most often begins after puberty and arises from a romantic friendship, which leads to sexual activity. The same is not true for homosexual men, the majority of whom privilege sexuality to the detriment of love or friendship. If we are to believe the statistics on homosexuality presented by Corraze,[51] 90% of homosexual men are used to encounters that are totally devoid of feelings of attachment and where conversation is kept to a minimum. This is especially true in special meeting places such as saunas or backrooms, which may not even be lit. A significant number of homosexual men, those at least who prefer to continue polymorphous perverse practices, give exclusive preference to this type of relationship. Infidelity is the rule for them (or rather the question of fidelity does not even arise), whereas, on the contrary, fidelity governs feminine homosexuality.[52] One may then ask why on earth fidelity should be considered a criterion of adulthood. And indeed, what is at stake is not so much fidelity as guilt. For the child, innocence prevails, everything is an entitlement, and the burden of debt and guilt only makes itself felt after the end of the latency period. The lover feels guilt by provoking love, and this guilt may then pressure them to be faithful.[53]

On the feminine side there is a stronger motive for valuing fidelity. 'Adult' feminine homosexuality is linked to castration anxiety and not to its denial. At the end of the latency phase, the girl expects to receive the penis from a man, but he inevitably disappoints because the first in the series is none other than the father. Endogamously, the latter refuses the penis to his daughter who experiences a more or less violent sense of rejection and reacts with a spell of homosexuality. In this case, loving a woman (as a man should have done) will serve as a fall-back and will function as the equivalent of having the penis. So *love* palliates castration anxiety and replaces penis envy; hence, the intoxicating madness of a young girl's love for one of her sisters, and this love, because it comes into the place of penis envy, will generate clitoral arousal of a phallic nature. But unlike the type of masculine homosexuality described earlier, it will have love as a prerequisite. This enables a better understanding of the fidelity of homosexual women; the condition of their penis envy is love, which follows directly from a fantasy of masculinisation. Masculine homosexuality, on the other hand, despite also playing out at the end of the latency phase, does not have love as a condition (love instead of penis envy) but involves an initiatory moment:[54] the boy accedes to virility by identifying with paternal impersonality or by loving like a phallic mother, forging homosexual bonds (active or passive) with other boys.

Disappointed by the father, young girls start to like other young girls, although more often than not, they are not disappointed for long and quickly regain hope. Not because a man knows how to show them a satisfaction of penis envy that is more in conformity with anatomy but because the exogamous man promises them the death of the disappointing father. So a kind of revenge against the father is a condition of the transition to heterosexuality (the father must cry bitterly on the girl's wedding day).[55] It may seem that the passage experienced by most women from homosexuality to heterosexuality is down to the passion of a man, who prevails over the homosexual inclination of the one he loves. But this edifying phenomenology, where the kiss of Prince Charming awakes Sleeping Beauty from her sleep of disappointment, says nothing of the unconscious fantasies that are at play here. The man loves a woman who, he senses, loves another woman. His love does not have the ethereal purity of children's stories but stems from a masculine fantasy that calls for two women. A 'masculinised' woman may love another woman out of spite towards her father. The man here may organise his heterosexuality through the love of a woman (representing himself) who loves another woman (like him). He needs two women in order to himself be a man. To love a woman who loves a woman thus corresponds to a male fantasy. And through him, the woman can also keep alive her dream of loving another woman. As if wearing her perfume, the man fits his homosexual inclinations into his heterosexuality. On the feminine side, feminine homosexuality does not disappear but is transformed into jealousy of the rival, which is never absent from even the most trusting form of love.

The importance of this relationship of heterosexuality to homosexuality must be recognised, and it is undoubtedly what led Freud to use a particular concept, that of 'retirement' ('Ausweichen'), in order to capture the specificity of 'adult' feminine homosexuality. In his paper *On the Psychogenesis of a Case of Female Homosexuality,*[56] Freud describes the case of a young girl who is prey to an unrequited and platonic passion for a woman who is still young but older than her. She is brought to Freud by her parents after a suicide attempt. Freud states that the girl's passionate attachment amounts to a masculine identification. Her change of gender and object choice occurred because she wanted a child from her father and was dismayed when her mother became her triumphant competitor, giving birth to a new baby. Freud writes: 'She changed into a man and took her mother in place of her father as the object of her love'.[57] The girl 'retired' in favour of her mother. As Freud puts it: 'If, then, the girl became homosexual and left men to her mother (in other words, "retired in favour of" her mother), she would remove something which had hitherto been partly responsible for her mother's dislike'.[58]

This inverted love not only seeks an identification with the father by loving women as he loves women but it also seeks revenge for a betrayal. The traitor must pay for his treachery. Hence, the constant effort to ensure that the father is aware of his daughter's homosexual loves.

The vengeful nature of her 'retirement' makes it more than a simple identification. The father is always, in some way, a traitor in the eyes of the daughter (or son) who loves him, most often without the father knowing it. The poor man has no recourse: either he is a traitor because he prefers someone else (usually a *fait accompli*) or he is incestuous, which is even more heinous. So there will always be a reason for exacting vengeance on the father, and the ostentatious 'retirement' through choosing another gender is one modality of this. Hence, the urgency that drives many homosexuals, at some point in their lives, to inform their parents of their choices. Heterosexuals rarely bother to do so.

Beyond this vengeful demonstration of the change of object, often played out directly to the father, the whole of society may need to become its witness. We should, of course, tread carefully here. Respect is due to the recent and justified revolt against age-old oppression.[59] But is there not more at stake here when we remember that the greater part of society today takes little interest in the sexuality or sexual 'deviations' of individuals, each person having their own? In a country like France, where secularism and unbelief have been pervasive for several centuries, everyone manages as best they can with their sexuality and does not usually wish to make it into a public matter.[60] The demand for recognition only becomes collective when the singularity of retirement is augmented by a transgressive wish that is specific to certain kinds of homosexuality (perverse ones, in particular). The exasperation which the father or, by extension, the patriarchal stratum of society then manifests, is proportional to what is felt as a provocation. The father's angry reaction to this demonstration has less to do with homophobia than with a wound from the loss of filiation, compounded by jealousy at seeing his daughter (that is to say, his son) go off with somebody else. This aspect of his anger is the sign of his own repressed homosexuality.

It is also important to note that 'retirement' invalidates any genetic conception of sexual maturation. There is no progressive pathway from homosexuality to heterosexuality. Children are not homosexuals to begin with before becoming interested in the opposite sex. On the contrary, the affirmation of gender is immediate, either feminine (loving men) or masculine (loving women) or different combinations that combine these two terms, according to varying positions as to gender and object choice. In these different combinations, the sexual identity of the lover is the point according to which the choice of love object varies (this is what happens in the phenomenon of 'retirement'). For example, a man who recognises himself as a man may for a time love men, then women or both. But his identity will only change relative to this choice of object, which does not follow a progression from 'less good' to 'better', from a first homosexual phase towards a heterosexual choice. It is in the space of this variability that fixation will occur, depending on the vagaries of love and history. Fixation is not due to some blockage in the course of a structural progression. Indeed, fixation on a particular object occurs just as much in homosexuality as in heterosexuality. The subject doggedly loves that which, in his or her imagination, completes them – the other in whom they hope to refind themselves. It is a love that comes before knowledge of what sexuality means; it is a choice that hurts, and sex soothes the pain as best it can.

It is important now to look in more detail at what we have called 'adult masculine homosexuality'. It does not attract a great deal of attention and is not at all militant, but it may well be the majority position. There are neurotic, hysterical or obsessive men whose homosexuality has its heyday in adolescence when it is the endogamous gateway to future heterosexual exogamy. This 'initiatory' moment is the motor of heterosexuality as the logical consequence of endogamous homosexuality. Besides these episodes of adolescent homosexuality, homosexual choice can persist transiently, cyclically or with greater longevity. In these cases, homosexuality requires love as a prerequisite, while sexual practices are only a contingent consequence and are usually limited (active or passive sodomy is generally excluded, except as an experiment). Fantasy love for men can flourish with a minimum of acting out or even entirely without sexuality. The sexual goal can be inhibited even if love is firmly established. We see here the difference from 'adult' feminine homosexuality, which is almost always accompanied by sexual excitement.

In neurotic hysteria (standard for men), repressed endogamous homosexuality pushes constantly towards exogamous heterosexuality. Psychoanalysts have perhaps been a little hasty when they find in the myth of Don Juan – the archetypal seducer – none other than an unusual homosexual. In fact, this mythical hero only demonstrates the role of the father in ordinary heterosexuality and how it spurs the conquest of each woman. The father imposes his law, whether he appears in the guise of the Commendatore (in Mozart's opera) or that of the Eternal Father of religion, when the repentant seducer enters a monastery (in other versions). This masculine hysterical position has the same objectives as feminine seduction and enacts identical scenarios. Love of the father pushes towards an imperative heterosexuality without excluding homosexuality, which remains its potential point of regression; whenever a situation requires the love of the father, the homosexuality of adolescence may rise from its ashes.

This fixation of homosexuality in hysteria differs from that at work in obsessional neurosis. For the obsessional neurotic, the death of the father is a matter of constant doubt, which may produce fixation to love for a man – either a ferocious father or, by reversion, a youth. But this love runs the risk of being strongly de-erotised by the transition to the adult neurosis. As a general rule, neurosis emerges in ambivalence towards the father, who is loved because he saves and hated because he is a rival. Love pushes towards homosexuality, while hatred creates a repression of love and pushes towards heterosexuality (this is the hysterical position). But in obsession, the love for the father is constantly accompanied by the fantasy of his murder, without either of these terms being repressed, driven by a perpetual doubt. The fixation point of obsessive homosexuality stems from a doubt concerning the death of the father, a symbolic event made uncertain by an incestuous proximity to the mother. This is quite different from hysteria: the mother of the obsessional does not put her child in the place of her phallus but in the place of a man who could give her the penis. So she eliminates the man who is her husband and who is at the same time the father of the child. The child would gladly put an end to the father, in accordance with the Oedipal wish, but at the same time, the father must live in order to play his role as a man with the child's mother. The result is an immense debt of love to the father since he must save the child, not from the position of being the phallus but from the position of being the husband of the mother. The father's quality as a man is desired *before* his quality as a father. Hence, a potential fixation in love for a man but a love that will be constantly in question and, therefore, inhibited because behind the man looms the father, whom the child hopes to get rid of. Love of the father pushes towards choice of a masculine object, and the murder fantasy, which would have favoured heterosexuality, is kept in check by this same love.[61] Sexuality is impeded and is often limited to masturbation. There is a link here between this inhibited love and the fantasy of the primal scene; witnessing a copulation becomes a kind of rescue obsession where the father is first and foremost a man before he is a father. So he becomes a sexual character – a real husband – and it is in this capacity that he elicits a strange love, which strives to pay the debt of the parricide wish; the obsessive plunges 'debt-first' into the primal scene.

Our conclusion then is that a certain number of homosexual positions may crystallise under the pressure of castration anxiety. Starting from a transsexual origin that is always retroactive, we described active feminine homosexuality and active and passive masculine homosexuality, relating all of these to the polymorphous perversion of childhood. After adolescence, we looked at the 'adult' scenarios of passive and active feminine homosexuality, as well as active and passive masculine homosexuality. There remains one last question to consider: can we say that coupling, even between two subjects of the same anatomical sex, still brings into play the masculine-feminine relationship? Does a homosexual couple not in principle presuppose such a pairing through the basic paradigm of possession? Certainly, any subject recognises him- or herself as one of the two genders, and even in a couple that is anatomically homosexual, one of the two represents the woman and the other the man since erotism is always aroused and motivated by the mirage of imaginary completeness. For human beings, sexual arousal has nothing natural about it. It results from castration anxiety, that is to say implicitly from a relationship to the other sex. If this were not the case, why would homosexuals frequently live in (often very conformist) couples? And we should note that homosexual couples often experience the same split between love and desire, the same jealousies, the same dreams of unbridled freedom opposed to a constraining and boring conjugality as are experienced by heterosexuals.

However, it is clear that in such a coupling, the 'feminine' no longer has any relation to the anatomical configuration of a woman (it may, perhaps, be a phallic woman). In the context of perversion, sexual arousal itself results from the denial of this implicit heterosexuality, the presence of which is, therefore, completely obscured; if either partner in a male homosexual couple is asked whether he is the man or the woman in their relationship, we are often told that each of them loves a man as a man. When two partners are of the same sex, their unconscious fantasies can nevertheless attribute opposite sexes to each other, with the difference concealed in the erotic activity itself, each treating their partner as they themselves had wished to be treated. A young man, for example, may treat another young man as a woman, that is to say as what he had failed to become himself, while his partner may do exactly the same towards him. So the masculine-feminine difference is indeed at stake in this homosexual relationship, but it remains invisible; each of the protagonists desires a man as a man. Difference is denied in this process, and this denial is what drives the erotic tension as such.

Finally, a remark on homosexualities from the point of view of psychoanalytic treatment. If homosexuality was to be considered a 'fixation' at some point in development, it would then be necessary to add that a development *without* 'fixation' – a 'complete and harmonious' development – should lead to heterosexuality, according to a natural pre-established sexuality. In this case, homosexuality would be a pathological accident which could be put right, and the subject would then evolve towards heterosexuality. This would be to treat homosexuality as a symptom which can be mobilized; transference entails regression up to the historical fixation point of the symptom, whereby the fixation is undone.

But homosexuality is not a symptom because it is a choice of gender and love object, which is an entirely different process. Regression under transference cannot liberate a subject from his object of love in the way that it liberates from a symptom. Transference regression cannot undo either the homosexual identification or its love object because these are not symptoms but the result of two determinations: of gender and of object. Once the subject's desire has been oriented in this way, desire itself maintains this fixation. This is in total contrast with the symptom, which is not fixated by desire. How would a fixation be changed when desire itself is what fixates it? A homosexual does not usually ask for his identity and choice of object to be changed and that is why he does not actually change them in the course of an analysis. He doubtless hopes for the alleviation of his sufferings and anxieties, but how could he ask to change his desire, when desire is precisely what sustains him? When changes do occur, they affect the flexibility of what Freud called 'retirement' and the avatars of bisexuality.

To conclude, we might note an infrequent but significant scenario: in analytic treatment transference, love generates trauma and disappointment, which sometimes take the form of a 'retirement'. Some men, for example, believe during their analysis that they have found themselves to be homosexual. This development, which is to be put down to transference disappointment, will be all the more insistent if the analyst has intimated to them that they need to take seriously any manifestation of their repressed homosexuality. At the slightest untimely acquiescence from the analyst, the patient risks becoming suddenly certain that the truth of his desire is same-sex love. It thus happens that analysands may take a sudden turn in their choice of object and restrict themselves for more or less time to a certain form of homosexuality and to assorted (often limited) sexual practices.

This will be due to the trauma of transference love rather than the revelation of the truth of desire.

Homosexuality shows the relativity and the evolution of norms

On June 27, 1968, a riot broke out in a gay bar in Greenwich Village. It was the first act of a movement that has been growing ever since. After much controversy, it was to lead, for example, to the demedicalisation of homosexuality, which was no longer considered a mental illness in the American classifications of the DSM-III.[62] Although the number of homosexuals has probably not increased, their place in the public arena is now much greater than before. The importance of the gay rights movement far outstrips its numerical weight.[63]

Why is this minority movement so important to the whole of society today? It could be said that everyone suppresses their homosexuality, so everyone feels concerned. But that has always been the case, so we need reflect on the specifics of the question as they present themselves now. It is worth reflecting here on the great upheavals that gradually delegitimised the *potestas* of the father of the family. In Roman law, the father was equal to God and had power of life and death over his *gens*. Nowadays, we have some insight into the psychology of this deification: when a son becomes a father, he does indeed dispatch his own father to heaven, and it is from this Eternal Father that he derives his legitimacy, which is fundamentally oppressive and murderous towards all who deviate from the patriarchal ideal.

Christianity adopted the principles of this domination in the name of God – a system where the guilt of the sons vis-à-vis their father pushed them to act for their redemption. As well as having children in the name of their fathers, the sons invented, built and manufactured in order to ensure their salvation. Guilt became the motor of ever more rapid progress, until the moment when this enlightenment machine outgrew itself and became counterproductive. God legitimised the patriarchy since the deity embodied the dead father, and science – his secular child – eventually showed that no Eternal Father could explain causation.

The unbearable patriarchal law pushed the sons towards the future, and some of them came to prefer women. The repressed homosexual bond of father to son gave way to heterosexuality and, more generally, to unrepressed sexuality. So we see what it is that has delegitimised the patriarchy since the Age of Enlightenment. Science has explored the sky, the seas, the earth, the economy, history and the psyche and has found no trace of God but only laws. The mathematical God who never dies and knows only these laws – the laws that govern the order of the universe – is the reverse of the eternal (dead) God of patriarchy and monotheism. The God of monotheism was the father who had to be killed (in fantasy) because of the sexual trauma he inflicted on both boys and girls. Once the patriarch had been dispatched to heaven, sexual desire in general had to be suppressed, or it was only lawful for the purposes of giving to the father a child bearing his name. All sexual activity over and above this modest allowance had to be repressed, and it was fiercely repressed. This father had been the object of a parricide fantasy because he had imposed castration, i.e., a difference made explicit by the difference of the sexes. So as soon as he lost his legitimacy, there was nothing to oppose the love of sameness. What is more, if the father no longer castrates, there is no bar to loving him and to being loved by him. The hegemony of a father who is as natural as he is scientific not only accords with homosexuality but it also invites the love of such a father who, moreover, can no longer be distinguished from the father of perversion.[64]

The problems of sexuality are foregrounded today as never before: everyone is preoccupied with the specificity of their way of loving rather than trying to make it fit with a norm. Moreover, the norm itself is valued differently: marriages for love have become the rule (previously, most marriages were arranged by families). The interest accorded to sexuality loses all selectivity; it is directed to infantile and feminine sexuality, heterosexuality, homosexuality as well as any form of perversion.[65]

Homosexuality has occupied a special and ever more important place in this liberation movement, as demonstrated by the end (or great reduction) of the stigma attached to it. Sodomites were no longer at risk of the stake since the French Revolution, but homosexuality remained taboo long after. This is much less the case in ordinary life today. But this progress has been accompanied by a truly astonishing particularity that has more to do with the ideology of society, namely, the kind of ascendancy, mastery, even occasionally, terrorism, which homosexual activism exerts on cultural and political life. This specificity goes beyond the simple marginalisation of patriarchal ideals. As we have said, the repressive Eternal Father of monotheism, who legitimised the *potestas* of patriarchy, has given way to a sort of demiurge of science, a reasonable god, legitimised by calculations and for whom Nature lays down the law.

This god resembles Spinoza's *Deus sive natura*, who in turn is not unlike 'the Supreme Being in wickedness' dear to Sade. Such a god, merged with natural forces, was the god of totemic societies like those of Greco-Roman antiquity, and it is surely no coincidence that in these societies, homosexuality had a very different and socially sanctioned status. The great Caesar was a man for women and a woman for men. For the Greek, the Roman, the Japanese samurai or the Maasai warrior, homosexual love was the norm. In antiquity, familiarity with the living father was compatible with sodomy. So if the same natural familiarities are found today, are we to think that the god of science would be nothing other than a sodomite? Have we then returned to the Hellenic dawn that Heidegger yearned for?[66] Not at all. What is occurring is not a reflorescence of totemism but a quite different and remarkable evolution. Homosexuality is idealised today in the wake of a secularisation of monotheism (that was not the case in the societies just mentioned). We are not regressing towards the past but advancing towards another horizon, the nature of which (as ever) we do not know.

With the twilight of religions, the dead father abandons the heavens. How are we to imagine a dead father (or rather his dead desire), a father who would henceforth live on earth? Nothing could be easier. It suffices to represent him as impotent or as a homosexual. This representation haunts the discourse of analysands, who for a time consider their father to be impotent or gay. Their belief stems from a wish: as the father provokes sexual desire and seduces his daughter or his feminised son but fails to follow through and act, he will be charged with impotence or suspected of homosexuality. This widespread belief is hard to shift because it gives a straightforward explanation of the neutralisation of paternal virility. The homosexual father? Behold our Eternal Father descended to earth![67]

Why, though, has this belief spread so widely? In monotheism, the two figures of the paternal complex were distributed between heaven for the dead father and earth for the living father. In postmodern times, these two figures are on earth, leading to a new distribution of the paternal complex (and new family distributions). Now the violating father is no longer dispatched to heaven; he wanders among us unpitied and hounded on all sides. In democratic, more or less atheistic, regimes, seducing fathers are dragged before the courts for the smallest suspicious gesture. Deprived of a religious outlet, the mass propagation of this fantasy implies that the dead father descends not just to earth but continues on to hell, where he joins his accomplice, the devil.[68]

This new staging of the paternal complex has multiple forms and sometimes presents itself in curious ways. For example, the prostitute has always been a way for men to circumvent the father's sexual repression (therefore, to kill him). This place of transgression is experiencing a remarkable evolution: many of today's practitioners of the oldest profession are transvestite men, and their clients – not unaware of the fact, even though the assumption of femininity is often perfect – are more than happy to go along with it. Beneath the transvestite, we feast on this *nouvelle cuisine* father, previously enjoyed thanks to women but now served up with a homoerotic sauce.

So the image of the homosexual now represents culturally a certain idealised figure of the father. Certainly, male homosexuals have an advantage in this role-playing game, but female homosexuality is also significant here and specifically the kind where 'activity' corresponds to a version-towards-the-father[69] (where the sexual position is also sustained by an identification with the father). Instead of viewing the current social status of homosexuality as one achievement among others of sexual liberation, we might view it also as an unexpected incarnation of the figure of the father, who has been saved *in extremis*. Taking over from the castrated and dead father, it presents in its own way a visible aspect of the paternal complex. Certain masculine and feminine homosexualities which are constructed on the traces of the perversions of childhood represent a last stand for the ancient father, bearer of the phallus, who reigned before our sickly Messiah. They are the last remaining domain where one does not mess with the phallus and where the worship of sexual potency is still central. To this extent, some forms of homosexual militancy can claim a kind of spiritual hegemony over society.

Old ideals have not disappeared, despite the obituary penned by postmodernism, but are directly actualised in the present. Their status has changed from future to virtual.[70] The ideal is no longer projected into the future, as happened during the era of modernity and the secularisation of ideals. Now the ideals might seem to have disappeared, but they are only in this state of virtuality where they are real-ised by a passage to the act. The cultural image of homosexuality thus represents a name of the father that has passed from virtual to actual, and as such, it functions as an ideal *in praesentia*, making its services available to the whole of society. To be the successor of a declining patriarchy is a hard task indeed. Seen in this light, the success of the militant wing of the gay movement far beyond American college campuses becomes comprehensible; the particular image of the homosexual here is linked not just to the prestige acquired in a struggle against oppression but also to the paternal figure, whom he represents, though no doubt without wanting to.

This is the context in which certain gay liberation groups in the USA have claimed the role of a vanguard or, in any case, have considered themselves to be the revolutionary catalyst for society as a whole. Their subculture not only militates for their own minority – an attitude that would give it a role in society similar to that of the women's liberation movement – but has also at times presented itself as a messianic[71] vanguard of postmodernity. Admittedly, the effect is more strik-ing in the United States than elsewhere since it is in the United States that gay and lesbian studies have generated the new concept of 'queer'.[72] For this movement, to defend the sexually marginalised is to defend everyone who is marginalised. The Marxist rhetoric of this proposition is patent: just as the liberation of the proletariat is equivalent to the liberation of society as a whole, so gay people fight for the liberation of all sexual oppression, that is to say, for the future of the human race.[73]

In the countries of old Europe, the 'political' has a meaning framed by a long past, and it might seem hard to understand how a claim concerning sexual identity could have such revolutionary significance. They will point out the existence of blatantly fascist homosexual movements in the United States and of some similar trends in France. To oppose the oppression of a minority is certainly a political act, but that does not entail that to be a member of this minority would itself be a political act and even less that it would be revolutionary. The 'transgender' of queer people seems to be a private matter: why discuss it in the public arena? Everyone manages with their sexuality as best they can, and any public exhibition might seem to some to be a perverse provocation of the law or a desire to make life harder for heterosexuals, as if the latter did not have their own problems with the law.

However, if the emergence of these claims is linked to the erosion of patriarchy, things get more complicated; a very real question does indeed arise because sexu-ality only remains a private problem for those who repress it, i.e., the traditional fraternal patriarchy. This repression certainly bears on homosexuality but also on sexual enjoyment in general and feminine enjoyment in particular – all this in the name of the father-son bond. So we do have a real 'political' problem, albeit in an unusual sense. An unexpected questioning of the traditional social bond emerges via claims which, although they may seem marginal, raise a fundamental problem. Love, long kept in the shadows, enters the political stage here.

The result is a knot between the public and the private that is difficult to disen-tangle and liable to generate explosive ambiguities. Homosexuality has become a sociological shibboleth. Countless studies have been devoted to it, although the psychoanalytical dimension remains little explored. The emphasis on the political dimension and the plethora of sociological studies have the strange result of erasing the psychical dimension and neglecting the avant-garde position that Freud once took. Everything is presented today as if homosexuality was a natural fact with little room for personal history – an ineluctable organic specificity, which somehow affects human beings alone of all the earth's species. 'Science' plays an important role in this: the 'homosexuality gene' has already been discovered several times or at least announced in the press. As if by way of exception to the sexual choices of the rest of humanity, this homosexuality-from-birth is presented with complete neglect of unconscious desire and the question of filiation.

For example, the position of homosexuals in relation to their family is barely mentioned. But according to the statistics already quoted, only 2% of the parents of homosexuals say that they accept their child's choice. One imagines the subjective suffering that this implies for all parties, and new legislation will hardly be able to settle these debts to parents and family and to obtain their recognition, notably by the paths of a filiation, which is securely present despite everything. Moreover, if we are to believe the same statistics, 70% of homosexuals questioned before the age of 25 would have preferred not to be homosexual, and they have found it hard to adapt to. If an enjoyment stronger than themselves propelled them in spite of everything towards what they did not ostensibly want, then this interdiction (the 'not wanting') may itself have exacerbated the enjoyment; it conditioned desire, and it was first of all *internal*. We can also understand what a relief it would be to make it external.

The more the liberation movement grows, the more the lack of an external obstacle that would relieve the internal pain may be felt. So a search for prohibition or even for repression may be an undercurrent of the liberation movement itself. In some instances, a taste for provocation may even prevail over the content of justified claims, as if purposely seeking their refusal. For example, the parody element in same-sex marriage, with one partner dressed in white, is not designed to attract sympathy. Liberation flirts with an impossible limit because for a brief moment, the limit fulfils desire.[74] A certain number of claims, such as that of marriage or the adoption of a child, might even be felt as a testing of this limit point and their achievement as not really being that important in itself or even obsolete once obtained. We might think that homosexuality is seeking here to mimic heterosexuality or to fulfil a contract that it made with itself for a return to 'normality', but this would be odd given the obvious fact that today more than ever, traditional norms are being exploded. Perhaps, then, there may be an element here of making the ordinary heterosexual uncomfortable, making him or her the object of ridicule and enjoyment in the name of higher ideals. In the early days of the French Republic, the Marquis de Sade showed to what use such beautiful ideals as liberty, justice and equality could be put, not because their scrupulous application borders on perversion but rather because perversion is never so exquisite as when it proclaims justice, freedom, etc. So conditions for enjoyment are placed in an embarrassing contiguity with a political problem because the ending of terrible oppression and the recognition of basic rights for gay people remain absolutely legitimate, even if they may sometimes advance under the flag of a manifest, even perverse provocation.

Notes

1   Gender attributes certainly do not spring from a natural identity. But can we say for all that, as Judith Butler does, that they are governed by performatives: 'There is no gender identity behind the expressions of gender; [. . .] identity is performatively constituted by the very "expressions" that are said to be its results' (Judith Butler, *Gender Trouble*. London: Routledge, 1990, p. 25). If, as Butler has suggested, the term 'performative' refers to Austin's 'speech acts' (John Austin, *How to Do Things with Words*. Oxford: Oxford University Press, 1962), we can note the exorbitant role given to such acts, which relegates processes of identification to the background. But then an insoluble problem arises: who will be the subject of this sort of discursive technology of nomination? Butler's claim is that the phallocentric patriarchy is the 'subject' of this discursivity. But then who names such a subject or subjects, etc.? The politics of the operation are of interest, but its theoretical basis is inconsistent.

2   'In all of us, throughout life, the libido normally oscillates between male and female objects [. . .] even in a normal person it takes a certain time before the decision in regard to the sex of the love-object is finally made' (Freud [1920], *The Psychogenesis of a Case of Homosexuality in a Woman* in *Standard Edition 18*, pp. 158, 168).

3   As suggested, for example, by Monique Wittig, *The Straight Mind and Other Essays*. Boston, MA: Beacon Press, 1992, p. 20.

4   Freud writes at several places in the *Three Essays* that this excitation poses a problem. For example, 'the process of sexual excitation – a process the nature of which has, it must be confessed, become highly obscure to us'. Yet he had already at least discovered its consequences since he writes a couple of pages later that neurotic symptoms result from sexual trauma: they are 'the counterpart of the influences which bring about the production of sexual excitation' (Freud [1905], *Three Essays on the Theory of Sexuality* in *Standard Edition 7*, pp. 204, 206).

5   The term 'genitality' is also infelicitous, but better use a more precise term than a vocabulary that would be poetic but confused.

6   Freud, *op. cit.*, pp. 142–143.

7   'Each of the two loves in the other the refusal of him or herself' (Georges Bataille [1944], *Guilty* (S. Kendall, trans.). Albany, NY: State University of New York Press, 2011, p. 96).

8   As Lacan writes: 'Castration cannot be deduced from development alone, since it presupposes the subjectivity of the Other as the locus of its law. The difference between the sexes [*L'altérité du sexe*] is denatured by this alienation. A man serves here as a relay so that a woman becomes this Other to herself, as she is to him' (Jacques Lacan, 'Guiding Remarks for a Convention on Female Sexuality' in *Ecrits. The First Complete Edition in English* (B. Fink, trans.). New York: Norton, 2006, p. 616).

9   As affirmed by this quotation from Freud (many others could be cited): 'The assumption that all human beings have the same (male) form of genital is the first of the many remarkable and momentous sexual theories of children' (Freud, *op. cit.*, p. 195). Similarly, in *The Infantile Genital Organisation*, Freud [1923] writes: 'for both sexes, only one genital organ, the male, plays a role. There is therefore not a genital primacy, but a primacy of the phallus' (*The Infantile Genital Organisation* in *Standard Edition 19*, p. 142).

10 This transgender primacy of the phallus breaks with physiology, shaped only by the desire of the Other, and it is what gives to human sexuality its skewed tempo. The penile or clitoral erogenous zone has an equal phallic value for both genders, and if girls seem to be a little worse off in terms of size, it is really enjoyment that counts here and this is equal.

11 And specifically, without any relation to an organic bisexuality.

12 Or to put it another way: from there being a single symbol, one would have to deduce that there is a single gender, a monosexuality of sorts, abandoning the precious bisexuality which Freud always insisted on.

13 Significantly, the word 'enfant' ('child') has no gender in French: 'We call "epicene" a word – noun, pronoun or adjective – which does not vary according to its gender: "enfant" can designate a boy or a girl; "toi" ["you"] says nothing about sex; "jaune" ["yellow"] applies to feminine or masculine nouns. Epicenes are the exceptions that confirm the rule of grammatical categorisation based on natural or conventional distinction. They are literally bisexual words, linguistic hermaphrodites that show the precarity of "gender identity" in the order of language' (translated from: P.-L. Assoun, *Masculin et Féminin*. Paris: Economica-Anthropos, 2005, p. 9).

14 Paraphrasing the Roman adage, the fallen angel may say to himself: 'Whoever is well punished will be well loved!' A punitive agency already makes its appearance in the nightmares of children.

15 'Blows' that are purely fantasmatic, which is why we put them in inverted commas. A father inspires fear, even when he is very nice.

16 This is how desire is structured: there is a masochism intrinsic to it, which can be found in the steady expectation of an imminent catastrophe and even at the heart of the most decided love. There will be more to say about this later.

17 One might think that, for the greater part of humanity, it is love that eroticises and that love is not masochistic. But even when shared, love also engenders a kind of suffering, which strikes a blow that is conducive in its own way to erotism.

18 'Nevertheless, it should be noted that the confrontation with this feminine, common to both sexes, does not operate in the same way in the subjective language of the man and the woman' (translated from: Roland Gori, *Logique des passions*. Paris: Flammarion, 2005, p. 97).

19 'At no time did Freud speak of a belief in a single organ, which would be the male organ; he spoke of a belief in the *phallus*, which, he points out, is not the penis' (translated from: Moustafa Safouan, *La sexualité féminine dans la doctrine freudienne*. Paris: Seuil, 1976, p. 58).

20 'Under the influence of seduction children can become polymorphously perverse, and can be led into all possible kinds of sexual irregularities' (Freud [1905], *Three Essays on the Theory of Sexuality* in *Standard Edition 7*, p. 191).

21 'The nucleus of the unconscious (that is to say, the repressed) is in each human being that side of him which belongs to the opposite sex' (Freud [1919], *A Child Is Being Beaten* in *Standard Edition 17*, p. 21).

22 This struggle does not necessarily involve fighting. Games where there is a winner and a loser will suffice.

23 'Not-all' feminine, to use Lacan's expression, which is often wrongly understood in a 'mystical' way, as if women were somehow outside the human race.

24 Schreber also defers his feminisation to a future date (Daniel Paul Schreber [1903], *Memoirs of My Nervous Illness* (I. Macalpine, R. Hunter, trans.). New York: New York Review of Books, 2000, pp. 254–255).

25 This implies a different relationship to the temporality of desire for the two genders. Men do not have time; they are always busy, always in a hurry, haunted by the fear of a sodomised passivity. The opposite would be the case for women if they were purely

passive. But they are not, and so their position is not symmetrical, although they might seem to be less pressed for time than men.

26 Ordinary language does not give a good account of the distinction between man and masculine and between woman and feminine. This needs to be emphasised whenever the constraints of the exposition cause us to write 'man' instead of 'masculinity' and 'woman' instead of 'femininity'. 'The man' is the hypostasis of a quality – that of masculinity.

27 Can passivity be equated with femininity? Freud states categorically: 'I advise you against it. It seems to me to serve no useful purpose and adds nothing to our knowledge' (Freud [1933], *New Introductory Lectures on Psycho-Analysis* in *Standard Edition 22*, p. 115).

28 'Active' and 'passive' nevertheless remain useful qualifiers because they index (as we shall see) a characteristic of the fantasy of seduction, where the genitive entails an active and a passive pole. Moreover, each of the fundamental fantasies unfolds in a passive or an active sense. To be seduced or to seduce, to beat or to be beaten, to annihilate or to be annihilated, to see or to be seen, etc. – all of these have active or passive implications, which are variable depending on one's specific personal history and on its fixations and repetitions.

29 'This is truly a confirmation that, when one is a man, one sees in one's partner what one props oneself up on' (Lacan, *Encore, Seminar 20* (J.-A. Miller, ed., B. Fink, trans.). New York: Norton, 1998, p. 87).

30 'The other of sex' is a broader formula than 'the other sex'.

31 Things might also go the other way: if to the (normal) feminisation by the father is added feminisation by a mother who seeks to enact a virility complex with her son, the latter may well be pushed towards passive homosexuality.

32 The scenarios deployed in the service of such maternal pederasty are sometimes subtle. A mother may, for example, push her daughter into the arms of the father, turning a blind eye to the father-daughter seduction. But then the father is no longer a father worthy of the name, and the mother keeps her daughter for herself thanks to this paternal failure. The daughter may, however, respond by identifying with the father she would have liked to have, i.e., by masculinising herself.

33 Freud wrote as early as 1905: 'Indeed, if we were able to give a more definite connotation to the concepts of "masculine" and "feminine", it would even be possible to maintain that libido is invariably and necessarily of a masculine nature, whether it occurs in men or in women and irrespectively of whether its object is a man or a woman' (Freud [1905], *Three Essays on the Theory of Sexuality* in *Standard Edition 7*, p. 219). Twenty years later, the same point of view is taken up again: 'All human individuals, as a result of their bisexual disposition [. . .] combine in themselves both masculine and feminine characteristics, so that pure masculinity and femininity remain theoretical constructions of uncertain content' (Freud [1925], *Some Psychical Consequences of the Anatomical Distinction between the Sexes* in *Standard Edition 19*, p. 258).

34 For some time, children see the difference but don't want to know about it. We can teach them how babies are born, the anatomy and physiology of sexual intercourse, etc., but this knowledge remains isolated from what they do not want to know, i.e., that their mother is castrated, that she does not have the phallus, which they are.

35 E.T.A. Hoffmann, *The Sandman* (C. Moncrieff, trans.). London: Alma Classics, 2013; Freud [1919], *The Uncanny* in *Standard Edition 17*, pp. 218–256.

36 'The masculine contribution to this image of insatiable female sexuality is not in doubt, specifically the contribution of castration anxiety, which builds a danger worthy of itself' (Jacques André, *La sexualité féminine*. Paris: PUF, 1994, p. 23).

37 It is in this 'visual' context that confusion arises over the word 'castration' since it suggests that women are deprived of what men have.

38 'In truth, the hope is a kind of denial, but one that, instead of addressing what the female subject *is*, instead addresses what she *will be*. So we now use denial as a generic term' (Safouan, *op. cit.*, p. 100).

39 'It follows that in any man who utters the other's absence something feminine is declared: this man who waits and who suffers from his waiting is miraculously feminized. A man is not feminized because he is inverted but because he is in love' (Roland Barthes [1977], *A Lover's Discourse, Fragments* (R. Howard, trans.). New York: Hill and Wang, 1978, p. 14).

40 'Do we need to recall: the "wanting to have it" that Freud speaks of, or penis envy, designates repressed unconscious wishes, which no observation has refuted and the intensity of which is commensurate with the keenness that the female analysand shows in asserting her femininity' (Safouan, *op. cit.*, p. 96).

41 The expression 'battle of the sexes' ('Kampf der Geschlechter') is used by Freud in his paper *On the Sexual Theories of Children* in the context of the 'sadistic theory of coitus' (Freud [1908], *Standard Edition 9*, p. 221). The *Standard Edition* English has 'sex battles', which is a misleading translation of 'Kampf der Geschlechter' (translator's note).

42 It is rare for the choice of sexual gender to change as a result of analysis, and such a change is not the aim of analysis.

43 We will put inverted commas around the terms 'homosexual' and 'heterosexual' when they concern relations within the family. Indeed, endogamy alone does not prejudge what will happen at the end of the latency phase, in a period when the adolescent often goes against what his family has programmed him to do.

44 Later, if the latter cannot go the distance, the subject may dream of a transsexual solution.

45 This is corroborated by statistics: 77% of homosexual women report an identification with their father compared to 15% of heterosexual women (Jacques Corraze, *L'homosexualité*. Paris: PUF, 2006). These statistics are certainly very approximate and are only relevant because of the significant differences which they reveal.

46 'Homosexualité féminine active' in the French. In what follows, I translate 'féminine' and 'masculine' as 'feminine' and 'masculine' and not as 'female' and 'male', assuming deliberate intention by the author, since French also has 'femelle' and 'mâle' (translator's note).

47 A bond which she will have the greatest difficulty in breaking (men are often only a safety belt to stop her from being swallowed up by this devouring passion).

48 The father is in place from the symbolic point of view (there is no question of psychosis), but it is symbolic with a step missing; he is in the place of the father who died before he was alive because, as to sex, his role is null.

49 These three types of 'homosexuality' function according to infantile sexual theories, in which the question of reproduction is settled by means of the drive (having a child-clone via the mouth or anus). Consequently, in these forms of homosexuality, the desire to have a child differs from what it is in neurosis, where such a desire is shaped by the attempt to resolve the castration anxiety provoked by the other sex. The desire for a child comes with a nostalgia for heterosexuality (a majority of homosexuals would have preferred not to be homosexual). It expresses a regret at not being able to settle a debt to the parents by giving them children.

50 See Benoît Jacquot's film *Villa Amalia*, based on the book of the same name by Pascal Quignard (Paris: Gallimard, 2006). A woman is suddenly confronted with her partner's betrayal. She abandons everything, wanders through Europe seeking to erase her identity and falls in love with a young woman who saves her as she is about to drown herself. In the final sequence, she meets her father, who abandoned her as a child – the probable cause of the repetition in her destiny.

51 Corraze, *op. cit.*

52 According to statistics, [homosexual] men have fifteen partners per year on average, while [homosexual] women have only one, and only 20% of homosexual women engage in such dating. Although the statistics are often suspect, the major gap between behaviours is significant of a clear difference in position (Corraze, *op. cit.*, p. 68).

53 All the more so since narcissism demands that love be unique and reciprocate such uniqueness.

54 'Initiatory' in the sense of crossing the no man's land of the parricide fantasy.

55 The phase of identificatory mourning for the father (a frequent cause of the mystical crises of adolescence) may not occur under certain conditions because there still has to be a father to kill, which will not be the case if there is a certain type of paternal absence (for example, a father who is not very present or is 'depressive', i.e., who does not desire his daughter). Everything then tends towards homosexuality, usually of an 'active' type.

56 Freud [1920], *On the Psychogenesis of a Case of Female Homosexuality* in *Standard Edition 18*, pp. 145–172.

57 *Ibid.*, p. 158.

58 *Ibid.*, pp. 158–159. The verb 'ausweichen' has a connotation of side-stepping that 'retire' does not quite convey. In a note, Freud gives another example of retirement concerning homosexuality: two twins are both keen to court girls, but one of them being more successful than the other, the latter 'retires' and becomes homosexual (*Ibid.*, p. 159).

59 In this sense, the 'revenge' aspect of the struggle is surely justified.

60 This is not the case in countries where religion remains dominant and where the law and opinion do not hesitate to interfere in the private lives of their citizens (this is largely the case in the United States, among other countries).

61 This is reminiscent of what Freud says about Leonardo da Vinci when describing a certain kind of family relationship found with homosexuals: 'In all our male homosexual cases the subjects had had a very intense erotic attachment to a female person, as a rule their mother, during the first period of childhood, which is afterwards forgotten; this attachment was evoked or encouraged by too much tenderness on the part of the mother herself, and further reinforced by the small part played by the father during their childhood' (Freud [1910], *Leonardo Da Vinci and a Memory of his Childhood* in *Standard Edition 11*, p. 99).

62 *Diagnostic and Statistical Manual of Mental Disorders III*. Washington, DC: APA Press, 1980, p. 282.

63 In France, the number of exclusively homosexual men has been estimated at 6% or 7% of all men, while among women, it is less than 2% (Corraze, *op. cit.*, pp. 13–14). The statistics are dated and probably incorrect, like the statistics quoted earlier, but it is the relative difference that is significant.

64 The ideology of science does not establish a new psychical reality or a new content of the fantasy, which remains unchanged. But this eternal fantasy is now denuded of the religious fictions that promised a future redemption by the dead father. Oedipus split the all-too-alive father whom he encountered at the crossroads in his myth into two characters: one living and one dead. The God of monotheism was represented by the latter. By mathematically exposing the fictions of the Eternal Father, modernity has deprived the patriarchy of its main asset, and the accelerating collapse of the patriarchy is revealing what it was intended to repress: female enjoyment and, more broadly, any evocation of erotism.

65 All sexual particularities have become objects of curiosity because they are likely to teach us something about the truth of enjoyment and because this curiosity is itself an enjoyment.

66 Who, in the event, had to make do with the impotent Hitler and his gloved and perfumed SA brutes.

67 It is in this sense that the inevitable 'homosexual friend' of many young women often has a paternal characteristic, which generates no conflict with his harmless sexual habits.

68 But there are always a few 'good fathers' (judges, educators, psychologists of all sorts, etc.) to set against these bad seducer-fathers. Whether they like it or not, the former are put in together with the impotent and homosexual fathers; they are the new defenders of the law.

69 'Père-version' evoking 'perversion' (a Lacanian word play) (translator's note).

70 'Virtual' means ready to be actualised in the present. What is virtual is contrasted with what is actual, not with what is real.

71 This role is a good indication of how homosexuality is functioning as a 'name of the father'.

72 'Queer' reappropriates an insult since the term was at times used pejoratively to designate a deranged or bizarre personality before being applied to homosexuals.

73 The American writer Dorothy Allison writes, for example, that the movements of internal revolution that have historically followed the end of ideologies act beyond homosexuality to break the chains of what has previously functioned as a model of sexuality (*Skin: Talking about Sex, Class and Literature*. Ithaca, NY: Firebrand Books, 1994). The point is to bring together those who are excluded from normative sexuality, and the movement's theorists militate in favour of transgenderism – the idea that a person's gender should not be linked to their biological sex. The means of its struggle are those of 'gender fucking', meaning the refusal of a precise sexual identity.

74 As Foucault has rightly pointed out in his works on transgression.

Chapter 4

The dangers of 'becoming feminine'

The 'internal' danger of feminisation

In French, we distinguish *demoiselles*, *dames* and *messieurs*.[1] This subtlety is surprising today, when the taboo of virginity is not at the forefront of people's minds, at least in appearance, because the *demoiselles* are perhaps those whose virginity blooms again as soon as it is lost. Age alone does not differentiate the *demoiselle* from the *dame*. An indefinable intuition sometimes leads one – without prior acquaintance and in ignorance of marital status – to call a 60-year-old woman *mademoiselle*, even if she is married, a mother and a grandmother, while some younger women may be called *dames* without a second thought. Who are the *demoiselles*? Are they women who remain their father's daughter, even when they turn their backs on him to become *dames*? Who are the *dames*? Are they those who are done with the torments of the *demoiselle*? Without answering these questions too quickly, we will hazard the supposition that these designations are intuitive gradients of 'becoming a woman'.

The choice of psychical gender challenges any unqualified definition of 'man', and even more so of 'woman', since the latter is searching for herself after having been, in part, a man. Freud writes in the fifth of the *New Introductory Lectures*: 'Psycho-analysis does not try to describe what a woman is – an impossible task[2] – but sets about enquiring how she comes into being, how a woman develops out of a child with a bisexual disposition'.[3] Men, too, must become men, in a constant effort to live up to their name.[4] But they reject what women have to deal with: women accept their feminisation up to a point, while men refuse it – not once and for all but in a day-by-day struggle.[5] It is easier to refuse feminisation (as men do) than to refuse it in order to accept it (as 'becoming a woman' implies). Similarly, if we were to equate becoming a mother with having the phallus, this would be easier than becoming a woman, which would involve asking for the phallus. Little girls indeed mimic motherhood before confronting the task of becoming women.

What is the feminine here? If anatomy doesn't define it, and if it can't be reduced to being the daughter to a father or the mother to a son, how could we describe it? There is only relativity here, nothing absolute, which compounds the mystery of the feminine, defined negatively as that which refuses the desire of the father. This mystery can in part be linked to the object of lack here – the phallus – which also

DOI: 10.4324/9781003519287-4

plays a part in the mystery of masculinity, that is, the femininity that men refuse in themselves. If we had to define it in terms of phallus envy, femininity would be relative to the man and, first and foremost, to the man that every woman, up to a certain point, is – and with all the virility of men themselves (the proofs abound). If a woman wants to reject this virility because she thinks it threatens her gender, her femininity will then be relative to the succession of men who have allowed her to renounce the father. One man will have given her a jewel, another a taste for wine, music, sport, a certain sexual practice, etc. This borrowed dimension of femininity would thus be constructed by successive grafts onto its own lack of foundation. But it is less a question of a true lack of foundation (a non-existence) than of the refusal to be feminised by the father, after having desired this in order to flee the maternal appetite. So it is a femininity inscribed in a becoming.

Change of erogenous 'zone'

Freud's two late texts specifically devoted to female sexuality[6] emphasise the difficulties of becoming a woman. He argues that since girls were, to begin with, boys loving their mothers, how does a change of object take place? Moreover, for Freud, the impulse towards the father will be accompanied by a change of erogenous zone. Love for the mother has to turn towards the father, and erogeneity pass from the clitoris to the vagina.[7] To be more exact, 'expecting the phallus from the father' is the essence of femininity (for both man and woman), and the corresponding erogenous zone is primarily the anus or the mouth – hollow zones that have already been erogenised by the drive and are apt for reception of this phallus.

If a 'change of zone' occurs, this happens after there has been sexual activity, namely, clitoral erotism, which nothing obliges to disappear. The boy obtains enjoyment with his penis and goes on doing so. The girl enjoys her clitoris and also has no need to stop doing so even when she has a man's love. Love is not enough to make a change, and the change depends on circumstances; it happens or not, depending on the partner and the time. Fantasy here may create a longing to be penetrated, to bring into the self, to swallow. It is a fantasy that turns activity into activity with a passive goal. This is even more true with feminised men, who enjoy anal sex as if they had a vagina. Women do not always have a vagina[8] – the hollowing out of the vagina depends on a wish for the penis. A feminised boy can enjoy anally and have an erect penis at the same time. Similarly, a girl can have enjoyment in her vagina while simultaneously being aroused in her clitoris. The erogenisation of a receptacle is added on thanks to fantasy and implies only a relative and not a categorical change of zone.[9]

An anal erotism exists in proportion to feminisation (for both men and women), and it precedes vaginal erogeneity, which is not known from the outset. The idea of coitus through anal intercourse psychically precedes coitus through the vagina for both genders, as suggested by Freud's less-than-elegant term 'sadistic-anal erotism', and this is true for both boys and girls. This erotism is the precocious representation of an 'activity with a passive goal'. Anality superimposes phallic erogenisation on the drive-charged ejection of excrement. The excrement smells bad to the extent that it becomes associated with guilt – that of separation from maternal nourishment. Food is permeated with phallic significance because the oral drive inflates the body to make it into the beautiful phallus that the mother lacks. This is why small children have difficulty ejecting and thereby separating themselves from their excrement; it is a guilty act, and the result is that children often become constipated. But since they expect from their father the punishment that would relieve this guilt, anality itself is drawn into an erotising and sadistic paternal seduction. So the anus becomes an erogenous zone ready to receive the paternal phallus, to the rhythm of a feminisation that applies to both sexes.

The excremental ejection of maternal food invokes paternal presence. Since the ejection is accompanied by the masturbatory act of separation, which causes the subject to pass from Being to Having, and since this guilty act calls for punishment by the father, the punishment itself is imagined as a sadistic but pleasurable anal intercourse by the father. 'Expect' in 'expecting the phallus from the father' does not conjugate in the future tense; it is what happens at each moment of clitoral masturbation or masturbation with the penis. It does not have to be waited for; it is already there. The seduction of the father is seduction by the father: 'to be taken, violated, penetrated'. From a practical point of view, it corresponds to anal intercourse since at this psychical age, ignorance of the vagina prevails (the vagina, unlike the anus, is not invested by a drive).

Similarly, since the paternal seduction scenario occurs as a consequence of anxiety of the mother's castration and her prevailing orality, fellatio functions as a key template of sexual excitement: penetration passes first through the mouth, through kisses and then by contiguity, through fellatio. The erogeneity of the mouth establishes penis envy, following the path of the oral drive towards desire, which goes from the mother to arousal by the father. Freud's intuition served him well when he noted an intimate link between erogenisation of the vagina and a change of the object of love: the love of the father hollows out a lack which hollows out the body. This passage from mother to father opens up a void and calls for a corresponding bodily cavity to fill. The absence of an object of desire echoes this.[10] The mouth serves as a template for this passage; kissing in a way allows discovery of the vagina. This metamorphosis of erogeneity is by no means guaranteed if the woman kisses her lover with pouted lips.

This role of orality as a key template shows that there is a kind of symmetry between the attraction for the penis on the feminine side and for the breast on the masculine side. The appetite of men for women's breasts corresponds to *Penisneid*, and the breasts must be veiled and revealed in proportion to this investment of desire. An envy of the breasts corresponds to penis envy, which also acquires its impetus from the oral drive.[11]

So practices such as anal intercourse and fellatio, supposedly supernumerary to 'normal' sexual activity, are in reality the most original forms (despite being proscribed by the supporters of the Good Book). Although 'envy of the phallus' erotises the vagina as the cavity which corresponds to it (after the mouth and the anus), this 'envy' is not in any way a result of feeling deprived of an organ. Women are not deprived of it; they do have an organ but only on condition of the desire that excites this phantom member. Some homosexuals feel an equally strong desire – desire for an organ, of which they are not deprived but which they want erect as a response to desire (and not as an organ which would be missing). It is, therefore, more exact to speak (as we propose) of an 'envy of the phallus' because both boy and girl have a penis, in either penile or clitoral form. The challenge is to have it erect in the form of the phallus (the erect penis). So this 'envy of the phallus' emerges from the fantasy realm of desire.

Change of object: from mother to father

For the growing child, renouncing the mother is in some way a consequence of the impossibility of enjoying her.[12] The child will have many reasons for breaking with her and turning to the father. And these reasons will appear all the stronger because the flame of the father's desire puts drive erotisation in the background and opens up the void of a desire without an object – a pure subject. These patterns exist for both boys and girls. This problem of a 'change of object' which consists in moving away from the mother and turning to the father is simplified if we think of the transitivism of the mother, who through her child relives her own childhood when she also grew up with the idea of a primacy of the phallus: she was a boy. This transitivism may take on such imperative proportions that she experiences through her child less what she has lived herself than what she has dreamed of. In this respect, a boy will satisfy her, but a girl may disappoint her.[13]

A girl is often disadvantaged in her relationship with her mother by her phallus-debt, a source of intense guilt when the mother does not find in her the boy she dreamed of being. A girl's 'change of object' may, therefore, be inhibited by this guilt. The daughter's anxiety about disappointing her mother grows out of this unconscious devaluation from the mother. In this case, she may remain fixed to the mother because she feels bound to remain her mother's phallus, a position, which inhibits her entry into clitoral enjoyment and, consequently, inhibits her erotism – a consequence which can go as far as an enduring frigidity, a frigidity that is not relative to fantasy, i.e., that is not only independent of partners and situations but also independent of their relationship to their own enjoyment. Many women can become aroused easily through masturbation and sometimes more intensely than with their lover. But this solitary relief is unavailable to others because of the guilt that inhibits them. They need a romantic fantasy, a lover's alibi in order to free themselves. His presence, perhaps also using a neurotic fantasy figure, provides redemption for a fault that masturbation renders too obvious.

Freud describes this risk of fixation using a term which occurs only rarely in his writings – 'pre-Oedipal'.[14] What is a 'pre-Oedipal' state if not the state of a child who is required to 'be the phallus'? A girl caught up in this Being will inhibit her enjoyment of Having, starting with masturbation. Most girls quickly find a way of dealing with this debt: when they mimic motherhood and play with dolls, they want to get rid of their own status as child by giving a child to their mother (initially, their baby is not 'expected from the father'). They do not dream of having a child with a little boy but 'for' their mother, in accordance with this 'pre-Oedipal' fixation.

But since getting rid of one's mother by becoming a mother oneself is a second-best solution – envisaged for the future – a parallel fiction is created in the present: would it not be better to be seduced or even raped by the father than to stay locked in this motherly embrace? Where does such a fiction come from? It comes first of all from the anxiety associated with maternal demand, which inverts her love into hatred. This aversion prepares the ground for seduction by the father and for the much-vaunted 'change of object', but this can only be allowed to occur on one decisive condition: that the seduction is undergone in spite of the girl's own self, against her will. The turn to the father is indispensable, but since this change of object is culpable, better clear oneself of blame by imagining that the father is a rapist. The invention of a paternal rape – the first lie, the *proton pseudos* of the hysteric – is preferable to a stifling maternal straitjacket. And finally, the daughter turns all the more resolutely towards her father because she expected from him and will get (not later but immediately) the phallus, in the form of access to clitoral masturbation ('Having' rather than 'Being').

Inhibition of femininity by the mother's desire . . . and by the absence of the father's desire

Guilt in relation to the mother can inhibit the daughter to the point of an insurmountable frigidity, and it is remarkable that this origin of frigidity is parallel to anorexia and bulimia ('eating behaviours' which are almost exclusive to women). The daughter's disappointment with her mother, which leads her to turn to her father, is clear in masturbation. It is less clear how it can be related to food. But the attitude to food corresponds to the 'pre-Oedipal' mother fixation since nourishment is the privileged drive path for the demand, addressed by the mother to her daughter, to be the phallus. It is the nature of this maternal demand that creates food refusals, anorexia or even delusions of poisoning (if food corresponds to a maternal demand to be her phallus, then it can kill since this is an annihilating identification). So the mother becomes a persecutor, a source of resentment and detestation.

This relationship between food, the mother's demand for the phallus, and frigidity is all the more striking since anorexia may only begin in adolescence, when the question of femininity becomes acute. The contrast between a complete 'pre-genital' anorexia and a 'semi-anorexia', which begins in adolescence at the time of becoming a woman, corresponds to the contrast between complete frigidities and those which begin at the same time as genitality and which are linked only to fantasmatic circumstances.[15] Some anorexias are entirely articulated in the mother-daughter relationship. These feminine anorexias are accompanied by a frigidity issue from an extremity of maternal demand, which moves from orality to sexuality. By contrast, the 'semi-anorexias' correspond to the refusal of oral violation by the father, a violation marked by deep ambivalence, as shown by the disgust at foods that derive from animals (red meat, for example, leading to vegetarian 'organic' choices, etc.). This disgust signals a taboo on the sexual totem of the father – the shadow of the paternal phallus falls on food.

Yet the 'change of object' from mother to father cannot be attributed solely to the transitivism of the mother towards her daughter. No doubt this leads to mutual disappointment, which encourages the girl to turn to her father. These motives also apply in part to the boy, who also refuses to be his mother's phallus. He fights against maternal control and turns to his father, although he also resists him. How can we explain the acceptance by the daughter of feminisation by the father? We have to take into account the transitivism of fathers with regard to their daughters and the erotised seduction that they feel towards them. The father feminises his daughter when his attitude towards her is seductive (just as he masculinises his son when he feels in competition with him). The father's seduction has a guaranteed effect and cannot be refused, although we should not overstate the case: the way of accepting it in order to refuse it will define what it is to 'become a woman'.

On the other hand, this seduction by the father may in some cases be lacking. Feminisation may then sometimes not come to fruition, and there may be the formation of a feminine 'virility complex'. The girl wants to escape from her mother. But if, at that juncture, her father takes no interest in her or, more exactly, in her femininity, then she will identify with the father she would have liked to have had. Although she continues to acknowledge her femininity, she will nonetheless be equipped with a strong masculinity complex, which will often lead her to take an interest in women (as she would have liked her father to have taken an interest in her).

To sum up the problem of the change of love object: both boys and girls are born to sexual desire through seduction by the father. This desire is extremely ambivalent, swinging towards hate (concealing love) for boys and towards love (concealing hate) for girls. But love for the mother, now desexualised by the emergence of the father's desire, remains for both sexes. Later, the final part of the Oedipal trajectory makes the mother into a rival for girls, but this rivalry is quite different from the confrontation between boys and their fathers. Both boy and girl retain the mother as love object and do so all the better because the father cleanses this bond of its guilt and erotism.

These explanations of the 'change of object' enable a better understanding of the 'change of zone'. This double operation engenders guilt in relation to the mother. To overcome it, the seduction by the father will have to be 'forced'; most often, it is imagined as a kind of rape, a basic matrix of subjective trauma. Since guilt inhibits masturbation, the latter will follow the path of object change, moving towards envy of the boy's penis. This gives the key to how masturbation evolves; initially, it may be completely inhibited due to guilt in relation to the mother. But after moving beyond this barrier, or rather, in order to move beyond it, the fantasy of paternal rape comes into play, whereupon a second kind of guilt is imposed because, in reality, it is the daughter who desires the father (even as she casts him in the role of guilty party).

There are two possible scenarios in this new situation: either the father is not at all seductive towards his daughter (he is not sensitive to her femininity) and masturbation continues more or less unimpeded or the father is sensitive to his daughter's femininity and a new kind of guilt leads to greater or lesser repression of masturbation. In the latter case, the envy of a man's penis – proportional to female castration anxiety, which is finally objectified – becomes an insistent preoccupation. Clitoral masturbation has in some way been transferred to a man's penis, which is then treated as property no less exclusive than the girl's own body. This 'envy' of the penis sometimes assumes frenzied proportions, to the point of consuming the whole of mental life, rendering the individual insensible to any other goal.[16] All the more insensible because, since obtaining this phallus requires symbolic conditions (love for example), the goal remains concealed from the person who strives for it. It would obviously be a mistake to take this deception literally. When a woman engages in unreasonable activities to the point of doubt being cast on her mental faculties, it would be wrong to think that she is crazy or stupid. On the contrary, she knows exactly what she wants.

Three degrees of femininity in search of itself

'Becoming a woman' involves the successive obstacles that have been described, each with its own implications. Paradoxically, the first stage concerns what might be termed a 'masculine' phallicisation, which is the condition of feminisation. This stage puts an end to a transgender drive enjoyment by means of masturbatory activity and thereby allows an escape from the excess which phallicises the whole body. This 'masculine' masturbation is the *basso continuo* of human sexuality, and it remains a helpful recourse in otherwise 'normal' lives. First pitfall: by seeking to escape the mother's dominion, this autoerotism generates a large dose of guilt, which can lead to a complete inhibition of femininity.

Once this stage has been passed, active clitoral phallicism can encounter a second cause of inhibition if paternal seduction takes an excessively incestuous turn. The fantasy of a paternal seduction takes shape even if the father sleeps. But he does not always sleep. This occurs when – besides seducing his daughter almost in spite of himself and because of the position he occupies – he seduces her actively. Girls who have been fascinated by such paternal activity will certainly turn out ultra-feminine. However, to the extent that they remain their father's partner, they will never be anyone else's.[17]

The excessive feminisation of an 'ultra-womanly' woman may leave her in a completely passive relation with the father, and the hallmark of this ultra-femininity is frigidity, which is always close to suicide, the last bastion of seduction (suicidal women have their passionate lovers). Undivided feminisation – a total seduction by the father – creates a sort of death before life since sleeping with the father amounts to taking the place of one of the parents, and such an act operates a kind of time travel to before one's own birth.[18] This total and vertiginous femininity fascinates at the same time as it is, to varying degrees, rejected.[19] 'Being a Woman' with a capital W is a limit identification, a borrowed exteriority, often staged through masquerade.[20] 'The Woman' here exists as a powerful though unattainable psychical ideal.

This femininity frozen by the desire of the father differs from the frigidity produced by guilt in relation to the mother. The former most often seeks a way out through transgression of the paternal seduction; it seeks intrigue and repeated betrayals, which is its best hope of relief. For example, a first husband will sometimes be treated as an enemy, pure and simple, and only with the second husband, thanks to the dismissal of the first, will erotism become present. Frigidity remains trapped in the nets of a paternal love that a husband can certainly oppose but at the risk of himself becoming an ice-cold father. Hence, the theatricality of the fast-changing intrigues which may then ensue.

The most seductive women are also those who can most easily say no, and it also happens that, even when they say yes, their frigidity confirms the no. From 'activity with a passive aim', they retain only the passivity. Their femininity here has been enmired in the risk of incest and sometimes of objective sexual trauma (if they were actually seduced by an adult). This event may inhibit them forever after, each man representing a potential father for them. But such an unfortunate configuration is not necessarily the result of a real seduction. It may be sufficient that the father did not intervene to protect his daughter against the solicitations of another adult or that he guarded his daughter too jealously, as if she was his wife.[21]

In contrast to the more or less active seduction of the father, there is an opposite pitfall when there is a total absence of paternal seduction. When her father pays her no attention and is never moved by her charms, a girl will lose the urge to strive for her feminisation and may continue on the path of a virility complex. Nothing will make her believe that she does not have the phallus, and she will make the best masturbatory use of it, not without some homosexual ambitions, especially if her mother has sexually seduced her to a greater or lesser extent (unlike her father who took care not to). This will not prevent her from being heterosexual, and she will prefer slightly feminised lovers, nor will it inhibit orgasm, as an effect of the partner's enjoyment. Women with a 'virility complex' are not shackled by inhibitions and do not necessarily have a masculine appearance (quite the contrary), and heterosexual love remains compatible for them with devotion to clitoral enjoyment. Although they have had no paternal seduction to eroticise passivity, they can love a man quite easily, although they are also not averse to women, and we often find this configuration among obsessional neurotics.[22]

Between these two extremes of an ultra-feminisation and a virility complex, there is a middle ground: that of women who do not renounce their original masculinity, the basis of their (initially) clitoral enjoyment, yet on the condition of having eliminated the agent of this enjoyment, namely, their father. They are, therefore, invested in the encounter with another man, and this expectation shifts the epicentre of enjoyment from clitoral tumescence to the vaginal receptacle.

In these three ways of 'becoming a woman', we can see the three instances of feminisation described by Freud in his text of 1932,[23] where the last of them is taken to be 'normal' (in the sense of including the contraries 'activity with a passive aim'). Each of the three possible paths of 'becoming a woman' has its degrees. The father's seduction of his daughter can range from zero to the full-on attitude of man to woman (not necessarily implying action). And similarly, the erotic attitude of the mother towards her daughter can go as far as lesbianism. Female bisexuality is inflected depending on these conjoined variables. As Freud writes: 'Some portion of what we men call "the enigma of women" may perhaps be derived from this expression of bisexuality in women's lives'.[24] It varies according to events, and this is what matters from the point of view of psychoanalytic treatment. Certain events repeat older traumas and can cause changes of orientation. For example, following a disaster in heterosexual love, a woman may turn to homosexuality just as she did in adolescence when she compensated for what she experienced as a betrayal by the father by identifying with him and falling madly in love with another girl (unless, by a mystical turn, she was able to find a more obliging Eternal Father through religion). It is worth asking, though, whether Freud, in exploring the prehistory of 'becoming a woman' (i.e., the feminisation of the little girl), may have underestimated the changes that occur at puberty and specifically that a woman emerges from her infantile neurosis no longer expecting a child from the father but from the man who would eliminate him. So the woman might go along (albeit belatedly) with a masculine fantasy, which represented a first real challenge to paternal seduction. The orgastic scenario of parricide may be played out more or less dramatically with this man (often through the jealousies of love). This middle way leaves femininity in constant contradiction with itself. It tends towards femininity only on the basis of a masculinity that is never entirely renounced.

So feminisation becomes entangled in this contradiction. It turns on itself. On the one hand, it must please, following the subjective genitive 'desire for'. But at the same time, it must defend itself against this seduction, following the objective genitive which pushes towards being 'desired by'.[25] It must seduce, but as soon as the seduction risks succeeding, panic stations. Life without desire would be a slow death, but being desired is dangerous, at least if the seducer wears the mask of a father. And whenever another man tries to seduce, he wears that mask, for a moment at least. Desire begins in the excitement to make the mask fall, and it is actualised when it in fact does fall. For how could a man discard it completely? This incestuous potential is at once exciting and disturbing. The sexual desire for a 'paternal' seducer (and every man is such, as long as he remains anonymous) is accompanied by the desire to reject him or even to kill him in fantasy, a death wish proportional to desire itself.

Following upon the 'desire for', the 'murder of' in turn bears the mark of both objective and subjective genitive. She who kills might well kill herself, and she sometimes does. But without going to this extreme, the double movement of pleasing and rejecting always risks inhibiting desire and freezing it into immobility. And risk itself may get the seduction going again. The 'murder of the father' happens on this border, where the danger of an inhibition revives arousal and penis envy. Joan Riviere described this agonising moment of uncertainty in her famous article, 'Femininity as Masquerade':

> She was an American woman engaged in work of a propagandist nature, which consisted principally in speaking and writing. All her life a certain degree of anxiety, sometimes very severe, was experienced after every public performance, such as speaking to an audience. In spite of her unquestionable success and ability, both intellectual and practical, and her capacity for managing an audience and dealing with discussions, etc., she would be excited and apprehensive all night after, with misgivings whether she had done anything inappropriate, and obsessed by a need for reassurance. This need for reassurance led her compulsively on any such occasion to seek some attention or complimentary notice from a man or men at the close of the proceedings in which she had taken part or been the principal figure; and it soon became evident that the men chosen for the purpose were always unmistakeable father–figures, although often not persons whose judgement on her performance would in reality carry much weight.[26]

In her lectures, this brilliant young woman outdoes her male peers. Why does her success make her anxious, if not because the father falls along with her peers, and her solicitations, the sexual meaning of which is unmistakable, testify to the revival of her desire?

So feminine desire functions by eclipses, alternating between rejecting and summoning. This ubiquitous, oscillating gesture is a general feature of femininity, which is both offered and withheld. It structures the woman's posture, gait, movements, her look and way of being looked at, her manner of dressing and even her style of speech. When expressed under the influence of the fantasy of seduction, feminine speech may unfold to a tempo that is quite its own – engaging but restrained, moving forward but snaring itself. Her rhetoric is a linguistic universal recognisable in all languages, whether expressed by a woman or, for that matter, by a man. It is exacerbated in the presence of the seducer, in proportion to the risk of desire.

Femininity – with no present other than a perpetual future

'The future of man is woman', Louis Aragon wrote.[27] It is also the future of every woman. If she moves towards femininity on the basis of a primary masculinity, she is in an active position which chooses a passive goal. 'Activity with a passive goal' involves an obvious contradiction which is often the source of feminine inhibition or, in any case, of constant complications in love life. To speak of 'activity with a passive goal' is to introduce a cascade of contradictions, each emerging from the other up until their eventual orgastic electroshock. The first of the contradictions is that the feminine subject of this 'activity with a passive goal' takes herself as object, a situation in which she loses itself, since she then becomes other to herself and can, therefore, refuse herself what she may nevertheless have wanted. In activity with a passive goal, activity and passivity function in constant discord in a way that is conducive to both excitation and inhibition.

What could be more exhausting than this contradiction? Seducing casually is a full-time occupation, particularly if you have ultimately to refuse yourself. The aim of passivity seems clear: to trigger desire in order to have the phallus. Indeed, being desired is already to have it, and many seductive women who reject the consequences of their manoeuvres could be called 'phallic'. A woman has the phallus as soon as she is desired, which requires some work (a lot, perhaps). By the gesture of offering herself in order to refuse herself, she becomes phallic with each erection she provokes. Her charm consists in having the phallus at this magical distance. One desiring look at her, and she undoubtedly already has it, even if it incites the wish to give it to her. The passive goal is a way of having it, of provoking desire, since the phallus is erected only in proportion to that.

The activity has thus attained its goal, which is never affirmed so well as in refusal. If men make war to deny their feminisation, women confront the father's seduction with other weapons. Once desire has been provoked, not only does refusal leave them with the phallus but it also floors the seducer, placed in the role of a father who has been castrated and slain. The outcome is total victory over the father, with whom the suitor was confused. Seduction can be satisfied or inhibited in this confusion between father and man, a situation which is unblocked as soon as the man distinguishes himself from the father or, better, as soon as he kills the father, if not in person, then at least in the guise of a rival who resembles him.

In this contradiction between activity and passivity, feminine desire is first expressed by a 'no' since activity precedes passivity, satisfying itself by provoking desire and finally saying no to its consequences. Hence, a certain complication of feminine desire, which runs the risk of inhibiting itself in its own movement, even when it is powerful. 'No' does not always mean no nor does it always mean yes. Only a yes could resolve the ambiguity, but it is less linked to excitement. This mismatch amplifies masculine arousal, and the paradoxical result of this 'false note' is a creation of tension in the lovers' desire. The false note here plays the role of tuning fork, which sounds before the musicians start to play. How a couple deals with this false note is another question.

Is the exit from the Oedipus complex 'masculine only'?

Freud sometimes simplified the Oedipus complex by presenting it in two versions: masculine and feminine. Men would come out of the Oedipus complex thanks to castration anxiety, while women would enter it due an identical anxiety, from which they never manage to extricate themselves completely. He says that for the girl, the Oedipus complex is not destroyed but, on the contrary, created under the influence of castration. One might then draw the conclusion that girls never get over the quest for the father, a bottomless demand for love, the violence of jealousy, etc. Simple and robust though they are, these schemas do not do justice to the problems. If we were to confuse femininity with women, these patterns would leave the latter at a lifelong disadvantage, forever relegated back to childhood and the love of the father. Admittedly, Freud contradicts himself by proposing this simplification, since there is no class which would bring together 'men', opposable to another which would bring together 'women'. Bisexuality is always present, and a man's virility asserts itself against his fear of feminisation, whereas a woman's femininity never does away completely with her primary masculinity.

The hypothesis that 'women' always remain children while 'men' reach maturity needs to be challenged, even if this view carries the weight of several millennia of the infantilisation of women behind it. Do men not also behave like children, albeit on another stage?[28] Women often play out their comedies on the boards of love and family, but are men more mature in the public space? Do men really get over their Oedipus complex so easily? Since they usually pursue their conflict with the father on a stage other than that of love, their entrapment in the Oedipus complex is less visible, but that does not make them better balanced than women. At home or in the city, the issue is always their clumsy love for the father. Men expend considerable energy on the stage of society in their fight against the danger of feminisation, in multiple clashes of castes, clans and classes, in times of both war and of peace. Women may sometimes appear immature in their relationships, especially with the man they love, but the same goes for men with the man *they* love (the head of their office, party, tribe, etc.), although this is less visible in the case of men since these allegiances tend to take place under the banner of social ideals.

The continuing creationism of the law and the feminine superego

The boy's refusal of feminisation is head-on. The fight begins against the father and his representatives. But the risk of feminisation remains because total victory is impossible against a father who is perpetually reborn from the ashes of guilt. So the battlefront moves, and the war unfolds between the boys to decide which of them is a girl (the defeated) and which a boy (the victor). Someone who watches children at play might suppose that their skirmishes are mere amusement, but the stakes are high because they concern the choice of gender, and they are even higher at a second level because the game is a displacement of the struggle against paternal seduction and entails a shadow parricide with all the resulting guilt. The games of boys engender guilt and reparative ideals in proportion to their obvious fantasy violence. This guilt born of a head-on refusal of the father's desire leads to the formation of a demanding superego.

Things are not the same for girls insofar as they accept feminisation, and their superego should not have the same reparative demands. The masculine superego is thus more visible than the feminine superego. But the latter asserts itself no less directly by taking the detour of love. Women overcome paternal seduction as do men but not by opposing it head-on; they take a detour via the man who frees them from their father in what we might call 'parricide by proxy'. Their knight and champion does the battle on their behalf. Their superego goes to work with less fanfare than that of men, putting itself at the service of love where it lays down the law with as much firmness as the major masculine ideals. Love plays for women the role of a superego which is as coercive as that of men. It has the same mainspring, namely, the redemption of a parricide. Loving a man eliminates the love of the father, but this means that a tribute must be paid. As on the masculine side, this superego demands reparation through ideals, but they are the ideals of Eros.

The function of love as a feminine superego is never so apparent as in maternal love. As we have discussed, before 'expecting a child from the father', the little girl already wants a child in order to get rid of her mother. When she plays with dolls, she behaves like her mother behaves with her. She is not expecting a child from the father. The wish expressed in games with dolls has nothing to do with sexual enjoyment. Once she becomes a woman, the order will be reversed: her sexual enjoyment will interest her before she wants a child (which can wait). For the woman, the priorities of the little girl are reversed: she first betrays her father for a man, and the child born from the desire for this man will make reparation for the parricide by proxy. When she becomes a woman, her desire for a child will be triggered by the desire for a man who, for his part, wants to pay his own debt to his father.[29] So the feminine superego asserts its rights twice over – once for love and once for the child. Through the byways of obstinate loves, foolish jealousies, stubborn preferences, irrepressible desires, relentless refusals – an apparently narcissistic path, far removed from the great masculine ideals – the feminine position imposes its own form of the law, which does without the father by making use of him (to paraphrase Lacan's elegant formula).

If this coercion of the superego has a close relationship with love, is it really narcissism? Such so-called 'narcissism' weakens in proportion to what it seeks, towards which it advances like a tightrope walker. It leaves the position of 'being the maternal phallus' but without any guarantee of getting to the other side where it will 'have' the phallus. A mere trifle can knock it off balance given its extreme requirements, both on the side of being (demand for love) and on the side of having (demand for fidelity, jealousy). This pseudo-narcissism runs between 'being the phallus' and 'seeking to have it'; it flees from an impossible position and seeks its salvation from whoever will be able to give what has been left behind. So it is in a dependency on desire and seduction, and one might easily confuse the beginning and the end – the demand for love and the envy of the phallus. But these sequences are quite distinct. The demand for love has no gender; it demands universal recognition at all times, from men and from women, and all without a sexual goal. The only imperative is to please and be at the front of the stage while at the same time fearing to be there. This oceanic demand, so prone to shipwreck, differs from the demand for a phallus made to one man and one only. The latter is a demand that cannot be universal – and, hence, anonymous – without a risk of depersonalisation. And since the enjoyment obtained thanks to this phallus only attains its orgastic dimension as a function of singularity (of the name, for example), the result is a total exclusivity, with no sharing.

It will be objected that such an imperative of exclusivity does not square with experience. Countless examples of bigamous, bisexual, etc., women would seem to refute it. But (apart from the fact that we are not talking about women but about the feminine) is a bigamous woman who plays one man against another not still pursuing a dream of exclusivity? She secures the love of one by using the other against him. She never drives in more than one nail. This rule of monogamy, linked to the conditions of enjoyment, requires that the same be rendered to her. If this structural jealousy is called 'narcissism', it is a misuse of language. In reality, this 'narcissism' articulates the phallus in the name of the father so well that the law follows from it without trying to do so. Its demands repeat the original drama of the Oedipus complex so much and so well that love alone manages to rewrite the law.

The requirements of 'becoming a woman' result in a continuous creation of the law. Their horizon is an absolute because no human being could tolerate total feminisation (incest with the father, castration). 'Becoming a woman' is a relative thing; it is correlative to the man who tears her away from the endogamous love of her father (and, behind him, of her mother). And this relativity of becoming a woman by becoming the woman of a man inscribes the murder of the father at the heart of female enjoyment. A female mystic eternalises the father right to the end and also marries him. Marriage rituals (still present in most cultures), which are symbolic stagings of the loss of the father's name in favour of the husband's name, show the power of this mechanism. Admittedly, the parricide fantasy disappears behind the love that the lovers devote to each other. Love makes a woman and does so in exchange for the phallus, which makes this condition bearable. This relativity of 'becoming a woman' makes it a daily gymnastic exercise – psychical work, in which the lover, the husband and the entire entourage are asked to constantly participate. Nothing is more socialised than this constant effort, which (everyone will agree) brings life to the world. The simple fact of a woman walking down the street speaks to all those present.

Does 'becoming a woman' have a historical dimension?

In the 19th century, in the context of the triumph of the bourgeoisie, young men received their sex education at the brothel, often at the instigation of their fathers. Did women benefit from this? Not much, if we are to believe Lélia, one of George Sand's heroines, who describes the ordeal of sexuality like this: 'I gave myself, turning pale and closing my eyes' and 'when he had dozed off, satisfied and sated, I remained motionless and dismayed, my senses frozen'.[30] But the prospects were perhaps not so utterly dismal, at least if we are to believe the reputation of George Sand herself. In any case, it seems probable that the fate of femininity has depended on the historical conditions which each century has given it.

In the fifth chapter of the *New Lectures on Psychoanalysis,* Freud drew attention to the age-old social repression of the feminine.[31] We cannot predict what women will be like once this straitjacket is removed. But we can see that its grip has loosened and hope that the process will continue.[32] Whatever successes these advances may bring, femininity will remain a more or less anxiety-provoking issue but now for men too. Men sometimes say that femininity is a mystery to them, and this is true, primarily, of their own femininity. That is something which will become even clearer as women's liberation gathers pace. The liberation does not mean that women will be freed from their femininity but that men will stop offloading their own feminisation onto them, making women pay a heavy price for men's castration anxiety while themselves paying the heavy price of misrecognising their desire. And what is this misrecognition, if not desire itself, which gives to the woman a paradoxical power just as she seems to be most oppressed?

When Pandora, an artificial creature born by the will of Zeus, comes to life and becomes human, her first gesture – the opening of her famous box – plunges men into such torment that they set to work. From the height of her beauty, she is none other than 'her ladyship',[33] through whose fault work never ends. Where does the fault come from, if not from the evil of desire itself, of which it would be vain to purge the woman? To want to rid her of it would be to kill her. And yet the dead woman, the woman-automaton, doll, mannequin, gynoid – the thousand incarnations of Sleeping Beauty – have always haunted dreams and literature.[34] Men dream of a woman who would not exist, a dead woman, but they do so not so much from their desire, as from this point where they would be rid of their desire, which, really, is to say rid of themselves.

In the Bible, at the foundation of the human race by Adam, Eve comes in second place after the nebulous Lilith, of whom no one says a word thereafter. This division of woman operates at the start, and we do not have to read much further to see it repeated; at the beginning of *Genesis*, Abraham awaits a son from Sarah, but she remains barren and only becomes fertile after letting him take his slave Hagar, an Egyptian, as a second wife. From her, he has a first son, Ishmael, the father of Islam. But Hagar is repudiated on all sides, including by the Koran. In the civilisations of the Book, such is the destiny of the other woman, thanks to whom enjoyment appears. Eve and Lilith or Sarah and Hagar, women are divided figures through whose fault the evil of desire arises (and whom, therefore, the father always believes that he has a right to punish).

Despite being denied, marginalised and demonised for millennia, the occult power of women has nonetheless always been suspected or recognised. Although they were excluded from the priesthood, St. John Chrysostom wrote of women: 'They are vested with such power that they cause whomsoever they want from among the priests to be elected'. The quiet war of attrition against the patriarchy has never let up (although its political expression is only recent) and has ensured a certain form of dominion for women, if only thanks to the avenging twists of love – love of fathers, lovers, husbands and sons. More than others, women relegated to the kitchens or maternal tasks take revenge on their children, encumbering their daughters with inhibitions or making their sons into men who, like themselves, love men.

In the city, women were perhaps considered as minors who had to be tolerated patiently because of their role as mothers.[35] Their chatter, intrigues, narcissism, envy, jealousies, unfettered passions and narrow minds had to be endured with no other prospect than desire and the obtuse will of love. The 'madness' of women, for whom feminisation (castration) has never been a fixed state but rather, an uncertain becoming, has always troubled the order imposed by men, in their own denial of their femininity. Women harbour a value that goes beyond them – the result of their internal struggle between masculinity and a femininity that they never fully accept. And by standing in this contradictory space, the figures of femininity – Athena, Mary, Marianne, the Good Mother – have compelled the city to teeter endlessly, with no hope of finding a perfect balance.

Notes

1 Roughly 'young women', 'ladies' and 'gentlemen' (translator's note).
2 This 'impossible task' corresponds in part to the Lacanian aphorism, 'The woman does not exist'.
3 Freud [1933], *New Introductory Lectures on Psycho-Analysis* in *Standard Edition 22*, p. 116.
4 This corresponds, in another vocabulary, to 'honour'.
5 In *Analysis Terminable and Interminable*, for example, Freud suggests that castration anxiety holds every subject in lifelong thrall (Freud [1937], *Standard Edition 23*, pp. 251–252).
6 Freud [1925], *Some Psychical Consequences of the Anatomical Distinction between the Sexes* in *Standard Edition 19*, pp. 241–258; Freud [1931], *Female Sexuality* in *Standard Edition 21*, pp. 221–244.
7 This project – which may take a lifetime – seems to supports Freud's propositions from 1903 on the choice of gender (Freud [1905], *Three Essays on the Theory of Sexuality* in *Standard Edition 7*, pp. 219–221). It has the merit of simplicity and in this respect it is valuable, but it gains even more clarity once we recognise its relativity (highlighted in the 1903 version) by replacing 'man' with 'masculinity' (activity with an active aim) and 'woman' with 'femininity' (activity with a passive aim).
8 'The genital apparatus remains the neighbor of the cloaca (and in the case of women is only taken from it on lease)' (Lou Andreas-Salomé, ' "Anal" and "Sexual" ' (N. Hausmann, trans.) in *Psychoanalysis and History*, 24, no. 1 (2022): 19–40, 28).
9 'an unawareness [. . .] of the fertilising role of male semen and, on the other side, of the existence as such of the female organ' (Lacan, *Seminar 4, The Object Relation*. Cambridge: Polity, 2020, p. 88).
10 The mouth is the main erogenous zone of the drive link to the mother, and the loss of the maternal object creates a psychical hole well before the anus, and then the vagina, takes on the role of this hollow. The phallus is initially expected from the father through the mouth at the moment of loss of the maternal object. So the passage from the clitoris to the vagina will follow the same circuit.
11 The oral drive seeks to make the body equivalent to the phallus, symmetrically connecting the mouth of men to the breasts or that of women to the penis.
12 As Freud writes, the child's sexual desires change according to the different stages of the libido and 'cannot for the most part be satisfied'. They provide many pretexts for the appearance of hostility towards the mother, and this impossibility is sufficient to programme a change of object: 'The estrangement follows inevitably from the nature of children's sexuality, from the immoderate character of their demand for love and the

impossibility of fulfilling their sexual wishes' (Freud [1933], *New Introductory Lectures on Psycho-Analysis* in *Standard Edition 22*, p. 124).

13   Freud notes that the girl turns to her father to escape the maternal hold: 'She enters the Oedipus situation as though into a haven of refuge' (*Ibid.*, p. 129).

14   'We cannot understand women unless we appreciate this phase of their pre-Oedipus attachment to their mother' (*Ibid.*, p. 119).

15   In his 1912 text, *On the Universal Tendency to Debasement in the Sphere of Love*, Freud insists on the role of fantasies in female frigidity and writes: 'Often she can no longer, afterwards, undo the link which attaches sexual activity to the forbidden and she proves psychically impotent, that is to say frigid, when this activity is finally permitted' (Freud [1912], *Standard Edition 11*, p. 186).

16   'A little girl behaves differently. She makes her judgement and her decision in a flash. She has seen it and knows that she is without it and wants to have it' and 'The hope of some day obtaining a penis in spite of everything and so of becoming like a man may persist to an incredibly late age and may become a motive for strange and otherwise unaccountable actions' (Freud [1925], *Some Psychical Consequences of the Anatomical Distinction between the Sexes* in *Standard Edition 19*, pp. 252, 234).

17   Think, for example, of Marilyn Monroe singing 'My Heart Belongs to Daddy'.

18   This moment 'outside time' is that of the hysterical seizure.

19   Jacqueline Schaeffer writes in her paper *Horror Feminae*: 'I would therefore argue that everything that the ego finds intolerable – passivity, loss of control, the blurring of boundaries, the break-through of penetration, misuse of power, possession' (all fantasmatic representations that solicit the man's penis) '– is precisely what contributes to sexual ecstasy. [. . .] "defeat" – in all its polysemy: undoing, getting rid of, being defeated – is a necessary condition for a woman to experience ecstasy' (Jacqueline Schaeffer, *The Universal Refusal: A Psychoanalytic Exploration of the Feminine Sphere and its Repudiation*. London: Karnac, 2011, p. 120).

20   See Joan Riviere, 'Womanliness as Masquerade' in *International Journal of Psychoanalysis, X* (1929): 303–313.

21   For example, when he prevents her from playing with boys, from dressing as a girl, from going out, etc. Or if he goes to the beach with her when she is a little older and is careful not to say that she is his daughter, etc.

22   As Freud writes, what is essential in this process is the lack at this stage of development of the thrust of passivity that allows the establishment of femininity (Freud [1933], *New Introductory Lectures on Psycho-Analysis* in *Standard Edition 22*, p. 130).

23   *Ibid.*, pp. 112–135.

24   *Ibid.*, p. 131.

25   In French, 'desire for' and 'desired by' are, respectively, 'désir de' and 'désirée de'; both use the preposition 'de', which, literally translated, means 'of' – a preposition with genitive (possessive) import. The person who *desires* (the subject) in 'desire for' is the one who is *desired* (the object) in 'desired by'. So 'de' in the French is a subjective genitive in the first case and an objective genitive in the second (translator's note).

26   Riviere, *op. cit.*, p. 304.

27   Louis Aragon, *Le fou d'Elsa*. Paris: Gallimard, 1963. p. 62.

28   'The real difference between masculine and feminine hysteria is the difference of social scenes: in its masculine version the passivation under the effect of trauma happens in the workplace or the battlefield, i.e., "in the heat of action" ' (translated from: P.-L. Assoun, *Masculin et féminin*. Paris: Economica-Anthropos, 2005, p. 49).

29   This is the sense in which the gift of the name of the father to the child has legitimacy.

30   Translated from: George Sand, *Lélia*. Paris: Dupuy et Tenré, 1833, pp. 10, 26.

31   Freud, *op. cit.*, pp. 112–135.

32   It is a mistake to think that sexuality, especially female sexuality, has been liberated over the centuries in a gradual historical process. A glance at Mesopotamian, Greek and

American-Indian pottery or at Tantric figures shows that our era has not invented anything new as regards sexual freedom. If there is a movement towards liberation today, it is in response to the massive repression engendered by monotheism.

33 'la bourgeoise' (translator's note).

34 See Catherine Bruno, 'Fabriquer la femme qui n'existe pas' in *Psychanalyse*, no. 14 (Érès, 2009): 57–74.

35 The learned Aristotle does not hesitate to affirm that 'the female is as it were a deformed male' (*On the Generation of Animals*, Book II, chapter 3 (A. Peck, trans.). Cambridge, MA: Heinemann, 1943, p. 175). Tertullian adds to this by writing: 'Woman [. . .] you are the Devil's gateway' (*De cultu feminarum* ('On Female Fashion') (Rev. S. Thelwall, trans.), https://www.tertullian.org/anf/anf04/anf04-06.htm#P265_52058, Book II, Chapter 1). Flavius Josephus, in the 1st century AD, wrote: 'The woman, says the Law, is in all things inferior to the man. Let her accordingly be submissive, not for her humiliation, but that she may be directed; for the authority has been given by God to the man' (Flavius Josephus, *Contra Apionem* ('Against Apio'), Book II, Chapter 201 (H. Thackeray, trans.). London: Heinemann, 1926, p. 373). The Bible tops all of these maledictions: 'Sin began with a woman, and thanks to her we all must die' (Jerusalem Bible, Sirach-Ecclesiasticus 25:24); 'And I find woman more bitter than death, for she is a trap, her heart a net, and her arms bonds' (Jerusalem Bible, Ecclesiastes 7:26).

Chapter 5

Fundamental fantasies, organisers of sexual desire

The 'Oedipus complex', nice and not-so-nice versions

The Oedipus complex is supposed to be the most important discovery of psychoanalysis, even though Freud never wrote a text devoted exclusively to it. For Freud, the Oedipus complex was a myth, a useful envelope for designating a contradictory truth that is stratified in several sequences and of which we often see only the final result (the 'nice' version of the Oedipus complex), thus obscuring the structuring of desire by a tangle of fundamental fantasies that link erotism to death (the 'not-so-nice' version). In order to understand more, we must see how the subject is pushed towards an impossible enjoyment, a quest that is never entirely relinquished. We must look first at the cascade of interactive events which lead up to the suspended animation of the latency phase. For this purpose, we will explore some elements the 'upstream' incidence of which has already been mentioned as relevant to the choice of sexual gender. We will then describe their 'downstream' extension – their impact on the structuring of sexual desire. We will do so by looking at the origin of fundamental fantasies.

As we have said, the subject initially takes itself as object in order to stop being the object of the Other's desire. The subject makes itself enjoy (actively) more powerfully than it is enjoyed (passively). To begin with, this masturbatory activity can occur at any erogenous zone and later is focused on phallicism – the symbol of the passage from being the phallus to having it. This activity certainly affords relief, but it is culpable since it leads to the discovery of maternal castration; to stop being the phallus is to deprive the mother of it. So this enjoyment searches, more or less openly, for the punishment that would exonerate it. But since this now beaten child fears the loss of maternal love, it is better that a third party administer the much-sought punishment. Enter the chastising father, whose (imagined) 'blows' afford relief to the rhythm of masturbation.[1]

We already considered this *first fundamental fantasy of the beaten child**,[2] and we emphasised that the 'blows of the father' have no more factual reality than that of fantasised seduction.[3] Nevertheless, the father inspires fear, even when he is gentle and even because he is gentle.[4] Once the line has been crossed from the passivity of Being to the activity of Having, children are doubly at

DOI: 10.4324/9781003519287-5

fault. Firstly, because they cheat their mother by ceasing to be her phallus. And secondly, because they might make incestuous use of the erectile member, with which they are now equipped. In this sense, the father's punishment has an eroticising effect that is twofold: not only do the blows accompany arousal but they also punish as if the fault had actually been committed. This is why many children seek reprimand to a point where the punishment exceeds the fault. The more unjust the sanction, the more it succeeds in addressing another hidden incestuous fault, which is situated 'upstream'. So the sense of having experienced a passive incest is turned into an active, exciting incestuous desire. *The punishment has given reality to a fictitious fault (incest).*[5] The blows transform defeat into victory; in reality, no incest was committed nor could it have been, but the punishment insists that it was.

This appearance of the father, pulled like a rabbit from the hat of guilt, brings about an immediate reversal of the situation; since punishment accompanies arousal, the father himself becomes the seducer, as if the punishment had caused the erection. The beating now appears to be the immediate cause of the arousal, and all the more so since it is imperative that the mother not be involved in all this. The redemption is total, as if the blows were the primary reason for arousal, and hence, the ordinary masochism of erotism, which is not an exception but the rule.

Thanks to this reversal of the situation, the metamorphosis of the penis into the phallus will be expected from the father, by boys no less than by girls. What better seducer could there be than the father since he turns the penis into a phallus, albeit through the painful expedient of a spanking? So the 'envy of the phallus' is initially actualised with the fantasy of the beaten child and then results in the *seduction fantasy***.[6] The arousal that accompanies the blows makes the father into the agent of a violent seduction, the virtuality of which intensifies the actuality of the first masturbation fantasies.

This blossoming of desire immediately establishes a *parricide fantasy**** since its emergence introduces the risk of an incestuous trauma. This extreme danger turns the father's seduction into a death wish against him. From violence 'suffered' to parricidal revenge, desire is torn between enjoyment and murder in a contradiction concealed by the guilt that leaves its stamp on human sexuality and in which being at fault is itself arousing.[7]

The subject of desire is thus *causa sui*, as we can see by a short recap of what has been described. For there to be a subject, that subject must first have separated from his/her mother. But this breaking free entails both fear of losing her love and a sense of guilt. So the subject will cast the father in the role of punisher. And since the breaking free will have been correlative to arousal, sexual seduction will now take a father as its agent, which the subject tries to get rid of through a parricidal fantasy proportionate to desire. The contradictions of this desire, which is linked to death, engender a purely subjective trauma. At the same time, this punishing father allows a desexualised love for the mother, which results in a secondary motive for the parricidal wish – the motive of keeping the mother for oneself, according to the manifest but misleading version of the Oedipus complex.

So we see a stratification of fundamental fantasies: that of the 'beaten child'*, the 'seduction fantasy'** and the 'parricide fantasy'***, which is its consequence. The three asterisked fantasies have a special place because they are foundational and interlinked. They are so much in evidence that, like the air we breathe, we no longer even notice them. But to hear somebody complain (*), just listen in on any conversation; to witness seduction in action (**), just enter a public space; and the parricide (***) is social life itself, beginning with the weight of religion that eternalises the father right down to his most secular avatars. To these fantasies, we should add the fantasy of castration, that of the primal scene and various subsets of these fundamental five.

Let us start with the least 'conscious' of the fantasies and one that has special psychical importance – the *castration fantasy*.[8] The father gives the phallus since his 'blows' make the penis erect, but the gift is accompanied by the wish to kill this incestuous father, so the final outcome is a father who is dead and castrated. Just as the wish to kill the father is a revenge for the incestuous risk of his desire, so the wish to castrate the father responds, boomerang-like, to the dread of being castrated. On the feminine side, to be castrated implies a violent desire to castrate. 'To kill and castrate the father' means 'to be excited by his blows, to be seduced by him in order then to eliminate him while keeping the phallus'. This group of fantasies corresponds to an extreme in the lived experience of love.[9]

The *castration fantasy* has a key place in the sequencing of fundamental fantasies. There is an enigma here because the term 'castration' evokes the cutting off of an organ, whereas what castration actually does is to arouse desire.[10] These pairs of opposites – risk of castration and sexual arousal or dread of feminisation and virility – seem irreconcilable if we consider only the outcome of the Oedipus complex (the 'nice' version). Yet they engender each other in the genesis of the same complex (the 'not-so-nice' version).[11] The father arouses at the same time as he punishes, and because of this condensation, punishment will bear on the organ of enjoyment, the penis, which is to say that the punishment will be represented as castration. When the time comes to assume desire, the subject will take on both guilt and the dread of castration. The nice version of the Oedipus complex condenses and greatly simplifies this process: it seems as if the father castrates in order to punish the son's desire for the mother. But this loses sight of the genesis of the complex and makes the erectile moment of desire opaque; castration appears to be an emasculation, whereas, in fact, it arouses to the point of erection. The father gives birth to a sexual desire that did not exist before, a desire that is henceforth oriented by both organ enjoyment and lack.

This desire does not initially have an object but only an agent, who becomes invisible in the very movement which gives birth to it. The cause of desire is so contradictory that its mainspring eludes consciousness as soon as begins to function. We see only the result: desire comes alive without knowing what it wants. Its arrow is ignorant of the target it flies to. It is stretched on the bow of fantasies at the moment when the subject chooses its gender. The mother was never 'genitally' desired; she was, is and will be this Thing of the drive, the Thing towards which we gravitate but always eludes us. Desire is not born because the mother has been 'forbidden' by the father. The father isn't bothered with this and may play his part even without manifesting any desire.[12] The point is that this father himself becomes the hidden cause of arousal or rather, he would be, if he were not immediately doomed to parricide.[13]

The sexual trauma issuing from the father crystallises structure; it establishes a subjectivity split between conscious and unconscious. The subject divided between active and passive lives in incomprehension of what has happened and is left desiring but unaware of what. The affirmation of desire, its *Bejahung*, takes hold on the background of this incomprehension. Is it, for example, comprehensible that blows engender desire? Or that desire entails a wish to destroy the figure who gave birth to it? Thought runs up against this opacity, or rather, it gains the very momentum it needs for thinking to occur, even if it is always thinking about something else. These disturbing contradictions of desire are what produce neurosis in young children, the solution of which is postponed until later.

Childhood neurosis and the nice version of the Oedipus complex

The 'nice' version of the Oedipus complex, which only appears at the end of this drama, has proved popular as a didactic simplification. But it was a late conceptualisation by Freud, much later than his treatment of sexual trauma by a violating father (the 'not-so-nice' version of the fantasy of seduction, which was at the origin of the discovery of a repressed unconscious). At the end of the not-so-nice version, the mother, as object of drive enjoyment, becomes inaccessible, while the father, as cause of desire, vanishes behind the seductive fantasy of his murder. What could have been the object of desire – the mother – fades away in favour of a desexualised love. The benefit is extraordinary! The father, as he generates fantasies of arousal, preserves and pacifies love for the mother, a love that is now safe, powerful, whiter than white, free of fault.[14]

Alone together, a mother and her child often become entangled in a bodily intimacy that verges on violence; there is tenderness but also anxiety, cries, promises, tears. The situation seems hopeless, and then, in Épinal's memorable image, the door slams, father is home and calm returns. What we must remember is that the mother is not the Mother but a woman managing as best she can with this function of Other, which has fallen to her as her lot. The effect of paternal presence does not follow from some patriarchal magic; all that the father does is to work against the impersonal power of the Other. He also is but a subject, and as he converses with this woman about ordinary, day-to-day things, they find themselves in a subject-to-subject relationship, which dissipates the violence of the Other. This father is not simply a 'third party', as sometimes gets said; he is a man who speaks to a woman. And here begins a new round in the game – that of love and its demand for exclusivity. The father, whose presence has calmed things down, then becomes a rival.

The classic Oedipal drama now takes centre stage, with the wish to marry the mother or to live with her forever, while a theatrical rivalry develops with the father. This pantomime confrontation conceals and justifies the initial parricidal movement caused by the seduction of sexual trauma. This is where ambivalence towards the father becomes so powerful since it is thanks to the father that love for the mother blossoms in all innocence. Obscured behind this stage scenery, the hatred of the father stems less from rivalry than from the desire he provokes. The father is a sexual seducer before he is a troublesome rival. The nice version of the Oedipus complex (the version found in textbooks and magazines) superimposes its triangle on that of sexual trauma, which is the true birth certificate of desire – unforgettable and insistent, although its traces are erased each time it appears, as guilt overshadows the parricide wish. Superposition of the nice triangle on the not-so-nice triangle creates an irremediable split between love and desire: love pulls towards the nice version, while desire prefers the not-so-nice. This split establishes the conflictual nature of erotic life: nice and not-so-nice may cross paths, but they can only coalesce in the sort of unreality which often accompanies love.

Dynamics of the seduction fantasy

The 'hypnosis' of seduction** results from the blows the child receives*. Born from the desire of/for ('*du*') the father, the genitive ('*du*') in the fantasy *of* seduction leaves the subject in doubt: am I seducer or seduced?[15] This question seeks resolution through establishing an *external* tension between masculine and feminine. The never-ending war of the sexes relieves the *internal* conflict of bisexuality. What is at stake for the man is to be masculine in the face of paternal seduction, and he displaces the risk of having been seduced (by his father) onto a woman whom he seeks to seduce. For the woman, there can be no question of accepting her feminisation without prior elimination of the father who was its first agent; this is the test to which she submits the man who seeks to seduce her.

From this seduction, sexual desire takes on an 'altruistic' tempo. 'Altruistic' in the sense that the subject feminised (castrated) by the father sets out in search of an *alter ego* to which to do the same in order to finally have a phallus instead of being had by this father. To have been seduced establishes the eternal activity of wanting to seduce,[16] wanting at all costs to receive the phallus or to give it. But since this having immediately entails the risk of being had by the father, one must immediately seek to give it in order to have it but, this time, on one's own account. An exhausting chase indeed.

All of us are grilled non-stop on these hot coals in relation to the other sex. This tension is always present in public and private spaces, ignited by the mere co-presence of bodies, driven by the denial of castration. It functions above all for itself, striving towards a single objective – that of selecting a gender. The primary objective is not sexual activity or 'genital' relief – merely to please is sufficient. This conflicting relationship endures for its own sake, endlessly transforming the active and the passive of the drive into the *internal* contradiction of bisexuality, then turning the latter into the *external* contradiction of the 'war' between the sexes – a strange combat, more akin to dance than to war,[17] and where the outcome is decided by the mere relationship between bodies, a situation in which each one decides on their gender at the expense of the other. That is all. The war is over as soon as it is declared and because it has been declared.

The bipolarity of the drive has been metamorphosed into the opposition between masculine and feminine. The bipolarity is not gendered in itself but becomes so as we subjectivise it.[18] This redrafting of the drive's hold on us using psychical gender equates 'activity' with the masculine and 'activity with a passive goal' with the feminine, which is to say activity linked to its own *negation*. This changes everything. With negation, a thought of something that 'should not be' underpins sexual arousal. At the very moment when desire is strongest, it can switch into its contrary, due to this internal obstacle, often experienced as a latent feeling that something is 'not right'.[19] And yet desire will still be directed to and obsessed by this same object.

By first saying no, seduction stages a repression of the drive. Negation means 'I am not an object of consumption'. A seduction is bound to involve a refusal, and for many men, nothing is more exciting than a woman who initially says no. Beauty, intelligence and moral qualities alone may be hard-pressed to trigger sexual arousal. But a woman who proves elusive can trigger the seduction fantasy. Most women prefer not to acquiesce too quickly to an eager courtship but hold back to the last moment and even to the point of acquiescing while still refusing. The difficulty or even the impossibility of conquest captivates many men, who are attracted by virginity and even frigidity; the infantile world desire stakes its claims, sure in advance that only what remains unsatisfied will last.

'No' is one of those layered words, each occurrence of which does not necessarily issue onto a 'yes' but onto a different kind of 'no'. A refusal keeps the greed of the drive at bay at a limit where (provided they go no further) a look, a brush of the hand or a sigh transforms the drive into a lack, from which the fantasy can then unfold according to its own contradictions. When a woman begins by saying no, she refuses to be a passive object and thus affirms her primary masculinity. So the thrill of the relationship consists in proving which of the two lovers is the man, offering a solution to the torments of bisexuality.

But there is more to all this because an infantile underworld looms behind the refusal; neurotic love is kindled as soon as a man feels rejected, just as he feared being rejected by his mother in early childhood. The expression of the feminine 'no' here also summons up a father, whose prohibition engenders a transgressive desire that rarely leaves a man indifferent. To confront this refusal in the present and go beyond it, even as far as the sexual act, is as if to commit violence, which is validated by the cries of pleasure in sexual enjoyment (so akin to cries of suffering).[20] In this neurotic enactment, man's virility asserts itself against a father who forbids him from enjoying a woman. In this infantile underworld, the impersonal father may well defeat him; nothing is decided in advance (defeat may, for example, be signified by premature ejaculation). If this fight turns in his favour, the man will think that he has taken the father's place, but it is an illusion that will not last long.[21] So we see how even the most inconsequential 'no' can evoke a legion of fundamental fantasies – the fuel of sexual arousal. This 'no' is less just a refusal than the contradiction of 'activity with a passive goal' – that is, a sort of presence of the father internal to fantasy.

A remark is called for here about a contradiction inherent to the seduction fantasy, which can be polarised as an opposition between masculine and feminine. As such, it should be most adequately discharged in a 'heterosexual' tension (including homosexual couples which encrypt a transvestite heterosexuality, one of the partners playing the role of the man and the other that of the woman). In this sense, the function of negation is specific to heterosexual love, so often plagued by these complications but benefiting, thanks to this difficulty, from a specific enjoyment which homosexuality short-circuits (except when it covers a latent heterosexuality). Heterosexuality stages a presence of the father (in internal exclusion) which burdens the interaction with its neurotic freight. This internal prohibition does not exist in homosexuality, thanks to which its sexuality is easier and lighter. Homosexuality presents fewer complications and an undeniable narcissistic advantage.[22] Conquests and sexual consumption may occur at high speed, without the painful melodramas of neurotic heterosexuality. The latter must face, in the latency of love, the dilemma of parricide, which gives a specific quality to its orgastic electroshock (the just reward for its pains).

Homosexuality can certainly lead to analogous results because nothing could be easier than to summon up a father; one has merely to transgress. But the enjoyment of the confrontation with the law is then *external* to the partners of the act and to their fantasies. This 'confrontation with the law' is not reduced to acting illegally (although that may be the case). It requires that the transgression be established in relation to an external prohibition.[23] The transgression may just as easily be satisfied with parodies, mockery, disguises and a derision of heterosexuality, but whatever the case, the connection to the parricide fantasy is not to be found in the fantasy tension of the sexual act itself, as in heterosexuality. For example, it never happens that one of the partners in a homosexual couple feels the need to take the name of the other, except by way of parodying heterosexual practice.[24] So the 'madness' of marriage loses its main mystery; it becomes nothing more than a contract.

Imminent disaster: the fantasy of abandonment

A variant of the seduction fantasy may occur which turns negation into the feeling of being rejected. It deserves special attention. As seduction rises to its zenith, as everything heralds its success, as love, attention, eroticism are all on the ascendant, the certainty of an imminent catastrophe suddenly looms. It looms because abandonment by the most loved person follows from sexual desire itself, as it first appears. For some women, there can be no better way to make this painful memory present than by choosing impossible partners, whether they are disdainful and uninterested or their family or geographical situation offers no hope of an ongoing relationship. Other suitors are uninteresting. But even when the desired man presents none of these disadvantages, there may be a certainty that his love will be ephemeral, that abandonment is on the horizon. And the expected disaster happens precisely because it was expected, encouraged by the very precautions that were supposed to prevent it. The love life of some women is a series of such programmed failures, and they sometimes understand themselves that nothing can ever excite them as much as this.

Why this enslavement to such painful repetition? Because the 'desire of the father', the driving force of seduction, has an incestuous dimension; rejection itself will become closely linked to what is most strongly felt in desire. Indeed, it is enough for a father to have actually rejected his daughter on a few occasions for this gesture to become the sign of desire. The seduction fantasy often does not correspond to any actual seduction. The charm of a look, for example, will have been enough to foment this first lie, the hysteric's *proton pseudos*, which desire turns on. And an actual paternal rejection, if it happens, will feed this (the father rejects . . . because he desires too much). The father's marks of disdain are interpreted as signs of their repressed contrary; this father likes his daughter too much and so he dismisses her because she represents a danger for him. The daughter's certainty of this grows in proportion to the desire that she herself represses, in a double reversal that affords delicious pain.

The function of 'rejection' in the masculine seduction fantasy is even clearer. For many men, their desire to seduce puts itself at the service of their own rejection. A man loves a woman, but he cannot help, when he is in her company, trying to seduce another (often random) woman. The woman he loves will, therefore, reject him, and only then is his passion ignited, sometimes too late. But the whole process is a source of enjoyment. In his childhood memories, his father was rejected by his mother, as he himself wished (whether or not this actually happened). When he is later on rejected, in a situation he has engineered, this identifies him with the father and reinforces his love of a woman who conceals his mother and eventually becomes as unattainable as her, assuming that a breakup is the outcome of his manoeuvres. This oscillation of seduction between acceptance and refusal (or both at the same time) takes many shapes in the course of love life. And each time, its rhythm triggers the same passionate suffering, conducive to sexual arousal. The fantasy of rejection runs like a *basso continuo* through subjectivity, which invents a host of retrospective justifications (philosophical, political, religious) in order to rationalise it. Solitude, dereliction and exile are the standard masks of the desiring hero.

Although only marginal in relation to sexuality, we should mention here a very masculine consequence of the seduction fantasy when it is accompanied by rejection, a consequence which deserves a broader anthropological treatment. For most men, the fantasy of the beaten child* is closely linked to that of seduction**; tormented by the conflicting pulls of his femininity and his virility, every man feels a strong urge to do battle, to confront a like-being and decide once and for all which of them is the woman.[25] This is the basis of every man's fantasy life outside the field of his relationship with women; you must uphold your honour and see justice done. In what we might call a 'vigilante fantasy', disaster threatens, but thanks to the lone hero, good prevails. From Western to thriller, this marginal fantasy is always a best-seller.

Seduction, matrix of space-time

When a man walks into a room, he looks around to see if there is anyone there he likes the look of. When a woman enters the same room, she makes a point of not looking at anyone but behaves as if she was the centre of attention, to such a degree that she is sometimes shy of entering a new space ('Why do they all have to look at me like that?'). In some cultures, this relationship to the body is so powerful that women must veil themselves from head to toe. Seduction sets the pulse racing, and there are countries not so far away where it is illegal to approach women in public spaces (in the USA, apparently). It is said that today, we live in a permissive world.[26] But why such quantities of alcohol, ecstasy and cocaine in places dedicated to sexual freedom, if not to overcome the negation inherent to fantasy itself? Why this carry-on, if not because seduction is dangerous, culpable, risky, heavy with the incestuous scent of the father? A woman seduces in the name of the devil, the chthonic confederate of God, and their conflict holds her in a strange torsion of space.

The presence of women organises space. High heels, flat or overcompensated, with straps or without, the rhythm of their steps in the street sets the tempo for men, ridding them of their emptiness. The world is organised through the rupturing of space by feminine presence, which insists under its multiple disguises. This presence makes a hole; it delocalises the bodily habitat. For a man, the desire to give the phallus starts from him. So he is where he is. For a woman, having the phallus is expected from someone who stands at a distance. A woman is not completely there where we see her, and in this distortion between herself and what she awaits, a rupture of space engenders, with the time of waiting and expectation, a particular sort of space-time – that of desire. The distance from Being to Having is intensified by this waiting, by the time it takes to fill this gap, by a duration that is never reabsorbed, leaving desire always in evidence. If woman could say 'yes' (to herself, first of all), the lips of time would meet. But she could not do it without departing from herself, which is to say without ceasing to exist. And so by first saying 'no', she turns the sandglass over once again to let another small measure of time run through.

Women have their acquaintance with Cronos, castrator of his father, who was himself the mythical father, devourer of his children, at the same time as he was the guardian of time. The female body seems to punctuate time, from lunar menstruation to fertility. But even more than their bodies, the desire which they arouse organises a space-time without relation to anything but itself. It is a time without regard for copulation or for reproduction. It cares for sex only abstractly; it can wait. Men gaze at this immobile clock, men who do not want to wait; unlike femininity, virility lives by urgency.

The fantasy of the primal scene

Looking at the simple (even banal) consequences of the Oedipus complex, we lose sight of the stakes of desire. The last phases of the complex already involve a repression. Take, for example, the primal scene fantasy: how can it make sense that imagining, seeing or hearing a couple engaged in copulation can provoke enjoyment or, at least, deep emotion? We register the fact without considering its origin; the child enters into masturbatory enjoyment on the fantasmatic background of a chastising father. The father beats the child as punishment for masturbation because this culpable activity risks depriving the mother of the phallus. But if she is deprived of it, how will she be able to recover it except by receiving it in copulation? And this reparatory copulation will have to take the same form as that undergone by the child. So it is, first and foremost, the mother who must be beaten; she must be beaten in the same way as her child and for the same reason: in order to have the phallus. This violent scene is at the origin of how the sexual relationship is imagined; the act of witnessing the scene corresponds to a desire since the sight signifies that the mother can recover the phallus, which means that this burden no longer weighs on the liberated child. This liberation legitimises the child's erection.

The relief that comes from the vision of the primal scene is all the greater because it alleviates guilt. What was the child guilty of, if not of depriving the mother of the phallus? So by circularity, at the same time as he punishes the child, the father immediately compensates the mother's lack by fornicating with her. The 'primal scene' dramatises a relationship between the parents in which the father plays a violent and castrating role.[27] The enjoyment of the sexual relationship itself remains unknown to children when they witness this scene.[28] All that they intuit there is an act of violence, which, certainly, resounds deeply in them and moves them; they recognise it without understanding it because it is what their guilt makes them dream of. The sexual relationship between the parents is first imagined as a consequence of the woman's castration, a scene that excites the child in its energetic masturbation. So that later, seeing sexual intercourse will cause erection, and the cry of pleasure is assimilated to one of suffering.

The fantasy of the primal scene establishes the junction between the dread of the mother's castration and castration by the father; it shows the dreamt-of moment when the father gives the phallus to a castrated mother at the same time as he beats her in a bizarre sexual relationship that is not accompanied by any enjoyment on the part of its protagonists. In reality, it is less the sight of a copulation that excites and leads to masturbation than masturbation that *produces* the fantasy by first engendering guilt and anxiety associated with the mother's castration and then taking away the guilt by making the father the agent of castration, as represented and compensated for by a sexual relationship.[29]

Subsequently, this scene with three characters is dumbed down in the 'nice' version of the Oedipus complex; it gets the seal of rivalry with the father and jealousy of the mother. But this version forgets the subject's own desire. The poor soul is taken to be the victim of an unequal struggle against the father, losing sight of the fact that nothing excites as much as this struggle. So that, in later life, the man or woman will look more or less consciously for triangular situations which incite their jealousy. They will endure all the suffering of love at one level while their desire is aroused at another.

The parricide fantasy, an outlet for the death drive

Human beings are rarely satisfied with autoerotism, despite its practicality, or even with autoerotism for two, which would suffice for the reproduction of the species. Their dissatisfaction reflects the annihilating force of the drive, which pushes towards excess and, therefore, towards death. The 'death drive' was not introduced by Freud in a text that deals with human sexuality *per se* but with sexual reproduction in general, making reference to the animal (and even vegetable) kingdom.[30] Each individual must die for the sake of survival of the species; sexuality is 'naturally' linked to mortality. But this 'natural' dimension slips into the background no sooner than it is invested by the sexual drives. Because if, in general, the goal of the drive is unrealisable and impossible, then the drive is pushing towards nothingness, although it does not attain that either (excepting the accident of suicide). In this sense, the death drive underpins each drive, as it moves towards mortal excess. The death drive works non-stop from birth and without any immediate relation to the end of life. It accompanies, step by step, the autoerotic emergence of each drive to the point of masturbatory relief and gives its melancholic tone to the latter.

But that is not enough for the drive; when it reaches autoerotism for two, the drive seeks to sate on another body the enjoyment which would have brought annihilation if exercised on its own body. So its horizon will be an eroticised aggression towards someone else, seeking to make him or her enjoy unto death. Two lovers can exhaust themselves in a confrontation where each seeks to consume the other. The being and nothingness of the drive's circuit become a life-and-death struggle between two counterparts (fought to a Hegelian tempo) with the difference between the sexes at its service. But the drive is no more sated via a proxy than it is when it turned back on the subject's own body, even though its unsatisfaction now has, as a pretext, the resistance of the lover, against whom it tries to force submission through degrees of passionate violence that range from moral sadism to attempted murder. The clinic and even daily experience show this dynamic clearly; the drive pushes unhesitatingly towards excess and from excess towards what we could call death by overdose.[31]

Some drug addicts come ever closer to overdose because of this secret correlation between enjoyment and death. If we are to believe what they say, a 'high' can be like an orgasm.[32] The fusion of desire and death, in their violent proximity, sideline sexuality as such. A dream of enjoyment is realised in the autarky of drugs. It has no script and tells no idyllic story of endless nuptials. In a journey towards annihilation, the torturous ordeals of desire are abolished, and its satisfaction is mimicked without any particular scenario being played out.[33] What is this death, this 'lowest level of tension', this paradoxical pleasure that the drive seeks? It is the realisation of the goal of the drive, namely, identification with the phallus of the mother – the object of her demand. Incest seeks to kill even before the beginning of life since it actualises a relationship from before one's own birth in this degree zero of repetition. This link between incest and death pushes the drive towards a definitive enjoyment. It is what is dialecticised, as best can be, in human sexuality by shifting the coalescence of being and nothingness onto the terrain of a masculine-feminine relationship, thanks to another body.

Since the relation of masculine to feminine is dependent on the desire of the father, and since this desire of the father ends in a parricidal wish, the death drive finds an extraordinary outlet in the murder of the father. This moment of civilising metamorphosis is characteristic of adolescence, when the meaning of genital sexuality is discovered. What the new enjoyment requires is not so much a physiological capacity but rather, a change of place – taking the place of the father or meeting a man who takes his place. This is a confrontation, and the role of the father, which had remained dormant until then, suddenly assumes its meaning. The sexual trauma of our early years and the fantasy of seduction now emerge from the shadows and are played out in the parlour games of love, which are now no longer games. Because everything changes when the boy imagines that he takes the place of the father or the girl imagines that she meets a man who supplants her father. This change, rather than the physiological possibility of reproduction, is what counts at adolescence. Until then, the fantasies had remained dormant because from the child's point of view, seduction, love, war all existed but still without being connected to what is essential; the parricide had no meaning, and without it, enjoyment remained a game.

Two distinct psychical acts frame this moment when the parricide fantasy takes on its meaning. Firstly, a desire from the father, which follows from a seduction between the father and child. Every father sexually seduces his child through his role as punisher. And secondly, a desire for murder follows from this seduction as revenge for the 'death by incest' that the child experiences because it is desired and, most of all, because it also desires. The second psychical act seeks to actualise this murder by identifying with the father through some trait, by taking his name and attempting to replace him, if not with the mother, then at least with a woman.[34]

Sexual desire transforms the death drive into parricide, making it necessary to 'kill the father' in order to leave the family and have the enjoyment of a woman without slipping into incest. This transformation gives a civilising power to sexual love so that the intimate mystery of sexuality can be played out in public space.[35]

The myth of Don Juan – that famous figure of desire in our culture – offers a fine example of how the death drive is transformed into the murder of the father. In Mozart's opera, with the libretto by Da Ponte, the story begins with a parricide. We then hear the list of Don Juan's conquests (1,003 names of the father in Spain alone), and finally, a father made of stone asks for the Don's hand (*'dammi la mano'*) and leads our hero off to hell. A son, feminised (castrated) by a father in his childhood, will seek endlessly to escape his own feminisation by seducing 1, 2, 3 . . . 1,003 women. Each seduction seeks to rid him of his feminisation, which is to say of his father – the hidden wellspring of his excitement. Active seduction appears as the negative of what it flees from. Its subject does not know what he wants, except that it must definitely not be the agent of this desire, i.e., the father. The father must not cause desire; he *must* not! But what must not happen inevitably happens.[36] The father remains in evidence as a kind of double agent of desire. Prompter and phantom of the act, the moment his blow is delivered, he vanishes in his own machination, eternal return of a cause that seems to be without cause. Desire imposes itself in a ternary movement, where the death wish activates repetition and is set free by the abandonment of each new conquest. The transgressive moment of murder constitutes the orgastic point of possession; in the moment when the places of feminised man and woman are reversed, the grip of the father from hell is loosened. But if the conquest of women is a means of escaping the dread of having been feminised by a father, the debt of parricide is merely displaced . . . and its payment will finally end the drama.

The innumerable versions of the Don Juan story differ in details, but they all share an accumulation of feminine conquests linked to a transgression of the patriarchal order. There is, however, a version which stands apart from the others, that of Stendhal in the *Italian Chronicles*.[37] François Cenci, the dramatic hero of one of these, surpasses any other donjuanesque figure in the art of transgression. He indulges in 'corruption for its own sake' in a 16th-century Rome, where, as Stendhal writes, 'It is to the Christian religion that I attribute the possibility of a satanic role for Don Juan'.[38] Indeed, a character such as Cenci would never have raised an eyebrow in antiquity, where the excesses of love were not seen as licentious. The Don Juan figure could only find a place in culture once the god of monotheism had appeared, introducing a limit. Don Juan is a Christian hero who defies a universal father, and François Cenci belongs to this world where transgression takes on its real meaning. He revels in debauchery and crimes, driving his own children to penury and even death, defying the Church and its commandments, pursuing sodomy and corrupting the young, including youths he introduces to his wife's bed. He is never happier than when publicly accumulating all kinds of turpitude, with prostitutes as the officiants. The reader has the impression of a Sadean monster rather than our Don Juan, for whom a female conquest would not count if he had to pay for it. Our Don Juan does not take pleasure in inflicting torment. He would not impose the slightest physical torture for anything in the world. The only sufferings he inflicts are the sufferings of love, which Cenci holds in contempt. Cenci has no interest in being loved. Did Stendhal's intuition let him down when he presented this character as the archetypal Italian Don Juan?

But the writer is justified by the story's epilogue. Cenci has a bad end, assassinated by his wife and his daughter Beatrice, who resolved to commit the parricide after their long exposure to their father's debauchery and even several attempted rapes by him. Do we not see here an invariant of the myth, which the male Don Juan, guided by the dread of his own feminisation, conceals? Beatrice here is something like the sister of Don Juan; she incarnates the seduced daughter who kills the father, while Don Juan, by seducing women one after the other, flees from and slays a father in each of them. Beatrice shows us an inverted image of the seduced son; she reveals the hidden mechanism which gives its feminine dimension to the Don Juan myth. Far from incarnating Don Juan, Cenci incarnates the incestuous father whom she kills. Like her, Don Juan is a son threatened with death by feminisation, a son who resists by accumulating conquests, only to finally be dragged to hell by a father of stone, a figure as diabolical as Cenci, officiant at an execution rather than at a seduction. But the destinies of Beatrice and Don Juan are not symmetrical, despite their roles as brother and sister in the myth. Stendhal's chronicle does not tell us so, but Don Juan will not find Beatrice in hell. She was executed for parricide but absolved by Clement VIII. So she went straight to paradise (assuming, of course, that the words of a Pope, pronounced at the moment of death, count as an entry ticket).

A few fundamental fantasies, with a lot of subsets

The fundamental fantasies unfold closely linked, starting with the beaten child, seduction from the father and parricide. Knotted in a tight ball within the cocoon of the Oedipus complex, there are only a few of them. However, their variants proliferate as consciousness erases their contradictions to prove the subject's innocence or modestly modifies their transgressive dimension; these bleached versions cleanse desire of guilt. For example, as already mentioned, the parricide fantasy is turned into its opposite, into the idea of having been rejected by the father ('Father, why have you forsaken me?'). Or an expert in transgression may be enthused by a fantasy of being a vigilante and redresser of wrongs, etc. Or yet another example, the fantasy of the beaten child may play out in humiliating situations, more or less disguised, such as having a partner who is somewhat unpleasant or whose behaviour is annoying (a little mortification can suffice). Similarly, the seduction fantasy has many subsets, such as the *adoption fantasy* (With an adoptive father, isn't everything allowed?). The adoption fantasy is almost universal, its finest example being the myth of Oedipus itself, who presents himself as a child threatened with death by a father, then adopted by another father, according to the stratification that has already been commented on.

The prostitution fantasy is one of the most common subsets. In what sense does prostitution connect with fantasy? Prostitution has been a sexual practice since time immemorial and has been practiced universally, so it seems. It is sex minus love; you pay to consume in the same way as hunger or thirst are satisfied, and beyond the register of need, the drive as such seems to feel at home with it. However, unlike drive satisfaction, the consumption involved in prostitution requires a partner and an implicit scenario. If it was only about the drive, masturbation would be a cheaper and equally satisfactory expedient. But prostitution leaves the field open to fantasy based on transgression, if not guilt, and based on the objectification of a woman – an obscenity capable in itself of generating pleasure. The scenario seems to involve only two individuals: the prostitute and her client. In reality, though, it also involves the client's partner, the prostitute's pimp, the men who have been clients before, as well as social opprobrium with its prohibitive function. Far from being some sort of pure 'drive', the enjoyment is linked to a displaced fantasy: the violence suffered, the money paid, transgression, anonymity. Prostitution is not a mere stopgap for the sexually homeless. It represents a specific and even unique enjoyment for some men, from all walks of life.

Behind the question of money, let us look at who enjoys and how in the prostitute-client relationship. Let us first ask ourselves whether prostitution is an enjoyment at all. That the prostitute should not enjoy is built into the contract.[39] She can, of course, pretend, but it would be unprofessional for her to let herself go with each client. On the other hand, she can derive pleasure from it; some prostitutes say that they ply their trade by choice because why should they not derive satisfaction as well as money from the desire they provoke? The absence of orgasm, which it is her duty to refrain from, does not rule out a pleasure similar to that of a man who may only obtain pleasure by giving it. There may be a pleasure in not giving but taking – in making a man spill out his humiliation, contemplating the impotence of his hasty discharge, where the man's anonymity evokes the father. What pleasurable revenge when she discovers such an ersatz father in one of her clients and which thus costs him much more than the rate he is paying. That increases the value of her fee, and in this way, the prostitute *dominates* her client.[40]

What is the meaning of this dominion? It is that the prostitute is offered to the universality of men . . . so her father could have afforded her too. The client may have the vague idea that his father came out of the door of the same prostitute just before he went in, so she has something in common with his mother: she is his father's wife.[41] The dominion of the whore over her client is, therefore, beyond measure, whatever the price he pays. The guilt is limitless, and his guilt is what makes him come. His father punishes him at the very place of the crime. This is a transgressive situation where premature ejaculation is guaranteed. It is as if an impersonal father had just carried out a sodomy. Parricidal guilt speedily engenders a premature ejaculation as the result of a kind of passive sodomy by a paternal ghost. In short, it is a type of feminine enjoyment. A man approaches something akin to female orgasm when he visits a prostitute.

The universality of prostitution led us to examine the masculine fantasy that corresponds to it. But the respective feminine fantasy is just as universal, although it only rarely translates into practice. It is a subset of the seduction fantasy; to give oneself to anybody is to give oneself in imagination to the father – that scoundrel who most probably frequents brothels.[42] A father who frequents places of ill repute and meets his daughter there is a commonplace of the Western novel, and there are several versions of it; the prostitute encounters her father among her clients and recognises him just in time thanks to some characteristic trait.[43]

Like most fantasies, this variant is played out without special pleasure and can even cause illness. For example, a woman may be unable to leave her house just because she is pleasing to men, as if showing herself and being seductive was equivalent to being a whore. The feminine prostitution fantasy is about actualising incest but without doing it on purpose and, above all, without enjoyment; the act must be performed without really giving oneself, and that can be done by taking payment, which is a good way of blocking orgasm and exacting vengeance through frigidity. We can see how widespread this fantasy is by considering one of the ambiguities of the relationship of men to women in our society. At the restaurant, on vacation or when settling daily expenses, it is often accepted that the woman does not pay, even when she could. There is a legitimate dimension to such a disparity; the masculine gift is the intuitive counterpart of the gift of enjoyment. However, the male expenditure opens the door to a prostitution fantasy. The ambiguity here varies depending on whether these payments or presents are offered by a 'father' or by a 'man'. When the present is offered by a 'man', it functions as a symbol of the gift; it has no price and does not pay for anything. But it cannot always be easily distinguished from the payment of a shameful father who seeks to buy. On the other hand, it is clearer on the feminine side that when a woman persists indiscriminately in making men pay, her seduction fantasy plays on the boundary of the prostitution and parricide fantasy, whereby it rejoins the 'masculine' position of the paid woman, whose partner enters the field of a passive enjoyment, at least when this does not inhibit their desire.

An exceptional *outsider*: the love fantasy

Based on the drive, love cannot be analysed or rationalised. One person loves another, often at first sight: a certain characteristic or aesthetic trait attracts, and most of these instant loves finish swiftly. People cross paths, they could have loved each other, but they move on. Sexual arousal, which depends on the fantasy and not on the drive, introduces other requirements. The problem is how love and desire can connect. Love does not necessarily have sexual consequences, and sexual desire can do without love because love is a destiny of the drive, while desire depends on fantasy. However, there is a connection between love and desire in the *love fantasy*, a subset of the fundamental fantasies which shape the whole of erotic life.

Sexual love is not usually classed among the fundamental fantasies because it develops at a distance from them and later on. In childhood, love is attached to a presence – first of all, that of the mother. Its unrivalled power shows the unfailing attachment created by the subjectivisation of the drive – that unparalleled deliverance from the deadly weight of the Other, embodied by the mother herself. The knot of an unfailing love is tightened between the mortifying maternal Other and the feminine subject that this mother also is. The result is a collar drawn tightly around nothing other than itself; this eminently corporal, bodily love cannot enjoy the body it loves. Love is a subjectified destiny of the drive that results paradoxically from a negativising of the drive. It is born from the presence of a body, the subjectivation of which gets rid of the demand for its physical presence, but this relief is an exile, a consciousness unaware of what it comes from and what it would like to fall back on but cannot do so without denying itself as subjectivity. Love is caught in this circle. The kiss would like to go back to biting and devouring, but it would not be able to do so without annulling the subjective distance that the kiss provides.

However, this initial foundation of love on the drive immediately encounters an exception: the father. His love is also engendered from a presence but a presence that results this time from the birth of desire as sexual desire. In reality, love of the father arises from a source other than the drive, and that is so much the case that the presence of a real father may be lacking, while his myth imposes itself as a necessity. A father always appears in thought as the agent of punishment, therefore, of seduction, therefore, of parricide, and it is only at this moment that he can assume a bodily presence. The love of the father, almost impersonal at first, does not emerge in a form that is directed at his actual person until the very last limit is reached, just after the fleeting idea of a murderous wish towards him; once the living father is slain in imagination, a profound gratitude immediately covers this wish. Love casts a veil over parricide; the father of the Oedipus complex is loved for having allowed himself to be symbolically slain. This special love gives thanks to the spirit of the father once the murder, which ensures identification and gives a name, has been committed.[44] Love for the father, although not born directly from the drive, emerges because it, too, is programmed by the establishment of subjectivity.

This recognition of the father, born from his function, cannot be reduced to a kind of spirituality because his role is situated at a dangerous crossroads where the agent of castration – which he embodies – runs the risk of simply turning into the cause of desire. So his seductive presence becomes the danger. It is what has to be destroyed in order to reduce this agent to his spirit. Danger is felt at the physical presence of the father, and the drive force operates here in a direction *opposite* to that imposed by maternal demand. The mother was initially the drive object and then this was denied. The father was initially the operator of this negation but then he became the cause of a physical desire based on the traces of a repressed drive force that is ready to make a return thanks to him but on the condition of his murder. This inversion explains what Freud described as *oral regression*; the father must be devoured, according to the template of totemic cannibalism, the objective of which is to destroy the carnal agent of seduction and thereby to set free the cause of an empty desire. This identificatory devouring produces both guilt and to a love that is a form of recognition for the birth of desire.

This genesis of sexual desire will return at adolescence in the love fantasy as a repetition of the very conditions that presided over its birth. At puberty, when the parricide fantasy flares up again, a young man falls in love with the woman who gives him a place equivalent to that of his father, and a young woman falls in love with the man who rids her of her father. Innocently murderous enthusiasm, on the one hand, counterbalanced by flamboyant love on the other; all we can see is the fire, when it is actually the father who burns. 'Parricide' might seem too strong a word to describe what happens. Suppose we talk instead about confronting the forbidden. When love is declared, it must cross a limit to become erotic; it takes the hand, steals a kiss, presses forward in transgressive stages, which stoke the fire of desire in a situation that calls for crossing a threshold. Love, in a way, flourishes in challenging the rules of morality or propriety (Juliet loves Romeo, a teacher her pupil, a lawyer her prisoner, etc., and above all, in a word: a woman loves a man other than her father!). What 'shouldn't happen' leads the dance, at least to the point where – the situation having normalised, the lovers being recognised and their relations becoming habitual – what 'should happen' now replaces what 'shouldn't'. The situation is reversed, and sexual excitement must find a new alchemy if it is to continue.

So this moment of an unknowing transgression when something of the father is reduced to his spirit marks a threshold. While remaining the son, the amorous subject changes places and confronts an obstacle that is internal to his own fantasy. A kind of passage to the act chacterises the breaking through of what resists, at the very heart of desire. It is the dark space where, the murderer changing places, the lover is suddenly other than himself; in this sense, he abandons himself to the impersonality of a desire that surpasses and manufactures him. In the intoxication of this impersonality, he becomes his own object and is thus finally able to rejoin himself, to enjoy himself, this body, which had always remained exterior to him since childhood. This almost unthinkable loss-of-self of desire would be unbearable if it did not at the same time involve a taking hold of and then a gift of oneself. This sort of annihilation is all the more easily experienced if it is felt as a gift. The lover loses himself or herself all the better in giving themself. To put it a little romantically, the lover turns loss into an offering.

So we might say that the love fantasy functions as a later subset of the fantasy of the father's murder, which is the universal stand-in for the excluded middle. 'Love fantasy' certainly means that love is kindled from the drive (beauty, charm, etc.) but that the beloved presents a trait, some *prêt-à-porter* that is conducive to fantasy and its parricidal version. Enamoration covers up this fantasy. Far from revelling in anonymity, the parricide fantasy demands a very personal relationship, it demands the singularity of a single love among the many that are possible. The anchoring of the subject's identity thanks to this fantasy crossing engenders a sort of love of the name[45] which (as we shall see) constitutes the other side of orgasm, at the final point of sexual excitement. This love in the singular upsets the codes of expected pleasures; it comes unexpectedly, even for those who thought they knew everything.[46]

The love fantasy is the last to appear, emerging at the time of the changing of places that occurs at adolescence. It functions as a *retroactive fundamental fantasy*, so much so that for the greater part of humanity, it is the only fantasy worth having and, in any case, the only one that is conscious. This is how adult exogamous love is distinguished from other varieties, notably, the endogamous type. It shines more brightly than the others because it contains the repetition of the infantile, which is thus brought to incandescence from within. On the one hand, it is the last in the series of fundamental fantasies which are layered beneath it. On the other hand, under its smokescreen, the previous fantasies continue to shape desire, and it is thanks to the love fantasy that the death drive can be directed towards orgasm. So parricidal arousal pursues its course, causing death to pass endlessly from one side to the other, from autoerotic drive annihilation to what should not be permitted, namely, orgasm; the utterance of a name that betrays another name behind it. Because to say 'I love you', or merely to whisper the name of the lover, betrays the love sworn before – the love of the father. The vow of fidelity to the beloved telescopes the vow that was secretly promised to the father. The love fantasy is not just another fundamental fantasy. It represses and redeems parricide; its singular demand is in discordance with the impersonality of the other fantasies (although, of course, they also can bring enjoyment). This is very similar to the dream of a great and everlasting love that is so often attributed to young and inexperienced girls. But in dreaming like this, the young girl already situates herself as a woman and, in this sense, as guardian of the law. Isn't the law crucial here since this love echoes the murder of the father and the sense of good and evil that is a consequence of its repression?

Because it derives from parricide, the love fantasy has a memory; it presents the programme of repetition in advance. That is not to say that love re-enacts infantile neurosis but that, on the contrary, it takes up the same unresolved questions with new data concerning the sexual meaning of paternal seduction.[47] The relief that it brings by offering a solution to the sexual trauma induced by the father, which had remained hitherto incomprehensible, is so great that everything which might otherwise separate the lovers is set aside. Why is it, for example, that the fantasies at play between two lovers so often coalesce?[48] It is because love intoxicates and masks their dissensions. Its alcohol is primarily the unreality of the change of places that brings the infantile into the present, at the same time as drive energy dreams of refinding its footing in the artful twists of love. The love fantasy intoxicates for as long as it masks misunderstandings. Under its rule, the discords of the fundamental fantasies (constant, not occasional) are muted. In principle, bringing one sex into contact with the other introduces a state of war since both of the lovers are struggling with their bisexuality, and their face-to-face encounter must decide who is the man and who is the woman. This war results in an efflorescence of fantasies, which are born precisely to the rhythm of bisexuality (of castration). Each fantasy has its own weapon, and all but one want war. Hence, the universal esteem in which love is held; thanks to love, we avert our eyes from the conditions of our enjoyment, to which loves generously opens the door. It does so, however, not without a touch of mawkishness, the mantle of love covering the perversity of the drive and the discordances of fantasy. This innocent last-born conceals the games of its mischievous elders.

Any fundamental fantasy has its own orgastic virtuality. No one (especially in our time) will maintain that only love can open the doors to seventh heaven.[49] A single fantasy is enough to construct a pleasant-enough scenario for us, so self-sufficient pleasure appears to triumph. The convenience of this is obvious. For example, the seduction fantasy or the beaten-child fantasy are quickly set in motion by chance encounters. But unfortunately, fantasies are closely knotted to each other, and since the parricidal fantasy crowns them all, certain symbolic conditions will ultimately control sexual arousal. So that, although it would have been nice to sit around a continuously simmering drive cauldron, sexual activity is reduced to, or even content with, an unrealised desire . . . which is still a desire.[50]

Not only does the love fantasy appear last of all but it also behaves like a spoilt child, having little patience with its elders, even though the latter are conducive to sexual excitement. It can silence desire and is not much good, for example, at tolerating wounds or infidelity, which might contradict it. The love fantasy puts up with some of these, however, by making them dance to its own rhythm and by retaliating in return; love, after all, can make the other person suffer.[51] It can transform physical masochism into moral masochism, assuming we agree that 'moral masochism' is a good description of the taste for sacrifice which haunts love – its obsession with a total gift of the self. Is it not the case that saying 'I love you' is to imply 'I give myself' or even 'In your presence, I am nothing'?[52]

Thanks to this sacrificial dimension, the love fantasy proves its innocence at the very moment when it makes its confession. Its gift absolves it of parricide; desire is consumed by consuming its own evil so that the gift is renewed in a vow of fidelity. Its promise wipes away the latent death wishes of passion, and this future is the guiding light of most couples. Indeed, this fidelity hardly needs to be promised; it is correlative to the confession of love, which promises a future redemption. This sulphurous, almost unreal enjoyment is such that other relationships and fantasies become less powerful. Even the demand for exclusivity is made redundant by this revival of sexual excitement in the very place of a potential fault. Far from being a moral duty, it moves from the fault to the sexual discharge that sets it going all over again. Seen from the outside, many couples seem bound by guilt; it appears that they stay together so as not to hurt each other, for fear of loneliness, for the sake of the children. But in reality, this latent guilt masks a debt and, with it, the relaunch of the fantasy. Because the partners would like to leave each other, the fantasies become discordant, inflamed and are relieved by sexual excitement.

Grounded in repetition, the love fantasy absolves its own debt in a potentially infinite movement. It offers connections with the other fantasies, although each of them functions alone.[53] All of the other fantasy activities involve some kind of fault, but only the love fantasy can find its own redemption within itself. Functioning for the greater part of humanity as a normalising principle for desire, the love fantasy offers a kind of forgiveness for the inevitable betrayal of the father.[54] And most of world literature will only grant respectability to sexuality when it is accompanied by the love fantasy.

Redeeming the murder of the father, the love fantasy is set 'for life' (until it refinds the father after death). This optimistic prospect, which orients (among other things) the viewpoints of Christianity, certainly does not take account of the lifespan of the fantasy, which has its own temporality. It obscures the fact that fantasy excitement only lasts in certain situations. A woman, for example, will desire a man less after he becomes the father of their children. That will not stop her loving him, but sexual arousal will be displaced, at least for a while. It often happens that love basks in interrupted sunshine, while sexuality has to put up with fog and rain. The vow of everlasting love, pronounced in the churches, eclipses this. An undeniable aesthetic of existence pleads in its favour, though it is an aesthetic to which one cannot be forced to adopt. But a lover may well agree that their love is 'for life' (meaning 'against death'), if not forever.

How the crisis of adolescence generates erotism from the love fantasy

Despite what the myth tells us, Oedipus did not solve the riddles of the sphinx; they were left for later. The hornet's nest of fantasy, discovered in childhood, remains dormant, and polymorphic perverse solutions prevail. The physical changes of adolescence offer new potential for sexual life, but the potential cannot be realised without the activation of fantasy. Age, as such, explains nothing, and the surge in erotic love may not in fact be forthcoming at adolescence. Witness the number of childhood neuroses that last to an advanced age. The physiological event of puberty only becomes operational when it is made part of a new set of psychical meanings. Why do fantasies that have been dormant since childhood suddenly burst into life? How does this eruption bring about a qualitative change in enjoyment, which is no longer a game and becomes a very serious matter, the demands of which outweigh everything else?

The passage from endogamy to exogamy lights the spark that ignites hitherto latent fantasies and propels autoerotism towards erotism. Sexual arousal in adolescence depends on a change of place, when the individual has to play a role equivalent to that of the father; enjoyment only changes its register on condition of the father's elimination, a change which revolutionises the regime that governs enjoyment as the young person, no longer a child, identifies either with the father (the case of the boy) or with the one who meets a potential father (the case of the girl).[55] 'Change of place' here means that the Oedipal triangle seeks to turn on itself; because of their love struggle, the child strives to no longer be a child but to take the place of one of its parents, changing the position from which the young person seeks love and the person from whom he/she seeks it. The son comes to the place of the man (his father) and the daughter to that of the woman (her mother).[56] This upheaval is accompanied by the inversion of two characteristics of love. Inside the family, love is given (a little or a lot) without a second thought. Outside the family, however, it must be fought for. A second characteristic is reversed as a function of the first. Inside the family, sexuality does not resolve the excess of love (such, at least, is the rule). Outside the family, on the contrary, sexual activity compensates for the narcissistic ravages of the struggle for love. The change of place and the inversion of these two features give fantasies a new meaning, a meaning that activates them just like a detonator sets off explosives

Certainly, children already know a simple kind of love that often accompanies their experience of the drive. This amorous power may fuel narcissism, but this 'narcissism' then encounters a limit on which it is either shattered or revived when, in the throes of jealousy, it demands fidelity. The rival must be excluded, and this demand instantly brings the triangular nature of the Oedipus complex into play. To fight for love is to fight against a rival, so it introduces a drama with three actors, as in the good old days of the Oedipus complex.[57] A kind of suffering begins to emerge, dragging pleasure down with the weight of enjoyment. It produces a demand for exclusivity, by which a man and a woman will prefer to stay together; third parties, who had previously been welcome, must be excluded, but even when they are off stage, they will always cast a shadow, even over the most isolated couples. The law is imposed and even issued anew by what we might call 'narcissism' but which, in any case, is always a demand for exclusivity.

Parricide – the detonator of every fantasy – had little significance in early childhood, when death (and enjoyment too) did not mean much. Dreaming of the death of the father had no more consequence than the story of Bluebeard. But when the struggle for exclusivity begins, parricide suddenly takes on a weight because to eliminate or be eliminated becomes linked to sexual enjoyment, so much so that supplanting a rival becomes a powerful stimulant in itself. The rival must be cut down to the size of a child and, in this process, giving oneself the place of a father. The battle against rivals summons up a parricide fantasy that frames the games of love.[58]

Let's zoom out from this scene in order to understand it better: two suitors confront each other to win the favours of a woman, but at the same time, each of them is in the grip of an internal conflict about changing places – leaving the position of the child to take up that of the man. So each suitor, in the face-off with the rival, unwittingly compares themselves to a father who is the unseen protagonist of the drama. The dominant force seems to be hatred directed at a 'brother'; it is all that we see, and it seems to be historically primary. But since, in this confrontation, the subject is seeking to take the place of the father and thus to 'eliminate' him, it is the parricide fantasy which is logically playing the main role, even though it remains invisible. Such invisibility befits the father, who is at his most powerful precisely when he retreats into that which cannot be named or represented.

The rage of the adolescent lover, insisting on the exclusivity of his love, is directed at the invisible father, and this can be applied more generally to all manner of sibling rivalries. The hatred unfolds on the background of a relationship with the father, in whose name the drama is played out. After all, there cannot be any brothers without a father. But the father is erased, his name is swallowed into oblivion; the parricide wish is repressed in the very act of taking the father's place, and the death drive is metamorphosed and civilised through this painless murder.[59] Sexuality then takes on a meaning that it did not possess in childhood, when the fantasy murder was easy and empty of enjoyment. Enjoyment only emerges under the weight of the father's death which hollows out its centre and gives it its importance.

The confrontation with rivals becomes latent once love is established; the lovers feel they are alone in the world. This wondrous blindness masks the elimination of the third party and hides the work of repetition. Love excludes, conceals and forgets the betrayal of the previous loved one – the love of the father that a woman felt and the love of the father that a man also felt. Love emerges against a background that has been covered over by the repetition of fantasy scenarios. Behind the scenes of the love scenario, there burns an infantile passion, which the change of places makes unrecognisable. This inner world of childhood is what gives love its surreal power. This immensity will ensure that love always occupies a special place, even when sexuality is felt as an agonising ordeal. Love will take precedence over onanism despite the obvious practical advantages of the latter.

In adolescence, the 'activation' of the fantasy means that the struggle for love engenders a suffering intimately linked to pleasure, an alloy that did not exist before – a certain enjoyment of pain that is a million miles away from autoerotic pleasures. It is something akin to violence, and it produces an incomprehensible carnal shock because the means available for understanding it vanish as soon as it arises.[60] The individual is thrown into adulthood by a factor quite different from physiology. What had remained obscure in childhood suddenly becomes clear. But the person to whom this happens ceases to be a child precisely when the illumination occurs and they immediately forget what they just learnt. The moment that this electrifying intimation arrives, he or she opens the door to a universe greater than anything they had experienced before but to which they immediately lose the key by an amnesia of their infancy. The conflict with the father now means something since the child aspires to take a position in confrontation with him. And this shock gives new meaning to the pleasure felt, to the point of being able to inhibit it or, by following the very thread of its contradictions, and not without some delay, going as far as orgasm.

In *Paris Nocturne*,[61] Patrick Modiano describes a romantic encounter that is unknowingly stitched onto the paternal scar which is its infantile source. One night, a man is hit by a car. The woman driver is also injured. They are briefly hospitalised in the same clinic and lose sight of each other when they leave, although their chance meeting had an indefinable charm. With only a few vague clues to help him, the man embarks on weeks of nocturnal wanderings around Paris in search of the partner of this brief encounter. As if in a dream, the face of this woman becomes superimposed on figures from the man's past and on reminiscences of the father's abandonment (But who abandons whom?). A detail – a scar similar to that of a young woman from his childhood – is part of this recovery of the past. A certain telescoping between infantile neurosis and adult neurosis crystallises in the trauma of the encounter. We understand that this chance accident is love itself, an accident which is perhaps guided by the father's star but which nevertheless escapes it.

From love to desire

It can happen that a woman met in passing can make us dream, even to the extent that we prefer this dream to its real-life cause. The idealised woman must not be allowed to descend from this oneiric heaven. Her real presence is avoided for fear that a word or a gesture might spoil the purity of her image. So love is satisfied with the dream; it expands and exhausts itself in the memory of what has not taken place. Such was the case of Beatrice and Dante and of Laura and Petrarch. Love is thus completely cut off from desire. Desiring and loving can be reconciled, entangled and disentangled without each other or against each other. Nevertheless, the part of humanity that tries to put them together is sufficiently large for their harmony to represent a certain norm, while other scenarios, numerous though they are, often pass for anomalies. When we consider what connects love and desire, we must first clarify what kind of love we are talking about. The verb 'to love' can take jam, music, sport and much else as its object. And then we also love *someone*. Why use the same verb for such a range of loves? There is a common denominator that qualifies this passage from something to someone: the subjectivation of the drive. We begin by loving someone for reasons that are close to the love of something. The first movement is triggered by a look, a gesture, poise, etc., just as the smell of jam makes your mouth water. The drive is the common denominator of these various loves. The future beloved is glimpsed initially against a background of reification, as a thing among things.

When matters go further and love declares itself, the love of someone is still based on the love of something. The subject has climbed a step, but it quickly becomes apparent that the beloved does not want this culinary love. They refuse it and ask to be loved 'for themself' – an extraordinary expression since it rejects the drive which is what first lit the flame. The flame of the drive would have consumed them, if they had been content with it. And so they declare that they want to be loved 'for themself', separately, in a way, from their sensory attractions. Who is this 'oneself'? A bodiless subject? Certainly not, but by denying the drive, this subject sets in motion the mechanics of fantasy. To reject drive fascination is to open up a lack. The excess of the drive, in full cannibalistic momentum, breaks its teeth on an immaterial obstacle, beyond which lack and excess receive a new impetus. Negation creates lack, the excess of which summons up erotic fantasies beyond this denied body, a body from which the lack still hopes to find relief; lack now gives rise to a lack of *another order*. The autoerotic drive excitation of the object corresponds to the excess of the drive (which could have been content with masturbation). This drive excitation differs from the fantasy excitation which arises from the lack created by its negation. Love makes do with little; as the saying goes, lovers can live on love alone.

Love creates a special lack, which differs from the lack of something or of the person themselves since it is felt even in the presence of the loved one. It is a kind of lack in oneself that results directly from the movement to possess. The drive here makes the subject exchange places with the object, thus losing themselves in their effort to possess. This lack produces the 'exile' that characterises the adventure of love and forms part of its happiness. So this lack can be loved for itself, for everything that it conjures up; some loves are sated with their own drunkenness, preferring ideality to the person who provokes such intoxication, as if to insure in advance against the risks and disappointments of the encounter itself. Take, for example, the woman who is passionate about a prisoner confined beyond her reach[62] or certain men who adore a woman only if other commitments make her inaccessible. This love continues indefinitely, even when its object is no longer alive. This 'creation of lack' does not arise from any sensory quality. The creationism of desire goes further since it concerns something beyond appearance that stirs up fantasies.[63]

A person who creates a lack in their own presence is producing beyond themselves an ideal that they are not, which has its benefits! The lack emerges between the person who is accessible on a drive basis and an ideal which is always at a distance – a constantly widening gap between consumption of the body and regeneration of the lack. This ideal is not to be spelt with a capital letter. It is not an aesthetic trait, a literary dream or an image of the absolute. It is a certain magic – a fantasmatic magic – that arises from the traces of the repressed. For example, the gesture made by a woman may trigger a waking dream if it evokes a gesture made by the mother. We must be careful here, though; this is not a repetition of maternal love but rather of what evokes it while escaping it. Or a man's posture may evoke an old obsession (positive or negative) with the father. But here also we must be careful because this may be about trying to get rid of what could not be forgotten. Whatever the trait in question, the hallucinosis of desire uses it to generate an intoxication, drawn from our perpetual childhood.[64]

This subjectivation of the drive is what characterises love; it is from its subjective abstraction that we reflexively 'have' a body as an external thing and can hope to enjoy it after we have lost it.[65] As soon as we are conscious, as soon as we speak or think, we forget our body. It tends to dissipate with our thoughts. We can seek to regain this lost enjoyment through the drive to possess another body and then we could say that in order to inhabit our body, we need another body – that our life begins in a couple. One and the same body, always already separated from itself, seeks to be reunited with itself. French has the expression 'To love one another à corps perdu'.[66] It finds its meaning here: we find each other thanks to the loss engendered by love.

So does the situation resemble two drops of mercury, which, as soon as they are close enough, merge into one? This metaphor would only add one more myth to the myths of love:[67] presence magnetising presence, like quicksilver. But this dream of harmony has so many exceptions that the exception is rather the rule; presence also triggers aggressiveness, which struggles against possession by the other person. It is not that presence magnetises presence but that a certain person creates a lack that magnetises us. In this provocation of love, the lack magnetises the lack, which is bound to entail misunderstanding since each protagonist is ignorant of what the other sees in them or, more precisely, beyond them. The myth is undone by the incommensurable relationship of two lacks, which come into *resonance* with each other.

We might offer another image here: one flower is extracted from the bouquet of possible loves, and its scent of absence is immediately conducive to fantasmatic intoxication. Possession as such engenders a kind of love, which is predatory rather than generous but which will serve as bait for the machination of fantasies, and the first of them to take this bait will be the fantasy of seduction. The other fantasies will group themselves around this first, depending on events.

Imagine one of these fantasy sequences: 'I like you, you like me, and we make this clear to each other'. But this simplicity is short-lived, and we move to 'I like you, but at the same time, you don't like being merely a coveted object. Even if I am to your liking, you take a step aside or backwards to escape this objectification. And a dance begins, to the rhythm of seduction: you both offer and refuse yourself, and meanwhile, my want of you increases and assures your dominion. The dance hurls me painfully in all directions, and the fantasy of the beaten child, master of a vengeful excitement, is triggered. I begin to understand, but what do I understand? I suffer from your absence in your presence. When you are with me, I do not know where you are. You dream . . . I am not enough for you: where are you? In your reverie, you have already departed with somebody else, and I sense both of you elsewhere, embracing each other. Driven by the anguish of a primal scene, which I do not even remember, I demand my place and begin the combat, without knowing against whom I fight. And from this uncertain struggle, guided by a parricide ignorant of itself, I will change my position, breaking the moorings of autoerotic love. Forgetting even your beauty, I am enamoured, beyond you, of the charms that you have evoked, of this underworld of my intimate life that I knew nothing of and that I encounter thanks to you'.

In this interlocking of fantasies, which may be interrupted along the way or return to its starting point, only the last step breaks with childhood – so sharply on occasion that it is accompanied by the desire for a child, which is barely expressed but nevertheless present. From childhood to the child, the fantasy codes its own conclusion. The infantile underworld of love seeks to emerge from limbo.

Is desire a consequence of love here? The creation of lack is equivocal. Its consequences may be erotic, but they may also stagnate in the inhibitions of neurosis. When it results from the lack of a certain person, excitement can be triggered as if the sexual act would palliate the lack, making up for the delay created by the ideal. This delay resonates with another delay because who has always been late in relation to the ideal, if not the child themself? A lover is a child when he or she abandons themselves in love. Their excitement stems from what has been repressed, and the ideal that pulls them ahead of themselves shapes this return to the past.[68] It can, therefore, happen that love inhibits the excitement it arouses. By its intrinsic movement, the drive to possess seeks to consume whoever it finds pleasing, and when it does not achieve its end, fantasy germinates in the gap that now appears. This creation of a lack is sufficient to arouse love. But there is no guarantee that it will ignite sexual arousal; a lover may find themselves at a loss in the presence of their beloved if their neurosis takes advantage of the situation in order to enact childhood figures of Oedipal frustration. In that case, neurotic love – the past in the present – inhibits erotism.

Experience shows that there is a path other than neurosis, but that path is not linear. When erotism is not blocked by a return of the past, the fantasies born of love, which are the motors of sexual arousal, encounter an obstacle that is internal to them. Take the fantasy of seduction: we have seen how the act of refusing oneself participates in the seduction itself, by activating collateral fantasies. In the scene of seduction, 'no' implies 'yes', without, however, excluding 'no', and this manoeuvre tortures the suitor, who is plunged into the place of the beaten child* at the same time as they don the mask of a rapist father worthy of the gallows. While this goes on, fantasy represses the drive, in the sense of demanding to be 'loved for oneself' and, above all, not to be consumed. But, of course, this is not a pure and simple negation of the body; if the fantasy is contradictory and says both 'yes' and 'no', its 'yes' remains constantly connected to the 'yes' of the drive which insists simultaneously.

A spatial representation helps to understand the process. The subject first says 'no' to the positivity of drive enjoyment, which is, therefore, repressed. The fantasy then propels itself horizontally; powered by its own contradictions which run from 'no' to 'yes', it surfs on the wave of drive enjoyment which persists beneath it so that it always remains connected, though intermittently, to the 'yes' of the drive (which is nevertheless heterogeneous to its own 'yes'). A woman does not lose the seduction of her body just because she once refuses to give herself. The fantasy oscillates between a positive and a negative pole, and its positive pole connects intermittently to the 'yes' of the drive, which is always ready to enjoy. So that the fantasy, which is 'outside the body, is nevertheless anchored to the concreteness of the body. Drive and fantasy are related like two sides of a coin because the demand to be 'loved for oneself' is far from making the person lose their attractions.

Desire moves against the wind of the drive (like an airplane taking off). Generating arousal, the (paternal) fantasy feigns the demands of (maternal) drive satisfaction. Sexual arousal capitalises on drive power but does so by putting that power at the service of *another* goal (between the sexes), which makes it unrecognisable.[69] The drives do not vanish in this operation; they light up again as soon as they are extinguished, like magic candles that cannot be blown out. They are the fuel for a repression that must be constantly recreated. The drive is the explosive power that never stops working against the fantasy.[70]

So love and desire are in a dynamic of internal exclusion. Desire takes off using the wind of the drive, from which love originates. Strange repression, indeed, since it never succeeds but has to be repeated endlessly. It propels itself like a rocket in order to move forward in the void. Desire escapes the gravity of the drive by a sort of antigravity; it tears itself away from the drive, endlessly taking off and taking with it what it pushes away. It tears itself away from what is prohibited, from the body, which is always too incestuous – which it would be best to forget but which obsesses and attracts it for just that reason in the form of the desired other.

This desired other is, therefore, never far from arousing hatred, and we see the proximity of love and hate – feelings which are, in principle, so diametrically opposed and which, in reality, do not belong to the same register but move in parallel spaces (drive and fantasy). The opposite of love is not so much hate as disenchantment or, more precisely, disgust – its drive antonym. Hate, for its part, is correlative to the extremity of desire, as is shown only too well by the universal hatred levelled at women throughout history, even as they are universally extolled. Love is primarily a rejected destiny of the drive, whereas sexual arousal depends on fantasy. Desire seeks to resolve a contradiction which is *internal* to it, and its partner only corresponds to it for as long as the partner represents the opposite pole of this contradiction. Arousal disappears as soon as the contradiction is resolved. For example, conflictual relationships often have a longer life than harmonious ones. In contrast, love dreams of an *external* object, and the encounter with that object does not guarantee sexual arousal. One can love all kinds of people without erotic feeling (within the family, for example). Unlike love, fantasy has no need to please; it might seek to do so, but rejection, complaint (even illness), aggression, deception, rivalry, insults (even blows) – particularities that are in principle dis-suasive – can, on the contrary, be powerful stimulants of fantasy. So love can be contradicted by sexual excitement, which is perfectly comfortable rubbing shoulders with hate.

A peg for every fantasy

In this way, the bouquet of loves has metamorphosed into a bouquet of fantasies, the virtual charms of which almost push the reality of the beloved into the background.[71] The lack essential to love is generated at the border between excess – which the drive seeks to satisfy – and the production of fantasies conducive to desire. The person who says no to the other's search for drive satisfaction triggers a fantasy in which they take the role of 'peg' or 'ready-to-wear'.[72] When a woman is surprised by male attention ('Why are they all looking at me like that?'), which she may in fact have tried to provoke, when she rebuffs modest solicitations, she becomes the 'peg' of fantasies that make her into a unique subject and no longer an object among others to be consumed. A charm is born from lack here, beyond the actual attractions of the person who refuses. Some women may be able to attract a bevy of suitors by dint of the fantasies they arouse, while others who have conventionally 'attractive' qualities may not. What matters for desire is just the tension of fantasy. If the fantasy is defused, desire collapses and even the most exquisite personal qualities risk counting for little.

It is almost as if fantasy had achieved self-sufficiency; it conditions sexual arousal and seems to enjoy nothing but its own drama. But if fantasy was so self-sufficient, no one would ever meet anyone, and we would all revel happily in our daydreams. Stirred up by a particular person but beyond that person, in the lack which they have created, the love fantasy could almost make do with itself: do we not then have solitary masturbation in the company of a fantasy rather than a romance between two people (in which the partner could even hinder orgasm)? Some women achieve satisfaction better on their own or even can only achieve it on their own. For men, masturbation is a traditional and welcome relief. And yet these convenient habits leave a dissatisfaction, precisely because they are ultimately inadequate to the fantasy, so much so that sooner or later, the solitary pleasure diminishes or disappears and enjoyment becomes increasingly difficult without love.

This is how the fantasy, hooked by lack, gets activated. It is only activated thanks to another body, which functions as its 'ready-to-wear'. Initial attraction comes from the drive, from the peculiarities and aesthetics of a body that instigate the drive to possess, but this attraction is also oriented by femininity or masculinity; a look, gesture, shape of hands, posture or style of speech mark this polarisation because a subject speaks as feminine or as masculine, and in speaking, they seduce or are seduced, pity or seek pity. In short, they generate a fantasy. Love is only marked by the drive for as long as it takes to arouse desire. As soon as someone displays their lack, they become a potential 'ready-to-wear' for the fantasy and that happens before any grasp of what the lack is about. A minor detail, a piece of jewellery, a fashion accessory, may signal a vague desire for seduction. And then this is particularised by, for example, a certain way of speaking, which indicates a lack of love or of sex. Aggression, humour, illness, etc., can also function as signs of lack.

Women nearly always display the sign of a lack, which, by the same token, is a call to fill that lack. Something in her clothing, jewellery and ornaments evokes it, and this low-level fetishism is supplemented by gesture, gait, vocal timbre, manner of speech, an elusive gaze and touching the hair. Something is at once offered and refused, without any conscious intention. Femininity exercises a fascination that cannot be explained by looks; its seduction is both a summons and a refusal. Men are constantly called upon to respond to this solicitation, which at the same time most certainly is not a solicitation, and they are on the lookout for the interval, the brief moment when her gaze no longer slips away, when it says something other than 'Yes . . . but not you, not here, not now'. The ready-to-wear of the fantasy clings to these signs of lack. They certainly have a general erotic sexual meaning, but insofar as the subject exists thanks to their actualisation, they can be satisfied by them independently of sexuality.

The movements of fantasy seem to follow their own course. And one might think that since they flourish in solitude, they could be satisfied by masturbation and that the encounter between a man and a woman could then be reduced to simple masturbation for two, spiced with a touch of the imaginary. The so-called sexual relationship would then never take place except as an illusion. But fantasies are never solitary; they hanker after their 'ready-to-wear'. What they are looking for is not so much another body as another subject, whom they dream of before any actual meeting. The fantasy ultimately cannot make do with itself, as it looks for a real partner just because the 'itself' only exists in this tension where it meets the other of its fantasy. This personalisation of fantasy takes a definitive turn in the fantasy of love, which imposes symbolic conditions and is never satisfied with just anyone. No one says 'I love you' to an anonymous partner, unless they are pretending.

Of course, given this symbolic condition, love's denial of its drive origin is disingenuous. But it escapes from that origin because it stakes a claim on another subject. It seeks to re-enact the most basic repetition, that of alienation and separation; this subject, which has passively undergone someone else's fantasy (of having been seduced, beaten, annihilated by incest), now actively restages it. So someone who has been seduced will seduce, someone who has been beaten will strike, someone who has been annihilated will go on the attack and so on. All that is needed is to find the right partner, the other self in this role-play, and his or her presence will be imagined long before the encounter. The fantasy is actualised according to the circumstances, according to a staging that externalises subjective division. The tension of the fantasy is internal, but this intimacy is externalised when another subject creates a lack where half of this contradictory intimacy can be exiled. The home of the fantasy is this other, who becomes its heart. The external intimacy of desire is exteriorised by this otherness. The actualisation of the fantasy seeks the other who will give it relief; its encounter is at first dreamt of in solitude, and the dream is never enough. It must be incarnated in a body, so it breaks away irrevocably from its apparent self-sufficiency. The other of desire embodies the division of the subject – the half of the subject's self to whom the subject now submits. This force field of fantasmatic attraction is vital for the subject because the subject only exists as sexual.

So how do the fantasies of two lovers resonate? Does this happen at all, or does one person's fantasy take advantage of the other's, or is it perhaps nothing more than a misunderstanding? To speak of resonance evokes the beginning of a concert, when musicians agree their pitch by means of a tuning fork.[73] But the resonance in question differs from the coincidence of musical chords. If that was the correct comparison, the seducing man would pair up with the seduced woman, the punisher with the punished, the man who thinks he is a father with a girl disguised as a woman, etc. We would then believe in 'complementarities' that produce harmony. But it is easy to draw up an equally long list of perfect discordances, disharmonies that make harmony and that produce enjoyment, whether positive or negative. Negative enjoyment has the advantage of showing the conjunction of fantasies, albeit fantasies that are disharmonious. Take, for example, a case where the frigidity of one partner is matched by premature ejaculation on the part of the other or when a man needs to be married in order to have a relationship with another woman, while his wife finds satisfaction only in her children, etc. When the fantasy finds a partner conducive to sexual arousal, it does not imply harmony. A man who makes women suffer and only desires them on that condition may well meet a woman who is fascinated precisely by men who reject her. Consciously, she will rebel against the injustice, but unconsciously, she might find that nothing will please her more. And the man, for his part, will make her suffer but (as he believes) without meaning to. They are not a sadomasochistic couple but the crossed pairing of a subjective division. They will perhaps create an impeccable erotic mechanism, though in conditions that are far removed from paradise.

In such resonance between fantasies, each subject encounters the half of themselves that they risked becoming.[74] This *alter ego* magnetises an excitement that hopes for relief. But this other is not a complement of the fantasy and participates in it only by initially refusing to participate. Correspondence between 'seducing' and 'being seduced', 'beating' and 'being beaten', etc., is what happens at the level of the drive and not at the level of the fantasy. In the functioning of the fantasy, on the contrary, what corresponds to 'seducing' is 'refusing to be seduced', and what corresponds to 'beating' is 'refusing to be beaten', etc. Negation is the index of the subjectivation of the drive and the sign of the division of a subject who participates all the better in the fantasy by denying it.

These types of resonance differ, as we have just said, from the active/passive reversals of the drive that are at work in sadomasochistic, voyeur-exhibitionist relationships; in these drive destinies, the subject becomes the object and loses their subjectivity. But in the resonance between fantasies that is the hallmark of erotic encounters, a crossed relationship is inscribed between the contradictions of the fantasies of two subjects, neither of which abolishes the other. Each fantasy has its internal discordance which is set in vibration by the resistance of the other and not by their agreement.

So this attraction for the other of the fantasy differs from the possessiveness of the drive,[75] where transitivism is about the discharge of an overflow. In fantasy, by contrast, it is the lack which has been created, and not an overflow, that sets things in motion. The goal of the drive is univocal and is accomplished through a permutation in which the subject is lost; its verb remains in the infinitive. On the contrary, the permutation that occurs in the fantasy is declined in the conditional tense. It is an act of the subject: '*I* would *rather* seduce than be seduced', '*I* would *rather* beat than be beaten', etc. The subject escapes into the conditional of 'rather'. The fantasy retains the contradiction of its genitive (Who seduces whom?), whereas the drive has no such contradiction. The actualisation of the drive desubjectivises, while, on the contrary, that of the fantasy subjectivises.

Moreover, drive repetition is transgender; in seeking to free itself, it repeats itself on a body, on another 'me'. It is a simple passage from passive to active. The repetition involved in the fantasy is of a different order. It does not concern the 'me' (a body) but subjective division (one 'half' of the subject is embodied in the other), and it is gendered. It elevates the passive and active of the drive to the height of feminine and masculine. So it stages the mechanism of desire between, for example, being seduced and seducing, loving and hating, etc., i.e., the very contradictions that split subjectivity. Since these contradictions bring the masculine and feminine into play, they are acted out on the stage of (manifest or latent) heterosexuality. The active and passive of the drive only take on the value of masculine and feminine in the fantasy.

The contradictions that are intrinsic to each fantasy aspire to a meeting with someone who can externalise their tension. The fantasy seeks to farm out half of its internal division in order to relieve itself of this discord. The quest for an other who would make an *internal* contradiction into an *external* tension is what pushes desire forward. Finally meeting 'the bearer of your fantasy' is a wish that comes true more easily than one would imagine, mainly because that other person thereby also finds what they are looking for. Far from the fantasmatic tensions being exchanged in an idyllic complementarity, they constantly try to 'assume' each other, not without some misunderstanding.

Everyone fantasises what they want, and as long as they keep it to themselves, misunderstandings are bound to arise between the lovers. Nothing obliges us to talk about our fantasies, especially since they most often elude consciousness. But the misunderstanding is less important than one might think because the fantasy is not an ideational truth that we keep to ourselves. Being so massively present that it prevents any conscious reflexivity, it is immediately staged and results in unmistakable enactments.[76] So the misunderstanding is a pure facade; it is merely a pretext for protests about deception, complaints that are themselves a part of the fantasy. Each partner quickly understands what the other wants, and the discord is then part of the actual fantasy staging. The term 'misunderstanding' is, therefore, inappropriate since it is essentially an exchange of discordances, which reconciles each with him- or herself rather than with the other, who remains fundamentally other. It is only this clash of strangeness, this spark, that has a future.

To represent this resonance schematically, take two subjects who are living the fantasy of seduction. On each side, there is a discordance intrinsic to the fantasy: to seduce/to be seduced. Neither of the two lovers can bear this contradiction, and each puts onto their partner the half that they cannot manage. At the same time, the first refuses to take on what the other puts onto them, saying 'no' to what they are trying to get the other to accept. So the internal contradiction of each gives its power to the desire of the other. The discordance itself calls for a partner of the fantasy, without which the fantasy cannot be actualised. The two subjects do not harmonise; they continue to differ, and they unwittingly assume their discordances. The erotic encounter is far from being self-sufficient; it is not a masturbation for two. It works, primarily, because each is fighting against that which, in the other, they find resistant in the other – precisely that which does not work. The fantasy stages its own discord, stages that which is not allowed and which the alterity actualises.

Possession initially created a lack for each of the lovers, and the two lacks do not complement each other, but the fantasies of each blossom in a certain beyond that is aroused through the other. The maintenance of this difference sets their contradictions alight in a mismatch that makes the internal conflict explode. Moreover, as we shall see, it is thanks to this breach that the drive – i.e., the enjoyment of the body – will then reach its greatest field of expansion.

So desire keeps moving thanks to another person; it always looks for someone who could serve as a peg on which to hang. This essentially 'altruist' fantasy, eager for someone to support it, is in action all the time. Any human body in public space is immersed in seduction; it shows itself, hides itself, displays itself in order to conceal itself or the other way around or both. Its looks consume or allusively acquiesce. No veil can resist it. Desire beats time to this infinite repetition – that of fantasy rather than of signifiers. And this desire is never quenched because it regenerates the lack from itself. There is always a size missing in ready-to-wear, so the game must start over with a new fitting session! Whoever seeks to escape from what they have undergone only finds relief for the time it takes to change places. And then they are back where they were, weighed down again by the lack of the desired person (the same one or another).

Desire is twice the bearer of negation, which relaunches it. To begin with, negation in the relation of subject to object since this object is in reality a subject who arouses the fantasy. And then negation that is intrinsic to the fantasy itself; being seduced is the motor for seducing, beating covers being beaten and parricide depends on love for the father. Each actualisation elides its opposite. If the subject as peg refuses to be an object, they relaunch the contradictions that are intrinsic to fantasy; two negations are better than one for the affirmation of desire for a certain particular person as opposed to anyone else. So the subject of fantasy actualises their improbable existence as a sexual being, by which they are constantly tormented. This trouble is the very life of the subject. The fantasy (or desire or repetition) sets itself the task of freeing 'the subject' from the mire of the drives. In this sense, the fantasy has no object other than escape from objectification. To make the point differently, no object satisfies it because its problem, its causality, comes down to its own existence. Satisfaction matters little or is even better avoided, as if there was a kind of fantasmatic levitation favourable to existence.

Every fundamental fantasy is polarised by a contradictory tension that one could formulate as a contradiction between 'minus' and 'plus', to borrow the vocabulary of magnetic fields. This analogy reflects the division of the subject; each of its halves is linked to the other by polarisation. Its split cannot be seen. Not only is the subject divided but it also seeks to free itself from this internal tension and does so by transferring one of its poles to an external person. Every subject is constantly 'transferring' one of the poles of its fantasy to somebody else. It does this without asking anyone's opinion and moreover without any awareness of this magnetisation.

It can happen that this external investment of desire finds someone to attach itself to. And the movement is sometimes reciprocal. For example, a man places his 'minus' on a woman, who places her 'plus' in him. Pursuing the magnetic model, this produces a crossed exchange of the opposite poles of the fantasy. Such a desire exercises a powerful magnetism even though each of the lovers misunderstands what the other invests in them, just as they are unaware of what motivates their own desire, except that they experience it. Bizarrely, this shared desire engenders not so much a harmony as a reciprocal alienation – a disharmony, therefore, for which there is only one solution, namely, the equalisation of the tension. Really, the problem of the internal division of the subject has merely been displaced because what do we now do, essentially? We *imagine* it.

This tension between the contradictions of fantasy generates an intensive work of imagination, an overabundant production of little stories, which are not the fantasy itself but a torrent released by fantasy. Whenever we meet someone, we spin a little story. Just passing someone attractive on the street – the mere exchange of glances – makes us dream of an idyll, of a passion and of its end, and all before we have turned the corner. Desire prolongs itself thanks to these superabundant imaginings. The impossible tells itself stories and comes to life all on its own.[77]

'Imagination', little stories, our intimate myths result from the internal contradiction of the fantasy. They encrypt discordant sequences in a single scenario. For example, the conjunction of desire for the father and his rejection makes us invent a story where an abandonment is followed by a refinding (in the stories of King Lear, Moses, etc.). The story is told in such a way that the subject emerges from it exalted and, above all, innocent, with the realisation of ego ideals on the horizon. In the myth of Oedipus, for example, the hero who is abandoned by his father goes on to kill him.[78] The same happens in everyday life, where we imagine our future activities based on our fantasies but give them an acceptable form. We then try to stage them. Will everything go according to plan? There is no guarantee because once the fantasy has made its entry on stage (what we ourselves wished to happen), it can suddenly impose its contradictory imperatives and thus cause the objective that was so much desired to turn into its opposite.[79]

Notes

1 The masochistic fantasy of the 'beaten child' is directly linked to the father's seduction. We can take as an example the childhood history of Freud's 'Wolf Man' patient: 'By bringing his naughtiness forward he was trying to force punishments and beatings out of his father, and in that way to obtain from him the masochistic sexual satisfaction that he desired'. So the child was naughty in order to obtain the desired masochistic satisfaction ('die erwünschte masochistische Sexualbefriedigung') and 'his screaming fits were therefore simply attempts at seduction' which 'would also have satisfied his sense of guilt' (Freud [1918], *From the History of an Infantile Neurosis* in *Standard Edition 17*, p. 28). See also: Paul-Laurent Assoun, *Le masochisme*. Paris: Economica-Anthropos, 2003, pp. 33–34.

2 In this chapter, for the sake of clarity, we will use asterisks to mark the first three fundamental fantasies, from which the others and their subsets follow.

3 When a child cries because he or she has been forbidden something, it corresponds to such a 'blow'. Real blows would fall into another register; they would radically change the fantasmatic framework and be experienced as a rape, a sexual relation.

4 A violence of some kind (an accident, a war trauma) can resonate with the fantasy of the beaten child, resulting in the nightmarish dimension of the post-traumatic neuroses.

5 In his description of the beaten-child fantasy (Freud [1919], *A Child Is Being Beaten* in *Standard Edition 17*, pp. 175–204), Freud explicitly writes that it is a female fantasy, and yet most of the examples he gives concern men. This is because the subjects feminised by the father's blows are men as well as women.

6 See the feminised and eroticised relation of the Wolf Man to his father in *From the History of an Infantile Neurosis* (*op.cit.*). Similarly, Little Hans says to his father: 'Oh, yes. You have hit me' (Freud [1909], *Analysis of a Phobia in a Five-Year-Old Boy* in *Standard Edition 10*, p. 42).

7 Seduction and murder will then imprint their ambivalence on erotism so that a person may, for example, go to great lengths to provoke desire but then refuse to go further. This might seem to be part of female seduction when it imposes a certain violence on men, even when this is not really aimed at them. But isn't it always aimed at them, however unintendedly?

8 'We know that the unconscious castration complex functions as a knot: (1) in the dynamic structuring of symptoms; [. . .] (2) in regulating the development that gives its *ratio* to this first role: namely, the instating in the subject of an unconscious position without which he could not identify with the ideal type of his sex or even answer the needs of his partner in sexual relations without grave risk, much less appropriately meet the needs of the child who may be produced thereby' (Lacan, 'The Signification of the Phallus' in *Écrits* (B. Fink, trans.). New York: Norton, 2006, p. 575).

9 For example, in Nagisa Oshima's film *Empire of the Senses*, which presents the striking shortcut of a woman killing and castrating her lover. The less radical expedient of
   spurning one or more suitors gives some women a subtle pleasure, which is sometimes
   enough for them. It simultaneously gives them the phallus and kills the father. Being
   attractive to all men while refusing oneself is a very feminine way of having the phallus – not without castrating the men. If, for example, fashionable clothes and a seductive
   walk appeal to all men, the father is included in that universal.

10 It never happens that a father threatens to unman his child. And yet anxiety about castration by the father – equivalent to anxiety about feminisation – accompanies erection,
   thereby becoming its cause in the retroaction of guilt.

11 The 'castration' is correlative to the erection since the punishment accompanies it to the
   point of provoking it. In the succession of events, the masturbatory gesture certainly
   precedes the desire for punishment. But from a psychical point of view, if the subject
   is keen to be punished in order to allow themselves to enjoy, the punishment itself will
   trigger the excitement by legitimising it.

12 'Just as Heraclitus, I think, says that even when they sleep men are workers and
   fellow-agents in all that goes on in the world' (Marcus Aurelius, *Meditations* (C. Haines,
   trans.). London: Heinemann, 1989, p. 153).

13 The father is the universal aphrodisiac of human sexuality, outclassing any neurotrans-
   mitters of pleasure. He is present in all religious systems. The 'Eternal Father' represents the father who is killed and castrated in the secret realms of each person's fantasy.
   The collectivised version of the fantasy thematises a knot of insoluble contradictions – a
   father who is at once castrator, seducer and crucified. His desire as such is traumatic
   because the subject who is sexualised in this way engages in a seduction, without which
   they do not exist and for which they must pay the price.

14 One can certainly say, as a shorthand, that the father prohibits the child's incest. In reality, though, he does not prohibit any such thing because the child lacks the means to
   carry it out. If the father felt moved to impose a mother-child 'separation', he would be
   more likely to take the mother to task since she might indeed have some overly erotic
   designs on her little one.

15 See earlier: Chapter 4, footnote 25 (translator's note).

16 So the excitement has followed a gradient. First of all, there is a passage from Being to
   Having. The denial of the mother's castration forges the sexual obsession of finally having the phallus rather than being it but this 'having' must itself from then on be invested
   in order to bear fruit.

17 This 'war' is only a dance, or even the dance itself: this *pas de deux* that gets its rhythm
   from the choice of gender. Perhaps a 'bad dancer' is one who gets entangled in his/her
   bisexuality.

18 The passive or active of the (autoerotic) drive transits from Being to Having, which is
   then subjectivised in the man-woman relation.

19 This upset can be expressed in many forms: 'I shouldn't have . . . you and me have
   no future. It won't go anywhere'; or 'By being with you, I am breaking a promise to
   someone else'; or even 'There's something about you – a physical trait, a way of doing
   things, an opinion, an attitude – that I don't like, and it always meant that it wouldn't
   last'; etc.

20 So it is with the sexual act when it mimes a certain confrontation that evokes the fantasy
   of the beaten child.

21 This conjunction of negations can affect desire to the point that some men only give
   their passion free rein when a breakup is imminent.

22 Freud was surprised that homosexuality, which is more practical, is not a universal preference. Heterosexual choice involves more problems. The human species has the seduction fantasy and not a reproductive instinct to thank for its survival.

23 Some homosexuals, for example, have an irrepressible urge to discuss their sexual habits with those around them (not just their parents but also their neighbours, etc.) in the hope of shocking them.

24 This exteriority of parricide to the sexual act may explain the claims and demands for recognition that certain militant homosexuals present to heterosexuals. They sometimes like to challenge and mock, as if such attitudes were a condition for their orgastic liberation, located in an external inclusion.

25 The insults, which are traded when an argument breaks out in the street, seek to feminise the opponent.

26 Although sex offenders now account for a quarter of the prison population in France.

27 Nothing proves this better than the often demanding attitude of the mother towards the father: if she feels the need to claim something, it must be that she has been deprived of it.

28 They may know about copulation from watching animals or television, although the heroes of children's TV (Tarzan, Bécassine, Spiderman, Lara Croft, etc.) are never interested in sexuality. What fascinates children is violence.

29 In his paper *Hysterical Fantasies and Their Relation to Bisexuality*, Freud says that when a person masturbates, he often 'tries in his conscious phantasies to have the feelings both of the man and of the woman in the situation which he is picturing' (Freud [1908], *Standard Edition 9*, p. 166). So the masturbator restores to its proper place the fantasy of the primal scene, which follows less from the sight of a real scene than from masturbation.

30 'The ejection of the sexual substances in the sexual act corresponds in a sense to the separation of soma and germ-plasm. This accounts for the likeness of the condition that follows complete sexual satisfaction to dying, and for the fact that death coincides with the act of copulation in some of the lower animals. These creatures die in the act of reproduction because, after Eros has been eliminated through the process of satisfaction, the death instinct has a free hand for accomplishing its purposes' (Freud [1923], *The Ego and the Id* in *Standard Edition 19*, p. 47).

31 The term 'overdose', which evokes drug addiction, here qualifies the purpose of the drive in general. Each drive has, of course, its own determinations, which attach it to the mouth, the voice, the excreta, the gaze, etc. But all of them are obsessed by the same extremity, this 'overdose' which is another name for an excess that can end badly.

32 'What we are witnessing here, in this truly explosive mutation, is the meeting of a lack and something which, through the drug-object, transcends this lack in and through a state that is absolutely unique for the human species' (translated from: Claude Olievenstein, *La drogue ou la vie*. Paris: Robert Laffont, 1983, p. 125).

33 Everything suddenly becomes possible, although nothing in particular entails action. Inhibitions are lifted, even if no one act is preferable to another. The drive sensations regain their fine acuity. Time can stand still and sometimes does. Why minimise or reduce to pathology this powerful link between erotism and death? Human enjoyment takes the risk of annihilation at every step so that annihilation itself exerts an undeniable fascination, which can lead to suicide. This is what lends allure to risk-taking or drug-taking, which would be incomprehensible without this annihilating vanishing point of pleasure.

34 This revival, which unleashes violent fantasies about the father or his representatives in society, claims its toll of adolescent suicides.

35 In which form sexuality has always been in some way consecrated by the churches and then by civil society.

36 So transgression imposes itself 'from below' as an internal threshold, as Foucault writes: 'Transgression, then, is not related to the limit as black to white, the prohibited to the lawful, the outside to the inside, or as the open area of a building to its enclosed spaces.

Rather, their relationship takes the form of a spiral which no simple infraction can exhaust' (Michel Foucault, *Language, Counter Memory, Practice. Selected Essays and Interviews* (D. Bouchard, S. Simon, trans.). Ithaca, NY: Cornell University Press, 1977, p. 36).

37 Stendhal, *Italian Chronicles* (R. MacKenzie, trans.). Minneapolis, MN: University of Minnesota Press, 2017.

38 *Ibid.*, p. 65.

39 A colleague who had a prostitute in analysis told me that she had orgasms from time to time. So there are exceptions.

40 And this power relativises the supposed masochism of a denigrated profession, which nonetheless discovers a secret of male desire.

41 The prostitute is a kind of vestal of the father (there were many forms of sacred prostitution in antiquity).

42 See Viviane Candas' film, *Les Baigneuses* (2003).

43 The father both plays with his daughter and plays her, replaying through her the son he once was and playing out the extensions of his tie to his mother.

44 It is only thus that the effective presence of a father becomes legitimate, generating a certain gratitude towards the person, thanks to whom sexual desire was born.

45 See Martine Broda, *L'amour du nom. Essai sur le lyrisme et la lyrique amoureuse*. Paris: Corti, 1997.

46 This stranger knocks at the door unexpectedly. He may come once and never return or he may settle in the house and impose his own life, rendering meaningless the autoerotic practices of the past, which were sometimes entertaining but are suddenly too flimsy.

47 A young girl, for example, will imagine being seduced by a stranger who has certain characteristics that revive the problematic of her relationship with her father. A man will be certain in advance that his wife will cheat on him or a woman will be certain that she will be abandoned, this rejection having a delicious similarity with the attitude of her father, who certainly loved her but preferred her mother. In each case, the template – even when seasoned with tears – generates sexual excitement. Deception and rejection, especially if they are imagined in advance, are often the best entry point to enjoyment, and of course, they may occur precisely because they are anticipated.

48 'But then, what can hold a man and a woman together? In the best of cases, it is called "the symbolic"' (translated from: Charles Melman, *La nouvelle économie psychique*. Toulouse: Érès, 2009, p. 41).

49 A spanking can achieve the same result. All sorts of practices – violent, nonviolent, solitary, collective, alcohol-fuelled or mystical (or a combination of the aforementioned) – can relieve fantasmatic tensions. Some of the fundamental fantasies function in relative impersonality, merely resonating with those of a partner who is almost anonymous.

50 The conditions are less drastic when a major claim of the parricide fantasy is satisfied. For example, when a certain monogamous stability (perhaps marriage or childbirth) is established; other fantasies are then actualised, possibly on another stage.

51 The arrow of Eros pierces beaten children, who may derive an enjoyment from their beating. Love is aroused in proportion to the blows it deals and the exquisite suffering it inflicts. In a word, its arousal is proportional to its sadomasochistic envelope.

52 Such a confession takes up the fantasy of the beaten child* and lights the masochistic touch paper of arousal. On the male side, the ensuing erection serves to reinforce narcissism. The subject, who has in a way 'sacrificed' themselves by confessing their love, has undergone a deflation of their phallic identification. They regain it thanks to erectile inflation. In this sense, sexual arousal is the counter-fire to the kind of consensual annihilation that occurs in the confession of love.

53 For example, that which involves humiliation or rape or the relationship to the father that occurs in a bodiless mysticism.

54 Don Juan, the uncompromising adherent of a never-dead father, would not tolerate it.

55 'So the elaboration, for each person, of his or her sexuation from the Oedipus complex, in terms of having or not having the phallus, links up, in adolescence, with what the sexual law establishes in the love relation as a dialectic of having and being' (translated from: Gisèle Chaboudez, *Rapport sexuel et rapport des sexes*. Paris: Denoël, 2004, p. 117).

56 These expressions in brackets do not correspond to a conscious identification; they are masked by the change of place itself, driven by a displaced repetition, itself activated by the struggle for love.

57 Autoerotism for two can transit into erotism in various ways, but let us imagine one example. In adolescence, a group of friends, boys and girls, have a lot of fun together. They dance, they laugh, they drink. Any sex that happens does not involve a great deal of commitment or enjoyment; it is just something that has to be done. Then extracting themselves from the group, a pair of male friends and a pair of female friends spend all their time together. They have just as much fun, but the more they laugh, the more the pleasure is eroded and the more jealousy and rivalry arise out of their banter.

58 A revolt against the father is characteristic of adolescence, marking a resurgence of this Oedipal drama.

59 The paternal totem thus functions as the universal transformer of the death drive (as religions in general show).

60 The traumatic dimension of many women's first menstrual period, for example, is attested less by the memory of a disagreeable sensation than by the inexactness of the memory; the date and circumstances often remain vague. Men are often just as vague about their first ejaculation.

61 Patrick Modiano [2003], *Paris Nocturne* (P. Weston-Evans, trans.). Newhaven, CT: Yale University Press, 2015.

62 See: Yukio Mishima, *Madame de Sade* (D. Keene, trans.). London: Grove Press, 1967.

63 Following this logic, desire can arise where it seems least probable because madness, illness and signs of suffering (for example) can easily evoke lack. What 'doesn't work' can trigger desire. Similarly, a woman's sense of being abandoned, worthless or unworthy may be what makes her seductive, sometimes much to her surprise.

64 'It is really as if I had been lost and they had come to give me some news about myself' (André Breton, *Mad Love* (M. Caws, trans.). Nebraska, NE: University of Nebraska Press, 1987, pp. 8–9).

65 This process is the same as that of the mirror stage; a child recognises itself in the mirror on condition of a subjectivation of the image, and the subjectivation happens as soon as the child is named by the person carrying it.

66 Literally 'to the loss of the body', i.e., impetuously, wholeheartedly (translator's note).

67 'This idea of fusion is really a myth inherited from the child's first relationship to the mother, where making One is evoked insofar as the child, in order to be desired, makes itself equivalent to the object of desire that it perceives in the mother' (translated from: Chaboudez, *op. cit.*, p. 133).

68 'Complete object-love of the attachment type is, properly speaking, characteristic of the male. It displays the marked sexual overvaluation which is doubtless derived from the child's original narcissism and thus corresponds to a transference of that narcissism to the sexual object. This sexual overvaluation is the origin of the peculiar state of being in love, a state suggestive of a neurotic compulsion, which is thus traceable to an impoverishment of the ego as regards libido in favour of the love-object. [. . .] What he projects before him as his ideal is the substitute for the lost narcissism of his childhood' (Freud [1914], *On Narcissism: An Introduction* in *Standard Edition 14*, pp. 88, 94).

69　Thanks to this continuous process, the death drive changes its meaning, becoming linked to filiation and paternity. On the occasion of this metamorphosis, the death drive provides the fuel for aggressivity against the father. The result is not death but the fermentation of fantasies that now have a sexual nature.

70　We will see that, in this sense, perversion provides a sort of underpinning of neurosis.

71　Many lovers no longer see their partner's defects or even forget some of their physical characteristics, such as the colour of their eyes.

72　See the short story by Nikolai Gogol [1842], 'The Overcoat' in *Petersburg Tales, Marriage, The Government Inspector*. Oxford: Oxford University Press, 1995, pp. 115–145.

73　In the Yunnan region of China, newlyweds have wishes for happiness fixed to their door, where it is written that two very different musical instruments can still sound good together.

74　'I'll tear myself to shreds, I'll kill myself for the Beloved! Of course. Just so long as the Beloved is the projected ideal of my own self, just so long as he or she is my thing, my property, myself' (Jean Anouilh [1948], 'Ardèle' in *Five Plays, Volume II* (L. Hill, trans.). New York: Hill and Wang, 1958, pp. 161–162).

75　Which consists in seeing instead of being seen, taking instead of being taken, etc.

76　'Passages à l'acte' in the French (translator's note).

77　This 'imagination' is not the imaginary – a synthetic quality that here leads to confusion.

78　Otto Rank [1922] showed the regularity with which this story is told in *The Myth of the Birth of the Hero*. New York: Robert Brunner, 1952.

79　For example, a woman enters a café imagining that she will attract a man (I). But if a man tries to start a conversation, she will spurn the advance (II), even if she finds him attractive, thus contradicting the first stage of her fantasy, which is not played out in either of the two sequences but in the on-the-spot tension between Act I and Act II.

Chapter 6

Where does the power of desire come from?

A desire that is always already there

Does the birth of desire follow the dramas of early childhood and then of adolescence? For adults who have already passed through these two stages – that of the Oedipus complex, then of puberty – the word 'desire' has, above all, the meaning of sexual attraction. And other forms of desire, actualised in creation, work, social ties or only in speech, are taken to be sublimations or else forms of repression or even perversions of an attraction that was originally erotic. This is a mistake. Desire is forged at the same time as the existence of the subject and only later does it find contingent and provisional relief in what passes for its 'genital' normativity. Certain theoreticians of psychoanalysis even maintain that desire is exclusively 'post-Oedipal' and results from some kind of prohibition of the enjoyment of the mother imposed by the father. As if it was enough to forbid something in order for desire to ensue, following what one might call 'the Parmentier principle',[1] whereby some meagre object would become massively important due to the barrier around it. If that were the case, desire would never be so powerful as when it is countered. We would then have to revert to the good old days when sodomites were burned and women of easy virtue stoned. But desire does not factor in social sanctions until quite late. To begin with, it depends on fantasy, and family or social repression belong only to a second phase, useful for escaping the intimate inhibitions of the first. Once it is marked by guilt and its contradictions, desire finds justification for its troubles in an external law; societies dictate variously that one must be monogamous, bigamous, polygamous, homosexual, bisexual, etc. What matters is the existence as such of a set of rules.[2]

The Oedipus complex is but a belated and unpredictable reworking of desire, which occurs precisely because desire precedes it and which occurs under the pressure of that desire. This constraint stems from primal repression itself. The autonomous existence of a subject presupposes repression by the subject of whatever objectifies him or her, i.e., of the determinations imposed on the subject by the maternal Other. To begin with, the subject is in a state of helplessness, *Hilflosigkeit* – the state of separating from what the mother would have wanted him or her to be: a sort of angel, her dream double, an 'ideal ego'. This is the separation of self

DOI: 10.4324/9781003519287-6

from self, which, as soon as a subject exists, engenders the first movement of desire by a knock-on effect; the subject will seek to recapture itself, to rejoin itself in this 'ego ideal'. The subject seeks to go back in time to the separation from this ideality of self that he or she was to have been to actively relive the trauma that was undergone passively. That trauma was nothing tangible or material since it was only the result of a separation of the subject from the ideal angel. That's why instead of this insubstantial trauma, any of the sensations that accompanied the experience of distress will be memorised 'passively'. They are the 'thing representations' that accumulate in the first moments of life and, indeed, throughout its course – whenever an incomprehensible event occurs and precisely because of this incomprehension. We remember the colour of the sky, a smell, a certain music, etc., in place and instead of an accompanying shock that remains resistant to understanding and incapable of representation.

From its very first sleep, the infant tries to catch up with itself by actively dreaming what it has passively experienced. The dream repeats, in what is a first hallucinatory realisation of desire. The infant does not dream of what was lost but of the 'thing representations' that accompanied the loss. This lost object is by no means 'the mother'; rather, it is that part of the infant's own self which would have given her satisfaction – the ideal double, which the infant seeks to rejoin. The act of hallucinating thing representations materialises desire and not the things themselves. Among the representations of things that make it possible to hallucinate desire, one in particular among the small objects that provide sensation will be privileged: the cuddly toy, the teddy bear that was offered, precisely, to calm the infant's distress. The teddy is the double of the self that the child has to take in its arms in order to fall asleep to invoke the host of thing representations that fill its dreams. The teddy is the first 'transitional subject', the prototype of the other of desire, the *alter ego* of the other sex, with whom, much later, the adult will like to fall asleep and whose contact, hands and body heat will, in turn, summon up the mass of suspended dreams and bring sleep.

The dynamics of desire, hallucinatory from the outset, are governed by repetition – by a movement that goes from passive to active with the aim of putting an end to subjective division or even of rejoining oneself. This is the wish that the desire of Oedipal, then post-Oedipal coupling will take up for its own purposes. This original desire is by nature unconscious because the subject, chasing after itself, goes beyond itself and loses itself by doing so. It is not even precise to say that desire here is unconscious; it would be better to speak of an *aphanisis* of the subject at the moment of desire or, to be even more precise, of a kind of first knowledge of death, an abolition of self at the heart of desire which, throughout life, never ceases to foreground death. This inexorable force is destiny – a power, which is neither before nor after but a perpetual present. Before, it is the place where the subject was awaited but from which it exiled itself. After, it is the hallucinatory materialisation of desire, thanks to which the subject seeks to rejoin itself. In between, this place of self-abolition of a desire that is always already nascent must be traversed. These three forces of destiny are the *Moirai*, the three Fates, with the difference that the third – the one that cuts the thread of destiny – is not at the end but right in the middle; the subject, at the heart of its desire, is impersonalised and automated beyond its will. Freud discovered this link between death and desire at the same time as he discovered the repetition compulsion. Paraphrasing what Deleuze wrote about repetition,[3] this annihilating power is the 'dark precursor' of the death drive at the heart of desire.[4]

The child who caresses the teddy bear and falls asleep, feeling the mass of hallucinatory memories that push towards oneiric life, seems far removed from the lover who becomes calm and falls asleep beside the partner who holds the same ideal power. Under the impetus of an original desire, the subject has advanced as far as the knot of fantasies of the Oedipus complex, which will bestow gender and erotise that desire. So desire, at first hallucinatory, is sexualised secondarily. The teddy bear of our earliest life is erotised under the influence of the Oedipus complex and assumes the features of the beloved. We had to leave ourselves as ideal (ideal of our mother) behind in order to find ourselves as subject, and the ideal has fascinated us since that time, taking on – with the blows and seduction inflicted by the father – the mask of an attraction for the other sex in the case of heterosexuality. But this metamorphosis of desire leaves room for other modalities of repetition which are not sublimations of sexual activity but different shapes of our original desire, functioning alongside its erotic form, not the least of them being speech, which is animated by the same dream of rejoining itself.

So erotism – sexual desire as such – prolongs the hallucinatory process that was first set free in dreams. The beloved makes you dream too. Not only does he or she let us to sleep but their presence also redirects the mass of dreamlike sensations that constitute our likes and dislikes, connecting them to our current perceptions of the world. We 'see' any spectacle better in his or her company or rather, thanks to it; we can bear the weight of the death drive – the anguish of the real – which our perceptions evoke. In this way, the beauty of things, which could at any moment suck us out of ourselves and destroy us, is kept at bay.[5]

Thus, what is excessive in enjoyment – the subjectivation of its hallucinatory threat – becomes dependent on the other of desire. Enjoyment makes a detour via another body in order to avoid hallucination. To make someone enjoy is already to enjoy, as if pleasure given or taken creates the only 'echo' that is worthwhile. This is because the echo was the first shelter of the psychical body, when it was first constructed outside of itself, in the Other. Its ideal transitivism was vectored from outside to inside. When a child hears another cry, it cries in turn, as if they were the same being. The child's lips move when it watches someone speak. This is the other – the child's sensory double, its dream twin – whom he or she will continue to love through each of their metamorphoses. Just as, much later, a man is transported by hearing the enjoyment of a woman. The other of enjoyment awaits us, first of all, in a dream; desire is hallucinatory and is incarnated as best it can be, more or less precariously, in the way that angels (masters of the aura) know how.

Is there such a thing as a 'pure desire'?[6]

After the metamorphosis of desire in the Oedipus complex, we see only its result – sugar-candy love for mum and ambivalence towards dad. One might deduce too quickly from this that desire now strikes out in search of some kind of untraceable mother and the 'lost objects' that go with her. But sexualised desire dissolves its object and is obsessed by the excess of lack from the moment it begins. When paternal seduction makes its entry, the enjoyment of the mother is reduced and becomes emptied out. The very means of enjoyment slip away since erection depends henceforth on the arousal of the father, leaving only an unshakeable and consoling but desexualised love to blossom for the mother. The phallic instrument of conquest becomes erect at the moment when its object slips away. The erection occurs in a vacuum. What it might have aimed for vanishes under the impact of the conditions that give birth to it. The lack of an object relaunches the excess of desire. It never ceases to be lacking, but what is 'it'? Something (But what?) that has slipped away during the vertigo of seduction.

So sexual excitement gets moving, but it has lost its object on the way. It is certainly true that this emptiness of the object depends on the whole of the fantasmatic structure previously described. It is a 'structural cause', which, no doubt, results from its various invariants. But none of them, nor their sum, is 'the' cause of desire, which is born fully armed from the gesture of a subject; it is him/her and it is his/hers, with no engine other than the subject's own existence. Immediately suspended in this infinite emptiness, desire does not know how to satiate itself on what lies before it, and if it turned around, it would not be able to say either what is pushing it. It is a cause which divides the subject at the very moment of the subject's coming into being. The desiring subject no longer sees who, what or how to enjoy, although it desperately wants to enjoy.

'What happens' will then give form to this formlessness; minor traumas take on a weight because of this emptiness, giving a *retroactive* cause to desire. History and its repetition flesh out *a posteriori* and give a form to fantasies, the emptiness of which seeks garments that are found along the way. Driven by subjective existence, reasons for acting always function in the retroactive manner of psychical causality because of this emptiness. One invents the 'why' of an event after it occurs, and what one constructs acts causally only in proportion to the emptiness which inspired it. And this invented 'why' will itself then start to shape what we actually do.

Desire takes to the road without knowing where it is going or why it has to go. Henry the Navigator wrote that 'navigare necesse est, vivere non necesse' ('To voyage is necessary, to live is not necessary'). So with our desire: it pushes us harder than our life. In reality, nobody compromises on their desire, even when its actualisation is a sure path to perdition. Desire always makes us yield – if necessary, in its symptomatic forms, which still give it a voice, if not speech. Desire itself never yields and pushes the subject blindly forward at the risk of life and limb, of accidents, of misdeeds, of disastrous or felicitous repetitions of destiny. It is bigger than our life, so much so that people have nearly always believed that real life only begins in the beyond, with a divine father, the father who first set desire in motion and died from it, rejoining the world of the Spirits where he will await us.

The object of desire vanishes in the time it takes to be born. Desire tends towards nothing. Its emptiness precedes any choice whatsoever. So its tension seems to result from an engine that is *sui generis*, from a naturalness of desire elevated to the rank of an *a priori* concept. But this apparently 'pure desire' is caught up in a mechanism – that of a fantasy activated by an agent, namely, the father who is eclipsed as soon as his erotic blow is struck. This second birth of sexual desire is less desire for what would always be 'something else' or 'beyond' than desire for what ought not to be – to be seduced by the father. This traumatic, initially paralysing seduction contains its own limit, counterbalanced as it is by a mystical murder, which makes the father into the eternal embodiment of an excessive desire that is endless because it is forever unrealised.[7] The apparent 'purity' of desire results from the parricidal wish that guides it.

This can be verified by everyday experience, when desire finds its way onto the stage via the seduction fantasy. Its erotisation can just as well provoke a withdrawal into the fortress of purity (frigidity or impotence are the outcome of a desire) as the triggering of donjuanesque pursuits, which express – more concretely, for sure – an erotic dimension linked more or less explicitly with the parricide wish.[8] The same wish is actualised in both cases.

No one shows this to better effect than the mystics, those zealots of a desire guided by its true object: to reduce the agent of desire – the Eternal Father – to a pure cause. They are never closer to an unrepresentable god than when they cancel out every last morsel of their pleasure and want to reduce themselves to nothing. To be only nothingness would to finally be close to the Most High – he whom no name shall name. So close sometimes to the Eternal Father that, Nothingness to Nothingness, God himself disappears at the same time as his creature. This nothingness would be his only possible apparition, if we are to believe Meister Eckart, the devotees of quietism or those who seek to equal the Buddha: 'Be still, become nothingness and the nothingness of God will inhabit you. No more difference between God and yourself. By following the path of such an artful parricide, you will find enjoyment in the depths of this abyss'.[9] The ways of God are certainly unfathomable, and there are many paths, which, by taking the way of an unrealised desire, nevertheless find enjoyment.

But in striking contrast, consider whether a practice such as that of the peepshow is not also the manifestation of such a desire. God forgive me, but when an almost naked woman dances surrounded by a circle of booths, each containing a man whom she cannot see, is the peepshow not staging the inaccessibility of the object of enjoyment: 'Enjoy the impossible itself, gentlemen! Flying through the air, I am your erect phallus far away from me. But no . . . I take a step back because I am, first of all, myself'. The dance is to the rhythm of a seduction that has been consented to and which says yes as much as it says no. Arousal contains its own end, and there is no further prospect to break the magic circle. Desire finds its satisfaction in that which, by keeping satisfaction at a distance, satisfies it. The dancer on the stage comes alive as if electrified by the gaze of the spectators, like a puppet on strings. An anonymous male community gathers around this purity that cannot be deflowered. At the centre of the peepshow, this putative Virgin reveals an inviolable dancing body that is exposed to the gaze alone; eaten up by eyes, it remains intact. She could indeed be a virgin; the men, locked in the circle of their fraternity, would derive no less benefit from her trance. They enjoy a woman who is taken up by this rhythm, mystical in the second degree.

The gaze here is underpinned by a fantasy of inexhaustible feminine virginity, reborn from all the acts of consuming we can imagine, in as many drive montages as one cares to invent. The woman remains a virgin for whoever contemplates her, and nothing can be taken from her. In the peepshow, as in prostitution, an ideal woman represents the dark continent where she is intimate with a satanic father. The feminine ideal projected from childhood is primarily this image, from which pleasure is derived via the eyes. If its presentation was more erotic, it would no longer be the ideal of a woman entirely devoted to the Father, a forbidden woman. And many men become attached to women whose distance or frigidity fascinates them and triggers their enjoyment more surely than if they were to enjoy them physically. The contradiction is striking between these figures, both of whom generate the tension of desire – the mystical Father and a Virgin mistress of enjoyments.

The *in situ* repetition of fantasy

Enjoyment imposes a primary impersonalisation under the sway of the Other. The obsession of desire seeks to transform this passive impersonalisation into action. To go by choice towards this loss, albeit reluctantly, is to no longer be lost. From the start, desire repeats in an intoxicating dizziness, running as fast as it can from passive to active in an infinite, invisible movement. For example, the active (masculine) part forgets – wants to forget – its initial feminisation, and this urge to forget excites it or is excitement itself. When first the child and then the adult tries to break free from seduction by seducing in turn, they pass from a passive to an active position. So they change places but will not beak free by this means.[10] At the same time, they are unaware that they are repeating because they change places while doing so; they replay on one half of themselves what the other half has undergone and do so in the hope of being free of it. This change of position perhaps offers momentary relief, but it does not reconcile the person with themselves. Desire will only have exacerbated the division that underpins it. Repetition redirects but does not purge division. This pursuit fashions desire[11] as an *in situ* repetition which functions as its perpetual-motion engine.

The dream itself is motivated by repetition. At night, we rid ourselves of the little traumas of the day, which are connected to their infantile elders. Repetition is not one more formation of the unconscious to be added to the dream, the slip of the tongue, the symptom, etc. Repetition establishes the dynamic which characterises the unconscious precisely because the subject does not succeed in realising itself there but rather vanishes.

So repetition insists without finding rest or resolution. It results from its very enactment; when it is successful, it fails in the sense that when the blow inflicted by the active subject finds its target, that subject is no longer the victim of a similar blow. This folly that is built into any success resists historicisation; we see where the fantasy comes from and how it works, but it leads only to its recommencement, to nothing other than the division of the subject by the subject's own desire, which the subject reiterates in order to be a subject. The better things go and the more the subject's fantasy unfolds, the more the subject divides itself in its own acts, objectifies itself, mortifies itself through the intimacy of what brings it to life, pulled along by its desire like a fish caught on a hook. Desire is constantly revived according to the cycle of Cronos, the time of the father devouring his children, and it is our time as we flee paternal seduction, following the thread of our sexual excitement.

The speed of desire is proportionate to repression. Not wanting to know anything about it activates the desiring mechanism, which is never relieved of this primary torment. The repetition of the fantasy engenders an endless loop: no sooner achieved, it must begin again. It is only abolished for so long as it takes to be reborn because what was but a marionette, an object, becomes the subject of what it brings into action. So the agent is the puppet of its own desire which it never manages to relieve; it enacts what activates it. It self-activates.[12] The success of the fantasy sounds the hour when it starts over again and gives to desire its infinite movement, recommenced no sooner than realised since this repetition constitutes the subject of desire as such. We are reactive subjects, given the subjective trauma which we have suffered. Repetition, by its nature, reiterates an emptiness of being to such an extent that it gives the impression of passing by its own life, of moving in a dream, whether heavenly or nightmarish. So desire lacks a positive definition; we can only say that it seeks to be sated, but we do not know what could appease it.

Seeking to be rid of a trauma that it reproduces in its own movement, the fantasy develops according to logical structures, predicated on a single cause: the existence of the subject. The fantasy is implacably actualised under the pressure of the psychical cause, which was unknown to Aristotle: the *causa sui*. As soon as a subject exists, the sarabande of fantasies begins because what is at stake are not merely fantasies in general but their articulation with each other.

Desire recommences in the movement which seeks to resolve the oxymoron of each fantasy. It is not 'prohibitions' that make forbidden fruit appetising but an internal contradiction that pushes each fantasy towards its relief. And if such relief is ever achieved, that is not the end of the matter because the relief precipitates a fall into the snares of the next fantasy. The contradictions of desire make it move from fantasy to fantasy. Seduction** hurts? Well then, here's the beaten child*. The unfortunate child feels enjoyment under the blows? Well then, here's parricide*** which comes to purge the incestuous risk. The guilt of the parricide precipitates anxiety? Love immediately puts the lid back on, relaunching the machinery of seduction**. Each fantasy has its outlets or its own symptomatology, from sexual pleasure to the suffering of symptoms, without forgetting death itself, which also actualises desire, since the other side of parricide is suicide, annihilation, a taste for danger or drug addiction.[13]

The fantasies are linked together in a circular structure: beaten child* → seduction** → parricide*** → guilt → (again) beaten child*, etc. Desire is the arrow that each fantasy fires towards the next. Desire is reborn with new traits beyond its goal as soon as it reaches the goal. It turns in a round, moving from one fundamental fantasy to another in a circularity that goes from seduction to the complaints of the beaten child and then to aggression. For example, whoever experiences a blow (perhaps in love) is seduced by it – a contradiction! The game of seduction then triggers aggressiveness – another contradiction! And aggressiveness entails guilt that brings him or her back to square one, and yet nothing has in fact happened, and often, nothing will happen. A certain *in situ* repetition of the fantasy corresponds to this stationary orbit. Is there some hidden process at work here? One might consider desire as that which – without being reduced to a single fantasy – infinitely traverses the cycle that links them together. In this obligatory entrainment from one fantasy to another, all of them can lead to sexual arousal provided that the fantasy does not get entangled in its own contradiction, i.e., that it is in its active phase. On this condition, 'repetition', 'fantasy', 'sexual excitement' and 'desire' are equivalent.

When desire remains in its passive phase and settles on a single fantasy, it internally combusts. Desire then appears contradictory; it becomes entangled in itself, loyal to its destiny as displeasure filled with pleasure. A woman may, for example, work hard to seduce but rarely reap the fruits of her efforts or even reject each suitor while suffering from her loneliness. The pleasure of her seduction actualises a desire, which is satisfied by its opposite. It aims, for example, at both purity and its contrary; the desire of the father is quite compatible with purity, as shown by the mystics, who make little secret of their enjoyment.[14] But this desire transforms quickly from purest to most perverse, and often, one cannot do without the other, as shown sometimes by masochistic practices (drinking the pus of a scrofula patient, etc.).

The internal contradiction of the fantasy leads to a remarkable result. In its ordinary cruise mode, it remains suspended, spinning in the stationary orbit of a latent desire. Its frequent non-realisation would be incomprehensible if we forget that such non-realisation is also a part of desire. This is in fact the usual way: unsatisfied desire derives enjoyment from itself, and its own dream is enough in the suspension of all practical erotism and of orgasm, delighting in its own tension and letting it increase, at the risk of becoming trapped in a symptom. Fantasies can be articulated with each other, but each of them has its own enjoyment, which does not necessarily lead to sexual excitement (for example, parricide finds an outlet in the gesture of war or in its representations). Each of them seeks actualisation thanks to a partner (in the same example, the enemy of the fatherland). Here, too, sexual discharge is not obligatory, and war finds in its violence alone an ersatz of satisfaction which ousts the sexual. The same goes for seduction, which manages effortlessly to satisfy itself (with an unrealised desire). Each fundamental fantasy is put into a state of internal tension by its own conflict, and this static energy gives to desire its power, which remains unsatisfied as a function of its own conflictuality. Looking more closely, we might say the non-realisation of the fantasy is the rule, except when – in certain circumstances – it is actualised by an encounter.

Desire is not a pleasure but a displeasure full of pleasure

At its starting point, desire results from a tension, so it is not a pleasure as such. And at its point of arrival, it misses its target because the tension is only discharged thanks to another subject and to a change of place. So it has to start over. Because desire attempts, by means of repetition, to treat sexual trauma, it creates a tension that is unpleasant but is nevertheless full of pleasure, true to the equivocation contained in the German word 'Lust', which means both excitement and discharge.[15] This contradiction between a pleasure and a displeasure finds a first explanation if we consider that the pleasure involves a relief compared to an earlier stage (better desire than remain in anxiety) and the displeasure results from the tension towards the next stage, which is still unsatisfied. It is, for example, a pleasure to pass from the alienation of Being the phallus to that of Having it ('forepleasure'). But the passage is still a displeasure in relation to what is not there: possession of another body and its penetration. There is a difference between the pleasure of the erogenous zones and the displeasure of not yet having been able to possess and then, when the latter is possible, of not being able to reach orgasm.[16]

However, this explanation is insufficient. As we just saw, desire can remain suspended, without progression or regression, so we cannot be satisfied with a model that would situate pleasure as the satisfaction of having overcome a stage, while displeasure would result from the feeling that one has not yet reached the next level.

In fact, unpleasure full of pleasure results from a principle that is internal to desire itself. Is it not contradictory that the 'blows' are correlative to an excitation, that seduction is correlative to a murderous desire, and parricide to love for the father, etc.? In this sense, would a 'balanced' subject be one who leans neither to one nor to the other side of their fantasy? The latent contradictions themselves can provide an enjoyment of the balancing act, by which many are satisfied. This enjoyment is the neutral, stationary point of the contradiction internal to each fantasy. For example, a woman who likes to please can be satisfied with that and refuse to go further. Thus suspended, the unrealised desire itself becomes an enjoyment; it is balanced by a negation, which gives it new impetus. Rich in a displeasure full of pleasure, desire can satisfy itself without seeking an orgasmic conclusion.[17]

So the contradictions of the seduction fantasy unite passivity and activity in a single knot – to be seduced and to seduce. This suspended desire is both a displeasure (a tension) and a pleasure, a 'tension full of pleasure'. Unpleasure corresponds to passivity and pleasure to activity. This pleasure itself remains ambiguous since it is a question of the balancing of tensions, of a zero sum of excitation, a degree zero which resembles death more than it resembles pleasure in the usual meaning of the word; it is indeed the meaning given by Freud to pleasure. Always preliminary to its own obliteration, it heralds the infinity of its repetition. The displeasure of tension vectorises a desire that pleasure does not satisfy. No sooner emerged from immobility, desire advances like a tightrope walker, hurrying forwards to avoid a fall. But what is it hurrying towards? Towards pleasure in the ordinary sense of the word? It may flirt with pleasure, but that is not its goal. In any case, it has no pleasure other than the relief of its internal tension. The internal tension itself is a displeasure, and the end of displeasure is not yet a pleasure. Always already preliminary, it remains unfinished, if not in an infinite openness.

The fantasy is plugged into history: it knots its subjective trauma to an objective trauma

The fantasy is animated by a kind of *in situ* repetition, which seeks to free itself from a trauma that was originally purely subjective. The subject was first caught up in paternal seduction, but this seduction itself resulted from the subject's own engagement in phallic enjoyment. It is not 'the father' who is traumatising but 'the father's desire', which is first and foremost the desire of the subject, and this desire is what, above all, cannot be allowed. So the birth of desire is in itself subjectively traumatic. If desire led to incest, the drama would be extreme indeed, but the fantasy is activated in the imminence of such a drama; it flirts with annihilation through incest. The subjective trauma is immediately caught between active desire and desire for what ought not to be (to be desired passively). This is why, bizarrely, desire can be satisfied by suffering, or more exactly, desire finds suffering without looking for it, like a familiar companion, as it travels on its way. We repress this subjective trauma by a simple process: by behaving as if it had been imposed on us. In this way, we repress our engagement so that desire appears subsequently to be an alien force which manipulates us in spite of ourselves.

Subjective trauma is different from objective trauma (if we use the latter term to mean an actual sexual assault). Subjective trauma is never lacking; it is the consequence of desire itself. It strikes when one no longer knows who desires whom; it concerns the desire *of* the father, with a genitive that is both subjective and objective. A fantasy of the murder of a father now stripped of his paternal majesty by desire is born in order to escape this shameful anonymity, this desire 'of' the father where one no longer knows who desired whom. Love and hate jostle and drag each other into a contradiction that renders this psychical event opaque to consciousness.[18] From this fall, desire retains the dimension of a violence unknown to itself, which cuts its legs from under it and breaks its momentum when it is at its strongest. This is the trauma that gives to the feminine its reputation for passivity. How are we to think, even fleetingly, of the murder of the very one who is desired, and how also are we not to think about it since to make love with one's own progenitor would be to never have been born. This depersonalisation of the unborn paralyses the body at the moment of an enjoyment that is not allowed.

So each subject scrutinises their history and seeks an objective trauma from the past, to which their intimate suffering could correspond. The intention is to be innocent of one's own desire by finding an external cause for it, in a paternal seduction. The subject will always find a greater or lesser sign of such seduction. The trauma remains invisible because it is purely subjective, but it will have been more or less shaped by a particular event in their history, to which the subject will have become fixated in early childhood. To begin with, the seduction fantasy is only a fantasy, but as events really experienced with the father unfold, and later in amorous encounters, the subjective trauma is objectified in stories, which *in turn* require their own repetitions, grafted onto the repetition of the fantasy. As a result, events that actually happened with the father will repeat themselves, according to his greater or lesser seduction, etc. The past in itself does not seek to come back to life, but a certain event insists because the force of the fantasy, which was its soul and its driving force, stages it. Indeed, if a trauma, even a serious trauma, falls outside the compass of a fantasy, it remains without long-term consequences. But if a real trauma objectifies its subjective twin, consequences will not fail to ensue.

Games of seduction repeat 'what was undergone' without knowing that they do so, firstly because the past event only put its stamp on a subjective trauma, experienced in a 'semi-conscious' way, if we can thus designate a fact that is fully recalled but without any knowledge of the desire at play. The certainty of having been sexually seduced in childhood may be based only on very vague memories. Something must have happened . . . but what? Memory flutters around uncertain images, and they are what impose themselves in the present at the time of a real seduction. A certain situation will, as if by coincidence, accurately play out what activates desire but without knowing the reason for it. And this repetition cannot abandon itself to a present pleasure without occasioning the replay of a scene that was once experienced as a brutal initiation.

Purely fantasmatic at the outset, desire repeats in the present not only the infantile but also any event that evokes it. Small details of history objectify it and do so all the more easily because the subject chooses to believe that what he or she underwent was due to external circumstances and not to their own desire.[19] No child is sheltered from their own desire, and they will always prefer their subjective trauma to take the form of an objective trauma, which he or she imagines or, if necessary, invents (this is the *proton pseudos*). We repress subjective traumas because they result from our own desire, and we may even repress objective traumas (resulting from real seductions) as if we were somehow to blame.[20] Repetition is then organised around a fixation of the subjective on the objective; from the psychical point of view, history and fantasy are not opposed. But the story – our life as we tell it to ourselves – only presents a version, from which the part of the fantasy that engages us has been, as far as possible, expurgated. The passive and active sides of the fantasy correspond to this repetition, which uses objective events to materialise the subjective trauma. The more real the trauma was, the more fantasy becomes fixated in its passive aspect, inhibiting the active aspect of desire.

We can think of this subjective-objective relationship as scales that find their balance at an ambiguous point. If a seduction by an adult really occurred, it will tip the scales to one side, cancelling out the subjectivity of desire, which is henceforth launched on a circular repetition of the objective trauma itself. For example, a very young girl who has been raped is at risk of being frigid thereafter. And it will be the same for all the events of family life; a certain presence of the mother or of the father or a fraternal rivalry will crystallise the traumas and be fixed in memory at the crossover of a subjective trauma (desire) and an objective trauma (the event).[21] The actualisation of fantasies is structured against the background of a story, of a certain type of attribution of roles. Then this drama repeats itself in a circle, powered by the motor of the fantasy, the impetus of which precedes any of its actualisations; whether he or she enjoys it or suffers from it, the subject finds him- or herself caught up in the very conditions of their coming into being, namely, the impact (prohibition and transgression) of seduction and parricide (under the mantle of love) and, ultimately, of the primal scene (under the cover of jealousy, which inverts it).

If this 'fixation' concerns facts that are often vague in memory, it is because in reality, what is being repeated concerns less these 'facts' than *situations* that have been prolonged over a long period of time. So that it is then types of desiring relationship that will recur. This is never so apparent as in 'situation eroticism', which is triggered by a kind of role-play. For example, the man who wants to make the conquest of his best friend's wife will no longer be interested in her as soon as he has obtained satisfaction and his friendship has been shipwrecked (an irreducible primal-scene fantasy shapes a desire that withers as soon as the fantasy is actualised). Similarly, the sexual solicitations of the man whom a woman loves may become intolerable to her as soon as he becomes her husband. Such scenarios abound. Consider only the prevalent example of desire that fades following paternity and motherhood, sexuality now being located in a different constellation; excitement dwindles while love stays keen because the first depends solely on the actualisation of fantasies, while the second is invariant. Desire changes according to situations that recall other situations. A woman who is desired in certain circumstances may no longer be desired if her place changes. She may provoke a storm of excitement for as long as she is courted by rivals, but desire dwindles as soon as she is seen to have been won.

A certain situation is sometimes in itself conducive to desire because of how it contrasts with the past: a girl from a bourgeois background will be attracted to an artist. Or a man will fall in love with the wife of his boss. Or it might be that a specific trait, which is not always conscious, plays a role. A woman has a penchant for men of a particular profession or men who have a particular trait (dark or blond, bearded, old, young, short, sickly, muscular, etc.). Some men always fall in love with the same kind of women – those who are forward or reserved, who wear a uniform, who are mothers or grandmothers, etc.

Like stationary engines, fantasies take hold of history, which then repeats itself, driven by their emptiness. Similarly, the resonance of fantasies between two lovers will use the repetitions of history, whether of the past in neurosis or of flight from the past (in this kind of normality of desire when it sails towards the unknown, either with the wind or against the wind). The lover excites thanks to the fantasy that he or she arouses, but since this fantasy is fixed on past traumas, it will burn all the brighter for showing its scars. Seduction will never be stronger than when it summons up some ghost of the past, cast in relief by repetition. So destinies seem to cross paths through misunderstanding; for example, someone who has been seduced wants to be a seducer in order to lead their own 'seducer' to perdition and often does so to their own chagrin, their only way forward then being to start over again. Reiterating the Oedipal triangle, a man may only take an interest in a woman if rivalry is involved; the situation excites him more than the woman herself. Where, then, does the desire come from: from a primal-scene fantasy or from the repetition of an infantile trauma? But there is no opposition between the actualisation of the fantasy and the repetition of the traumas of history. The fantasy is already a repetition *in situ*, to which the repetition of past events become linked that were only traumatic because of their connection to the fantasy. Desire is set alight by a particular person, selected among others for one of their characteristics, the scope of which, moreover, often remains unconscious. The scars of the stories we tell are clues to the fantasy beneath them. So the fantasies of two lovers resonate thanks to the details of circumstance and the features of their history.

A woman who, for example, was raped in her childhood may be sexually inhibited if the subjective dimension of her fantasy has been fully objectified in this trauma. But depending on her encounters after adolescence, this destiny may be shifted and generate 'new' repetitions. Repetition leads to a certain way of acting but then this new action itself may have traumatic consequences and may repeat itself, taking on a life of its own, apparently different from its initial source. So a harmless scene of childhood seduction may be replayed in adolescence in another directly sexual language, and it is this second event that will then be repeated and will orient the person's love life.

Moreover, traumas with no apparent relationship to sexuality, such as accidents or real physical violence, will repeat themselves in a way that is occasionally nightmarish and that cannot be got rid of because a small feature will be seized on by the subjective traumas of childhood for their benefit. Past history goes in a loop around such accidents. Since purely fantasmatic repetition (fantasy is the beating heart of repetition) has no consistency in itself (it is the void of desire), it will attach itself to any objective event so that a false connection (*falsche Verknüpfung*) becomes its only truth. When it becomes looped around a past trauma, particularly a trauma from infancy, this (now neurotic) fixation weighs on every current situation. The subject seeks to get rid of it by re-enacting certain situations, shifting from passive to active. But because he or she changes places, the subject fails to recognise that they are repeating. They have the impression of a liberation even as they run along the same rails. It is not such a bad outcome – release from prison as often as you want, thanks to an act that puts you back in prison.

The traumas of history reiterate themselves to the rhythm of fantasmatic repetition, and they inhibit or unblock their actualisation as a function of *present* circumstances. Another example: a child whose guilt has been relieved by purely fantasmatic 'blows' will take special enjoyment in conditions of at least moral masochism or with the help of the fantasy of being tied up, humiliated, etc. On the other hand, if the child was actually struck, the fantasy shifts and may be reversed into actual violence. Other modalities highlight the repetition of subjective division. For example, a woman's 'penis envy' is actualised by claiming exclusive rights to the penis of a particular man. She thus assures herself of her 'masculinity' against her own femininity. So her jealousy of other women corresponds to her own internal division between masculine and feminine. And even when she has no reason to be jealous, she may fantasise the presence of a rival, even during lovemaking. What is more, the same fantasy can also reverse its masculine-feminine orientation based on the accidents of her own history.[22]

The lifespan of the fantasy

The short story by Tolstoy, *Family Happiness*,[23] offers a fine account of how the love fantasy evolves depending on events, all the more so because it is expurgated of any sexual details or links to the desire for motherhood or paternity. Moreover, the mystery of this love is sanctified by a religious dimension: that which has been consecrated for millennia by the Churches, as if they alone could bear witness to this kind of madness, set ablaze against the backdrop of a love of the father whose sacrament they are well placed to confer. In Tolstoy's story, a man becomes acquainted with a woman, Masha, when she is still only a child. He is a friend of her father and assumes the duty of guardian when the father dies. As Masha grows up, she develops a strong passion for her guardian, Serge, although she sees him only on the rare occasions when he comes to manage the estate and her property. From their increasingly frequent encounters is born the plenitude of a manifestly shared happiness, a rare aesthetic dimension, a power of feeling without any hint of erotism – no touching of hands, no coquetry or seduction, no stolen kisses. Cut off from the world, this is a perfect love but one that is nevertheless driven by a secret temporality; Serge thinks that he is too old to be a match for Masha, and although it is not spelt out, he feels that he is invested with a paternal aura and so ought not to go further, even though he is burning with an enthusiastic passion.

When the day comes to declare that his duty prevents him for continuing these meetings, and to take his final leave, the exact opposite happens and they decide to get married. This is something like a sacrament of what should not be permitted in the name of the father! The few years of conjugal happiness that follow are gradually undermined by Serge's feeling that his wife is bored in the countryside and that they must move to Saint-Petersburg, city of glamour and allurements. We are told in passing (in no more than five lines) that one, then two children have been born, but they are looked after by nurses, and these events, major though they are, seem to remain peripheral to the evolution of a love that is steered by its own compass. Serge brings his wife to the city, where her beauty is feted and her grace acknowledged. He encourages her here, much as a good father might have done. She is flattered by the tributes that are paid to her, and he finds himself blaming her for it; he reproaches her for what is the work of his own desire since he himself pushed her into the seductions of Saint-Petersburg life and encouraged her to put herself in situations where he finds himself confronted with male rivalries, which he eschews. He turns away from this ternary desire, which might have revived his jealousy and his erotism. And his reproaches gradually erode his love for his wife, even though he has nothing to reproach her for. The epilogue of the short story suggests that conjugal happiness is to be found in a happiness centred on the family, an idea that has, of course, been central in the patriarchal family until today.

Tolstoy's short story shows the 'temporality' of the fantasy; beyond the general circumstances of the narrative, we should add its 'age', which mean that its objectives change depending on the time of life. A child actualises a different scenario from that of an adolescent, which in turn is distinct from that of an adult, etc., all in respect of the same fantasy. Curious as it is, this notion of the 'age' of the fantasy is nevertheless of great importance; it does not always correspond to the person's life age, so an adult can, for example, actualise adolescent or infantile fantasies, etc. Repetition changes, it differs from the past event that it blindly recalls. More than that, it engenders its own expanded repetition; once the fantasy has been staged with a certain person, it repeats itself, according to scenarios that emerge one from another. For example, once he has won the affections of a woman, the lover may want to become the husband, and once he achieves this new situation, he dreams of becoming the father, etc. Such sequences can only be attempted, and when they fail, back to square one. Illustrating this temporality, myths often present the functioning of the unconscious in reverse. This is true of Sleeping Beauty, awakened by Prince Charming: in psychical reality, on the contrary, she *falls asleep* after meeting Prince Charming so that she can continue to dream. Or a princess kisses a toad that turns into Prince Charming. In reality, it is often the opposite: a young girl meets Prince Charming who, when she kisses him, turns into a toad. The girl will then set off in search of another Prince Charming or even ask the toad to realise another fantasy – that of being the father of a family, for example. Then this father will not make the grade, etc.

The libido seeks to realise itself in a way that is also sequenced towards the future. For example, a young girl seeks to know love. When she knows it, she wants to get married, then to have a child, etc. Each mode of realisation begets a dream about a later stage; current disharmony begets the dream of future harmony. At each stage, the libido continues to push towards the resolution of the current stage, for so long, at least, as inhibition does not stop this movement, which, in fact, nothing can stop because if a 'stop' occurs, it regresses into a symptom.

According to its age, the fantasy actualises not only its own repetition *in situ*, which sets it free, but also effects an actualisation that is a function of its own past history and of the traumas that shaped it. It does this whatever the circumstances; it uses what has already happened, growing as a function of its successes or failures. The motor of desire would not run for long without misfiring if its actualisation did not climb upwards by degrees, according to the different times of life, and if it did not accomplish a 'progress' which renews it, even though it remains fundamentally identical. This progression offers hope to the subject who tears himself away daily from his neurosis, in a sort of race against the clock of 'counter-neurotic' repetition, which might perhaps pass as a definition of 'normality'. These successive actualisations climb, in a way, the steps of a narrative. Each love is a novel: it develops according to its own logic. It progresses by walking along its own branch. Each of the events is reiterated in how it is then used, constructing its own destiny. The subject learns a lesson from a particular love story which makes them take a further step, or a setback puts them on a different path.

The fantasies emerge from each other like Russian dolls. Love, far from proposing a static ideal, wants to achieve a certain goal, and then another, unless it is inhibited in its journey or unless it fails, in which case, it goes back to square one, with the same partner or with a different partner. This does not mean that love has failure built in but that levels are crossed in a sequence which is not infinite. Time suspends its flight for a moment when the fantasy comes true. In this moment of epiphany, we no longer know if we are dreaming or if what is happening really is happening. But this intoxication does not last long; another fantasy takes over and stretches the thread of time once more. But this psychical time always has an end, at least for most people, and so a lateral question arises: does a moment not come when psychical life has run through the potentialities of repetition (for example, from the son to the father, then to the grandfather) and when the final bell sounds? Geneticists tell us that soon, we will be able to live longer or even forever. But will desire subscribe to this programme – desire that carries its own end within itself from the very beginning?

Restricted and expanded repetition

Repetition seems to have a frightening power. It certainly has the ability to widen its scope, change its costume through the ages and appear different, but it animates desire so strongly that any resistance seems useless. Can we change this apparent automatism, or do we simply have no other prospect than that of enjoying our misfortunes – of being like Dante who, having lost Beatrice, loved only the loss itself? We must note first of all that 'repetition' certainly does not mean the same as 'catastrophe'. It can create an ordinary happiness. For example, when someone wants to have a child, he or she represents the person whom they would have liked to be: they repeat by proxy and, for the most part, are quite happy doing so. But whatever the outcome – contentment or misfortune – the dice seem to be cast once and for all.

However, there is a huge difference between two modalities of repetition: we may act in order to repeat a traumatic event from the past or, on the contrary, in order to escape from it. So we distinguish a *restricted* repetition of (neurotic) infantile material from an *expanded* repetition ('expanded' in the sense that it offers something else), which seeks to reverse the constraints of the first. When repetition is restricted, the scenario remains the same. When, however, it is expanded, it escapes this limited staging, which remains its negative determinant but without determining what will happen. For example, instead of looking for a woman who is like his mother (good luck with that!), a man will prefer one who is completely different from her (this offers greater choice). The term 'repetition' still applies in the second case because the maternal imprint – *quoad matrem* – continues to play a role, albeit only reactively. Desire then plays the card of a 'counter-determination' at the junction of restricted repetition and expanded repetition. In the restricted repetition, desire maintains the infantile neurosis and erotic problems accumulate, or it may even happen that a total sexual inhibition sets in, often alongside a passionate and exclusive love. In these circumstances, sexual desire, as incestuous, flees away and wavers, reversing itself into desire for non-desire. The contradiction of the fantasy puts desire into an equation with non-desire, but this is an unstable equilibrium and can lead to entanglement; 'non-desire' aims to avoid the incestuous danger but thereby authenticates it. So desire might then seem to swing suddenly towards its opposite.[24]

Love creates a lack, which, as such, does not stem from neurosis but may put neurosis back on stage. Because it is the lover's lack, the lover's own ghosts – the obsessions by which the lover is haunted – reappear in this abyss. A similarity with the past is sufficient for restricted repetition to be triggered. This bizarre superimposition corresponds to the scenarios of neurosis, when, for example, a woman has something of the mother about her or when a seducer reminds a little too much of a father. An infantile reminiscence ignites passion here. So lack itself assures the dominion of the infantile in the present, feeding on its own fire, sometimes for a lifetime.[25] All that is asked of the beloved is to re-evoke a ghost from the past.

Such, for example, is the case of men and women who can only be passionate about impossible partners, with whom they have sometimes had almost no actual relationship. What happens is that the past lack from childhood provokes love, rather than love engendering lack. This is a type of repetition of lack, which inhibits or even suspends sexual desire. The lack of possession has certainly fomented love. But certain features of the same person may, therefore, engender a neurotic love – a love that is frozen in restricted repetition.[26] The feature that is fixed upon may be miniscule. What generates neurotic repetition is small details and not such self-evidences as, for example, a man of a certain age and a certain presence who might be expected to evoke the father or even a woman whose particular skills evoke those of the mother, etc. In contrast, love escapes neurosis to the extent that it deviates from this schema. This is expanded repetition. Here, love and sexual desire get along more easily. If a relationship between lovers lasts, it is because of a relationship between love and desire. It is expanded repetition and not restricted repetition that allows life to flourish.

We enter into this repetition, for better or for worse, because we seek to escape from the compulsion to repeat the same thing. Desire repeats by repressing its cause, which seems empty, following the blind propulsion which counter-determines human freedom. For example, the intoxication of love floats in complete unreality because its waking dream replays and releases another scene, giving repetition the status of an act. That being so, why should we care that it is confused? The conditions of the repetition (of desire) are also the conditions of a repression of what determines it. The subject forgets that he or she is repeating in the very act of repeating.

The passage from restricted to expanded repetition relieves the entanglement of desire. In restricted repetition, neurotic guilt inhibits sexuality or makes it symptomatic. In expanded repetition, if sexuality crosses a transgressive space, it simply declares itself guilty. And nothing prevents us from enjoying the guilt itself, even to the extent of seeking it out. Indeed, the orgasmic moment itself is linked with this guilt. For instance, a woman can become ill from her own seduction (in restricted repetition). This seduction may keep her at home, unable to get dressed, put on make-up, etc. – difficulties that entail being late for every rendezvous. But later on, she may find the games and intrigues of the same seduction highly entertaining. Guilt may inhibit, but it may also procure pleasure (in expanded repetition).

As we will see, the 'situation' that pushes excitement to its orgasmic resolution will depend on the fantasy and on history, as they unfold in expanded repetition. The key is to escape from restricted repetition – that is to say from the family, less by 'assuming' the guilt which is a consequence than by enjoying this guilt. For example, a frigid woman, entombed in the amorous sugar-coating of restricted repetition, may find enjoyment with a stranger who makes her suffer: the suffering pays the price of her guilt. A contradiction that requires resolution is thus brought into focus. Frigidity is more often relative to certain situations than absolute. It is a problem of subjective position: the sense of doing something wrong may inhibit, but it can also be enjoyed. This passage to the 'enjoyment of being at fault' occurs when the objectification by guilt is overcome thanks to a certain subjectivation of guilt, which means being able to take enjoyment in oneself just as one has been enjoyed as an object.[27]

Repetition establishes its rhythm when we emerge from childhood. Desire then looks for a direction and moves towards erotism. By repressing childhood, this change of place initiates, outside the family, what was already once played out within the family, and it does so in the form of either a restricted repetition or an expanded repetition – a repetition that sets its course towards the unknown. This change sometimes generates such a sense of freedom that it can orient desire all on its own. Jettisoning what is infantile may be so intoxicating that, later on, desire will itself repeat this moment: it will need to quit, leave behind, let go of everything that resembles a tie or bond. Ardent love affairs sometimes end suddenly, perhaps because the loved man or woman fell back too quickly into the formats of the past, turning one's life into a repeated exile from childhood. Certainly, desire cannot be reduced to the relief offered by such a repetitive exit from the infantile. And yet this permanent exile represents a kind of paradigm of desire in the West, much vaunted in Christianity, which describes it in many myths (notably, that of Don Juan) that model the passage from restricted to expanded repetition – repetition that revels in recurrent breaks with the same partner or with several in a series, following a scenario that women act out no less than men, when the first kiss turns the lover into the father.

A new world opens up only at the moment of expanded repetition, when the struggles for love, its conquests and its rivalries reactualise the drama of the Oedipus but in a mode that is both misrecognised and restaged by the change of place; infantile claims continue to impose themselves behind the struggle of the adolescent so that events unfold against this background. But now they take on a depth and a seriousness that the tenuousness of childhood could not know. Everything suddenly becomes more pressing; each fact takes on a hidden meaning. The force of expanded repetition orients the subject towards a new sexuality, served by a new fantasy appetite. This repetition, apparently devoid of meaning, pushes towards this new world that is completely unknown and even frightening in certain respects and through which one must travel in disguise.

Repetition pursues its course here while remaining hidden and becomes entangled in imitations of sexual templates so that the new pleasures ring false at first; they seem impractical and anxiety-provoking. They are, after all, less convenient than masturbation, which is quick and problem-free. And yet! To hold a body in one's arms – even with slight or feigned pleasure, even in the name of an awkward love and rudimentary tenderness – opens up another time within time. The present is intensified by a never-fulfilled dream of infancy, and the space that this opens up, difficult and symptomatic as it may be, will be given immediate preference, if one can call 'preference' that which submits to the demands of repetition.

Αντέρως (Anteros) – 'counter-love', the motor of expanded repetition

In Plato's dialogue, *Phaedrus*, Socrates argues against the thesis of Lysias (not present but much cited in it), who considers it prudent not to respond to love with love: 'favours should be granted rather to the one who is not in love than to the lover'.[28] At a certain point in the discussion, Plato introduces a curious term, that of 'counter-love' ('Anteros'). He uses the term after mentioning Lysias' idea that it is preferable to reject love and only to take advantage of sexual desire. The term 'counter-love' refers to the beloved (not the lover), when the beloved falls in love just because he is made so much of;[29] he is intoxicated by the powerful feelings that are directed towards him and set alight by them without realising what is happening to him.

What we are to understand from this passage is that somebody who is loved to excess may in turn burn with love but for the benefit of somebody other than the person who lit the flame. This is, after all, a banal characteristic of passion – a person lavishes love on somebody who does not requite the love but finds in this love received the strength to love somebody else. So a third party is brought into the love relationship in a chain-like process: someone loves someone, who loves a third person, etc., in a broken circularity, which, step by step, could include all of humanity. How splendid this universal, painful and magnificent process would be, if it did not so often become entangled in its neurotic dimension.

What lesson can we draw from this? The person to whom love is addressed is loved for more than what he or she is,[30] and in order to shake off this burdensome alienation, they love in their turn but somebody else. This process enables the person to move from a passive position, that of 'being loved', to an active position, 'loving', which rids them of this objectifying love. Is this push of love towards counter-love not precisely what happens in the passage from endogamy to exogamy? The term 'counter-love' emphasises that exogamous love is constructed in counterpoint to the aspect of love formed in the family. It also emphasises that exogamous love will always be tormented by a force that runs counter to it and that emanates from its place of origin (but then an aeroplane always takes off better against the wind). We get a sense of the importance of this process: counter-love, 'anteros', is what lends strength to the libido. 'Libido' for Freud is not a vague term but a concept in its own right. It describes a force that is directed initially from the mother to the child. But its violence is such that the child cannot tolerate it and turns this libido outwards, towards its own drive objects, one of the destinies of which is none other than love.[31] Children direct their love outside their family from an early age, and nothing offers them greater relief. Counter-love is situated at the crossing point from endogamous to exogamous love. The strength of the acquired libido is what decides the operational capacities of children.

How are we to understand the specificity of this process? Parents transfer their unrealised fantasies onto their child. They play out with their children the share of their own Oedipal desires, which they have renounced, dedicating to them a love that has been desexualised by repression but that, in reality, blindly transmits a concealed eroticisation. This 'pure' love has a subjective consequence for the child: it is strongly eroticised even though it has no sexual consequences. This the 'subjective trauma' of childhood, distinct from the 'objective trauma' produced when, unfortunately, there is real sexuality between an adult and a child. So libido is directed (sexually, at least) outside the family and seeks to escape the weight of eroticised parental love or rather, to escape its repressed incestuous dimension. Libido is propelled exogamously in proportion to the positive sexual trauma that parental love engenders.

This process is even clearer when we look at its opposite: an insufficiency of parental love creates an absence of counter-love, a stasis of the libido, and this is the foundation for another far-reaching concept – that of inhibition. Inhibition is the result of a 'trauma of the absence of trauma', which can result in a certain drift of the body, left floating because the parents did not traumatise their child in the sense of a subjective trauma. This notion of a 'trauma of the absence of trauma' corresponds to the lack of eroticisation, implying that there has been nothing to give rise to a seduction fantasy. The child's body left the parents cold.[32] The child was not loved to the point of revulsion, as are most children, where the excessive love they receive propels towards other horizons. The more a child is loved by his parents, the easier it will be for that child to overcome their inhibitions; parental love is a passport to action.[33]

Desexualised parental love and the desire to have a child

Is sexual desire oriented quite simply by a natural goal, namely, the reproduction of the species? Is 'what should not be' opposed by 'what should be' – a desire aiming at procreation? It is certainly true that sexual desire sometimes connects at a particular moment with the desire for a child. But too many exceptions prevent us from thinking that what is in question is an innate instinct. Biology, the church, the state, etc., want reproduction to be on the agenda of people who have sex. But experience shows that people who want children are not initially driven by a procreative instinct but most often by unconscious motives. Sexual arousal is relieved without concern for reproduction. Not only is erotism active at every hour of the day with no procreative aim but it also does not even seek pleasure either. We see only the fixity of a desire that ignores its own object.

The desire for a child is but a (relatively late) subset of desire as such and of the fireworks of fantasy that actualise it. The miracle of birth is an accidental extra in a nest of fantasies, for which the reproduction of the species is of no concern. Does it ever happen that lovers, in the first moments of their love, think of having a child? A path must first be followed, the pitfalls of which cause the idea of the child to germinate. Seen this way, a certain failure of love also enables a progression.

The desire for a child certainly has an entry point determined by the drive, when there is a desire to create another self, a narcissistic clone – a desire that is already at work in the dreams of very small children. But once this stage has been moved through, the desire for a child is linked to the fantasy realm of sexual arousal. Evoking parricide, sexual desire summons up the desire for a child as payment of the debt owed to the father. Through the vehicle of love, the desire for a child can seem like a gift – a sort of response to orgastic loss. From a transgenerational point of view, this desire is marked by a more or less pronounced ambivalence. On the one hand, the child is the payment of a debt to its grandparents; the parents make good on a vow of love to their mothers and pay a debt to their murdered fathers. But on the other hand, the desire for a child arises from a subject seeking to escape his or her own childhood and dreaming of how the newcomer will be spared the difficulties that he or she experienced with their own parents, starting with the torments of seduction.

This is where the repression of sexual desire in its paedophilic dimension finds its most powerful motive. Parents repress their incestuous desire towards their children because they want them to have a destiny different from the one which they believe was theirs. The little innocents are, therefore, invested with a strongly desexualised love, but from the depths of their purity, they will be no less seduced by it. Because nothing exacerbates seduction as much as the purity of love, its purity itself being conducive to angelic erections. This sexual repression on the part of the parents towards their children is sometimes so powerful that it inhibits the children's own sexuality. So endogamy can repress erotism, and the famous prohibition of incest is less a law than an avatar of the repressed seduction fantasy.[34]

How much is love opposed to desire?

It is worth running through the characteristics of this parental love. It is quite different from exogamous love, which has sexual consequences. Not only is it distinguished from desire but it also represses desire due to an initial opposition between desire and love. It is not a result of the Oedipus complex but an opposition that is present from the outset. This initial split can be summed up very briefly: the desire for a child precedes and surpasses the parents who are its bearers. And their love then seeks to repair the damage caused by this transgenerational desire.[35] Parents want children under the impulse of a desire that goes beyond them and that has an objectifying dimension. And their love takes up arms against the annihilating effect of this desire. When they educate their children, make them eat, clean them, etc., this drive education is beyond them and operates through them. Sometimes they give their children orders that make them cry, but no sooner have they done it than they regret it and console them in a movement that shows clearly the opposition between a desire that is always other and parental love. Because their own attitude is beyond their conscious control, they then repair what they have themselves provoked. A way of characterising this oblative parental love would be to say that they take pity on their child.

Parental desire is initially propelled by the violent and incestuous desire of the Other. It plunges the child into distress (*Hiflosigkeit*), which gets taken for a lack of autonomy when it is in fact the mental distress of being only an object and of refusing to be that object. Maternal love then steps in to oppose the objectification involved in this desire, and it is in this sense that maternal love resembles pity or oblativity. Listen to a mother speak to her child, and you will always hear that note of pity and compensation. When a mother realises the morass in which she enmires her child and against which the child struggles, she moves from the position of big Other to that of subject. This is the moment when the child recognises its mother and is recognised by her. But this pity does not accord dignity to the one to whom it is addressed. This is why it engenders a counter-love, which flees away from the indignity of endogamous love.

The parents' gift of love inflates narcissism, which may go elsewhere to be deflated.[36] If such love/pity is wanting, the power to act will also be wanting.[37] The loved child acts without caring about this love or even in ignorance of it, considering it as what is due to him or her, in return for their coming into the world, designed to complete the desire of the Other. This love settles the accounts. Counter-love is based on this love, which gives force to its forgetful, ungrateful action. It enables counter-love to act with the force of forgetfulness[38] – perhaps not without knowing what it is doing but at least without knowing why. Endogamous love, the vector of counter-love, is variable. Unlike the desire of the Other, parental love is not always present, but when it is, it has several levels:

1   Parents may not love their child and make this evident to the child
2   Parents may not love their child and hide it from the child
3   Parents may love their child but not give signs of this love, whether in the form of small gifts or, especially, in the form of words that declare this love (gifts sometimes seek to replace words; we then fall back into case 2)
4   At a higher level, they may love their child and give signs of love
5   They may then love and give signs of love but prohibit counter-love by prohibiting activities outside the family
6   Finally, they may love, give signs of love and allow exogamous action (the 'paradise' scenario)

A stronger or weaker fixation in structure, i.e., a greater or lesser inhibition of action, will depend on these six variables. It can also shed light on the degrees of fixation in neurosis or psychosis. There are different levels of intensity; a large number of psychotics or neurotics are not ill to the extent that their activities are not inhibited. Various authors refer to 'schizoid' or 'paranoid' personalities, etc., by which they mean that the individuals in question are not suffering illness in the psychiatric sense of 'illness'. The same applies to hysteria and obsessional neurosis; most hysterics and obsessionals are far from being grounded by their symptoms. They are able to act. The lifting of inhibition allows these people to get out of their psychosis or neurosis in their day-to-day lives. So these gradations of illness depend on a trans-structural gift of love, which has the same beneficial effect whatever the structure. For example, a psychotic child may be much loved or, on the contrary, unloved. A distinction must be made between, on the one hand, neurotic or psychotic structure and, on the other hand, their varying degrees of intensity depending on the love which the individuals in question received. One might describe six levels of neurotic or psychotic fixation, going from a weak to a high level of intensity, according to the six gradations of endogamous love.

Total inhibition of the passage from infantile to adult neurosis – i.e., degree zero of the gift of love – would correspond to perversion or, as we might say, to perversion that survives from the polymorphous perversion of the child (if we are to believe a remark by Freud in the *Dora* case, where he notes that adults do not *become* perverse but *remain* so because inhibition has kept them trapped in childhood).[39]

Finally, a last comment on the desexualisation of endogamous love: a mother does not give the same kind of love as that offered by a father. The mother's love counterbalances the annihilating effects of narcissism,[40] and in this way, the first condition for the possibility of action is obtained. But a second condition is necessary in order for the action to begin: the subject must bear his or her own name; that is to say they must be able to identify with the father, to 'kill' him and take his place. With the mother's love, the vehicle is ready to run, but the driver must be able to drive it. The existence of a subject is one thing, but for the subject to be able to bear their own name is quite another. A subject may consider him- or herself anonymous if their father does not allow them to take his name (for example, by preventing the subject from acting, playing, studying, going dancing, getting married, etc.). A subject already exists just in relation to structure and the love of the mother, but inhibition is only overcome to the extent that the subject bears the father's name, according to the law of a fantasmatic parricide. The mother's gift of love concerns the ego,[41] while the father's gift of love concerns the subject.

Love and counter-love present themselves differently in the two cases. The mother's love provokes a lifting of inhibition, which sets in motion the vehicle that would authorise action, if there was a subject capable of using it. But the father's gift is not symmetrical; the father's love (that of the actual man who embodies the paternal function) counterbalances what is too violent in the relation to the mythical father. His love does not directly generate a counter-love, but it counteracts hatred and the murder fantasy. The father's love wipes away the hatred that the anxiety of castration by the father provokes; he has no reason to feel pity, but he forgives.

If the father's words do not forgive the hatred which is unconsciously addressed to him by the son, this hatred does not reach the turning point where it recognises itself in love,[42] and action remains weighed down by castration anxiety. The father remains in the mythical state where he signifies only what is forbidden, with no possible reassignment of the resulting anxiety. So a certain forgiveness by the father is the passport to effective action. If it is not present, the subject tries to force a way past the unforgiving father, and action will seek to force this passage in spite of itself, without taking enjoyment in anything. This produces men who spend their whole lives in a state of war. Their ambivalence in relation to any figure of authority is relentless and unflinching, from school to university to the workplace, etc. Transgression becomes the rule, and its goal is to personalise the father – to fashion a figure who would no longer be mythical and who would localise anxiety in a specific person or institution.

Pity is the mother's part; forgiveness is the father's part. These presentations of their love include as many combinations as are permitted by two times the six entries described earlier, without any particular privileging of the father or mother over each other, because a father may love a particular child whom the mother does not love, etc. The result depends on a balance of power, and one does not make up for the other. The love from the father does not occur after the love from the mother but may or may not be contemporaneous with it. Counter-love takes its strength from these feelings.

The passage to exogamous love

Initially, love generates an impersonal counter-love; an inner obligation to love comes before the love of anyone in particular. This love and counter-love appear differently inside and outside the family. In the family, the equal love of the parents works against what is annihilating in narcissism. Outside the family, by contrast, loving someone depletes and impoverishes or even annihilates the person who loves.[43] The love felt for someone outside the family takes on the proportions it does due to an overvaluation[44] of that person, who is both themselves and the ideal that they evoke. In any case, exogamous counter-love alienates;[45] it provokes a narcissistic loss which is the opposite of endogamous love. Here, there is no pity and no forgiveness. This is why the subject seeks to make up for this loss thanks to sexuality, which recovers erotically the enjoyment that was lost in this narcissistic haemorrhage. The eroticism that is concealed in the family is unmasked outside the family due to this change of position. So love is sexualised; what is endogamously repressed is exogamously actualised. Erotism is always based on the prohibition of incest.

But why does a subject expose him- or herself to love outside the family, if that puts them in such danger? Why not do without it and stay in the endogamous love of the parents? This is just what some people choose to do; parental love is their rampart. This preference is also definitive of neurosis, when it actualises the parents' love using partners other than them. Why should one love? What is to be gained by it if not that, thanks to love, the drive is subjectified? Love propelled by counter-love is not narcissistic; it is the most subjective of acts, which consists in giving back what one has lost. Love is an act, perhaps the only act in the full sense.[46] Always already subjective to begin with, love actualises the freedom of the subject against structure, even when it is trapped in neurotic repetition, even though love is never triggered so powerfully as when it is impossible. Subjectivity is further affirmed in this suffering itself, which is the suffering of the subject struggling against his or her determinisms; it is the subject's way of treating with what has been given up in their alienation.

This love is not a product of narcissistic satisfaction, even if such a satisfaction – a dream of completeness – would be its means of realisation. It results from a narcissistic fracture; not only does narcissism not cause love but it is also not its end either (or when it is, it leads to annihilation). Narcissism is only a means, a reflexive stage, the finality of which is not animal or instinctual satisfaction but the realisation of the subject him- or herself, their separation. Narcissism is only the middle term of love, its *pneuma*, because it follows from the act of a subject. One can no longer speak of an 'object' of love when the fantasy is actualised in this way. The 'object' of love is in reality a subject, the subject who recognises themself. For this reason, the subject seeks to love despite the risk that it involves.

Otherness is sex

We are able to recognise someone different in the world around us because we are different from ourselves. The birth of otherness results from the division of the subject since we are constantly the prey of an internal splitting.[47] Our parents wanted us in a certain place, and we began by contradicting them. Our existence is affirmed by pronouncing this 'no', which is our first name and which remains so. Our family name drives us on and makes us eternal travellers. But this inner splitting does not allow us to recognise otherness. On the contrary, we gladly run from same to same in order to forget our difference from ourselves. We forget it through being part of a crowd and through the love of our neighbour, preached by Christianity, which set so much store on this similarity. But is it really so certain that we love our fellow beings?

For Levinas, the discovery of alterity – the face of our fellow being – is made in the name of a divine transcendence, a big Other who is present at the face-to-face with the fellow being. This recognition of others has an impact on the one who makes it, and the awakening of consciousness is the 'first movement toward the other, the traumatism of which is revealed in the Intersubjective Reduction, a traumatism secretly striking the very subjectivity of the subject'.[48] But we no more know where this trauma comes from than we understand what pushes us to confront it, if not an ethical choice of mysterious origin.

The nature of this trauma becomes clear if we relate it to the sexual trauma of early childhood and then to its erotic consequences in adulthood and, finally, to its consequences in the relation to difference, which is based on the difference of the sexes. The fellow being no doubt pre-existed this moment of violence but only as the other of narcissism with whom one can amuse oneself, enjoy a little or a lot and then fall back into oneself until the moment when the solitude of childhood is broken. One day, the subject learns what otherness means, taught forcibly by the encounter with sex in a kind of violence where the third party is a part of the subject's intimacy.

The difference of the sexes imposes the experience of a formidable otherness – that which each of us maintains first of all with ourselves. It is not simply that 'man' has to discover 'woman' and vice-versa. What is at stake for each of us is castration, bisexuality and the existence of the feminine.[49] But this conflictual recognition of the other sex remains correlative to the affirmation of gender. And otherness will be discovered in a quite different dimension as soon as erotism is actualised in the games of love.

The presence of a third party is always implicit in love, at the same time as the demand for exclusivity. It is by counting to three that the 'us two' of the couple can be constituted. Love brings sex out of its anonymity; it forces a choice *against* a third party, and enjoyment takes on another meaning by bringing prohibition into play. This is how the narcissistic relationship of autoerotism, always capable of reducing the two to one, is broken. The exclusion of the third person is how alterity appears at the heart of the couple, and it is never revealed so well as when there is a rivalry that ends in defeat. This present trauma recalls those of the past and actualises the fantasies which they gave rise to. To see a rival victorious is to confront something like a primal scene, and the suffering of this defeat puts us in mind of and makes us understand the seduction suffered in childhood. The adolescent only recognises this when he or she sees someone who resembles them falling prey to this same seduction. In the *Studies in Hysteria*, it is when Katarina sees what her father is doing with a girl her own age that she falls ill because it is then that she remembers how her father tried to do the same thing with her in the past when she did not understand what he wanted.

Most often, the father of the sexual trauma, he who has been thought of at least once in a daydream as a potential rapist, imprints a subjective trauma when nothing has actually happened. It is the father's love itself that engenders the reverie, but its sexual consequence is unbearable; it demands revenge for the very enjoyment it provokes – the enjoyment that ought not to be. Consciousness is unaware of this conjunction of love and hate until it is directly presented: when, without purposely meaning to, a fellow being reveals this suffering, which is also an enjoyment. Confronted with the victory of the rival (male or female), his or her enjoyment – the enjoyment that should not be – is imagined, and copulation ceases to have the comic dimension that it had when the child was told about it. It is because, before the subject's own eyes, it is another who experiences enjoyment, and because this enjoyment that the subject covets traumatises, that the subject suddenly grasps what the relationship to the other sex signifies. This suffering seizes the subject quite suddenly, without their understanding it, except that it takes them back to their childhood, where this obscure seduction, the effects of which they feel today, occurred.

Otherness is only discovered after learning to count to three, and even when the context is not unhappy, love's demand for exclusivity nonetheless programmes a script for three $(2-1 = 3)$, which rekindles the Oedipal drama all the more vividly when the excluded third party is a person with whom one can identify. Through this transitivism, the trauma becomes pleasurable, to the point that betrayal is sometimes sought for its own sake and to the point of creating delicious suffering, often dwelt on for years afterwards. Remembering the trauma is the latent content of any form of jealousy. It exteriorises castration – i.e., the anxiety of feminization – which is the central motif of difference, of otherness.

The 'primal scene', which involves three characters, is an internal event first of all; another person is introduced in order to represent this violent moment when the enjoying body separates for a moment from itself. At the same time as a woman reaches orgasm, the orgasm happens to someone other than herself. And orgasm only happens for a man through the woman that he risked becoming and whom he rejects into the one he loves. This staging of sexual love reveals a third person; separated from the incestuous dimension, this third person *is distinct from the father*. It is an otherness born at a far remove from him and that gives rise to the relationship to the fellow being, to otherness.

The 'third person', central to jealousy, is born from the internal division of enjoyment. Each erotic partner is in some sense already coupled and, therefore, carries this third person with them. Jealousy 'makes a scene' in the literal sense; it constructs otherness, which colonises orgastic impersonality in advance. Otherness is thus what the encounter with the other sex reveals in more than one sense. Each of us, in our relationship to erotism, differs first of all from ourselves. And the lover then duplicates him- or herself with a third presence in relation to the one they love. The man presents beyond himself that which, from the death of the father, engages him in the sexual act. The woman divides herself between herself and the other woman – the woman who would kill her or prevent her from enjoying if she was equal to her. Sexual enjoyment imposes this recognition of difference, a recognition that is almost unbearable and immediately concealed, because it is too strange that the same person can be both him- or herself and somebody else. The division of the body by its own enjoyment gives rise to an otherness where each person in the couple is divided by the encounter with the other. On the feminine side as on the masculine side, the third emerges from the two. The 'third' person brings out the otherness of the woman, while on the masculine side, the death wish and its predictable punishment rid the man of the paternal figure.

The otherness just described seems to be limited to the narrow sphere of private life. What could be more intimate since such otherness does not even concern all of our loved ones but only the (often unique) person with whom each lover generates this third – this effective but inscrutable presence? This is a definition of otherness that bears no resemblance to current conceptions. What then of all the people we encounter without the slightest erotism? Does the question of otherness not arise with them? Do we only recognise them vaguely, as scenery in the world through which we move? Yet the third party who emerges from the most intimate part of sexuality is anonymous. It is nobody and then it is anybody – the Person with a capital 'P'. Any woman potentially incarnates the other woman; the clothing and manner of that other woman might then be passed on from one person to another. Any man carries within him the war of the son against the father – the conflict that the political edifice of brothers is based on. Any woman can split into a multitude of women. And this otherness gradually contaminates the millions of our fellow human beings. They become linked to the secret of our erotism, which remains as foreign to us as they are foreign to us. When we hate them for no reason, we attribute to them our own foreignness to ourselves.

The relation between the sexes produces this ternarity, the 'third' term of which is not one person more who could be added to the relation of one to two. The third is unequal to the one and the two, who, without it, would collapse back into each other. An infinite third assists this strange relationship. It gradually infects the totality of humans, none of whom can be excepted. Whenever our gaze settles on a fellow being, he or she falls under the scope of our own division and thus into the field of our sexual obsession. We take shelter from this fellow being. No doubt, he or she has no truck with us, but we do not forget them when we close the door behind which we experience this strangeness to ourselves.

Notes

1 Antoine Parmentier was keen to introduce the cultivation and consumption in France of potatoes, but his enthusiasm was not shared by society. He overcame the prejudice by putting fences and guards around his fields. Potatoes then became desirable because they were forbidden.

2 In some countries where polygamy is the norm, it is forbidden to cheat on your wives, etc.

3 Gilles Deleuze [1968], *Difference and Repetition* (P. Patton, trans.). New York: Columbia University Press, 1994, p.119.

4 The *Moira* is, for example, the hallucinatory flash by which a hysterical seizure brings to life a scene from the past in the scene which is unfolding in the present.

5 See: Thomas Mann [1912], *Death in Venice* (C. Koelb, trans.). New York: Norton, 1994.

6 See: Bernard Baas, *Le pur désir. Parcours philosophiques dans les parages de J. Lacan.* Louvain: Peeters, 1992.

7 'This marks – more than it reveals –the true function of the Father, which is fundamentally to unite (and not to oppose) a desire to the Law' (Lacan, 'The Subversion of the Subject and the Dialectic of Desire' in *Écrits* (B. Fink, trans.). New York: Norton, 2006, p. 698).

8 As in the opera *Don Giovanni* (the Mozart/Da Ponte version of the Don Juan story).

9 As Madame Guyon wrote in a letter to Bossuet: 'Desire in God no longer has the vivacity of a desire in love, which does not enjoy what it desires, but it has the repose of desire that is fulfilled and satisfied' (translated from: Catherine Millot, *La vie parfaite. Jeanne Guyon, Simone Weil, Etty Hillesu.* Paris: Gallimard, 2006, p. 99).

10 If, in admiration of a father who seduces him, a boy tries to seduce a girl, whom he invests with what he was for his father, he will not be rid of his anxiety about feminisation.

11 This is why 'wanting one's own desire' – a wish that can signal the end of an analysis – is such a difficult thing to do since it a question of freeing oneself from a guilt that is internal to desiring, a guilt quite different from that linked to an external prohibition (social or familial) which one has to transgress.

12 We will see that what remains unsatisfied at the very heart of satisfaction forms the kernel of the 'actual neurosis', which is never sated. At the heart of the greatest erotic happiness, sexual excitement carries this opacity, this internal core that nothing can pacify.

13 Lifting inhibition, calming anxiety or providing intoxication are not the only motives for taking psychotropic drugs. The self-destructive act fascinates in itself, as an incestuous extremity of desire, while at the same time bringing liberation from that extremity: the harm and the remedy in a single gesture.

14 Intense silent prayer brings them to 'transverberation' – the specific term, which is used to describe their experience and which expresses so well their penetration by the Word.

15 Freud often uses a specific word – '*Entlastung*' (literally 'unburdening/unloading') – to express the concept of discharge (Freud [1905], *Three Essays on the Theory of Sexuality* in *Standard Edition 7*, p. 210).

16 'The former may be suitably described as "fore-pleasure" in contrast to the "end-pleasure" or pleasure of satisfaction derived from the sexual act. Fore-pleasure is thus the same pleasure that has already been produced, although on a smaller scale, by the infantile sexual instinct; end-pleasure is something new and is thus probably conditioned by circumstances that do not arise until puberty. The formula for the new function of the erogenous zones could therefore be stated as follows: they are intended to make possible, thanks to the preliminary pleasure which, as in infantile life, can be derived from them, the production of the greater pleasure of satisfaction' (*Ibid.*, pp. 210–211). 'This last pleasure is the highest in intensity, and its mechanism differs from that of the earlier pleasure. It is brought about entirely by discharge: it is wholly a pleasure of satisfaction and with it the tension of the libido is for the time being extinguished' (*Ibid.*, pp. 210).

17 The hero of Goethe's tragedy, *Faust*, says in the 'Forest and Cave' scene: 'I reel between desire and enjoyment, and in enjoyment languish for desire' (Johann Wolfgang von Goethe, *Faust I & II* (S. Atkins, trans.). Princeton, NJ: Princeton University Press, 2014). The Faust character is the perfect illustration of a transgression which prolongs a desire that is itself an enjoyment and, therefore, is not linked to orgasm (and even less to reproduction).

18 True to Aristotle's logic, consciousness does not admit contradiction.
19 A boy, for example, will prefer to hate his father as if he had been tortured by him rather than recognise the risk of his own feminisation by him (see: Franz Kafka, *Letter to the Father*. New York: Schocken Books, 1966).
20 Thus, for example, a little girl who has been molested by a stranger might be ashamed to complain about it to her parents.
21 Flight from a bourgeois father will be actualised, for example, by the seduction of a social misfit. The young man whose mother was a cook will be aroused by the sound of pots and pans, etc.
22 For example, as we have seen, a woman who has been disappointed by a man may switch from heterosexuality to homosexuality; she will behave towards a woman as the man ought to have behaved towards her.
23 Leo Tolstoy [1859], *Family Happiness and Other Stories*. Minneola, NY: Dover, 2005, pp. 1–66.
24 When, for example, a lover's enthusiasm is suddenly horrifying: Prince Charming turns into a toad more often than the reverse.
25 See Wong Kar-wai's film *In the Mood for Love* (2000).
26 If, for example, a man falls in love with a woman who has the same look as a friend (a boy) from his early childhood. A family man of 50 may abandon everything and leave home when his son of 20 is about to do so, reliving through the son what he would have liked to have done at his age; the man repeats, but he is completely unaware of this. He could not have replayed this scenario earlier, and his experience is of no use to him. Similarly, a woman may attach herself to a man less for what he is than for his race, his religion, an accident, a real or supposed misfortune, a divorce, etc.
27 We will see that this is ultimately a relationship to the name.
28 Plato, *Phaedrus* (H. Fowler, trans.). Cambridge, MA: Harvard University Press, 1925, 227c.
29 'So he is in love, but he knows not with whom; he does not understand his own condition and cannot explain it; like one who has caught a disease of the eyes from another, he can give no reason for it; he sees himself in his lover as in a mirror, but is not conscious of the fact. And in the lover's presence, like him he ceases from his pain, and in his absence, like him he is filled with yearning such as he inspires, and love's image, requited love' ['anteros', more literally 'counter-love' (translator's note)], dwells within him' (*Ibid.*, 255d.).
30 As Freud writes in *Mourning and Melancholia*, the melancholic 'knows *whom* he has lost but not *what* he has lost in him', which would be the object of the fantasy (Freud [1917], *Standard Edition 14*, p. 245).
31 As Freud suggests when describing the cotton-reel game played by his grandson (Freud [1920], *Beyond the Pleasure Principle* in *Standard Edition 18*, pp. 14–16), the child does not merely play with objects because he has been abandoned; he exogamically 'marries' the reel, and this offers him relief because he thereby moves from the passive position of being his mother's reel to an active position. He lets go of the Thing in favour of things.
32 This lack of interest has no structural implication; it does not decide whether the subject will be on the side of psychosis, neurosis or perversion.
33 'If a man has been his mother's undisputed darling he retains throughout life the triumphant feeling, the confidence in success, which not seldom brings actual success along with it' (Freud [1917], *A Childhood Recollection from Dichtung und Wahrheit* in *Standard Edition 17*, p. 161).
34 This universal fact established by anthropology is not a law but a consequence of sexual trauma, from which each generation strives to spare the next generation. Totemism, as a consequence of parricide, also assumes its universal value due to this psychic reality (*pace* Lévi-Strauss).

35 'I will write the following sentence: "Jouissance [enjoyment] of the Other", of the Other with a capital O, "of the body of the Other who symbolizes the Other, is not the sign of love" ' (Lacan, *Encore*, *Seminar 20* (J.-A. Miller, ed., B. Fink, trans.). New York: Norton, 1998, p. 4).

36 If we want to relate this process to castration, anxiety concerning maternal castration generates a debt that pulls the subject backwards and prevents him/her from acting; it pulls them towards drive-based regression. Maternal love makes it possible to overcome this retrograde force. The greater this love, the more strength will accrue to the action.

37 The distinction between the love and the desire of the other means that we must differentiate the sources of anxiety. There is an anxiety that corresponds to the installation of structure, but there is also another form of anxiety that results from lack of love, entailing a lack of exogamous pressure [French, 'pression'] of libido and of action. It is perhaps the only acceptable definition of 'de-pression' [French, 'dépression'].

38 We may note here an amusing dimension of the split between love and desire: the theoreticians of the major currents of psychoanalysis (i.e., the IPA and the Lacanians) have emphasised either love or desire. Many Anglo-Saxon authors have emphatically chosen the side of love (the 'good-enough' mother or the 'rejecting' mother, symbiosis, holding, etc.). Ferenczi, Winnicott and most of the Anglo-Saxons neglect the implacable and structuring aspects of desire. By contrast, the Lacanians insist on desire, often neglecting or reducing love to narcissism or to the imaginary.

39 Freud [1905], *Fragment of an Analysis of a Case of Hysteria* in *Standard Edition 7*, p. 50.

40 i.e., identification with the maternal phallus, the lack of the Other.

41 'le moi', literally 'the me' [translator's note].

42 'Not to know hatred in the least is not to know love in any way either' (Lacan, *Encore*, *Seminar XX* (J.-A. Miller, ed., B. Fink, trans.). New York: Norton, 1998, p. 89).

43 'Only an hour after that woman had entered my room, I had thrown my life away and was running amok, careering into empty space' (Stefan Zweig, *Amok*. London: Pushkin Press, 2017).

44 'This sexual overvaluation is the origin of the peculiar state of being in love, a state suggestive of a neurotic compulsion, which is thus traceable to an impoverishment of the ego as regards libido in favour of the love-object' (Freud [1914], *On Narcissism: An Introduction* in *Standard Edition 14*, p. 88).

45 'The subject who is seized by passion appears to his own eyes and to those of others as dispossessed of himself, no longer having control over either his thoughts or his acts' (translated from: Roland Gori, *Logique des passions*. Paris: Flammarion, 2005, p. 32).

46 That is not to contradict Lacan, who proposed that the only successful act was suicide. On the contrary, it emphasises that love and suicide have some features in common (echoing Freud's view that narcissism may collapse as a consequence of love).

47 This is surely the experience that Lacan was alluding to in the May 8, 1957, session of the seminar: 'Everything indicates that this *thou* is the limit signifier. [. . .] This Other is already within us in the form of the unconscious, but nothing can be accomplished in our development if not through this constellation that implies the absolute Other as the seat of speech' (Lacan, *The Object Relation, Seminar 4*. Cambridge: Polity, 2020, p. 363).

48 Emmanuel Levinas [1991], *Entre Nous, Thinking-of-the-Other* (M. Smith, B. Harshav, trans.). New York: Columbia University Press, 1998, p. 88.

49 It goes without saying that homosexuality does not invalidate this recognition of otherness.

Chapter 7

From perversion to neurotic perversity

Perversions

The word 'perversion' started out with the simple meaning of a sexuality that does not correspond to the laws of nature. And yet this was applied first of all by psychoanalysts to the sexuality of the child, which has no connection with genitality or reproduction, and then also to adult sexuality which is built on that of the child. What is 'sexual' for the child are the drives, which push the body to identify with the maternal phallus. This eroticises the body from the outside and immediately shapes a sexuality that is indeed 'unnatural' and that deserves the label of perversion; if erotisation depends initially on the destiny of the drives, it loses all relationship with genitality and reproduction. This, at least, is what is shown by the multitude of perversions which, using drive objects such as the gaze, the voice, excrement, fetishes, etc., achieve a complete sexual discharge without any thought for genitality and even less for reproduction. The purpose of the drives is to identify the body with the phallus. But since this phallus has no consistency in itself, this goal falls back on the drive so that the latter takes over the copulatory value of the phallus, with no other support than itself and, in this sense, is autoerotic.

The existence of a 'polymorphous perversion' in the child dedramatises perversion as such. By showing this source of perversion, Freud removed the forensic cloak by which it had been covered by Krafft-Ebing, among others. Far from being pathological, this childhood perversion is a necessary passage that maintains its prerogatives for life. And far from ratifying the morbid classifications of perversions, facts considered abnormal are integrated into the cruise mode of normal eroticism, which is constructed with or against them. And yet even today, perversion retains a pejorative, if not criminal meaning, even though most perversions are harmless. But then why should we see the diabolical side of desire as innocent? We would do better to acknowledge that it will be present in any kind of structure. Still, the assertion that innocent toddlers deserve to be called 'polymorphous perverts' requires explanation, and the explanations given to date have not gone down well.[1] This is something that has to be reflected upon several times before one starts to understand – and then forgets – before finally having some insight into a strange area of sexuality that most people would prefer to remain ignorant of.

DOI: 10.4324/9781003519287-7

For we are not 'subjects' on the one hand and 'sexed' on the other. We are quite simply 'sexed subjects', and our cognitive capacities go no further than our modes of enjoyment. Once certain choices have been made, they are so firmly attached to our identity that we believe we were born that way, with a gender, feelings and tastes that are our 'nature'. It is indeed true that they become our nature once these choices have been made. But it happens that we suffer, sometimes seriously, from forgetting what made us become what we think we are. We made a choice and then we acted as if we had had nothing to do with this choice, dreaming of an innocence that is in fact highly perverse. So what is so resistant to understanding that psychoanalysts themselves (human beings, after all) constantly put it in question? To begin with, how are we to understand the 'primacy of the phallus'? Why is it said to be the only symbol? Because as we have seen, children are, to begin with, the phallus of their mother, who desired to have a child because of her *Penisneid*. Their mother has a phallus because the child is that phallus! This belief, which denies castration and is, therefore, perverse, is deeply rooted and has significant effects throughout our lives. It is a split belief: knowledge of the anatomical reality changes almost nothing, although it adds to the perplexity. Nor is much changed by the fact that this split aestheticises the glory of the female body, which structures our experience of space and time.

It is worth reviewing once again the background here that we have already described in order to emphasise its 'perverse' potentialities. The *denial of maternal castration* (the axiom of perversion) is, in a way, a necessity of existence, but it also pushes towards enjoyment of the organ in order for the subject to Have the phallus rather than to Be it. All forms of active masturbation seek to demonstrate this 'having', and they offer liberation from a passive alienation in the maternal Other. The enjoyment of the Other inevitably goes too far; the second gulp of the mother's milk is already almost enough and the excess seeks discharge, but its own pleasure-induced passivity blocks it and the task is modified into that of becoming the agent of this inevitable excess, becoming the active party, which can be achieved through the onanistic grasp of a part of one's own body. This active masturbation begins as a play with the drives, which are thus earmarked from the outset for perverse pleasure. But as we have said, this liberation generates intense guilt, which requires punishment for its relief. So that every child, from very early on, seeks to be punished, giving to masochism its original sexual inflection.[2] To be punished, to suffer, is a source of enjoyment. This is how sadomasochism becomes the formal envelope of the perversions and, ultimately, of erotism as such.

This brief reminder of how the subject enters into enjoyment of the phallic organ brings out the key elements of perversion. We will first define its formal envelope (sadomasochism), then its means of actualisation (the drives) and, finally, its goal or what one might call its 'keystone' (the fetish).

1   The entry into phallicism occurs under the aegis of a punishment that the child, driven by guilt linked to the anxiety at maternal castration, actively seeks. In

order to keep maternal love, the child gives the father the role of punisher, but (and this is the key difference) the father may be disqualified from this role by the mother, thereby creating a future dividing line between neurosis and perversion as such; in the latter, it is the woman as the angel of punishment wielding the riding crop who is centre stage. Punishment is necessary, but its agent is contingent; the role of (mythical) punisher is not always taken by a father.

Later on, in a reversal of this initial masochism into sadism, the accounts with this ghost will be settled on the back of an *alter ego*, with whom the initial scene is repeated. The subject strives to make this *alter ego* undergo actively everything that he or she previously underwent passively, enacting this repetition with a fellow being who must be forced to change places.[3] So the reversal is *transgressive*, and any transgression can bring enjoyment. This use of the other follows from drive alienation; in all perversions, a mute violence, even when it is consensual, is a precondition for the formation of a couple (a voyeur must exercise some kind of violence, as must an exhibitionist, etc.). This violence will always be present, even when it is muffled or regulated by a contract.[4]

2   Perversions are actualised by the drives. It is a fact that some subjects can achieve full enjoyment using objects, artifices or situations that have nothing to do with coupling between human beings. That a partial drive – the gaze, excrement, the voice, etc. – can provide sexual enjoyment is incomprehensible if we forget that the purpose of the drive is to identify the body with the phallus, and that, as a consequence, if this drive is redirected in order to instrumentalise a fellow being, this will cause erection. The catalogue of perversions[5] is a list of the enjoyment of various drives, the goal of which – the denial of maternal castration – only appears in their paradoxical result, which is erection.

To instrumentalise an *alter ego* is to take another self as support for this relieving actualisation. When the drive fails in its purpose using one's own body, it seeks to possess a body that resembles it. What we have here is not an additional drive but rather, the fact that each drive seeks to take hold of another body as soon as it misses its goal on one's own body. It may, for example, seize on a playmate, on whom perverse polymorphism exercises its (generally innocent) talents. Perversion would lack visibility and meaning if it did not seek to satisfy itself on a fellow being. All the drives can redirect themselves towards another body (I). And since, at the same moment, the drive excess engenders excitation of the penis or clitoris (II), this capture is accompanied by phallic excitation (I) + (II). Seizing hold of – violence as such – is accompanied by sexual arousal. How else are we to understand the fact that sadism and masochism, voyeurism and exhibitionism can have an erectile consequence?

The 'seizing onto' doubles the destiny of each drive, or rather, it redoubles it by means of creating a couple, a process that occurs at the very point where the drive misses its goal. If the drive reached that goal, the subject would be annihilated (by identification with the phallus). For this reason, the death drive haunts the field of 'seizing onto' or 'possessing', giving perversions the morbid intoxication that makes them potentially dangerous and not so far removed from drug-induced impersonalisation. The autoerotism for two of the perversions sta-bilises phallic signification through a kind of complementarity: the sadist seeks his whipping boy, the exhibitionist seeks the person he will surprise, etc. It is never the masochist who seeks out the sadist or the voyeur the exhibitionist, etc. The transfusion of the drive from one body to another depends on the use of force. It leaves itself behind on one side to appear on the other side but can only do so on condition of a violence. The two poles of the drive that habitually alternate for the same subject, oscillating between being and nothingness, are divided here between two subjects, one of whom forces the other to take upon themselves the first's share of nothingness.

The reversal of the drive to possess transforms the masochist into a sadist through an intermediary, while the masochist himself is eclipsed as a subject at the time of the painful ritual. Even more instructive is the reversal that occurs for the voyeur, who experiences enjoyment at the moment when he is caught looking; in this case, the consequence of the passage from drive passivity to activity is immediate in the form of an erection. There could be no clearer dem-onstration that drive excess (Being) is relieved thanks to the opportunity offered by enjoyment of the organ (Having). No special drive corresponds to erection, and one wonders how the gaze connects to the penis, which never fails to erect on these occasions. The connection happens because the prime goal of drive energy is the phallic fetishisation of the body. This is their excess. So relief from the excess is obtained by conversion of the phallic body into an erect penis. The excitation of the penis corresponds to the passage from 'passively being' the phallus (the whole body) to 'actively being' it (the penis only) but now as an erection, conditional on a change in the vectorisation of the gaze. The subject who 'was' now 'has' by putting the other in their place. This reversal comes with a moment of impersonalisation because the subject exchanges their place for that of the victim, the other. This impersonalisation means that no one did anything; it just happened.

To describe this enjoyment of the pervert as 'pleasure' is not quite accurate because the feeling of compulsion is so strong. This 'pleasure' is intense, forced and depersonalising; its effect is to liberate rather than to provide enjoyment. The subject to whom it occurs often wants to change their ways; they promise themselves that this time will be the last. But this pretence is part of the pleasure. The subject is unable to master this force, which produces the restricted repeti-tion of a violent pleasure felt in childhood, fixed in memory and then reiterated in a pattern not dissimilar to the repetition of war traumas. The action takes place in spite of its agent, who will sometimes feel that the fault lies with the victim. And the victim often feels guilty as well, as if they were the cause of what happened.[6] This impersonality of perverse drive discharge contrasts with the subjectivity of erotism, and this results from the lack of the requirement of one specific person and no other.[7]

This enjoyment is not obtained thanks to the enjoyment of the partner (as in neurotic orgasm) but is carried out against them by doing violence to them (or a

semblance of violence, if the partner is consenting).[8] The enjoyment is liberating due mainly to the transitivism of the relation. The object (the partner) must
be transformed forcibly into the subject that one risked becoming, and this is
to be done by surprise, in spite of the partner, and in this sense, it is an infraction – against consent, with which neurosis, in contrast, is satisfied. The pleasure is accessed to the rhythm of transgression. The prohibitions that exist at a
particular time and place are to be defied; conformity and social norms are to be
opposed, and that includes the norms of persecuted groups, which approve the
exploration of 'deviant' practices such as group love, homosexuality, bisexuality, etc. Relieved of the torments of love, this extension of the limits of prohibition offers the benefits of an undeniable freedom in pleasure.[9]

But due to its impersonality, this relief of drive tension cannot rid the person of the pain of their existence because it does not legitimise their name, as
erotism is able to do. A perversion does not require any recognition and works
with a multiplicity of partners; all that counts is their annihilation at the moment
of the exchange of places. In this autoerotism for two, the partner is taken as
the pure object of the actualisation. This annihilation of the partner's subjectivity is part of the enjoyment or even the whole of it. Perverse assassination, as
portrayed in the murderous scenes coordinated with orgasm that are described
by the Marquis de Sade, is a (fortunately rare) form of this depersonalisation.
This impersonal neutrality – 'apathy' as Sade would have called it[10] – explains
the fascination that perversion holds, which is exalted to a sort of ideal by some
neurotics.[11]

3 The fetish represents a sort of keystone of the perversions; each seeks complete
   sexual satisfaction thanks to a drive *object*. But since the *goal* of each drive is to
   identify the body with the maternal phallus, and since the fetish symbolises this
   goal, it represents a sort of objective (at least virtual). It gives visible form to the
   denial of maternal castration, whereas the other perversions hide their aim; the
   sexual excitement that an isolated drive is able to provoke remains a true mystery since its phallic motivation remains latent and only appears in its result: an
   erection, which, once again, is the real enigma that denaturalises sex.

This fetishism has a real theoretical significance since it demonstrates retroactively
the importance of the phallus as the sole sexual symbol in the first periods of life.[12]
There is nothing in the initial mother-child relationship that can demonstrate this
role since the child him- or herself is too young to say anything about it. This pri-
mordial role of the phallus can only be assessed by its consequences; if perverts use
fetishes, representatives of the maternal phallus, the absence of which they deny,
it is because they originally *were* the phallus for their mother. The use of a fetish
shifts the phallic investment of Being onto this object, whereby the fetishist's interlocutor can Have it. So the recourse to the fetish triggers an erection.

Why does a fetish excite? Not because of its use value but because of its
exchange value.[13] It is an object invested by reminiscences, especially if it has
served in the past to adorn the mother's body image and thus symbolise a lack.

The mother wore jewels, hats, gloves, etc., to order to entice, to provoke in men the erection of what she did not have, and so these symbols were suffused with desire and took on the value of the phallus, which she still did not have. The fetish functions as an ersatz of the maternal phallus and denies her castration; on the one hand, it masks it, while on the other hand, it acknowledges it. A screen both hides and shows. In reality, the fetish itself would be nothing were it not for the promise of an erection. Between being and nothingness, this dynamic makes it exciting. It is a border crossing, a contraband the efficiency of which comes from how it is imposed; a shoe, for example, has nothing erotic in itself, but when a woman is asked to put it on, this constraint feminises her, while her partner tries to become masculine through his act of domination. This violent transition from the use value of the shoe to its exchange value is what gives it erotic power.

Fetishism, like other perverse pleasures, achieves enjoyment without fantasy thanks to a scenario that involves a forced exchange of places. It reiterates the entry into phallicism; a subject who has been the mother's phallus elects a fetish, which symbolises this phallus, and imposes it on somebody else so that the first subject no longer is the phallus but has it. This liberation creates an intense but illicit pleasure, which is deliciously guilty, and the woman solicited to help carry out this little scene might then administer a light (or not so light) spanking to her playmate, perhaps with a riding crop, which may then itself become a fetish object (or even function as the sole fetish). The punishment can vary, from insults to beatings or be limited to a moral reproach, and this introduces a second discharge of tension, that of guilt. The ensemble might then be crowned with an ejaculation, a high point of pleasure which is also its endpoint. This finale is equal in intensity to orgasm but without involving the dimension of subjectivity and the relationship to the name. The result here is certainly comparable to those that would mitigate the contradictions inherent to fantasy. If they were to be listed on the stock exchange of Eros, perverse pleasures would undoubtedly be valued as more practical and easier to manage than the pleasures of love. But apart from the fact that they require a special aptitude, they leave crucial matters – such as subjectivity – unresolved. Matters of subjectivity are best treated through sexual love but not without bathos and pathos, which make the guilt-ridden neurotic a difficult partner.

True perversion

The passage from childhood to adolescence modifies the place of enjoyment for neurotics. Seeking to 'have the phallus', the denial of castration is now filtered through the relation to the sexual other, from whom this phallus is expected. This displacement of the phallic quest to the zone between masculine and the feminine (of which parricide is the condition) entails repression of the 'polymorphous perversion' of the child. What remains is an ordinary perversity which underpins neurosis. It is distinct from genuine perversion, which involves the monomaniacal activity of an adult, characterised by complete discharge of pleasure with ejaculation and without any help other than that of a partial drive (the gaze, excrement, blows, etc.) or a fetish. What might function as a preliminary condition in neurosis serves as an end in perversion, which is defined by this complete discharge thanks only to partial objects. Such a pleasure that goes directly to discharge does not exist in the polymorphous perversions of the child nor in neurotic perversity. Perversion as such results from fixation of the modalities of infantile sexuality, whether it be drive enjoyment, transitivist identification (perverse homosexuality)[14] or the taking of a child as sexual object like the child the person once was (paedophilia).

Contrary to neurotic sexuality, which runs on the fuel of fantasy and, therefore, depends on subjectivity, perversion is regulated by the objectivity of the drive in a circuit that doesn't break down or misfire. What could be more practical, for example, than a fetish? One wonders, indeed, why the polymorphous perversion of the child should ever pass to the more complex territory of genitality. But one wonders, too, why, in certain cases, the polymorphous perversion of the child is continued as adult perversion. Is this a simple extension of infantile sexuality? Yes, from the point of view of the relation to the object, but no, from the point of view of the sexual goal. If we consider drive pleasure and the object it brings into play (fetish, gaze, voice, capture, etc.), it remains identical to that which once fixated a traumatic pleasure. But the subject has grown up since the moment of psychical shock, and the sexual goal has been considerably modified. In childhood, the sexual goal offered relief along elliptical lines, so faint as to be hardly perceptible – pushing and shoving, blows, a few sexual games, touching, rather than outright masturbation. Adults saw nothing untoward: who would have thought that these innocent games had sexual goals? The qualitative leap from childish perversions to adult perversion reflects a complete change of the sexual goal; now discharge is the priority. This goal resembles that of genitality, from which it nevertheless differs, because autoerotism can only win freedom by force; it takes everything and gives nothing. If the goal now calls for penetration, this must involve a violation, or at least a verbal one. For a paedophile, for example, the object remains the same. It is the child he once was. So to begin with, he will content himself with touching a child who resembles himself as a child. But since the sexual goal has changed, penetration will later give another dramatic form to this violation.

The fixation to a scene from childhood is repeated according to a transitive autoerotic pattern, to which the partner must not consent. The partner must be forced, even if they do in fact consent. And this consensual rape is sometimes institutionalised by the signing of a contract. The purpose of such a contract is not to ape the law; it is a means of obeying a past scenario, of putting oneself at a distance and imposing a certain mechanical impersonality, which makes it possible to enjoy, at least from afar. Perversion is a kind of slavery to which the pervert must submit (with the apathy dear to Sade), as if to say, 'This is how things have been arranged. It's the routine'.

Count Sacher-Masoch, who gave his name to masochism, made his companions sign such contracts which imposed, in certain circumstances, the repetition of a scene from his childhood when he was given a beating. His memory of the scene was as follows: one Sunday afternoon, as he was playing hide and seek with other children, the young Sacher had hidden in the cupboard of an attic room. One of his aunts, the Countess Zenobia, a strong-willed beauty, entered the room followed by her lover, with whom she immediately gave herself to the pleasures of the flesh. As this was going on, her husband pushed open the door, but far from avenging his offended honour, he received a hail of blows from Zenobia. What is more, the wretched man seemed to derive pleasure from his chastisement, stammering incomprehensible phrases between tears and supplications. Finally, the young Sacher was discovered in his hiding place and also subjected to a beating, pinned to the ground under the heel of the Countess, in which position he experienced sexual enjoyment for the first time in his life.[15]

Did this single burst of pleasure alone fix the scenario of its future repetitions? We must add to it the latent spectacle of a husband humiliated by his wife. This context determines the fixation; Oedipal confrontation with such a father loses all its meaning because the parricide has already been carried out, not by the child but by a mother figure. The mother (identified here with masculine power by the violence which she administers) steals from the son the final act of the Oedipus complex – the murder of the father on which 'neurotic' genital assumption depends. The father who should have been confronted has disappeared! Genuine perversion imposes itself in this devaluation of one of the paternal functions, which may be broken down by the mother. Such a devaluation may mean that fantasies remain in their dormant state, the state they were in during childhood, prolonging polymorphous perversion. Fantasies will lack the parricidal dimension, which they take on for neurotics in adolescence. For the latter, the confrontation with the father is the necessary and sufficient test which allows them to move from the polymorphous perversion of childhood to the neurotic regime of the adult. Parricide introduces a new regime of enjoyment; guilt represses the drives and, therefore, also represses perversion, which will continue to appear in the return of the repressed that is neurotic perversity.

This paradigm of perversion is even more striking in the case of Sacher-Masoch in the fact that at birth, he did not receive his father's name but that of his mother's father, and this in order to perpetuate the lineage of his grandparents which was threatened with extinction.[16] Enamoured of a woman of noble lineage, the commoner father accepted that his son would bear the name of his wife's father, a condition that he had to accept if he wanted to marry her. In this sense, the father of Sacher-Masoch was deeply humiliated – humiliated to the point of the extinction of his name. In the scene of fixation, it is Zenobia, this mother-by-proxy, who 'kills the father' instead of the deed being done by the son. The son remains at a distance from the act that he needed to commit and that he should have committed. And it is in this distance that the pleasure is subsequently repeated; he enjoys the sexual rapport *from the outside*, for which he is at the same instant punished, like his father, with whom he identifies in being beaten. Punishment thus becomes in adulthood a contractually guaranteed right. To be beaten and degraded like the father is, in the very last extreme, to take, if not his place, at least his posture, and, therefore, in this limited sense, to kill him. This second-order parricide gives the punishment its orgastic outcome.

Perversion is indeed in this sense a 'version towards the father'[17] as Lacan said. But it is an inverted version towards the father in comparison with neurosis. In neurosis, it is the 'perversion' of the father (his role as punisher) which triggers the series of neurotic fantasies that go as far as parricide. In contrast, in perversion, the subject constructs the 'version' towards the father from scratch because he lacks a 'father for killing', his mother having done the work for him and right in front of him. His only expedient may be to identify with her in various scenarios, to result perhaps in some forms of homosexuality or paedophilia or indeed the various montages designed to support a father as ferocious as he ought to have been in order to merit execution.[18]

Paedophilia, an avatar of the desire 'for' a child

Paedophilic acts, especially when they have a dramatic outcome, produce all the more disgust and revulsion because they go to the heart of the child in each of us. Paedophilia, more than any other perversion, shows the neurotic the repression of his or her own perversion. This proximity can be illustrated with the expression 'desire "for" a child' and its equivocations. First of all, there is the ambiguity between desire to have a child and sexual desire for a child, the one not being entirely unrelated to the other.[19] The ambiguity of the expression 'to want a child' lets us develop the dialectic of desire depending on whether it remains incestuous or, on the contrary, represses its sexual dimension. The socially accepted aspect of the 'desire for a child' is to have a child, while its socially reviled aspect is to sexually desire a child. These two aspects are not contradictory. The fact of desiring to have a child does not exclude desiring it sexually, but of course, this wish is generally repressed.

We thus see the complexity of the desire 'for' a child. A child very quickly wants to have a child in order to stop being one. He or she begins by producing fantasy children, either 'oral' or 'anal',[20] in order to make a break with childhood as such.[21] We leave this forgotten child behind us from our very first days in the world; it is our ideal 'self', our guardian angel. This rejected double embodies what we were to have been for our parents: a dream child. And it is this child we remember when we want to procreate. But at the same time, always in the hope of gaining separation from his or her own childhood, a child treats other children as he or she feels themselves to be treated, in a kind of sexual mimicry that is unaware of its goal. For example, the little girl who has been seduced will be seductive with other children, etc. So the 'double desire' of the child functions very early on, and a wish to procreate later will depend on how this has been organised. The wish has three objectives: firstly, to have a child similar to the one we once were; secondly, to have a child *for* the father or *for* the mother, in the sense of a transgenerational debt;[22] and, finally, to have a child with your sexual partner for the sake of love. Only this last case, that of love, represses the incestuous dimension of the desire for a child.

'Making a child' to settle a transgenerational debt follows from the parricide wish, which itself stems from a fantasy of seduction and violation, linking together the two components of the desire 'for' a child. These two components, erotic and procreative, are linked together by paternal castration, which creates sexual desire from scratch but transforms the father into a seducer, running the risk of incest that turns seduction into a desire to commit murder. Love becomes entangled with a death wish, and from this knot, there will arise both sexual desire and the desire to have children. The child, declaring war on the father, is seized by a kind of hypnosis and downs weapons for long enough to be seduced again, then to take up arms again, etc., not without the latent thought of having suffered a violation that paedophilia can repeat in order to relieve it. On the one hand, there is the threat of this desired violation, on the other, the revenge for this violation. An indeterminate fault excites,[23] and the wish for redemption arises from the depth of this sin. How is the forgiveness of this desired father, of the Minotaur always lurking in the depths of the labyrinth, to be obtained if not through the offering of a child who will bear his name? The conferment of the father's name pushes the 'desire to have a child' violently forward – in men but no less powerfully in women, albeit through an intermediary.[24] So the 'desire for a child' (sexual) will thus be repressed in favour of the 'desire for a child' (to have a child) in proportion to the magnitude of the parricide fantasy.

But repression is not abolition, and adults are overwhelmed by infantile fantasies. On the one hand, they repress their own polymorphous perversion so that by defending the innocence of childhood, they reinforce their own repression. On the other hand, sexual issues are always present between adults and children in the form of a transgenerational repetition; 'incestuous desire' remains incomprehensible unless we recognise that a man can play the part with his daughter that he failed to carry through with his own mother, just as a mother can see in her son a man like her own father and seek to seduce him. Transgenerational desire introduces this dizzying change of place which leads a son, when he becomes a father, to have sexual feelings towards his child, not as a father but as the son of his own parents. How else are we to understand that an adult can experience sexual arousal from holding an infant in their arms? In this change of place, which obscures it, incestuous desire invests the child's body by secretly skipping a generation. Eluding the consciousness of the parents, a rejection with all the violence of a murder imposes itself silently, addressed to what is incestuous in their desire for a child.[25] The fight against Thanatos amplifies the love of parents for their child. They must first protect the child from the darkness of their own desires. Each word of love and each gesture of tenderness help to exorcise this dangerous imminence. As the repression of incestuous desire gives way to a desexualised erotisation, the infant's body is eroticised by the parents in 'normal' fashion; this is how their repression in relation to their own parents is transmitted. In this respect, repression is the very transmission of a desexualised erotism, which draws children into desire in a positive way. The child grows with the strength of what the love from its parents and the love between the parents covers over and contains.

What is an adult's sexual desire for a child? When a child who has become an adult desires children similar to the one he or she was, they continue the momentum of their infantile sexuality; the polymorphous perversion of the child is transformed into perversion as such, the latter resulting from fixation of one of the modalities of infantile sexuality, whether it be drive enjoyment (exhibitionism, voyeurism, sadism, etc.) or transitivist identification in the form of loving someone like oneself (in one form of homosexuality) or loving a child similar to the one we once were (paedophilia). The paedophile continues his childhood by seeking in minors the child he once was because the paternal seduction did not push him to the parricide fantasy, therefore, towards guilt, therefore, to the redemptive gift of a child. He continues to haunt his childhood in the absence of the act of blood, which initiates the Oedipus complex and is repeated in adolescence. Paradoxically, he lacks the *subjective* fantasy of being seduced by the father, either because his father really was seductive towards him (when there is a real act, fantasy is cancelled out) or, on the contrary, because his father was completely absent from any erotisation (again, absence of fantasy), leaving him bound hand and foot to contend with his mother, who accomplished the parricide in his place. He will then have to deny the anxiety of maternal castration by various perverse methods.[26] In either case, the weakness of the seduction fantasy will lead to the same result, namely, fixation of infantile perversion and its transformation into adult perversion (which gives it a genital appearance).

The perversion becomes 'adult' by its application to the body of a being like oneself, who is a fantasy of the past. It obtains enjoyment (genitally, like an adult) but does so solely by way of drive preliminaries (like a child). So the adult remains obsessed with the child, keeping the same *object* despite the change of sexual *goal*. This means that whereas the sexual goal of the child is played out in voyeurism, exhibitionism, masturbation (usually no more than touching), the paedophile is not always satisfied with these relatively harmless games. When an adult feels sexual desire for a child, a child disappears; the paedophile starts by identifying himself with the child, whereby he himself disappears. And it is when he is in this depersonalised state that he may kill a child who has already disappeared, who has evaporated in the sexual act itself. An impersonal murder is the orgastic equivalent of this extended incest. If a paedophile kills his victim (fortunately, a rare occurrence), his act strikes the child he once was and does so in a moment of quasi-depersonalisation, taking to an extreme the logic of incest, by which to make love with a parent is to die before you are born. This murderous erotism corresponds to what neurotics repress and exchange for a gesture of protection; every child awakens in each of us the child we once were. No one is indifferent to this presence, and this emotion is at the heart of every normal relationship with a child.

Why is the polymorphous perversion of the child transformed? In adolescence, the demand for exogamous love, the demand for fidelity, and current rivalries re-enact the triangular structure of the Oedipus complex. The re-enactment is played out between the loved person and the wish for exclusion of the rival just as in early childhood, and (in a dramatic twist worthy of theatre) the sexual role of the father suddenly becomes understandable, provoking a sudden outbreak of ambivalence towards him. This renewed and sometimes violent aggressiveness produces guilt and a sense of a debt, which shapes the desire (sometimes quickly acted upon) for a child. So we see how childhood branches off towards another age, driven by a debt contracted through the detour of love, which revives and conceals a parricidal wish; behind this screen of love, the desire to have a child grows. With great effort, it buries polymorphous perversion, which remains its negative. The repression may occur all at once or little by little in the course of a life.[27]

The debt to the father is linked to the castration anxiety that he provokes, to produce a specific demand – that of having a 'child-penis' (*Penisneid*) in the case of a woman and that of giving this 'child-penis' in the case of a man. The desire to have a child corresponds to the debt owed to the father and was for centuries organised through marriages arranged by families, the priest or the rabbi. That has changed historically since love became a dominant force in forming couples; it subjectivises the drive that expresses polymorphous perversion. The repression of the drive by love is the result of the passage from endogamy to exogamy, which is accompanied by a sort of exchange of polymorphous sexuality for love. As we discussed earlier, the family guarantees a certain amount of love but sex is forbidden. Outside the family, the opposite is the case: love must be fought for, and its wounds are healed through sex.[28] The passage from endogamy to exogamy represses the perverse drive on the other side of genitality.[29] Love represses the endogamous roots of the desire for a child up to the moment when each of the partners in a couple has the idea of having a child, not in the abstract but specifically with this man or woman (and with no one else); it is the wish to have a child 'for life' and against the spectre of death that love always carries. Such a child makes the lovers forget the transgenerational dimension of their desire, their narcissistic wish to duplicate themselves, the payment of the debt and the anxiety of castration vis-à-vis their parents, although these motives remain powerful and active under the mantle of love. This subject of repression is the same as the subject of love; it does not know what it is looking for, only that it is looking for it.

Why have we insisted so much on the duplicitous destiny of the 'desire "for" a child'? Anyone who opens a newspaper will notice how stories about paedophilia have increased. In the past, the misfortunes of children drew crowds. In the 19th century, for example, the Paris morgue was a place for family outings, to gawp at unknown dead children who were put on display. We may wonder at a medieval episode as extraordinary as the Children's Crusade, when people allowed their children to depart to probable death with the blessing of the Church. Think also of the paedophilic excursions made just a few decades ago by major European writers, for whom the exoticism of the colonies was spiced by the ability to satisfy their inclinations. At that time, no one raised an eyebrow. What has changed today is that the hunt is on for the father, the rapist father, of course, but through him for the father in general.[30] The new attitudes towards the child have to do with what is happening to the father complex.

The progressive secularisation of society, resulting from the discourse of science, has gradually sapped the power of the patriarchy, which was legitimised for millennia by religion. But it was never 'the father' who founded the law. Rather, the law results from the guilt of the subject who represses a parricide fantasy. Each son dreams of the death of the father and seeks to make reparation for his murderous wish through the desire for a child, so through love. It would be fairer, therefore, to say that love, rather than the father, founds the law. The triumph of this law over that of patriarchy characterises the time we live in. Most couples today come together due to love rather than patrimony.[31] To say that this reorganisation corresponds to a 'decline of the father' fails to capture what is a double movement; while fathers who owed their legitimacy only to the patriarchy are in crisis, the paternal function as such is valued ever more highly. The decline in the power of patriarchy in no way calls into question the paternal function. The image of the father as legislator is receding, but at the same time, fathers have probably never been so conscientious in their function. They take care of their children much better than most fathers of previous generations, who tended to be more interested in racing, war, cafés, brothels, etc., than in the education of their offspring.

In the patriarchy, the link of the son to the father prevailed and women were disadvantaged. So love itself was not so highly valued. But it is thanks to love that the polymorphous perversion of the child is repressed. When their love for a woman wanes, men return to the café; they relapse into their polymorphous perversions, their attraction to little girls or boys. These inclinations are part of the operating pattern of the patriarchy, incestuous for the girls and murderous for the boys who are sent off to war. The more the love of women increases in intensity, the more these features of the past become visible. Paedophilia is not more prevalent today than it used to be; it is just that today, we notice what in the past remained unnoticed or was judged unremarkable. One cannot attribute paedophilia to a decline in the paternal function since, on the contrary, paedophilia becomes visible proportionally as the paternal function takes a different place, a place which owes more to the love of woman than to a debt towards the father.

This new visibility of paedophilia has emerged as the existence of a different prepubescent universe has come into view (in large part, thanks to Freud). Children have been treated with more respect, whereas not long ago, they were treated even worse than adults.[32] And yet, paradoxically, the supposition of the angelic nature of childhood has emerged from this progress stronger than ever. In the name of the protection of children, and of a so-called 'symbolic', different species of integralism fly to the aid of an ailing patriarchy. The child may be a subject, but he or she must remain innocent. All kinds of psychologists are called up as reinforcements to help build a protective wall around childhood. The sexual fantasies of minors are taken as proof of an intrusion by adults into their psychical virginity. Practitioners are now expected to report the sexual fantasies of children as if they were realities, and it is not always easy for them to distance themselves from the role of a 'thought police'.[33]

In societies increasingly obsessed with the purity of the father (not only in Protestant territories), accusations against adults who allegedly abused their child increase, sometimes years after the 'facts'. Moreover, accusations are brought against children who are judged to deviate from the ideal of innocence.[34] Between renewal of the paternal function and the hunt for paedophiles, society's contradictions seem to reflect the ambiguities of the desire 'for' a child. 'Wanting to have a child' covers over the dark and murderous version of 'sexual desire for a child', turning incest into horror of incest, drive autoerotism into heterosexuality, paedophilia into the wish to have a child and obsession with the dead child into an ideal wish for the living child's happiness.

The beautiful remnants of repressed polymorphous perversion: neurotic perversity

The chastising mother who 'kills' the father instead of leaving that task to the child is certainly only one example of that which leaves a subject in the perversion of childhood. Other configurations can lead to the same result, in particular, an inhibition resulting from a lack of love (and, therefore, of counter-love), which prevents the subject from taking action, starting with the action of parricide. This lack of confrontation with the father to the point of a death wish – to the point, therefore, of repression, which buries childhood at the same time as the father – lets the genuine pervert play out the prolongations of childhood so that the second phase, that of adolescent parricide, does not occur. When, however, the repression of the drive by fantasy plays its role, 'polymorphous perversion' loses its goal of transgender enjoyment of the phallus. This enjoyment moves onto a new stage – that of desire between masculine and feminine; the phallus now becomes what is at stake in a war between the sexes.

But the drive continues to exert its pressure, in the field of 'forepleasures' in the process of relating sexually to another body – a dimension which thus leaves room for a *neurotic perversity*, which will continue to play its role as the other side of neurosis. In short, this perversity functions as a return of the repressed drive; whenever the love fantasy fails or loses its power, neurotic perversity take up the baton of sexual excitement. The love fantasy covers over the claims of the other fantasies and renders innocent whatever it touches, including the perverse dimension of other fantasies which reappears as soon as the love fantasy fades. Yet despite the universal paeans sung in its honour, love is not always there when we want it. We dream of it; we know from books and songs that this wonderful feeling exists. We expect it, but it often fails to materialise so that, perhaps with regret and certainly with a measure of guilt, a part of humanity takes its pleasure instead in perverse scenarios.[35]

Today, a lot of people no doubt express their sexuality through love. Most encounters begin by paying Eros for their entry ticket. That is how they begin, but what happens next? At the moment of satisfaction, the other fantasies will be called to the rescue, both for sexual excitement and for its discharge. The drive energy within them, that is to say their 'perverse' dimension, will then take centre stage. This is not genuine perversion but a perversity that is present in all fantasies, except for the love fantasy,[36] which alone symbolises the gift – the tribute of parricide.[37]

This is so true that, without love, the other fundamental fantasies only allow orgasm if there is a transgression. Any fantasy can trigger sexual arousal, so enjoyment can always dispense with love, which, despite its undoubted charm, may sometimes seem dull. Such loveless eroticism may be a risky game, but it is often enough simply to stage a transgression that takes the place of parricide. Indeed, nothing could be easier! All that is needed is to flout the current practices or morals of society. Such is neurotic perversity.

Each fantasy has its own agenda and seeks to actualise itself without any particular emotional state (especially in our time). There will always be a devotee of spankings, chains, leather, blows, etc., or a curious girl ready to dress up as Vampirella, a nurse, etc. And when the escapade is over and done, everything is quickly forgotten in the fog of the Internet and the nocturnal metropolis. These practices generate their own latent guilt, the result of small, innocent parricides. Transgression itself is pleasurable, and it takes advantage of a guilt that lies at the very heart of pleasure, to the point of taking its place. The heart of the fantasy beats at a transgressive limit: the cries of the beaten child, the jealousy of the primal scene, the promise of the rope and whip. The artifices of a now banal licentiousness offer a low-cost substitute for declarations of love, which sometimes seem a little flat. This game with the forbidden is most evident in perverse practices, which are never so delicious as when they defy the law.[38] Transgression counts as a murder of the father 'outside' the fantasy. Furtively or in broad daylight, committing its offense openly or under the cover of a lie, through pretence or even by means of a game or a contract, transgression dispenses with love and plays the parricide card on another table.

The power of this *père-version*,[39] this strange enactment of the denial of maternal castration, is thus found in all structures, coupled with a certain satanic impulse that strives to bring the original punisher to life, all the better to slay him by transgressing.[40] The committing of minor transgressions (enough for the police to be called) is a common form of neurotic perversity. The prevalence of such staged misdemeanours shows how widespread this appeal to the father is – so widespread that we often pay no attention to it.

As we already mentioned, the masochistic practices of the mystics, alternating with prayers addressed to the father, are even more demonstrative. Their perversity never appears as clearly as in their immoderate taste for suffering. From cold to fasting, beatings, flagellation, piercing of the skin, prayer marathons, no suffering can discourage them, and no expenditure of care on the sick and the dying is too much. Mystical enthusiasm turns the pleasures of the drive – 'maternal' earthly goods – into their opposite, as if this was enjoined by an absent and spiritualised father, levelling enjoyment with suffering and thus waging a constant struggle in his field and, ultimately, in his service. The 'version towards the father', this Sadean love of God, has always made the female mystic a somewhat satanic child of the Church. The absence of a violent father is palliated by apparently self-punitive acts – acts that he should have committed. Reproducing on oneself the blows he should have administered makes him briefly alive, for just as long as the pain – proof of his existence – lasts. In true Sadean fashion, evil proves the exist-ence of God, whom goodness would cause to perish irrevocably. This mystical ver-sion towards the father is in this respect exemplary of a modern experience; great catastrophes, genocides, nameless misfortunes, far from nourishing atheism, on the contrary nourish the glory of He who is without name and prove His existence. As evidenced by the almost incredible fact that the extermination camps have often been called 'the holocaust', which is to say a sacrifice made for the glory of God.

Faithful to its formal sadomasochistic envelope, genuine perversion constructs a punishing father figure. Such a figure is not lacking in the neuroses, but (this is the difference) in neurosis, such a father is present without needing to be constructed. Moreover, this presence is what generates the parricide fantasy. So we find the same figure in genuine perversion or in neurotic perversity. This secret connection explains the undeniable fascination that the pervert exercises on the neurotic, a fascination of which the pervert takes advantage for purposes of manipulation.[41]

We might take pornography as an example of this ascendancy of perversion over neurosis. Pornography works well. Does it represent the expansion of a perversion through a disoriented society? Erotism requires time and energy. It results from a situation which is given meaning by a fantasy. If this situation changes, the erotism is displaced or vanishes. Pornography, on the other hand, enjoys the body in all the drive scenarios in which the body can be caught. It seems so much more conveni-ent. And this apparent neutrality of pleasure would be emptied of meaning if it did not possess a shocking, transgressive dimension, which shows the ascendancy of exhibitionism over the voyeuristic perversity of the neurotic. The drive quality of the spectacle is magnified by its being shown to spectators who watch it while hid-ing, when others, who do not want to see it, protest and call for it to be banned. The latter participate in the enjoyment of the former. That adds up to a lot of people.

Pornographic films traditionally show super-potent men interacting with women who are offered to anyone and at any time in a scenario that seems to be drive-based since it does not require any subjectivity; excitement is produced on its own, inde-pendently of persons, situations, prohibitions and their transgression. What we wit-ness is the discharge of a surplus rather than orgasms brought to the boil by love. That is all it takes for porn stars to show us the ideal of an enjoyment that has finally been mastered and objectified. What the actor defies by their performance is not so much morality as ordinary human capabilities. How could one gather any real enthusiasm for sex when surrounded by light and sound technicians and with a director barking instructions? To be able to do so would be a fine example of sex in a 'state of nature', free of the psychical work that ordinary mortals carry out in order to occasionally achieve the same result.

But it is not just a question of pure drive here, as fantasies are nonetheless pre-sent, we have to factor in the fantasies of the director, the actors, the spectators and also those of the non-spectators – the immense public consisting of those who cover their eyes and condemn such exhibitions (while thinking about them) and thereby reintroduce the forbidden and its transgression into the anonymity of dimly lit rooms and internet networks. This is far-removed from a simple reduction to the drive. On the contrary, this huge fantasy montage requires a considerable number of participants. We see only the screen and forget what happened before, during, after, behind the scenes and in the dark space of the room where it is being viewed. What finds relief here are ordinary fantasies rather than a perverse voyeurism, which instead requires the real presence of those it takes by surprise. The porn star appears as an ideal for so long as we know nothing of their exhibitionist impulses nor of their fantasies of sodomising the spectators in whom they induce enjoyment – a crowd that may include their father or even their mother, who suddenly recognise their son or daughter at the moment of a finally shared orgasm. Because even though they are displaced and kept in check by the distance and the anonymity of the spectacle, the conditions of orgasm will nevertheless be present, and these are hardly 'natural'.

The porn film shows in a repetitive loop an undefined copulation, returning to the same scenes, a 'ready-to-wear' for the fantasy that any spectator can make use of if they wish. They can discharge on the spot and often do so. They see everything except what excites them. Their fantasy is lodged in the interstices of something impossible to see, which exacerbates their voyeurism. If there is an event here the cause of which escapes the viewer, it is the erection of the actor, which results from a desire that is almost impossible to represent. Has any film (pornographic or not) ever shown not so much the tumescence of a sex organ as what actually provokes it?[42] How would it be possible to see at the same time that which causes the erection along with fantasies and a repetition of the past that cannot all be present together on the same stage? The fantasies date from an earlier period, or they are projected to a later time, or rather, they are as such timeless. And the spectator will be all the less able to see this superimposition because he or she is themselves a part of the scene. They take advantage of what they cannot see in order to project their own fantasies. What causes the actor's erection escapes them, but in its opacity, they feel the slow erection of their own organ.

So pornography functions in an in-between space: it could be perversion, but it also appeals to the dream of the neurotic, who would like to have done with the harsh subjectivity of lack. It does not offer a marginal solution, to be thrown into the hold-all of perversions, but offers the mirage of a mechanisation of enjoyment, free from emotional entanglement and from passion.[43]

Pornography marks the historical moment when, in the spotlight of the Enlightenment, the vision of bodies finally focused on its true object: sexual enjoyment.[44] We might say that, before this date, pornography was displaced and transposed. If we consider the pleasure of seeing a body enjoy, even in spite of itself, as 'pornographic' or if the spectacle of suffering is a psychical equivalent of enjoyment, then the gladiatorial games of Rome, the tortures of the Inquisition, a crucifix, the beatitude of a martyred saint are so many pornographic spectacles (as are the works of art that depict these scenes). In this sense, genuine pornography gives the truth of such spectacles: the unbreakable night core of sexuality (to paraphrase André Breton). It focuses on what it is at stake without trying to show anything else. Postmodern in its genre, its narration is impoverished, looping around obsessions, the images of which are forcibly inserted into the ideational networks of ordinary perversity.[45] This forces the viewer to look directly, on an innocent stage, at a spectre that haunts us all. So it works for the truth, although it has no use for the philanthropic dimension which that implies. It puts the sufferings that were inflicted in the past in their proper place, when their sexual meaning was not recognised.

The existence of such displays then appears as a sign of progress rather than of decadence. For these are only spectacles and watching them does not lead to acts because they take the place of the act.[46] They are fantasies, staged to be seen, for the purpose of an enjoyment complete in itself, just as desires come true in dreams.[47] Seeing is an act. The spectacle does not push the viewer to imitate any more than a reader of detective novels becomes a murderer. The fan of murder-mystery novels would perhaps be horrified at the sight of a drop of blood. But the adept of porn films has a head start because the millions of lovers of detective novels, of murders that occur during the pursuit of the culprit, of innocent victims taken to be assassins, are unaware of the enjoyment that fascinates them. The reason why murder appeals to them so much is because, like the paedophile, they need transgression (killing) in order to enjoy. Not so long ago, earthly enjoyment was conditional on despatching the father to heaven, so as not to be disturbed. We no longer believe in that, and since this father has returned to earth, stories of the living dead and murder have become an obsession, as seen in the emergence of vampire stories and then of the detective novel, centred on guilt and its resolution.[48] The taste for crime, born at the same time as pornography, is a phenomenon of modernity. What does this showcase of corpses amount to if not, again, an excess of enjoyment taken to its limit?

The detective novel and pornography are both examples of a transgressive perversity, situated at a kind of crossroads. The modalities of enjoyment bear the mark of their time. In our society, enjoyment is presented as a spectacle between crime and pornography. In our immense film and print production, crime belongs to glorious enjoyment, while pornography remains largely shameful. Reading about the events around a murder in a novel is not a crime. Killing someone is a crime but not dreaming of it. In contrast, making love is not criminal but showing it is. Murder belongs to our 'civilised' fantasy world, but the same does not apply to pornography.[49]

Pornography and the detective novel are 'spectacular' examples of the ascendancy exercised by perversion over neurotic perversity. To this mass fascination must be added the banality of a 'practical' perversity, as shown by the important role of fetishism in ordinary eroticism. The fetish is the keystone of perversion, but its empire extends much further. To what extent is a gift (a frequent preliminary to love) linked with the fetish? A jewel or a valuable present takes its investment from castration and from the desire that castration establishes. Similarly, the fetish symbolises an absence, and its use value is irrelevant. Many items of clothing, indeed, have no practical value and are designed only to please. We see that far from being limited to the framework of 'perversion', a latent fetishism exists everywhere.[50]

We can find as many examples of it as we wish in fashion, in accessories and the way they are used, the eccentricities of which add spice to a well-tempered perversity.[51]

Each new fashion offers its little denial, which turns our heads. This erotic demonstration of lack through the adornment that conceals it is to be found in any civilisation. An aesthetic dimension serves as a pretext for this latent fetishistic perversity. The 'beauty' of a garment, a piece of jewellery, etc., masks this directly erotic function. Sandals, lingerie, furs, ties, etc., contribute to this discreet fetishisation in fashion. The constraint it involves is as violent as it is invisible, and no canon of feminine beauty can dispense with it. Who is behind it? If the fetish is its manifest content, some father must be at work behind it. This fetishism is smuggled in under the finery of a beauty that is never naked. Who can explain what a tie, high heels, sumptuous fur, etc., are for? Framed by fetishism, aesthetics stitches this hem of discreet perversity around ordinary erotism. It is true that the characteristics of 'what pleases' require criteria that are recognised by third parties for a certain time (for as long as the fashion lasts). The fetishised adornment is designed to please everyone during this time. Its anonymous erotic function, destined to participate in general excitement, is not addressed to anyone in particular. We see clearly here the double-sided relationship between neurotic perversity and the love fantasy. 'Fashion' seeks to seduce everyone but does so furtively until the moment when seduction chooses one person and one only. This choice of this particular person is accomplished by repression of the perverse dimension evoked by the fetish, with which most women are adorned. In this sense, by conceding its favours to one person only, innocent neurotic perversity has denied itself. So the 'aesthetic' criteria of fashion have the latent function of subjectifying the force of the drive, which, against its will, becomes the messenger of Eros. The drive pressure has not disappeared, but it has been pushed back to the other side of neurosis.

This latent fetishism of fashion does not merely entrust to the good offices of the community the task of stoking the fantasy of seduction. It also corresponds to another problem – that of the division of each woman between herself and an image of womanhood that eludes her. When she puts on make-up, certain clothes, particular shoes, jewellery, these anonymous fetishes of femininity, far from being reduced to a masquerade, exhibit the division of the female subject – the subject whom an anonymous father could love – between performing womanhood and her own self.

The trinkets of fashion have the great interest of putting aesthetics back in its place and bringing out an underlying dynamic. What relationship, after all, exists between the appreciation of beauty and the denial of castration? Does what is considered 'beautiful' not conceal lack while at the same time unmasking it, as does a fetish? Why does a certain spectacle, a certain object, appear so 'stunning' to us, like an opiate that puts our erotism to sleep? Where does this taste come from that divides the world between what pleases and what displeases and does so as if it the division itself was a natural one?

The fetish results from the phallic cathexis of an elected object. It crystallises in itself the goal of the drive. Before any particular object occupies this place, the drives in general shape how we perceive the world around us. The signification of an imagined body is reflected in the world, and a latent sexual excitement invests this archaic drive relationship to our environment. Are not all of our perceptions intensified by the drive, that is to say by the desire of the Other? The most elementary sensations – the wind, the sky, the sound of water, of leaves – have a sexual resonance that draws the subject out of him- or herself. The beauty of the world triggers daydreams that invite the subject to escape: 'Come with us, leave yourself behind, lose yourself in us!' When the wind in the branches innocently excites him, the walker sees woodland nymphs or the god Pan, who is always ready to sodomise passers-by of either sex. Just as the child seeks freedom from the grip of the mother's drives through masturbation, the daydreamer's impromptu erection puts him or her on their mettle. This empty excitation allows them to resist being swallowed up by the drive.

The trinkets of fashion and *objets d'art* give an orientation, a framework and, above all, a signature to this diffuse emotion. Does the aesthete contemplating his or her favourite object feel the same emotion as a walker in the forest? There is a difference because a work of art does not show directly the beauty of the world; an artist signs the work of sublimation, which then circulates in a market where it takes a place and assumes a value. A subjectivation and rules of exchange are added to the simple drive relation to the world around us. The work of art possesses a phallic value conducive to fetishism because of this sublimation, by which the artist projects in creation the drive that threatens to consume his or her body. The work has no fetish value for the creator him- or herself; it will only acquire such value for the aesthete (via the art market, for example).[52] At one level, the work of art is priceless; its value for the person who appreciates it is that of a fetish.

Does the pleasure itself of this aesthete here correspond to a sublimation? The term is better suited to the creator. An artist sublimates his or her drives in a work, which he or she frames and signs. We can only speak of sublimation in a very rough sense when the act of seeing or hearing is at the service of an indirectly sexual excitation. Rather than sublimating the drive, the aesthete enjoys it little by little, sometimes with more directly sexual consequences. Some aesthetes are overwhelmed by powerful excitement when in the presence of their favourite works, excitement that can go as far as complete enjoyment. It is hard to say whether this peculiarity is widespread because those who experience it do not make themselves known and they are of no concern to the police. The popularity of museums suggests that it is not so rare, and although it is unusual to meet a purely aesthetic pervert, a certain aestheticism coexists happily with perversion. Moreover, this knotting becomes universal in the case of neurotic perversity. The artistic patrimony of humanity would undoubtedly be meagre without this aesthetic dimension, which, by claiming and cataloguing the works that it chooses, creates the last civilised bastion against nothingness. The work of art frames that which would otherwise obliterate us.

Notes

1 'But it is in fact self-evident: if a child has a sexual life at all it is bound to be of a perverse kind; for, except for a few obscure hints, children are without what makes sexuality into the reproductive function' (Freud [1916–1917], *Introductory Lectures on Psycho-Analysis* in *Standard Edition 16*, p. 316).

2 See the qualifiers of the fantasy given by Freud: 'being gagged, bound, painfully beaten, whipped, in some way maltreated, forced into unconditional obedience, dirtied and debased' (Freud [1924], *The Economic Problem of Masochism* in *Standard Edition 19*, p. 162).

3 The place in question is passive and, in this sense, feminine. 'Lacan, in saying that feminine masochism "is a fantasy of the desire of the man" [*Guiding Remarks for a Convention on Female Sexuality* in *Écrits, op. cit.*, p. 615] gives us the key to the situation' (Colette Soler [2003], *What Lacan Said About Women* (J. Holland, trans.). New York: Other Press, 2006, p. 78).

4 Or even in gallantry because an excess of thoughtfulness towards women may be equivalent to treating them like fools.

5 Two works are essential in this respect: Richard von Krafft-Ebing [1886], *Psychopathia Sexualis* (C. Chaddock, trans.). Philadelphia, PA: F.A. Davis, 1894; Marquis de Sade [1904], 'The 120 Days of Sodom' in *The 120 Days of Sodom and Other Writings* (A. Wainhouse, R. Seaver, trans.). New York: Grove Press, 1966.

6 The victim is sometimes unable to bring allegations or even to talk about this moment with their own family.

7 This should be emphasised, as some writers maintain that the difference between pornography and erotism is purely cultural and depends on the habits of an era (see: Ruwen Ogien, *Penser la pornographie*. Paris: PUF, 2003; and Michela Marzano, *La Pornographie ou l'Épuisement du Désir*. Paris: Buchet-Chastel, 2003).

8 There is also a dimension of going beyond in neurotic orgasm, but as we shall see, it depends on the internal contradictions of the fantasy. In perversion, on the contrary, this dimension has to be constituted in relation to some norm (often social).

9 At least for those who can manage it because others dream more than they act, tormented as they are by love, which makes them lose their taste for these amusements.

10 Marquis de Sade, *Three Complete Novels*. New York: Grove Press, 1965, p. 580.

11 Objectifying the sexual offers many benefits. It puts a stop to the otherwise endless battle between the frenzy of drive excitement, on the one hand, and the anxieties and precautions of love and the idealisation of the person, on the other.

12 'An investigation of fetishism is strongly recommended to anyone who still doubts the existence of the castration complex' (Freud [1927], *Fetishism* in *Standard Edition 21*, p. 155).

13 We use these terms, with their Marxist connotations [use vs exchange], deliberately, evoking parallels between the efficiency of the fetish and the fetishism of the commodity (see: Karl Marx [1867], *Capital, Volume 1* (S. Moore, E. Aveling, trans.). Ware: Wordsworth, 2013.

14 This is not to say that homosexuality is a perversion because the choice of a sexual object of the same anatomical sex does not necessarily mean that the object is of the same gender as the chooser. We will find homosexual object choices in all clinical structures (neurosis, psychosis and perversion) that are discussed here.

15 James Cleugh, *The First Masochist. A Biography of Leopold von Sacher-Masoch*. New York: Stein & Day, 1967, p. 14.

16 'It should be noted that the father, named Sacher, was given the mother's family name, Masoch, at the same time as it was conferred on his first-born son. The destiny of the name is doomed to antonomasia: it is this "paternalised mother's name" that gave rise to the eponymous perversion' (translated from: Paul-Laurent Assoun, *Le masochisme*. Paris: Economica-Anthropos, 2003, p. 22).

17 'père-version', literally 'father-version', in the French but including 'vers', which means 'towards' (translator's note).
18 Getting yourself imprisoned for life or sentenced to death belongs to this construction of 'versions towards the father'.
19 At the same time, the 'for' expresses a strong equivocation in the vectorisation of desire; we cannot know in advance who desires whom between adult and child. Both possibilities can be envisaged, right up to the precarious equilibrium of a reciprocal virtual desire.
20 For example, by swallowing a cherry pip, or by being constipated, etc.
21 As do adults, for whom children in general represent their own rejected childhood (any child in the world moves us).
22 Or not 'for' but 'with', sometimes not without serious symptomatic consequences.
23 A fault in relation to the father, as shown by the Christian religion in the form of a mystery so opaque that believers will never make the connection between their sexual desire, their death wish against a violating father and their faith in an Eternal Father. This lack of knowledge opens up the abyss of belief.
24 A woman marries a man who kills the father, according to the structure of Corneille's *Cid* (Pierre Corneille [1636], 'Cid' in *Cid, Cinna, The Theatrical Illusion* (J. Cairncross, trans.). London: Penguin, 1975).
25 Many ancient civilisations sacrificed the first-born to the totem of the ancestor, and today, the desire to have an abortion often sacrifices on the same altar (the number of abortions has not declined, even though ways of avoiding pregnancy are far more available than previously).
26 The extent to which the two absences of the 'seduction fantasy' lead to different modalities of perversion is worth investigating.
27 Neurotics repress their perversion throughout their lives by means of love or work. Not that neurosis would metamorphose into a perversion if these safety valves were to fail. Rather, the drive would fall back on the symptom (falling back on the father) which is capable of repressing drive perversion.
28 Love inflicts a narcissistic deflation; the lover is no longer anything before the beloved and seeks to compensate this loss of phallic value by means of organ enjoyment (penis or clitoris).
29 Passion reverses the autoerotic impasses of childhood; the paternal toad becomes a prince charming, desire awakens the sleeping beauty, etc.
30 Much of the controversy around Bill Clinton's affair with Monica Lewinsky showed that women in his country are widely regarded as minors.
31 In 2009, more than 50% of children were born out of wedlock.
32 In France, thanks to the work of Maud Mannoni and Françoise Dolto, children are not perceived in the same way as in other countries with the same standard of living (in the United States, for example, carers do not make a special effort to speak to babies in maternity wards, hospitals and institutions). The child has gained status as a subject that it previously enjoyed only for its mother, who was herself often regarded as if she was a child or a half-wit (who, after all, would speak at length to a baby who lacked understanding?). Children were abused in a thousand ways, as was a good part of humanity: women, the underprivileged classes and the so-called inferior races, who were also considered to be children. Psychoanalysis can pride itself on having obtained recognition that, although they may be minors, children are no less subjects.
33 The terms of Ségolène Royal's 1997 circular required all officials 'to notify [. . .] the public prosecutor [. . .] as soon as a pupil has reported facts of which he or she claims to have been a victim'. The vagueness of this requirement led to an increase in unfounded accusations. From 1997 to 2004, 75% of 849 paedophilia cases that were investigated were not pursued. But the human damage (exclusions, suicides) was done.
34 For example, an 8-year-old boy was summoned to a Paris police station after the mother of a little girl complained that she had caught the pair in a state of near undress.

35 The patriarchal family, which arranged marriages according to criteria that one can hardly claim to have satisfied the 'symbolic', falls into these categories.

36 Anyone (not only a pervert) who watches a pornographic film is solicited by it. Jean-Jacques Rousseau, the great paranoiac, needed a little spanking to get himself in the mood for erotic activity. He was not, however, a pervert.

37 So the love fantasy occupies an exceptional retroactive position; it is at once a safety valve for the fundamental fantasies, the chain of which reaches back to it, and a universal transformer of the death drive.

38 It does not matter what kind of law – whether it is legal, only moral or even immoral. What matters is the defiance. Discharge is dependent on there being a prohibition, shame, disgust, repression or mockery.

39 'version towards the father' (translator's note).

40 'Nevertheless, as we know, this current perversion, which has become so frequent that it can be described as ordinary, needs to be distinguished from perverse structure strictly speaking, to which it does not seem to correspond' (translated from: Jean-Pierre Lebrun, La perversion ordinaire. Paris: Denoel, 2007, p. 309).

41 The Marquis de Sade put his chief talent to use for precisely this end; the long list of perversions which he enumerated omits one, namely, his writing, by which he has sodomised innumerable neurotic readers via their latent perversity for more than two centuries.

42 This is also true of the fantasmatic conditions of enjoyment in general. Catherine Breillat's film The Last Mistress (2007) is rare in showing the fantasmatic contradictions in which a woman finds herself caught, right up to the explosion of her pleasure.

43 The pornographic film suggests that sexuality will resolve their uncertainty. These films are classified 'X', which is of interest when we remember that the same letter designates the unknown quantity in a calculation as well as an unknown surname (the name is lost in the ocean of a proscribed pleasure).

44 The term does not appear until 1769, in the writings of Restif de la Bretonne.

45 This provocative dimension suggests no great distance from pornography to certain features of contemporary art nor, in another sense, is it unworthy of the ideology of neuroscience which also mechanises sex, reducing it to hormonal flows and their wiring.

46 If it was true that porn stars encourage imitation, those most at risk would be the members of censorship boards.

47 The violence of certain pornographic films, the titles of which alone turn the stomach, would limit this liberal point of view (see, for example, the reflections of Michel Houellebecq, Rester vivant. Paris: Libris, 1991). However, some horror and war films are more than a match for the porn genre in this respect, and yet they do not provoke the same outcry.

48 See Jean-Claude Aguerre, La naissance du vampire au XVIII siècle, unpublished dissertation, University of Paris VIII, supervised by F. Châtelet, 1981.

49 In this regard, we will see later how orgasm and the name of the father are two sides of the same coin.

50 'To the extent that this term "fetishism", coined in the framework of a theory of culture, has found itself at the centre of psychoanalytic conceptualisation, it must also be examined as a "bridge" between "psychoanalysis" and "culture"' (translated from: Paul-Laurent Assoun, Le Fétichisme. Paris: PUF, 1994, pp. 4–5).

51 In Freud's words: 'In the world of everyday experience, we can observe that half of humanity must be classed among the clothes fetishists' (Freud, 'On the Genesis of Fetishism, Minutes of the Vienna Psycho-Analytic Society, February 24, 1909' in Psychoanalytic Quarterly, 57 (1988): 147–166).

52 Where art is fetishised in a way that is very close to what Marx wrote about commodity fetishism.

Chapter 8

Orgasm, perhaps

The music

Freud made a few remarks about orgasm here and there. His followers had little to add,[1] as if there was a difficulty talking about it. So where are we to find some documentation? Pornographic and erotic literature has been around for a long time, but it was mostly written for solitary consumption – to be read with one hand, as the saying goes. And such works, intended mainly for a male readership, are confined to an erotism that is always preliminary. But since when has literature spoken not of pleasure (it has undoubtedly always been evoked) but of this acme of arousal, which is short-circuited and returned at the moment when the same happens for the partner? Descriptions remain approximate; they are interested in the arousal rather than its resolution. Lots has been written about arousal, not much about orgasm. Sade, for example, speaks heavy-handedly of 'discharge'.[2] But can this moment be written about at all? In any case, even before anyone tried, it has almost always been obscured, even as everyone thinks about and strives, with either more or less success, to reach this point.[3] Only a few avant-garde writings, those of Breton, Bataille, Blanchot, Leiris and some others, have evoked the proximity of sexuality, transgression and the death drive in works which continue to inspire psychoanalysts.

There is certainly no shortage of references to sexual enjoyment[4] in psychoanalytic literature. But most articles concentrate on its pathological consequences and its symptomatic offshoots, leaving the question of orgasm itself unexplored, as if it was a physiological response of the organism which is sometimes inhibited but would otherwise be natural. We might ask, though, whether animals experience anything resembling an orgasm? Their arousal is regulated by the reproductive clock. And their pleasure – if they have any – ends with the discharge intended to perpetuate the species. It is true that psychoanalysis differs from sexology and that the Freudian conception of the sexual includes both the symptom and the mystical impulse, without needing to collect details on the nocturnal activities (if any) of analysands. After all, as we will show, the sexual rapport is homothetic to speech, which, moreover, conditions it, and we have already made progress by recognising

DOI: 10.4324/9781003519287-8

speech's value as truth. Be that as it may, after more than a century of publications, the question posed by orgasm still calls for clarification.

Our postmodernity puts eroticism and pornography on display to the point of satiety, making it hard to find an adequate definition of transgression. You can read recipes in magazines for how to achieve orgasm – the ideal norm of a civilised sexuality. A strange ideal, if we had to stick to these recipes, which are so far removed from the 'unbreakable core of the night' evoked by Breton.[5] A few books manage to go further,[6] notably, that by Yukio Mishima, *The Music* (1964),[7] in which the author dares to speak in the name of psychoanalysis, as if he realised that Freud's followers still had much work to do on the matter. The novel's hero (the first-person speaker) is a psychoanalyst working in Tokyo by the name of Shiomi Kazumori. Reiko, the young woman who is the central character of the novel, comes to the analyst complaining of frigidity (But is she really complaining?). The subtitle of the novel states that it concerns 'a case of female frigidity observed in psychoanalysis' and, therefore, as the publisher notes, of a scientific study based on real facts. However, in spite of this supposed scientificity, the unpoetic term 'orgasm' is infrequent under the pen of the author, who prefers 'the music' – a music, which may or may not be played, may be heard or remain inaudible. It is an enjoyment that is just as much heard as emitted. So the essential point is captured in the title; a subject plays or does not play this music, which is always already exterior to them and which comes to them in spite of themselves. The subject has first to hear it from another desire before reacting to it with their own.

As if instinctively aware that orgasm imposes itself from outside, Reiko does not begin by talking about her frigidity. She complains of a specific deafness. She says that she has come for consultation because when she turns on a radio or when an orchestra starts playing, she hears nothing. She remains deaf to the music; the exteriority of its harmony does not vibrate inside her. She takes her time before speaking of her own music, the music that seems to elude her in pleasure. She does not accuse anyone of wresting it from her or of not giving it to her, as can happen to women (something she is aware of). We also learn the circumstances of her presence in Tokyo. She came there on the pretext of studying, when in reality, she was fleeing from her home province, where she is awaited by a fiancé, who, as we will later learn, more or less raped her when she was a teenager. She remains bound by a family arrangement to this man whom she silently loathes, without, however, having broken with him. We also find out that she loves another man in Tokyo, with whom she is in an ongoing relationship but without experiencing the slightest pleasure in his arms. She is also afraid of getting pregnant by him.

Having learnt of these circumstances, the reader has already understood that music is a metaphor for sexual pleasure, a rather heavy metaphor in the (justified) opinion of Dr. Shiomi, who wonders, 'Was there not some symbolic link, difficult to grasp, between the "music" that she evoked and the orgasm that she ardently desired?'[8] But can we speak of a metaphor since the thing, unnameable in all languages (more so even than the name of God), has no consistency other than its sonority – that of a cry echoed by the infant's cry at birth, of which Freud wrote in the *Project* that it was already only the memory of another cry.[9] Music is the first phrasing of the cry in the infant's babbling. It is the child's humming in response to the desire of the Other. Without this desire, the child is silent. Thanks to this desire, the child modulates its cry, vocalises it and, from then on, expects from the other the measure, tone and rhythm of their own pleasure, a pleasure sealed by the first loss, the loss to which the child consented in answering it. This shaping and kneading of the cry signifies a knotting which is the result of multiple meanings that are fitted together, come apart, oppose one another, inhibit each other depending on situations that make the person hear or not hear what is there, as relevant for the deaf as for those afflicted by the hallucinations of love. So what it is that makes a person deaf to the music, to the point of not being able to play it, be played by it or enjoy it more strongly than their own self, is to be found in the constellation of the Other and the accidents of filiation.

Once this powerful symbol of music has been framed, the details of Reiko's story come into perspective. Is it really true that Reiko cannot enjoy? That would be to believe that frigidity is not part of enjoyment. Our first thought might be that her frigidity offers her revenge on a generic figure of the man, embodied in the present by her current lover. She loves him for the hurt she does to him, for the blow that she inflicts through him on a ghost. But this revenge comes at a price for her, and this guilt freezes her pleasure. She is in pursuit of a pleasure that she holds back, a 'little death' which would relieve her of the ghost that haunts her, finally laying it to rest. Her revenge hesitates on the threshold of this death, and in this sense, her frigidity resembles a cold but continuous orgasm, of which her lover pays the price after each of his vain attempts. 'The idea that frigid women made men slaves without letting themselves be imprisoned by them seemed to bewitch her like a beautiful poem. She perceived this as a crushing female victory in the realm of love'.[10] There are indeed some men who prize frigidity, tormented by the effort to make women enjoy, faithful for an eternity that lasts as long as the suspension of pleasure, with the thought, 'Tomorrow, it will happen!'

But circumstances show that the unfortunate lover is not the only one waiting for Reiko's 'music'; he is kept company by the psychoanalyst. Mishima imagines a truth that may well be relevant to the theme of the analyst's desire. Because the analytic cure relaunches indefinitely (*unendlich*) a rapport that was stolen from the sexual and displaced onto the symptom. Dr. Shiomi makes no mistake when he writes, 'I had every reason to shudder before the action, like that of an icy poison, which this hidden trouble called "frigidity" exerted on me and on others'.[11] Shiomi, intent only on listening (in a certain position of sainthood, which Reiko's frigidity allows him to grasp the meaning of), also has his dreams. The metaphor of music, of an immemorial cry which is both that of orgasm and that of birth, affects him, too, his function being to hear. He dreams of the endless trajectory of a needle on a broken record:

The crackling didn't stop, and when my ear caught it, I had the impression that it had been the only sound since an eternity . . . the music of this record had stopped in a past so remote that my memory could not go back there.[12]

And how could memory have gone back to what is not a source but an in-between, a pure relationship, that of speech and that of love? Can speech make a rapport? Can love?

The music of the voice is there, but it is difficult to place between emitting and hearing. The child who utters a cry hears it as something external, which comes back to them charged with the other's desire, and they continue to cry because they forget the first cause of their cry. So the origin of the cry is immemorial. The cry is itself divided, and if memory tries to remember the origin, it finds something but always something else. It forgets what it is looking for as it advances, circling round this opaque memory.

For the child who hears it, their own cry comes back to them heavier than when it was emitted, like a boat that has been loaded elsewhere before returning to its home port. And it has, indeed, been loaded, because it has taken on a meaning for the mother and comes back bearing her messages. A crying child may have had its reasons for crying, but it forgets them because of what returns. Its cry, which began with a complaint, comes back to it like an injunction of obedience to the mother's demand – and, hence, to her enjoyment. The child cries because it now hears the imperative in its own cry, ordering them to enjoy beyond what the child is capable of. The message from the Other should have been the happiness of no longer being thirsty, but the child prefers to be thirsty. Satiety would entail non-being.

Similarly, any cry, heard anywhere, has an immediate impact because it reminds us of the message of this other enjoyment, an enjoyment that is extreme because it signifies a sort of doubling, a splitting that goes as far as depersonalisation. This immemorial cry is carried with us throughout life, and remembering it, the lover enjoys hearing the pleasure they provoke, as the infant cries hearing its sibling cry. There would be no such feeling without this echo. Just as, for the child, the cry is divided between its emission and its reception (which nevertheless seem to over-lap), so the pleasure of the body depends on another body; the bodies do indeed overlap. The other body seems to respond to the first, but it then becomes its source because of this past that it evokes.

Where does the 'music' of the lovers' enjoyment come from? It seems to come from the woman rather than the man, or it seems to be torn from her, but by whom? Should we say that her lover is the craftsman of this enjoyment? No, because he, too, is surpassed by this music, which grips him when he hears it, even as he seems to provoke it. The cause goes beyond the rapport between the actors who are present; it conceals its own beyond outside the scene, which, in this sense, is 'ob-scene' because the cause cannot be seen, even by staring directly at what seems so physical.

A child awakened by the lovemaking of its parents, caught in this scene without understanding it, will always instinctively pretend to be asleep. Confronted with this nocturnal theatre, the child at once finds the path of pretence. What has the child seen and heard that at once imposes silence, unable to distinguish pleasure from pain in what seems to be simultaneously a game and a face-to-face encounter of the most serious kind? The greatest truth seems to be played out in this strange drama. How are we to understand this contradictory struggle, this apparent suffering accompanied by words of love, if not as the miming of something else? What resemble blows perhaps evoke for the child other, fantasised blows that punish when the child touches itself, escaping the circle of filial love, and it is the same pleasure mixed with violence that the child contemplates without understanding it.

The psychoanalyst listens to Reiko's story, which describes her love scenes, but as if in slow motion or frozen. And he, too, is caught up in the same sense of something immemorial, repeating it without knowing what it is. As she talks to him, his patient reveals the same repetition, and as if this dimension had to be made to appear clearly, she keeps a false diary, in which she describes her analyst as a 'perverse, erotomaniac and ridiculous' seducer who tries to abuse her. Why does she do this? Because she knows, with feminine intuition, that her lover will read this false diary, that he will be furious, that he will seek out this perverse psychoanalyst, that a combat between the two men will ensue and that the fate of the 'music' will depend on the outcome of this struggle. Only one of the two, either the lover, unable to break the ice of her frigidity, or the analyst, described as a perverse pleasure-seeker, will be left standing when the fight is over. And is it not from the destruction of one of them that the music will come? The aim is to establish an asymmetry between a dead man and a living man in a masculine world which offers nothing in itself, as if enjoyment had to arise from the macabre outcome of the combat. Admittedly, Mishima does not formulate the problem in these terms, but it is certain that a father (or a stand-in for the father) has to die in order for exogamous enjoyment to follow from his loss.

This tension remains the theme until the end of the book; Reiko sets one man against another in a variety of circumstances in the secret hope that a 'murder' will finally set her free from her ice prison. But the sought for combat seems fated never to begin. She remains in wait for an incestuous father whom a lover would confront head-on and overcome, like Corneille's *Cid*.[13] One way or another, successive lovers seem destined to nothingness, either by frigidity itself or by the dream of their suicide, their illness, their impotence. We may well recall that nothing excites Héloïse more than Abelard's actual castration. Similarly, Reiko's music begins to flow in a chance encounter with a man who is impotent and whom she saves from suicide. Her enjoyment is provoked by the opposite of virile power. Other than that, nothing helps; the young woman stages almost every scenario imaginable, but the corpse is never the right one, or love always brings it back to life, still frozen.

And Dr. Shiomi, despite being well placed by his profession to embody the corpse, does not allow himself to be 'killed' any more than the others. After the episode of the false diary, he lectures his patient in an effort to explain why she went to so much trouble to write these slanderous pages about him. She wrote there that he succeeded in making her enjoy, precisely by listening to her like a saint, and his interpretation is that she wrote the diary, knowing that her lover would read it and expecting that he would understand her to be saying, 'With you I feel nothing, but on the other hand, with another man'.[14] The situation then seems blocked because the analyst himself has obstructed the movement of the analysis.

At this point, news comes of the fiancé who had been promised to Reiko by the family arrangement – the rapist, who all this time has been at home in the country. We learn that he is suffering from an incurable disease. 'I am drawn to illness and the sick',[15] says Reiko and immediately flies to the bedside of the dying man. In a few days, she undergoes a complete transformation. The fetid odour of the cancer-stricken man is like incense to her. Female mystics were always fond of human suffering, and hospitals were their preferred purgatories. Christian mystics are foreign to Reiko's culture, but she follows their example nevertheless. 'Day by day I saw my image change in the patient's gaze: I became a true saint, haloed in light'.[16] Religion is conducive to miracles and to none more than the miracle, which religious historiography mentions only metaphorically, of the orgasm. The rapist fiancé, previously so maligned, is on his deathbed; he is dying, he is dead. And immediately, the music starts.

When death comes, as was to be expected, the hand of the dead man does not have time to grow cold in that of Reiko before the long-awaited music is finally heard. 'I heard, not with my ears but with my body, with an ineffable sense of happiness, the "music"'.[17] With the dead rapist before her, the music resounds, while Reiko stands crowned by the halo of sainthood. The sacred halo of one who is blessed rids her at last of her hysterical aura, her dizziness, her suffocations, her clouded eyes and the turmoil in her ears. The music carries her off without delay to the realms of enjoyment. The step from the halo of sainthood to orgasm was taken via the body of the rapist – the object of a love that carried execration within it.

So enjoyment was possible. But what was enjoyed? The man, certainly, but in a relationship outside the body where he is divided between his carnal presence and his being for death. What, then, is at stake here if not the paternal legacy – his name, the name to which he is reduced at the time of his departure? This truth is more evident in Japan than elsewhere because Japan is a country where the highest name is assigned to a person at their funeral. Unlike the provincial lover, the Tokyo lover does not die. He does not render back or give his name. He is, therefore, incapable of generating enjoyment. For this lover, the orgasm would attest less to his amorous abilities than to the value of his name. If this remains elusive, his existence falters, postponing its proof until tomorrow and postponing his excitement. The name is what the father extracts from his own animality, and it is given in love at the moment when the lover is called by their name. It is the name that makes a rapport.

A few weeks later, back in Tokyo, Reiko's black clothing barely conceals the happiness she has known. What she mourns is not so much the dead fiancé as the moment of happiness when the music was heard. Everything has been described clearly, and yet no one is any the wiser as to the source of this shift. But does this joy she has now experienced not call for repetition? 'Someone else must accept to die for me so that I can keep this feeling alive'.[18] In that case, the 'music' would be simply a funeral song, requiring an exhausting, repetitive dramaturgy, because it would seek a death to respond to this death which is not the end of life but the symbol which pre-exists and outlives it – the totem that is always already deceased, reborn from its ashes on the day of the wedding. This dramaturgy, the *basso continuo* of hysteria, stirs the ordinary sexual excitement of the human species, the condition of its reproduction in the name of a father who is never sufficiently symbolised, never sufficiently slain, exorcised since time immemorial by means of religion and propitiatory rites. Killing the father in each lover through frigidity leaves less room for musicality than seeing him really die. Reiko, in a dramatic confusion of death and what it symbolises, does not know how to write their rapport, yet it is on this that orgasm depends. And so the spiral continues ever further, without ever meeting the protagonist that it needs; instead of confronting the (potentially dead) father, it knocks up against the brother (the living man).

This is Mishima's extraordinary intuition; since childhood, Reiko's sexuality has been in a deadlock with a fraternal rather than a paternal figure.[19] Her elder brother was the first man who made desire manifest to her. Was there nothing before? Perhaps seduction by the father in early childhood had some importance. How could she not have experienced this purely subjective, fatal seduction – that precisely which an orgastic parricide would free her from? In any case, no evocation of the father in childhood has emerged up to this point in the narrative. However, there has been a brutal freeze-frame memory of a scene with her brother, a collateral but powerfully concrete trauma, which absorbed vague daydreams of a fantasy of seduction by the father. What happened? On a journey in her early childhood, it had been difficult to find rooms in a hotel, and she had slept in the same room as her older brother and one of her young aunts. In the middle of the night, in the dimly lit bedroom, her aunt reached orgasm, and the image of the entwined couple had remained etched in her memory with all the force of an episode from a dream – uncertain, perhaps, but nevertheless shattering.

Prior to this reminiscence, the novel had seemed to go in circles, but here, suddenly, the drama thickens and spirals downwards, pushing Reiko in search of this brother, who has disappeared and of whom it is known only that he lives as a *Yakuza*, sunk in vice, in a part of town that is dangerous to visit. Reiko wanders through this underworld, like a lost woman 'delivered to hell', in search of her brother. She wants to rediscover the unforgettable childhood feeling that she knew thanks to him, as if only such a dreadful situation could make her approach the music and, ultimately, sanctify it. Because such is the power of repetition, which can no longer make do with micro-dramas, where successive lovers come and go almost unmarked.

Reiko eventually finds this brother. And as if it was inevitable that the earlier drama be repeated in inverted form, it is now she herself who is raped in front of a woman, raped by the brother himself. It was he who stood in the background of the successive seductions, and what had been fantasised earlier is finally projected onto him: a brutal incest of sister with brother, in a drunken state, in front of his female companion, probably a prostitute. The repetition changes the places of the first seduction which Reiko underwent as a child, when she was only the dumbstruck witness of her brother making love to his young aunt, her *alter ego*. This woman had orgasmed in her presence, and now this same brother rapes her in the presence of another woman.

The rape by the brother 'had gone beyond obscenity to take on the dimension of a sacred ceremony [. . .] the feeling of immeasurable debasement, which Reiko experienced, had quickly changed into a memory of sainthood'.[20] This mutation would be incomprehensible until we realise that, behind the rapist brother, stands a father who would otherwise be unrepresentable. The metamorphosis of memory repeats the thread of lived history in reverse. This brother, a damnable rapist, 'would perhaps reappear one day, debased, before her, with the freshness of a divine apparition'.[21] The father complex, divided into two people – the rapist father of the sexual seduction, on the one hand, and the father murdered as the price for this trauma and then sanctified, on the other hand – are telescoped together and duplicated in a single figure, that of the brother (then men who resemble him).

From halo to orgasm, from redeeming works with the sick to excursions into the underworld, from the murderous dream to its forgiveness, extremes oppose each other without being able to mediate each other. In this sense, the only harmony is based on a rupture of harmony – a unique musical moment, relentlessly sought after. The disjunction, the short-circuit, the rhythmic syncopation of the various scenarios pursue 'the music' until a murderous, delicious enjoyment – an enjoyment that should not be – imposes itself. The multiplication of these scenarios traces carbon copies of their invariants, engineering a short-circuit of the extremes of the seduction fantasy: to seduce and to be seduced. But since to be seduced is to die incestuously, the seducer must be killed, at least to the extent that he is the father, and the living man must be enlisted against him, or alternatively, the illness, impotence, suicide, etc., of the living man must be enlisted against that same man. To these constantly repeated oppositions of contraries we must add that, if the father seduces, it is against the background of the enjoyment he gives to the other woman in a primal scene, where violent blows seem to be inflicted on her – against the background, therefore, of the masochism that captivates human eroticism. When Reiko seems to hold on to life by only a thread, this thread still guides her to the bottom of the labyrinth where her music awaits her. Perhaps an abyss of despair has a power identical to that of the orgasm itself (if not its value), and its nothingness is sometimes preferred to the labyrinth of love, with its inevitable Minotaur.

What would be the resolving short-circuit for such a tangle of fantasmatic contraries? This opposition of contraries escapes reason, and this is no doubt why the word 'orgasm' has not existed for long in any language and only appears relatively recently in French, based on commentaries on Hippocrates that dealt with other (medical) problems. The music imposes a rapture on the body, shaking it and gripping it in the gap that opens up, but thought cannot grasp it entirely from any angle. Words fail and their referent resists, even more so than the woman who is supposedly not all. She also is unable say it, despite her relentless urge to stage the implacable drama where it happens – this thunderbolt at the heart of language. Indeed, it is not so much the woman's enjoyment as feminine enjoyment that is at stake here and which concerns both sexes; a certain woman may (occasionally) obtain the liberation of this orgastic knot which concerns her femininity but which also concerns the femininity of the man who enjoys it through her.

A woman's femininity, caught in this oppositional knot of the living and the dead, cannot be grasped in terms of a linear, non-conflictual causality. As Mishima's psychoanalyst says:

> A woman's body, in many respects, resembles a city. [. . .] That was how I saw Reiko, lying there in front of me. Her being contained all the virtues and all the vices. Some man or other could probably fathom it in part. But, in the end, he would never know all of it, nor the real secret.[22]

A desire born in the depths of the father's seduction is no sooner born than it is lost because its incestuous impulse is immediately shattered on its prohibition. In almost the deepest cavern ('almost' because, for Reiko, it concerns her brother and not her father), the opposition of the saintly and the diabolical is inscribed in its original form. The father dies like a saint because of his diabolical desire, and it is he whom Reiko does not know how to represent and, therefore, never attains. As unrepresentable, he is 'sacred' (*sacer*) in the original sense of the word: both rejected with horror and religiously venerated, taboo.

But this unreachable father, the ghost of his rejection, immediately becomes the cause of an endless desire. He forever excites the girl who no longer knows how to represent him and who desires without knowing whom she seeks but only that she cannot help but seek. This excitement can be called 'holy' if we take desire in its pure point of departure, but it is no less sexual. This absent father provokes an erection; he gives a phallus of which he thus finds himself deprived, castrated. The dead father, untraceable, the cause of desire, is castrated in the same parricidal movement. 'I think I've always been looking for scissors that would play music',[23] Reiko says. Why should castration have such a power of seduction, to the point of governing the whole machine of desire? The father excites inevitably and cannot help doing so, even if he sleeps. Even when sleeping, a role will be given to him whether he likes it or not – the role, namely, of punishing the first sexual excitations. So that punishment – castration – accompanies desire from its beginning, giving to desire its masochistic impetus, not without the powerful counter force of a parricide wish, which definitively binds desire to the law.

In the Shinto shrine of Tagajo, the men venerate a phallic symbol in their temple, while a pair of scissors is exhibited in the women's temple. For Reiko, the scissors from her childhood games were called 'Cisabelle', which was the name of a woman who, like scissors, had nothing between her legs.

> What if one day I caught my dad with Cisabelle? [. . .] The only man who must not be cut was my father. But I had the right to attack any other man, so as long as I did not feel for him a love strong enough to replace that which I dedicated to my father.[24]

Ultimately, 'femininity' is another name for this castration, to which no human being consents. Women have to struggle with this burden a little harder than men – and much harder if men make them carry their own share of it. Castration conditions desire but at the cost of a feminisation which traps that desire. A certain desire for non-desire thus becomes its permanent torment. This snare should drive us mad, and so it does if we call this will for a desire for what should not be by the name of 'madness'. A desire sealed by its own evil, which carries it, powered by a few fantasies: seduction, primal scene witnessed by the beaten child who takes revenge by the eye-for-an-eye principle of parricide, taking revenge for his or her own desire. So the death of the father is linked to this infernal desire, sexual desire linked to the wish to strike the father in the man, if he has not already done so himself. When Euripides stages the infanticide of Medea, who seeks to strike the father through her children, he might have presented this monstrous mother as the negation of the most basic humanity. But instead, he remembers that Jupiter will absolve Medea of this irremediable evil. As Medea says: 'We are women, unable to perform great deeds of valour, but most skilful architects of every evil'.[25]

One last page of Mishima's novel remains to be turned. After the memory of the rape has been sanctified, the brother will reveal the paternal essence that he contains in a final episode. Reiko sets off again in search of the brother, despite the rape scene or because of it. After wandering through the most disreputable neighbourhoods, she finds him living in poverty, once again in the company of a prostitute, but now he has become a father. The last word of the story introduces paternity – that which should have emerged first, long before the erotic trauma of the love scene between brother and aunt. With the staging of fatherhood, the story takes a romantic turn that brings resolution. Reiko weeps at the sight of her brother as father and gives him all the material support she can, paying, as it were, a debt that is at last directed to the appropriate symbolic place. And now things seem to settle. Reiko's Tokyo lover, who never disappeared from the story and who always kept Reiko's love (although he was never able to break her shield of ice), suddenly comes back into the action. There is a healing now and this lover, who has always been faithful, reaps the benefit. With him, Reiko finally achieves harmony, in the musical sense of the term, and the book ends on this note, a note that is, perhaps, exaggeratedly optimistic. It is, after all, difficult to believe that a man who has paid no other price than that of patience can have knowledge of such musical scores, with all their syncopations and dramaturgy.

Orgasm, a word impossible to say: does it resonate with the taboo of the father's name?

'Pleasure', 'enjoyment' and 'orgasm' are terms that do not have the same psychical impact nor the same place in the history of language. Enjoyment has always been taken into account by religious systems down through the centuries. It is not that religions aimed to govern sexuality in the manner of a moral power that regulates certain behaviours from the outside but rather that the 'mysteries' of sexuality have been integrated into theology. Although the empire of religion was exercised above all for the benefit of the patriarchal family and heterosexual masculinity, the narrow path along which sex and theology could keep company corresponded to social customs that reflected the general repression of desire rather than being solely imposed by the Church. It is hard for us today to imagine what the agony of an almost total absence of sexual freedom must have been.[26] In just a few decades, this painful reality has been turned upside down, and everyone can act as they please, within the bounds set by their superego, for which (thank God) the Churches no longer play the role of relay as they did in the past.[27] Everyone can do as they please, provided they do not harm anyone else.

However, a new imperative has emerged: not only does everyone have the right to benefit from the new freedom but they *must* also do so. An imperative to enjoy has imposed itself as the new *Credo*.[28] What it imposes, at the simplest level, is that you must be in good health, enjoy your body and cultivate your potential. This emphasis on the healthy body seems so natural to us today that we find it almost unimaginable that such emphasis was actually frowned upon in the past and that illness was even considered a sign of divine favour in certain religions, including that of our culture, which gave pre-eminence to hospitals and ministrations to the sick and dying. The deified body, today at its zenith, eclipses the fetid odours of sickness from yesteryear, as if illness was no longer an ever-present recourse against the excesses of enjoyment. The symptom, after all, has the practical function of limiting pleasure by a suffering which is really only the excess of that pleasure.

So enjoyment as such contains an evil. *Jouissance*, the French word for 'enjoyment', differs markedly from *plaisir* ('pleasure'), to which it adds a pinch of excess and prohibition. The original meaning of 'enjoyment' was the taking advantage of a good. The word has been used in this way to refer to pleasures, and since sex takes pride of place among them, other uses of the term have diminished under its hegemony. Finally, since sexual pleasure is never realised so well as when it is prohibited, enjoyment has been touched with the scent of transgression.[29] With much imprecision, psychoanalytic jargon casually uses the word 'enjoyment' to mean orgasm, which is really a distinct event. There is, of course, a temporal succession between enjoyment and orgasm, but enjoyment does not cause orgasm. Orgasm is not what occurs at the top of a *crescendo* of enjoyment. Orgasm comes from another place. We cannot treat them as the same; enjoyment is always ready and present, without necessarily setting itself free in orgasm, which sometimes remains always out of reach. So there are several degrees between pleasure, enjoyment and orgasm.

Enjoyment oozes from all sides: it is enjoyment of the body, generated by the drive, and it is phallic enjoyment, which seeks to relieve the drive. It is the enjoyment of language, actualised in each sentence, and the word 'enjoyment' itself seems almost supernumerary, even misleading, because enjoyment in itself has no substance but resounds like a sort of *basso continuo* that is present everywhere, through passive or active vectorisations. Enjoyment is parasitic and constant, and we may well wonder whether it ever achieves its goal. After the orgastic short-circuit has interrupted it for a moment, it immediately pursues its quest. There is no escape; we are enjoyed or we enjoy according to an actualisation that is summed up in the Word itself.[30] 'Enjoyment is the Way', the Taoist would say if he thought about it, to which a devotee of the Bible might respond, 'In the beginning was the Word'.

The word 'orgasm' came late to the French language and is not to be found in Latin nor in the two other 'mother tongues' of our culture, Greek and Hebrew. There is no such word in the Bible.[31] The demotic languages derived from Latin and from Celtic and Germanic idioms are also without it, as is Arabic. We may wonder whether there was an equivalent in the old spoken languages, but in that case, it might have survived like other words which have remained in use, though absent from written language. The word does not appear in any ancient, autochtho-nous form in the various languages when we look for it. The orgastic event seems to have remained an unnameable heart, elusive in each of its beats.

The word 'orgasme' is recorded for the first time in French in 1612 to describe a discharge of passion, specifically a fit of anger, and in this, it is faithful to the meaning of the Greek words 'orge', 'orgasmos', which is 'to simmer with ardour, with desire'. It owed its appearance in French to commentaries on Hippocrates, who himself used the word but in a different sense. For Hippocrates, 'orgasm' describes the tension and excitement of a function or an organ but without any sexual meaning.[32] A dictionary of ancient Greek indicates that 'orgasm' is a derivative of 'orge', meaning 'anger'. Its link to pleasure is obscured by violence.[33] 'Orgy' probably has the same source as 'orgasm', and this is an interesting parallel since an orgy transgresses habits and cus-toms, just as orgasm includes a moment so transgressive that languages were unwill-ing to have a word for it. If, in Greek, 'orgasmos' derives from the verb 'organ', it means 'to be full of juice and sap'.[34] It, therefore, does not yet designate the acme of pleasure but only a tension towards its realisation. This Hellenism, as it was initially used in French, designated a fit of anger and, at the same time, qualified the highest degree of physiological (not just sexual) excitement. It takes on the latter meaning from 1623, without supplanting the first meaning (a fit of anger), which remained for a considerable time. It did not have or at least only confusedly had the meaning of a height of sexual enjoyment since an ambiguity remained between the excitement and its endpoint (as is also true of the German word 'Lust').

In French, the word 'orgasme' continued for many years to designate a state of tension, excitement, turgidity of an organ.[35] It was only from 1777 and at first sporadically and in parallel that it acquired its modern meaning of a peak of enjoy-ment, making French the first language to give a name to this exquisite moment. Its new use to qualify the high point of sexual enjoyment initially referred only to male ejaculation. After 1830, sexual satisfaction became the main meaning of 'orgasme'. As late as 1920, one still finds uses in literature of the word 'orgasme' to describe a tension, but today, it is definitely a question not of tension but of its resolution. 'Orgasme' continued to evolve in a purely sexual sense, and from des-ignating the culmination of enjoyment for both sexes, it gradually became more associated with the female side of sexual experience.

So the word appears late in French, where it is a borrowing made by pre-classical French from ancient Greek. It entered French by chance due to an erroneous translation of Hippocrates, under the pen of an obscure 17th-century scribe. It was then inflected through use to designate what people had not previously dared to name. We should add that all the other 'Western' languages now also use the word 'orgasm' to describe this event.

We might take a short excursion here into a culture distinct from our own. In Chinese, 'orgasm' has recently been written using a set of three characters, which are rendered in pinyin 'Xing Gaochao'. 'Xing' denotes spirit, sex or quality, and 'Gaochao' has the sense of 'rising tide' or 'paroxysm', breaking down into 'Gao' ('high', 'upper') and 'Chao' ('tide', 'wet'), a term with demeaning implications. 'High', 'upper' sits oddly alongside a word with such implications, but that is perhaps in the nature of the thing. 'Xing Gaochao' is, in fact, one of the thousands of neologisms that were invented after China came into contact with the West[36] and is meant as an equivalent of the English word 'climax'. This notion of 'rising tide' seems inadequate to capture the essence of orgasm since it connotes a continuum with a relative lack of distinction between pleasure and its end.

There is an older term, which must, however, be relatively modern since it comprises four ideograms. In pinyin, it is rendered 'Yusi Yuxian' and has the meaning 'near to dying' or 'near to become immortal' (one can indeed become immortal in this life before life that incest implies). The repeated word 'Yu' represents lack or desire. According to Rainier Lanselle, who translated some erotic writings from the Ming period into French, the orgastic moment is evoked rather than named, in particular, by the expression 'Dia' ('to lose oneself') which is interesting since it evokes depersonalisation. The character 'Xie' ('to emit') is used for both men and women. A range of metaphors appear here, but a specific term is lacking.[37]

This quick overview highlights a linguistic fact that seems universal. Why such silence about such an important phenomenon for so long? It seems that, with the progress of History with a capital 'H', the meaning of orgasm was gradually clarified and discovered. The greatest enjoyment only found its concept very late. There is, indeed, no direct symbol of the orgastic moment, if we can be allowed to use 'orgastic moment' as a periphrasis to designate precisely that which generates the invention of the symbol – this psychical short-circuit of *Versöhnung*, reconciliation, which no language has ever invented. To this linguistic peculiarity, it must be added that the word 'orgasm' is of extremely rare occurrence in the conceptualisations of psychoanalysis itself, appearing only a dozen times and often incidentally in the work of Freud, who prefers the unfortunate term 'end-pleasure'.

What status should be given to a psychical fact as important as orgasm since no word designated it for centuries and it has only recently made its appearance in various languages? In Arabic, Chinese, Russian, English and German, it seems that people have been unable to designate this extremity of enjoyment, the unpronounceability correlative to the loss of consciousness that occurs in this moment, if 'loss of consciousness' can appropriately describe what is a moment of depersonalisation (the name being the condition of consciousness). What are we to make of this silence? Has the phenomenon of orgasm been known at all times and in all cultures? Its power has certainly always been sensed and repressed. For example, the excision practiced in certain regions of Africa seeks to prevent female enjoyment. But there are many other ways to stifle its voice. When, for example, in the 19th century most bourgeois sexual activity took place in brothels, orgasm was probably hardly visible. *Demi-mondaines* and, even more so, prostitutes take care to refrain from it since it would be unprofessional and since they are paid in order not to indulge in such excess. Such an impressive silence is the result of a knot of fantasies so unconscious and so contradictory that we dread to even designate it.

As we will try to show, orgasm is a taboo in the strict sense of the term because it concerns the ghost of the father at a moment of conjunction-disjunction of Eros and Thanatos. Similarly, the name of God was for a long time unpronounceable in the Bible religions,[38] reflecting the taboo of a father who has been made eternal. But what then are we to say about the other side of this taboo – the orgasm, which has not even been formulated in language? Is this absence of the word not similar to the sacred name of God, unpronounceable because it evokes a murdered father? This comparison of the two taboos is not that convincing because we can in fact pronounce the name of God, we can read the tetragrammaton YHWH ('Yahweh') and we can enumerate the thousand epithets of the Most High. 'Orgasm', on the other hand, remained inaudible for millennia, as if it was a word even more taboo than the name of an eternalised father. Today, if this word designates a specifically feminine moment, it is a seizing by the father that is at stake yet one which allows a breaking free from him, following the thread of an enjoyment, which, to reach its culmination, must cancel out its own agent: he whose name cannot, therefore, be spoken.

The masculine conclusion of enjoyment

The title of Sandor Ferenczi's article, 'Pollution without Dream Orgasm and Dream Orgasm without Pollution',[39] shows that psychoanalysis, from early on, made a distinction between the psychical value of orgasm and the physical discharge that it involves. Many patients have nocturnal pollutions although the accompanying dream, which they remember, is devoid of erotism. Viktor Tausk noticed that pollutions followed 'dreams of doing things' (mending, cleaning, etc.) and thought that the compulsion to be busy represented sexual activity. But here, too, there was no orgasm in the dream itself. On the other hand, we sometimes have sexual dreams that culminate with an orgasm without there being any actual physical discharge. Even a dreamer who is frigid or impotent can have a dream in which they reach orgasm. Some Anglo-Saxon authors have referred to these as 'phantom orgasms' (by analogy with 'phantom limbs'). This might suggest that orgasm is not a peak of sexual development which some individuals attain after a long journey but a potentiality of fantasy that is present from early childhood. A psychical orgasm may occur during sexual intercourse, or outside it, or even without the slightest pleasure, or finally, in a symptomatic form without ejaculation (in epileptic seizures, for example). We may wonder whether other kinds of purely psychical orgasm also exist – operating, for example, by simple resolution of the internal contradictions of the fantasy – or when desire has disconnected from its sexual dimension. The question is also linked to certain forms of drug addiction, where users sometimes declare that their drugs make them experience an orgasm superior to sexual orgasm. We can at least agree here that there is a link between the extremes of enjoyment and the death drive.

On the masculine side, orgasm is too quickly confused with ejaculation – a simple physiological discharge that signals the end of pleasure. But that is assuming that there is pleasure because masculine pleasure is no more self-evident than female pleasure, even in the event of an erection and ejaculation, the occurrence of which may seem well-defined and clear. Men sometimes carry through the sexual act without enjoyment or orgasm and without experiencing any pleasure other than that of their partner, which is often sufficient for them. In this, they resemble many women who consider themselves to be sexually fulfilled because their lovers seem to be content and who only discover the delight and excess of orgasm late in life, through some chance adventure.

Masculine frigidity, often overlooked in standard 'psychopathology', differs from problems such as impotence or premature ejaculation. Some men report feeling as if their penis is made of wood when they make love, and they do not complain about this insensitivity unless it is only occasional because, if it is permanent, they do not even notice it (and their partners don't complain about it). This degree zero of masculine pleasure is perfectly compatible with sexual discharge, and the absence of pleasure shows that there is a clear distinction between orgasm and ejaculation.

This masculine 'frigidity' contrasts with the excess of pleasure involved in premature ejaculation. Some men always enjoy too early and complain about it (as do their partners). Others enjoy too quickly despite themselves but only with a certain partner and when that partner begins to express their own pleasure or (bizarrely) when the partner is frigid. Others only reach orgasm when their lover has reached it. Such variability shows clearly that masculine orgasm is something other than physiological discharge. It is important to note that premature ejaculation is an intense discharge that occurs when it should not and brings displeasure. It is, therefore, linked directly to the forbidden, and as such, it represents a paradoxical paradigm of masculine orgasm. Orgasm occurs on the basis of pleasure but, in such cases, precisely because it is countered by the thought that 'it should not happen'. In premature ejaculation, the thought occurs that it is really not the moment to let go and, at once, that is exactly what happens.

We can find this role of prohibition as the detonator at the very heart of pleasure in other forms of orgasm too. It may happen, for example, when the orgasmic moment is accompanied for a woman by the idea of being tied up or beaten or the thought that the lover is unworthy of her favours, that she should not have made love with him or that he has some intolerable flaw. It may happen that a woman has her first orgasm on the occasion of a rape or the equivalent of a rape, when she lets herself be used to a certain point but does not want to go further or when her partner does not please her or even, in some way, disgusts her. The orgasm may be enabled by various transgressive practices which often result from passages to the act[40] that bypass the person's conscious intentions. The subject feels overwhelmed but goes there anyway, despite a promise made to themself not to do it again and with the thought, 'This will be the last time!' What 'should not happen' ranges from ideas of violence to shameful images accompanied by crude language ('I take you', 'I eat you', 'I beat you', 'I tie you up', etc.) or even the playing out of these scenarios. Such more or less civilised perversities ought not to be evoked, but they are precisely what hastens the conclusion. The fantasmatic short-circuiting of pleasure by 'what should not be' precipitates the conclusion.

What are the invariants of such a short circuit in premature ejaculation? When orgasm is triggered at the start of sexual relations, in the first expressions of pleasure by a woman, the first question is this: what puts her in this state of pleasure? Where is she, and who is she with? Whom exactly is she enjoying (the question is particularly relevant if her eyes are closed)? What is for sure is that she has gone elsewhere, and the premature ejaculator will think that she is taking her pleasure with another man – with the man she has left in order to be in his arms, namely, her father, the man who eternally remains 'the man before'. This is at least what the premature ejaculator will sense, and he will sense it all the more easily because his own fantasy concurs with it; he is himself in fantasmatic rivalry with a father at the moment of the conquest of a woman. And this father comes out the winner when the woman begins to take pleasure.

The fantasy is all the more powerful if, in his own rivalry with a father, he has remained in an infantile position in which he is feminised. So his untimely orgasm in response to the expression of female pleasure occurs because it makes him feel feminised and that feminisation is precisely what 'should not happen'. In every psychical reality, rapid ejaculation results from sodomy at the hands of a father.[41] It might be objected that other men suffer from premature ejaculation even though their wives remain wooden in the sexual act (something that does not prevent them forming strong couples). In fact, though, the scenario is the same: a frigid woman remains with her father, who has locked the door, and the door cannot be broken down without bringing him back to life.

There are other varieties of premature ejaculation, but we will find without exception a powerful guilt, constant or occasional. The orgastic dimension of male ejaculation is always linked in some way to a moment of passivity where the subject is not only overwhelmed but also feminised. Premature ejaculation represents a kind of *feminine orgasm,* and it is not a source of pleasure since it provokes anxiety about virility. For the premature ejaculator, each of these symptomatic crucifixions is accompanied by suffering, which purges his shame about a threatened feminisation. Men here experience a form of orgasm when their repressed feminisation returns. It may take the form of epilepsy, anger and sexual symptoms. It has often been observed that the clients of prostitutes are overcome by such guilt that they sometimes do the deed in a matter of seconds. Contrary to the clichés about the sexual misery of venal love, a visit to a prostitute may involve orgastic enjoyment that is superior to what these men experience with their wives, to whom they often do the honour with statutory regularity but with a pleasure less than that of the transgression. The visit to a prostitute lets them experience a 'feminine' orgasm. The intense anxiety and displeasure of premature ejaculation are proportional to this orgasm because, when it happens, the feminine part of a man enjoys in defiance of his gender, plunging him into shame.

Beyond the field of premature ejaculation, a man can, in a way, enjoy feminine enjoyment through an intermediary – the woman he makes love to. He thus experiences a certain degree of impersonalisation. But this impersonalisation does not divide him, at least so long as he enjoys as a man. The division only catches up with him if he enjoys as a woman (rather than enjoying the woman), as happens in premature ejaculation, which functions as a kind of feminine orgasm for a man. This is why it provokes his anxiety, despite and because of the enjoyment that it releases.

Premature ejaculation illuminates the psychical conditions of male orgasm through contrast. Triggered by the thought that 'it shouldn't happen', which makes it happen, it gives the index of the fantasmatic contradiction which provokes it. Most men at the beginning of their sex life have a problem with premature ejaculation, but it diminishes with age. This evolution may give the measure of their progress in their fight against the father and in distancing themselves from their feminisation. But premature ejaculation is not necessarily something that passes with time; it may continue to occur even if a sexual relationship endures for a long time. Indeed, however long a relationship lasts, orgasm can always come too quickly because of the thought that 'it shouldn't happen' – the encounter with a father (the eternal ghost). A long-distance race well run does not guarantee against failure at the finish line. So a last-minute rush avoids or replaces a feminine orgasm.

We see the difference here between the premature ejaculator and someone who only comes because his partner reaches orgasm. If his lover has arrived this far, it is because each of them went their own way until this short-circuit where she disowns her father at the same moment as he defies his own father. A double parricide occurs. A son supplants his father at the same moment as his lover takes leave of her father. But is orgasmic enjoyment not on one side only? The enjoyment is undoubtedly valid for the two lovers, who are both motivated in equal measure by their bisexuality (their castration), but only the feminine part reaches orgasm – a promised land that the masculine part can only contemplate.

The debate over feminine orgasmic pleasure (vagina vs clitoris)

In the absence of a definition of orgasm, many clinicians have fallen back on descriptions of physiological discharge. It should also be pointed out that almost all of the current literature on the subject concentrates on the feminine orgasm, as if there were a kind of intuition that only femininity knows orgasmic enjoyment. And indeed, most of the complications that arise from the debate on this aspect of femininity (see Karen Horney,[42] Melanie Klein) result from the affirmation of one original gender: man or woman. But the choice of gender is distinct from the anatomical reality of the sexes. This conceptual weakness surely explains the difficulty of reaching an outcome in debates between proponents of the vaginal orgasm and proponents of the clitoral orgasm.[43]

Marie Bonaparte believed that clitoral sensitivity had to be completely suppressed in order to achieve vaginal orgasm. Indeed, many analysts (including women analysts like Jeanne Lampl-de Groot or Ruth Mack Brunswick) have tended to class clitoral orgasm as genital immaturity. However, some of them, including Helene Deutsch, qualified this position and asked questions that remain relevant today. As Deutsch writes:

> All waves of sexual excitement, often very strong and urgent in women, flow into the clitoris, and only subsequent more or less successful, communication of this excitement to the vagina secondarily incorporates this organ into the sphere of sexual experience.[44]

If we wanted to content ourselves with surveys, does what a woman says about her pleasure prove anything? Tenderness, desire and enjoyment can be at a premium without resulting in orgasm, and as long as this event has not happened at least once, a woman can think that she knows it without in fact knowing it. And since the satisfaction of the lover may itself provide a certain contentment, a relaxation of tension may pass for the vaunted orgasm.[45] For as long as she has not experienced it, a woman may sometimes consider that the pleasure she has in sex corresponds to what others call 'orgasm'. So there is a difficulty in relying solely on actual testimonies.

Since anatomical physiology is so often used as a reference, we could take a look at the famous Kinsey report (the first of its kind).[46] There, we read that a dissociation is made between the organic repercussions, which are always vaginal but sometimes unconscious, and the conscious sensation, which may remain localised in an erogenous zone. All orgasms cause vaginal contractions: 'the spasms that accompany or follow orgasm involve the vagina'.[47] We deduce that if these contractions always involve the vagina, the psychical orgasm may sometimes be lacking. The Kinsey report confuses 'contractions' with 'orgasm' and fails to note that these contractions can occur in other parts of the body. In this sense, a calf cramp (quite painful as such) may serve the purpose of orgasm. And how can one call a non-conscious physiological event 'orgasm'?

For Masters and Johnson, clitoral stimulation is the primary cause of orgasm.[48] This excitation concerns an organ that can only claim to be one on psychical grounds, exactly like the phallus, which, after all, is the phantom limb *par excellence*. Women have access to phallicism like men, clitoral excitation having the same value as penile. And clitoral excitation remains, throughout life, a preliminary and an accompaniment to the inconstant and unpredictable vaginal pleasure. This purely psychical quality is illustrated in the case of circumcised women, who are able to reach orgasm thanks to an excitation of that which they have been deprived.[49] It is not so much the erogenous nature of this part of the body that counts but rather, its role as a phantom member of virility. So long as it is not erect, the penis is also no more than a phantom phallus.

Maximum vaginal orgasm is obtained by clitoral stimulation, and Masters and Johnson also consider that all orgasms generate vaginal contractions (even when this is not perceived). They describe three stages of orgasm. First, a sensation focused on the clitoris, then a feeling of engulfment, of opening, and finally, the 'pelvic palpitation' of vaginal orgasm (also not always conscious). These observations tell us little except that the various testimonies of the women who were interviewed reflect the physiological phenomena differently.

These specialised discussions have led to classifications 1) of purely clitoral orgasm, 2) of clitoral orgasm leading to vaginal orgasm or vice-versa with variants regarding the means and moments of excitation. But 'physiologically' erogenous zones such as the vagina can, of course, remain insensitive to any excitation, while locations unrelated to 'natural' sexuality can be a source of pleasure; there are orgasms stimulated by other parts of the body (the breast, the mouth, etc.), and the classifications have been relativised accordingly. The same person can experience these different types of stimulation at different times.

These copious reports only confirm, if confirmation were needed, that there is no physiological model of orgasm.[50] It is not news to anyone that sexual relations may occur without any vaginal sensation or that the clitoris can be stimulated without any pleasure being obtained. What is most astonishing about these studies is that their authors seem oblivious of the main characteristic of orgasm, which is to be a conscious event.[51] But extracting the essence of these painstaking studies, we can learn at least one lesson: orgasmic discharge occurs starting from active zones (the clitoris) and proceeds towards zones which are passive (the vagina), that is to say by following the gradient of 'activity with a passive goal' created by fantasy.[52]

Anatomy is only the place (admittedly irreplaceable) where a psychical event is staged, and it is in fact the discharge of fantasmatic contradictions that gives *unity* to orgasm. This discharge can rely on various organs of the body or even on none (for example, in the mystical ecstasy of the dead father or the high of the drug addict). A passionate phone conversation can trigger a vaginal orgasm. Will we then say that the ear is a branch of the vagina? Such questions make it obvious that the orgasmic event is created in the place of fantasy, all the way to its final tidal wave.

To be more precise, the polarisation of the fantasy between activity and passivity has consequences for the anatomical investment of this or that part of the body, depending on whether it is hollow or pointed. The more the fantasy is directed towards activity, the more the enjoyment will be 'clitoral'. The more the fantasy prefers passivity, the more the enjoyment will be 'vaginal'. These 'organs' are stubborn carnal metaphors of active and passive. Insofar as an 'activity with a passive goal' orients feminine enjoyment, the active and the passive come in a series, but the active will always come first (the clitoris is the trigger for enjoyment, according to the harmonic of feminine bisexuality), while the passive (vagina) will remain contingent. The 'change of erogenous zone', which, according to Freud, defines the transition to femininity, follows a sequence from activity to 'activity with a passive goal' since all girls were boys to begin with in the sense defined above and remain so to a certain extent.

This movement from activity to passivity is the orgastic nodal point, never established once and for all and variable according to age, partners and situations. When it is not inhibited (in complete frigidity), feminine clitoral activity is the rule of a first 'masculine' identification – or more accurately, an identification that is transgender. For it to reach its point of conversion into passivity, an obstacle must be overcome, a wall of prohibition, a limit that should not be transgressed (actualised, for example, by the representation of a rape). This overcoming is accomplished by force in fantasy scenarios or by the strength of love, which leads to a certain degree of identification with the lover. By means of this amorous transitivism, the woman becomes her own object (she identifies herself with her lover and makes love to herself). To this extent, orgasm does not result just from any intercourse with any bearer of the phallus.

Psychical sensations differ according to their physical localisations, but they can converge towards the elected site of the active or the passive. A 'vaginal' orgasm can result from touching or stimulation of the breasts or merely from a look or a voice (even at a distance, over the phone, etc.). Similarly, an anal orgasm can result from the excitation of these various erogenous zones provided that they are connected to a fantasy or several fantasies. Or what is called a 'clitoral' orgasm can trigger an 'anal' or 'vaginal' orgasm. This succession of localisations depends on the sequence of 'active' and 'active with a passive goal', which provokes a variety of sensations, so that there seem to be different types of orgasm. But the orgastic engine itself runs on one fuel only, that of fantasy, which liberates drive enjoyment thanks to its internal contradiction.

That said, it is certainly true that this drive energy is best set free thanks to an organ – the vagina – which embodies a sort of 'black hole' of the drive.[53] Much has been made of the erogenisation of the vagina, and Freud has been criticised for underestimating it. But the vagina has no drive reality, and for this reason, girls remain for some time unaware of its role. No special wisdom is needed in order to realise that this cavity (like others) is only erotised as a function of fantasy. Sexual arousal depends less on anatomical erogeneity than on fantasy. It is obvious to anyone that, without fantasy, the excitability of organs disappears. The pleasure of the kiss vanishes if it is not the desired person who is kissed. This pleasure is even reversed into disgust if the kiss is with a stranger. Some fantasies erotise the vagina, while others block access to it. It is discovered only in proportion to the enjoyment expected of it. Otherwise, it remains insensible.

From childhood onwards, the anal drive invests (as its name indicates) the anus, and its erogenous nature is, therefore, quite understandable. But the vagina does not correspond to any drive, as shown by its minimal cerebral sensory projections. It is a kind of psychical 'externality to the body', the purely fantasmatic cathexis of which represents the most passive, most empty point of drive energy. The weak innervation of the vagina (noted by the Kinsey report) matters in an unexpected sense here because this is precisely what makes it suited to represent the over-whelming part of enjoyment. It becomes the elective place for discharge of the erogenous overflow, which converges towards this sort of epicentre outside the immediate field of the drive. If we can risk a metaphor, this eye of the hurricane – a vaginal void almost without innervation – centres the nothingness of phallic signi-fication, making it a sort of symbol for the envy of the phallus.

Having established the unity which the orgasm obtains from fantasy, we return to the field of lived experience; some women only reach orgasm through clitoral masturbation, while for others, it only happens on condition of a penetration. As we have said, it is not a matter of two kinds of orgasm but of an orgasm which fol-lows an indirect route (the woman, in virile fashion, possesses herself through her lover, with whom she identifies) or a direct route (the woman identifies herself with the woman whom her lover possesses but resists this identification to a greater or lesser extent). It would seem that the indirect orgasm (clitoral) is less intense than the direct one (the orgasm that can be described as vaginal).[54]

As we noted, the debates over feminine enjoyment which have occupied psy-choanalysts for the last fifty years have treated orgasm as if it was self-evidently women's experience. And this assumption seemed to erase its own historical dimension since the word 'orgasm' only entered usage a short time ago, with the emphasis on its feminine specificity even more recent. One might even wonder if the experience of feminine orgasm is not an equally recent phenomenon, pro-portional to the relative freedom of women in modern times in comparison with earlier epochs. It is certainly impossible to verify this, but it might be asked how women could have experienced enjoyment in sex when they lived in conditions of slavery. In the Aboriginal societies of Australia, marriages are so minutely regu-lated between clans, sub-clans, sub-sections of clans, etc., that one wonders how love could play a part.[55] Objects of trade, reduced to the status of bargaining chips between families, barely recognised as human beings by the fathers of the Church, what could women hope for? All that was left to them, it might seem, was the con-solations of motherhood, sugar-coated revenge on their sons, and frigidity. How might they have experienced their bodies and offered their love and their enjoy-ment with the freedom which the giving of a gift requires when they were slaves and even slaves of slaves (if their partner was himself a slave)? We might think that the Sovereign Good of orgasm was perhaps reduced to a barely glimpsed dream at best.

And yet its occurrence is attested at all times and in all places because orgasm does not result from a decision or a voluntary offering that a woman would refuse to make if she found herself in conditions that humiliated her. It is something that escapes her and humiliation can, on the contrary, favour its occurrence, just as some men can only find enjoyment with prostitutes or with women who disgust them. Orgasm can occur in conditions most contrary to love because it responds only to the solicitation of fantasies, and the fantasies of the beaten child and of parricide adapt very well to humiliation and hatred. It is not something that can be consciously willed, and it imposes itself either within a relationship or against a relationship. A woman can enjoy in spite of herself the man who enslaves her or whom she does not love, and on the contrary remain cold as ice with a man who is loved and freely chosen. Women experience something that goes beyond them, a force greater than themselves that may cause them to enjoy, under certain conditions, with a husband in whose selection they have had no say or with someone else. Every woman knows that she is the custodian of this thing, even if she never manages to give it. She knows it without knowing it and begins by protecting this Good even before she is acquainted with it. Similar to the warrior who spends his whole life preparing for a fight that he may never fight, the woman walls her fortress around a treasure that she is all the more unaware of (at least to begin with) because its value only appears in being given.

It may be true that frigidity was more prevalent during the millennia of patriarchal oppression. But feminine enjoyment must nonetheless have made itself heard as the absolute power of someone who is without rights, who is intractable, uncolonisable, a pariah perhaps, but nevertheless mistress of that which cannot be shared and which is only obtained through giving. In times of slavery, under the dominion of the fetish, the flag or money, this negative power (we speak, too, of 'negative theology') governs without governing. Even when they were treated like commodities, exchangeable at will, those by means of whom this power was actualised – beaten, veiled, fetishised perhaps, used as pawns in a patriarchal symbolism, no doubt – still occupied a central position. The 'making' of love resounds through the whole gamut of human activity, from the creation of things to fetishism, from fetishism to the manufactured object and to the price paid for this object, which conceals its basic perversity.

Universality of the infantile origin of orgasm

The clinic (and everyday experience) shows that the orgastic event may or may not occur depending on circumstances, age, lovers, etc. But while orgasm is a precious and sometimes rare commodity, the same cannot be said of its infantile origin, of which it is the distant and relieving echo. Children have small orgasmic equivalents, yet they are psychical and without physiological significance. The existence of early orgasms demolishes the organicist and sexological explanations of enjoyment. It is, of course, true that the organism must grow to a certain physiological maturity first, but the body remains the serf of desire, and it can only actualise the potentialities of the dream.

From childhood onwards, orgastic equivalents correspond to a moment of drive relief at the point of discordance between enjoyment and the excess of enjoyment. In this sense, there are as many kinds of infantile orgasms as there are drives threatened with implosion by their own excess. An oral pseudo-orgasm in infancy has long been documented.[56] Similarly, certain drive dynamics provoke an 'aura', which may result in an epileptic moment, an asthma attack, a migraine, etc. These moments of crisis are repeated until, in adulthood, sexuality takes over and erases their effects by superimposing sexual difference. Until that time, drive energy has no need for the difference between the sexes. It can make do with bodily stimulation and the enjoying liberation which this allows (this is the credo of queer theory). Drive autoerotism involves a form of orgasm different from that of erotism; its discharge is a result of the passage from being to having the phallus – a liberation that explains why masturbation is so common in the psychoses, for which orgasm in sexual relations represents a danger.

These 'pseudo-orgasms' of the drive, which can translate into symptoms (such as asthma or epilepsy) are more or less resolutive. They differ from the 'pre-orgasms' of childhood which conclude masturbatory episodes and already influence genitality. The pseudo-orgasms of the drive differ from pre-orgasms because genital excitation acts precisely to counter drive excitation. The masturbations of childhood end with these pre-orgasms, if we can use the term to describe the drop in tension, the quick recovery of a self that has finally shaken off what was dogging it. What occurs is a moment of relief, a moment of certainty of giving or taking (and not of 'having' as opposed to 'being'). And this happens thanks to fantasies.[57]

These childhood orgasms demonstrate the purely psychical nature of this relief, which has no physiological cause. The orgasm of childhood discharges the guilt that accompanies the transition from passive (being the phallus) to active (having it) and then to the affirmation of gender. Its pleasure is that of a liberation. More than that of the boy, the feminine orgasm of childhood prefigures the features of the woman's orgasm of adulthood. It is certainly still clitoral, but it already has the character of a surprise, of an unexpected rupture, which doubtless owes much to the guilt over an active masculinity that is suddenly contradicted by a latent femininity. Girls are initially boys in the sense that they have the same enjoyment. But it is as girls, most often identified with their feminine gender, that they experience this enjoyment of the organ. Hence, the shock of surprise; as boys, they suddenly find themselves as girls.

What the adult adds to this relief is a change of place; it is no longer as a child that the adult finds relief but by occupying the place of the father or, in the case of a woman, in her relationship to a man who rids her of the father. This change of place validates the parricide fantasy and only then gives sexual enjoyment its meaning. The orgasm then takes on a new meaning; it actualises a hitherto dormant fantasy by taking account of the contradictions between masculine and feminine, which then configure the resolutive moment. The drive orgasm of childhood underpins this process, remaining in some sense its initial driving force.

The universality of this vector from childhood can be summed up in two words: 'sexual trauma', resulting from paternal seduction. The Oedipal, infantile fantasy of seduction is oriented by a constant pressure until its release in adulthood. Orgasm may not always be on the agenda for an adult, but there is an unconscious knowledge of its possibility since the sexual trauma of childhood which concerns each and every human being. From that moment on and in every dream, a latent orgasm pushes towards liberation from the contradictions of desire.

Children of both sexes struggle with seduction by a father which results in a 'subjective trauma' since the child's desire is solicited but cannot be realised without mortal risk. There comes a time in the unfolding of the Oedipus complex when the father wears the mask of an impossible seducer. At this point, if the father's sexual desire were to be actualised, it would lead to a depersonalising vertigo,[58] and hence, the parricide wish that is formed as retaliation against this lethal desire. This childhood trauma happens for every subject, and it corresponds to the division of the subject, torn between two contrary movements.

We see this relationship of desire to subjective trauma in the fact that the beginning of sexual life involves something like an intimate coercion. It has to be gone through even though anxiety is acute. And this coercion does not concern just a few individuals but entire age groups. Both boys and girl feel they must go through it however great the associated anxiety may have been. When boys are brutal and clumsy, it is under the influence of this anxiety. The same goes for many girls who experiment with love affairs, breakups and adventures, accessing multiple models of masculinity, from the young to old, from truck driver to teacher, alone or in groups, with or without drugs and alcohol. Might the extreme and sometimes systematic nature of these forays suggest something like a self-rape, where pleasure remains secondary? The subjective trauma is repeated in this trauma of self by self. It echoes the first moment when the agent of excitement, the father, was also the agent of an incest that resulted in a death wish. It is this conjunction of sexuality and death which seeks resolution later in orgasm, although the latter proves to be a contingent event that is often inhibited because sexual desire, so closely linked to the thought of murder, is oriented according to a wish that may run counter to it. Hence, the relative rarity of orgasm compared to the universality of childhood sexual trauma. The final act, this lethal blow against the father, cannot be delivered so easily.

Orgasm seeks to relieve the tension of sexual trauma in a distant aftermath of the fantasy of seduction. But this fantasy was only traumatic *in its feminine aspect* ('to have been seduced'). This is why no woman accepts her femininity completely, and each woman keeps to herself a little or a lot of her original masculinity. Each woman stages this splitting of the sexual trauma, whereas masculinity, on the other hand, rejects its own femininity onto women, and men are then tormented by the obsession of making a woman enjoy (because their own improbable masculinity is at stake). In this sense, feminine enjoyment cannot be reduced to an 'additional' or 'other' enjoyment; it purely and simply *is* orgastic enjoyment. *There is no orgastic enjoyment other than the feminine kind* – a liberation from the contradictory knot of the seduction fantasy. Men get rid of this knot by pushing it onto women, so it is women who enjoy. If it happens to a man, it will be in a passive, feminine moment, when he is overwhelmed. Otherwise, he only has pleasure. That pleasure, no doubt, goes as far as a certain level of enjoyment, but orgasm is reserved for the feminine.

To summarise, every subject is traumatised by infantile sexual seduction by the father. Most then repeat the trauma symptomatically or else replay it in their love lives. The trauma of childhood is transmitted from dream to dream all the way to the adult sexual relationship itself, and some finally break free from it in the orgasmic discharge (although alas, even they are not exempt from either repetition or symptoms). In childhood, the universality of the trauma linked to the fantasy of seduction remains latent until adolescence. It then inscribes its contradiction in the suffering of the symptom. After this, it may be a particular event in love life that will bring the release of orgasm.

The 'making' of pretence

How long does it take to reach orgasm? The relevant sections of women's magazines suggest much uncertainly in this matter. They advise women with sexual difficulties to 'let go', to let themselves be taken out of themselves, espousing the idea of a passive feminine sexuality that depends on the goodwill of the gentleman. The weekly abundance of such advice gives the impression that many women are frigid at the start of their sex lives, just as men are so naturally prone to premature ejaculation that they have to work on it for a while before they can make sex last for any significant time. We may wonder whether this frigidity concerns only young female readers, yet looking at the advice given – to accept penetration, to relax, to think of a beautiful landscape, the sea, etc. – it soon occurs to one that this frigidity may also be an issue for the women of a more advanced age who dispense such fatuous advice while also insisting on an inalienable right to orgasm.[59] When doyennes of the sex and love columns, who are supposed to knew the score on these matters – at least for themselves and a significant sample of women – spout nonsense about the morphology of the vagina, the best position in order to minimise discomfort, the necessary duration (at least twenty minutes for an orgasm), etc., it is difficult not to think that frigidity may be an issue for the majority of women. Either that or that words fail to describe orgasm or, perhaps, that words only pretend to describe it.

This *pretence* is so much in evidence that one gradually comes to the conclusion that it concerns the thing itself: are the first pleasures of autoerotism for two not based (for an extended period in some cases) on the repetition of acts that are without enjoyment and, therefore, on a pretence? The descriptions of enjoyment that we are given in magazines, 'scientific' reports and sexology books, brimming with neuroscience and statistics, tell us less about pleasure than about what goes on adjacent to it – postures, circumstances, anatomy, the noise it makes. Everything in these descriptions may be true but at the same time false, and all the more false because the only 'falsity' which really needed to be talked about is ignored. There is indeed a pretence of pleasure that follows the path marked out by pleasure itself – a pleasure in repetition, in doing what one has read about, what one has heard that one should do, a pleasure which resembles that which others took before, and which leads to imitation of what they did, to doing what they (the adults, the parents) did, if the child accidentally caught them doing it. The first erotism – autoerotism for two – travels along mimetic tracks, not so much because it imitates what friends tell each other, what gets written in magazines or seen on television, as because it actively mimics in the present a shock that was experienced passively in the past. So there is a pretence of pleasure, although the first sexual experiences may have been far from pleasurable and sometimes involved suffering or at least anxiety, even when there may have been a certain enjoyment involved.

Defloration (on which there is a substantial literature) seems to have little traumatic impact. Female analysands hardly ever mention the moment when it happened. It was, no doubt, important but not as important as the first love. Perhaps defloration only takes on the dimension of an event because virginity is never really lost, because femininity remains impenetrable despite everything. Its 'dark continent' regenerates as quickly as it is conquered. Moreover, physical penetration, even when it causes pleasure, takes second place behind the discovery of the world of love – more important than the first sensations, which are far from convincing in many cases. When we learn that 'it was very good' right from the first time, we do not know exactly what was so pleasing. Was it the discovery of another body which enjoys thanks to her? Was it the gift of oneself, or the possession of the other, or both at the same time? Or perhaps pride at having taken this initiatory step? Or even the pleasure of telling friends that it has finally happened?

If the first pleasure is linked to an anxiety or even pain (that of the first penetration, psychically violent even when it is gentle), it is associated not surprisingly with blood. How could such an effraction fail to come as a surprise even for someone who wanted it? And what the woman releases in a cry goes back to the bifidity of the first cry: that of the primary psychical distress of alienation joined to the pleasure of the call which lifted the weight of the drives. Their pleasure works against the distress granted by love, just as the shock of being penetrated may be forgotten in the happiness of the embrace. If this penetration elicits a cry of surprise, or even of pain, and if this cry also simulates pleasure, the woman to whom this happens will believe that she has met the norm of sexuality – the norms, the descriptions of which she knows, or which she has actually witnessed. And yet this simulation is triggered like a *reflex*, and even when it is not accompanied by any pleasure, its emotion opens a channel towards enjoyment. The first cry of pleasure is based on a cry of pain; it echoes other cries heard in the past.

This conjunction of pleasure and pain goes back a long way; it evokes the first subjective drama of seduction, fantasised as a blow received from the father. A pain engenders pleasure, just as the child who masturbates dreams of the father's blows, summoned up to purge the child's guilt in the first days of subjectivity. This applies to both girls and boys because they both commit a kind of rape in repeating a psychical rape since the sexual seduction by the father occurs for every subject. But when the subject chooses the side of masculinity, they will feel particular resentment towards the father or towards those in society who represent the father.

When the fantasy of seduction is staged, the pretence – the factitious dimension – already belongs to the 'making' of love. Girls may sometimes simulate pleasure, as do boys, and boys also pretend that they are the cause of the pleasure. A woman can pretend to enjoy in order to please her lover (in order to be loved, in short). But this pretence is absolutely coherent with the truth of seduction. Its duplicity sets in motion a fantasy which leads to enjoyment thanks to appearance alone. To deceive is already to enter into the contradiction of love and pretence. It is already to kill in thought. It is to declare a truth – the truth of sexual trauma, which is thus demonstrated retroactively. It hardly ever happens that a father has really seduced his daughter or son, and yet a semblance of rape has been installed in memory. The physical shock of taking, given as if for pleasure, recalls the suffering of a love that has never been resolved. A pure pretence, like many other simulacra, ends up more real than what is real. The dream, for example, or the thought (even unconscious) of a murder was doubtless only a simulacrum, but the pain of the symptom punishes it as if it had been an act. Pretence alone can generate guilt that is strong enough to generate symptoms. And the same is true of enjoyment.

The first sexual relations may seek to imitate a scenario known by hearsay or from books but that does not prevent enjoyment emerging from the traces of this pretence, or at least, it may take the same path. The cry of the infant in distress, counterbalanced by maternal tenderness; the fantasy of the beaten child, who at the same time enjoys the blows; the cries of maternal enjoyment which evoke the suffering of a sexual act that was heard or glimpsed – all these cries echo each other and are set off again at the moment of the first sexual experience and the surprise that it provokes. As if the pretence of pleasure or displeasure would lead to pleasure, the pretence imposes itself like a reflex. Pretence is the performative of the orgasm, at the moment of passage from a 'false pretence' to a 'true pretence'.

Something factitious is set up early on and anticipates a sequel that comes later – either immediately afterwards or after a long time. This facticity of 'making', which does not know where it comes from, also does not know where it is going. Pleasure can certainly be imitated, and sometimes is, but this 'pretence' is not mimicry because it masks a repetition that ignores what it repeats to the extent that its violence is now linked to pleasure. The reflex simulation of sexual pleasure quickly forgets to imitate the visible erotic practices of adults. It repeats without knowing what it repeats, recapitulating a past that is forgotten precisely as it is replayed. Nothing stops it, and it must be run through. Even anxiety is transmuted into pleasure (and so into enjoyment) in relation to the trauma it evokes. The simulation here is part of the enjoyment; it is a 'pseudo-simulation', a redoubling of the false, where the false cancels itself out in its performance.[60]

This painful surprise, this false pretence of pleasure, this interplay of pain and pleasure precipitates an enjoyment that no longer mimics the supposed details of sexual love – descriptions in magazines, specialised books or what friends say. This gesture, this vocal miming of an 'appropriate' enjoyment immediately evokes an enjoyment that ought not to be, a distant pain (delicious at the same time) which has remained unechoed until now. The inescapable suffering of the first experiences of distress, of the first seduction thus suddenly find their meaning as simultaneously an intense pleasure, a lost love, a guilt and the dreamt-of blows that exculpated the guilt. In reality, nothing concrete may have happened in that distant past other than a diffuse excitement, a fear of losing love, anxiety of a feared punishment, without knowing the reason for this. Nothing happened, but it happens now, in a carnal reality borne by the unreality of a much older dream. And throughout life, sexual excitement sparks the resurgence of the same dream, without ever dispelling it.

Pretence awakens the distant echo of a trauma that was not a trauma. So from that moment onwards, 'doing as if' summons up the excitation which it has not actually reached.[61] From the distant launch pad of autoerotism, the factitious summons up pleasure and, in its wake, an unexpected enjoyment. As Marie Darrieussecq writes: 'In any case, the real simulators are women who enjoy. The others only produce crude imitations'.[62] She points out in the same short story that pretence invokes the paradox of the liar. Does Epimenides the Cretan tell the truth when he says: 'I am lying'? If he is telling the truth, then he is not lying. And if he is lying, of course, he has told the truth – or almost because . . . etc. In the same way, following the slope of an unintentional lie about enjoyment, enjoyment finally arrives as something external. Pretence here actualises the truth of the psychical body, which was initially hallucinated. A drama would ensue if the pretence took the body away from itself – a separation from oneself in a pleasure that would remain that of the past (incestuous, before life, hallucinated). It would be an enjoyment but depersonalising and ghostly.

The 'battle of the sexes', result of the co-ownership of a single phallus

The internal contradiction of the seduction fantasy ('Who seduces whom?') is intensified by the external opposition of masculine and feminine, producing a 'struggle' that goes all the way to the sexual relationship itself: who makes love to whom? Which one is the man and which the woman? The passage from autoerotism to erotism is characterised by this tension between masculine and feminine in what might be called a confrontation engendered by the co-ownership of a single phallus. The fundamental fantasies, few in number, put each body in the field of an active and passive polarity: to be seduced or to seduce, to be beaten or to beat, etc., associated in each case with a feminine or masculine identification. The 'battle of the sexes' which then gets started is about each of us separating out our original psychical bisexuality. We need to know who is on the masculine side and who is on the feminine side, and this is not something that could be decided through masturbation.

The first movement of organ enjoyment, a desire (never satisfied) to have the phallus, drives autoerotism, then autoerotism for two and, after that, erotism in its entirety. The desire to have the phallus – by giving it – corresponds to masculine desire (a gift without which desire does not achieve erection). This desire is also actualised on the feminine side by receiving the phallus (provided that an erection is elicited). If we only used the expression 'penis envy', we would make the mistake of thinking that what is in question is a desire specific to women.[63] Some men (many even) imagine that they have the phallus. But that is no magic solution because they can only have this phallus – i.e., the erect organ – on condition of someone's desire, without which the penis is reduced, if not to nothing, at least to a mere promise.[64] Men strive to have the phallus, just as women do, and their desire keeps them constantly on their toes precisely because they do not have it. They seek to have it by giving what they don't have, which allows them to pretend that they do have it.

A *Phallusneid*, a desire for the phallus, masculine as well as feminine, is at the heart of a desire that can never dispense with a partner who validates it.[65] Perversion – polymorphous or otherwise – is no exception to this rule; an exhibitionist, for example, must show the phallus which he does not have in order to then immediately have it. His erection depends on somebody else's gaze. The phallus only takes shape (if we can put it like that) on condition of desire.[66] It is a good that must always be shared in principle; no one keeps it for themselves. Neither men nor women have the phallus, so the 'envy' for it is never satisfied.

If the female 'desire for the phallus' is linked to male erection – of his penis becoming phallus – the masculine-feminine difference is no longer definable in terms of having or not having (since no one has it without the other). Rather, the distinction is between *the act of giving* and *the act of receiving*. A woman often knows how to provoke a man's desire and make love to him actively with his own penis, which has become hers (in which case, her orgasm will be secondary to the feminisation of her partner). Similarly, male premature ejaculation has more to do with the position of receiving, or even that of being taken in spite of oneself while, nevertheless, having sought it.

Because this 'desire for the phallus' develops proportionally to anxiety about the mother's castration, it is then articulated in the second degree to anxiety about castration by the father and, through the father, to the series of fantasies that activate the usual course of erotism, which we have detailed earlier. There is a feature of erotism that testifies to this passage from anxiety about maternal castration (being the phallus) to that concerning castration by the father (wanting to have the phallus). When enjoyment passes from drive energy (particularly oral) to wanting the phallus, this movement is ignited at the junction of oral pleasure and a sort of 'passion' for the phallus. This intersection makes fellatio so intensely pleasurable that it can trigger an orgasm not just of the person who enjoys it (that would be unsurprising) but also of the person who performs it. Fellatio does not only aim at the pleasure of the partner who receives it but also of the partner who gives it.

At this level already, the phallus is erect, and so at the moment of penetration, this one phallus is enough for two.[67] In this sense, the woman is erect with the same phallus as the man,[68] who often loses control of the organ that seems to belong to him but that goes its own way. Far from the usual clichés of the passive woman and the active man, both are more or less active in the 'making' of love. Each of them operates with this phallus, the erection of which depends on a presence and on the fantasies which that presence conjures up. The fantasy of each of the lovers retains its original bipolarity: each is now taker, now taken. But in this confrontation, only the masculine party manages to free himself from his potential femininity, while the woman will be concerned with the internal negation of activity with a passive goal. Girls are also boys to begin with, and when they become, to a certain extent, women, they retain a modicum of virility, which may be useful when they want to take their lovers.

Some stereotypes would have us believe that it is up to men to possess women, but this is to forget that women can possess no less than they are possessed, using the phallus which is erected through them. They do this all the better if they identify with the man they want to possess. So really, they possess themselves – vaginal pleasure is indirect, biased by a fantasy of penetration 'from' the man. In this reflexive way, the contradiction of masculine and feminine detonates for women and for them alone; they are woman and man at the same time, as shown by the banality of the fantasy of rape during lovemaking, which is found in many women. This contradiction will function as what detonates orgasm and will do so all the more powerfully because this contradiction unmasks another contradiction: that it is not the father who penetrates but he who offers deliverance from the father. The orgasm is, in a way, the explosive resolution of a contradiction with a double trigger (to which a double degree of enjoyment undoubtedly corresponds). The masculine/feminine contradiction piggybacks onto the contradiction between man and father.

The bizarre enjoyment of the phallus, which can be experienced only by giving the phallus, is distinct from the orgastic conclusion of such enjoyment, which requires another parameter – that of the contradictions of fantasy. Is it not a commonplace to observe that desire is structured by a violent internal contradiction, the relaxation of which is precisely what marks orgasm? When enjoyment rises, when it approaches its point of impersonalisation, its resolution requires a contradictory shock (the transgressive gesture or thought) at the same time as a repersonalisation – for example, to pronounce the name of the lover.

This actualisation of the fantasy and the discharge of its internal tension are unpredictable. A one-on-one with God may be suited to some, while for others, the alchemy of a group will achieve the same result. Nor can it be known in advance where the implosion will occur – whether it will it be vaginal, clitoral, anal, mammary, buccal, aural, etc. – or whether it will involve a man who is hated or loved, a frigid woman or a prostitute, clothed or naked. All depends on the contradictions of the fantasy and on what resolves those contradictions.

It is precisely this contradiction, the resistance to femininity that masculinity keeps up right to the last, which induces orgasm. Each fantasy is polarised by an active and a passive pole, and the short-circuit of discharge depends on the avatars of this distribution of charge. Breaking the continuity of sexual excitation, the spark of the fantasmatic poles provokes a psychical orgasm that is purely feminine since it is only the feminine that maintains the masculine-feminine opposition. What men do here is unload, in the sense that they unload their femininity onto women.

The obsession of the feminine,[69] the last frontier before orgasm

The 'making' of love generates a battle of the sexes and always involves an activity, whether it be an 'activity with a passive goal' or an 'activity with an active goal'. Activity with a passive goal does not necessarily apply to the woman; she may want to give the phallus, i.e., work actively to provoke an erection in her partner, who, for his part, is not always in an active position because some men prefer activity with a passive goal. A man who is virile in many ways can also be delicately feminine. In this case, he receives the phallus that he gives; his female companion provokes his erection with his more or less relative consent if he is in that feminine moment of the seduction fantasy where the 'no' must be pronounced before the 'yes'.

The 'active' woman just described might evoke the image of a greedy mistress poised to devour a passive lover. But this needs to be qualified. Such forms of activity might achieve the same goals through pretence. A woman can provoke her partner's desire very actively by a myriad of means – by arousing his jealousy, subjecting him to verbal abuse, being late, losing the keys, etc. When it comes to the male party's revenge – most successfully taken by erotic means – the man will perhaps be under the impression that it is he who desires, whereas he will in fact have been artfully guided into this position.

One might think that a woman so taken up with the conquest of her lover will experience only a limited pleasure, hardly more than that of men who benefit only from the pleasure of their companions. Will her enjoyment not then be analogous to that which a man has to make do with? That is to say, will it not be limited to clitoral pleasure, certainly experiencing much in giving pleasure but without going as far as orgasm? Her 'activity with an active goal' seems to reduce enjoyment to what it often is on the male side: that of a confirmed virility and pleasure given rather than orgasm.

Women are also often preoccupied with the enjoyment experienced by the man they love. Being active (one might say 'virile'), they love to give pleasure, and this sometimes satisfies them even without orgasm (a fact that some men find difficult to accept). If they meet a man who is also interested in his lover's pleasure, love can become a struggle where each of them tries in vain to make the other enjoy. In any case, by going only halfway along the path of 'activity with a passive goal', some women are just as active as men, or even more active than some men, endowed as such women are (thanks to the men) with the appropriate organ – a kind of psychical penis, the impregnable 'phantom limb' of every subject.

However, the intensity of this activity may be reversed through an identification with the feminised man. The orgasm still occurs but with a reversed direction: everything happens as if the active woman was in some way made love to by herself. In her enthusiasm, she causes the enjoyment of a fantasy-woman with the profile of her own 'activity with an active goal'. In the background of her fantasy, her companion is in the arms of another woman who is herself – that part of herself which is always already lost in a feminine anonymity. This 'activity with a passive goal' reaches its orgastic denouement split into its two halves.

So a woman's hyperactivity remains no less feminine when it somehow exceeds its purpose and returns to its agent through a kind of boomerang identification with the man's passivity. 'Identification' here means that it is conditioned by a transitive love. The success of this 'feedback' depends on the woman's amorous transport rather than on her response to the man's feelings. She uses the man to rejoin herself as a body, taking herself vicariously and jealous of his own fantasy of penetration. In order to take this passive part of herself, her activity unfolds firstly in the surge of clitoral pleasure, the pleasure of the vagina and of penetration being only a potential consequence – a pleasure that waits for the chance moment of a reversal. The passive aspect of 'activity with a passive goal' does not entail a renunciation of activity. It is simply a matter of letting oneself be carried away by its momentum, until the situation turns around – until, by dint of activity, the woman rejoins herself in the dimension of passive object, along the complex path of a femininity that is denied and that is orgastic under the impact of this very negation.

Does this mode of female activity occur with just any lover? We may well think that the man will have to be able to bear, at least for a while, the passivity of being possessed. Things will be more complicated with a man who is 'active with an active goal' – what gets called a 'real man'. The pleasure will perhaps be present, but its orgastic reversal will be difficult with someone who does not allow himself to be possessed – a predator who does not know how to share, who is interested only in possessing, fascinated above all by the music of enjoyment. How can she then abandon herself without the feeling of being abandoned in love or even rejected in a rejection that has always been a sign of the father's desire? He rejects his daughter precisely because he desires her. The orgasm then becomes something perilous; it takes on the meaning of defeat.

This bringing into play of female division echoes the two sides of fantasy, passive and active. What is the aim of the fantasy if not to free oneself from sexual trauma by actualising it through another body?[70] The child who has experienced seduction passively will want to seduce actively. Later, a man will replay the same scenario by seducing a woman. He is active in order to be rid of a latent femininity which haunts him, and he becomes obsessed with a woman's body (a body that is initially headless, a Venus de Milo, a gynoid). And a woman can want this, too, also relying on a woman's bod – her own perhaps, presenting it as itself divided. She shows 'herself' here, but who is this 'self' that she shows? It is herself and it is not herself but another self disguised as a woman or even as a woman whose image she borrows. She might mimic a model woman, like a fashion model, a woman to the end, dead because seduced by a father a long time ago yet in an ever-present time.

The risk of desire falls on this other in a vertiginous division that may initiate the meeting of a woman with herself. Could 'the Woman' here always be the site of a kind of splitting into this anonymised space? Can we say that she shows herself if she only sees herself through this image? It is only the feminine part of every woman that enjoys. It happens or does not happen to someone, to another woman who is herself at that moment, depersonalised by her own enjoyment. Orgasm never happens directly to a woman, or it only happens through a fantasy where she enjoys what she gets rid of, namely, of a seduction by . . . by who? Don't say! At the moment of this detachment, this explosion of a renounced incest only happens at the price of this splitting. This female body, always already ideal, obsesses both men and women. It is not the body of anyone in particular; it is the body that would undergo paternal incest in order to refuse it. This enjoyment of the father, rejected though desired, is set free in the orgastic disjunction. It is accomplished thanks to its own refusal in a cry which actualises it at the very moment when the cry says 'no'. This only happens to the woman dreamt of by the father, and the man enjoys it through her when he contemplates this transport; it only comes to him through his feminine part, the part that he renounces in order to be a man. A woman's enjoyment obsesses him as if it was his own – the enjoyment he would experience if he consented to be a woman. He seeks this enjoyment in his own other 'half', the part of himself that he rejects. That half experiences what the other half has, in fact, sought.[71]

Because they obtain their masculine credentials by refusing to be feminised by their father, men cannot know this enjoyment, which is in principle beyond the reach of the masculine.[72] Rejecting their feminisation, they only know orgasm through the woman as intermediary. This vicarious enjoyment frees them for a moment (a result that cannot be achieved by masturbation) by assuring them of their gender and of their name. And most male lovers are only satisfied if their female partner enjoys what they themselves do not know. Many men are obsessed by their partner's orgasm and so little interested in their own satisfaction that they prefer to hold back until their partner reaches that point. To take pleasure alone would be shameful. This modality of male desire provokes an orgasm that is the 'alibi' of the man who cannot know it. So he assumes a mask of anonymity, and the woman becomes the sole subject of the orgasm. But this subject is without a name. The subject of the orgasm is qualified by a certain amnesia of identity.[73] With impersonality on the one hand and depersonalisation on the other, the name becomes what is at stake in the sexual relation. This double division, feminine and masculine, explains certain oddities of human erotism, such as the case where the male partner is both actor and spectator of a scene where, in his fantasy, his lover would find enjoyment with another woman.[74]

The feminine orgasm, therefore, serves both parties and takes on immeasurable value because it assures the man of his own identity: that of his gender and that of his name, which can also serve both parties. It is the Sovereign Good since it governs the possession of any other good. Must a subject not be sovereign of their gender and name first of all if they want to appropriate any other good (starting with the good that is their own body)? Such is the Good of the transcendental subject, a sovereignty so great that whoever accedes to it already reigns and would renounce everything if it were not for the desire that pushes them to prove it once again: a testimony *semper incertus*, like the *Pater* who vanishes in the act.

Orgasm, the other side of the parricide fantasy

Let's try to summarise the movement of desire because its evolution bears the seeds of its eventual orgastic resolution. In the standard version of the Oedipus complex, parricide seems to result from the desire for the mother, even though she has never been desired in the genital sense of the term, with a sexualisation that only emerges with the paternal function. Castration – the 'blows' administered by the father – is what causes desire, and the goal of maternal drive enjoyment is now diverted to phallicism. It may be true that the castrating 'blows' are a punishment for masturbation, but they are administered at its pace and will themselves generate organ enjoyment. On the one hand, they have a feminising effect, but on the other, they provoke an erection, i.e., they masculinise. Castration both masculinises and feminises; this is the very definition of 'psychical bisexuality', which resolves its internal contradiction by the creation of an external tension (between two persons). The quest for the phallus is henceforth pursued between a man and a woman but on one condition: the father must be eliminated. Because if the father is the agent of desire, he must not become its cause, on account of the incest risk. The condition is, therefore, unambiguous: the father must be killed. The coupling of man and woman accomplishes this murder. In order to get out of the family and to enjoy with a man other than the father, it is necessary to terminate this first seduction. Sexual coupling repeats this scene indefinitely.

If the agent of desire also became its cause, incest with the father would have the effect of annihilation of the subject through lethal enjoyment, and on the masculine side, this feminisation would also cancel out virility. So the final relief of sexual excitement remains inhibited unless the agent of desire is suppressed. The problem of erotism is to preserve the cause while getting rid of the agent; if the father – the cause of this enjoyment that one should not have – does not die, orgasm will not be forthcoming.[75]

The quest for the phallus through the Other of sex initiates an excitement that could last endlessly, delaying the moment of discharge ever further. A parricidal meaning must be added to this, which would amplify the fault right up to its final reversal and its sometimes melancholic climax (*post coitum semper*). From the outset, this quest for the phallus bears the mark of something like a preliminary guilt, which saturates passive enjoyment (receiving blows), and orgasm produces a sudden passage to the active side of the parricide (dealing blows). From an enjoyment that is always already passive (undergone) to its orgastic conclusion that is on the opposite, active side (even if it seems involuntary), the cycle of fantasies runs through the whole of its arc until the arrow is released.

The orgasm resolves their contradictions by choosing the solution that is not allowed: to leave the father. This murderous abandonment triggers the shock and delight of a consummated fault. Pleasure reaches its epileptic peak thanks to what forbids and counters it. At the centre of the orgasm, there is a parricidal wish, which both shuts down enjoyment and realises it. This enjoyment is so paradoxical that it can at any moment become entangled in its contradictions. It remains an enjoyment even if it does not go as far as orgasm. So when a woman cannot leave her father, her position involves an incestuous vow of fidelity. In this sense, frigidity is also an enjoyment, though it is a 'frozen' enjoyment since prohibition wins out and inhibits the orgastic release instead of provoking it. In any case, the desire of/for the father, the first motor of phallic excitation, is only relieved when linked to his fantasised death, which thus becomes the condition for the possibility of orgasm. Either the father must be killed or she who enjoys must die, unless she prefers to inhibit her orgasm.

In neurosis, the figure of the father coincides with that of the man, and the orgasm has to rid the man of this incestuous double. If it explodes, it does so on the reverse side of a parricide fantasy.[76] The choice is simple: either an incestuous enjoyment kills before life can begin or this enjoyment passes to exogamy but on condition of the parricide fantasy that is predicated on incest while denying it. It actualises 'a little death'[77] by the doubling of a conjunction; the death that risked occurring due to incest is mitigated thanks to the murder of the father, eliminated by the man who supplants him. The man with whom a woman repeats the trauma of sexual seduction is precisely not her father, and therefore, from the point of view of desire, he chases the father away. In parallel to this, the man, in his own fantasy, ousts the father who would forbid him to enjoy in sex.[78] The linking of these two fantasies – masculine and feminine – implies a parricide, a relationship to the name, to debt and, therefore, to a gift. The lover has not replaced the father (except in the case of neurosis), but he has symbolically supplanted him by actualising his (the man's) desire *for* a woman and the recovery – through an intermediary – of his own enjoyment. For a woman, he remains a man as long as he does not replace the father (the temptation of neurosis), a requirement from which the dramatic collision of desire proceeds.

Parricide and the taking of the name that testifies to it is the exogamous condition of enjoyment, which itself reproduces the parricide (before reproducing the species). The orgasm orchestrates this reversal. This enjoyment of escape from a lethal being-enjoyed and the reversal which the escape involves amount to taking on one's name, to knowing who one is. But the guilt remains and reignites the engine of a desire that is still intact. So the parricide fantasy is the underpinning of orgasm, and it involves a depersonalisation since it coincides on the feminine side with the loss of the father's name. Opposing the father, a woman gives his name to the man she calls by name when making love, but by so doing, she loses her own. In most cultures, and until today, women have taken their husband's name for the benefit of their enjoyment, far beyond any submission to patriarchy (under French law, they have never been obliged to take their husband's name). The name, which serves both parties, thus inscribes the invariant of the sexual relationship.

Can we really speak of a 'fantasmatic parricide' that occurs at the moment of this reversal of enjoyment into orgasm? Is the expression not rather grandiloquent? It would be if this parricide consisted of scenes soaked in blood. Really, though, it is soluble in rose water. The 'parricide fantasy' does not present itself in murderous form. From childhood onwards, it is covered over by the love of the father. Provided that the father first allows himself to be killed, he is then loved, in recognition of his symbolic function as the initiator of desire. In short, the parricide drama can be played out entirely on the stage of love.

This will be even more obvious from adolescence onwards, when 'killing the father' comes down to replacing his love by that of a man. Is the father not thus well and truly abandoned? But this kind of murder is also covered over by love; the love of a man covers over that of the father who lets his son or daughter love someone else, that is to say, who lets them escape from him or who accepts a kind of symbolic death. A parricide is concealed under a fig leaf of love.[79] Loving another man or woman betrays a father who ends up in the grave, covered by the cloak of these beautiful feelings. The very confession of love conceals and fulfils this drama. It may happen, for example, that saying 'I love you' triggers orgasm at a certain moment in sex. Any murderous enactment disappears completely behind this tender confession. Far from any acute dramatisation, the confession of love seems the simplest act, as if declaring love was sufficient for the past – and, specifically, what the declaration denies – to be forgotten so that the lovers enjoy each other as if it was the first time, or at any rate, they situate themselves in a point of origin, which is that of their rebirth.

This parricidal dimension of orgasm, obscured by love, is barely visible in the snapshot of fantasy. The still is not enough to understand the film. It is not so much this love which covers things over as the actual script – the sequence of events – which reveals the parricidal undercurrent of the film. We have to see the sequence of the story unfold in order for the term 'fantasmatic parricide' to take on its meaning. The actual drama has several acts that make it more visible. The standard plot is that of Corneille's *Cid*: the young suitor kills the father of his beloved in a duel in the name of his own father's honour.[80] But real stories seldom follow such a neat scenario, and there are many more frequent (but also more convoluted) sequences that lead to the same result. For example, the first man whom a woman loves will be absorbed – within the constraints of a restricted repetition – by her love of the father that was designed to allow her to escape maternal capture. Sexual pleasure is unlikely to find satisfaction in this imposition of the father on the man. But more erotic conditions will be met if a rival eliminates the first love in this festival of phantoms.

Some women thus endlessly pit two men against each other in the melodrama that plays the man against the father. They eliminate the father thanks to a lover, who immediately takes on the features of the father,[81] etc. One clown chases off the other. The woman sometimes only finds her enjoyment after a long series of these pantomimes, and happiness often only comes unexpectedly or when she has given up looking for it. With each new love, this repression of the past functions as a kind of shroud – another metaphor for the fantasmatic parricide. A certain feminine donjuanism, drawing acidic pleasure from instances of betrayal, probably has no other source than an enjoyment that denies itself to one lover in order to bear fruit thanks to another. In this respect, it is symmetrical to male donjuanism, where the hero – the sex symbol of our culture – takes fewer detours in order to display the confrontation with the father. Do these remarks on Don Juans of both sexes imply that they do not enjoy, that they are engaged in a hunt for orgasm that is doomed to disappointment (unlike monogamous couples, married in church in the name of a father who was betrayed and crucified once and for all)? But they do, in fact, enjoy on occasion, not, though, without learning the lesson that orgasm only comes at a price, a price that neither tears nor even blood can succeed in lowering.

In his book *The Name on the Tip of the Tongue*,[82] Pascal Quignard writes of the forgetting of a name when a couple is about to be formed. A young woman loves a man who vows that he will marry her if she manages to make him a copy of a precious woven belt, bearing representations of various scenes. Can the embroideries that she will weave correspond to his fantasies? It is an impossible task of bringing fantasies into harmony, and the young woman cannot succeed at it, to her great despair. She is on the point of giving up when a knight dressed in black, Heidebig de Hel, knocks on her door one night. The reader senses at once that he is an avatar of the devil. As a mark of his gratitude for being offered shelter, the dark knight gives the lady a belt identical to the one she was unable to copy but on condition that, when he returns in a year's time, she will remember his name. If she does not remember, then he, Heidebig de Hel, will consider her to be his and carry her off wherever he pleases – to hell, as the reader suspects.

This satanic encounter was necessary in order for the phantasmagoria of the belt to be duplicated and for the weaving of another belt to enable harmony; the two young people are married. And as if the name of the Evil One was locked away as soon as the union was consummated, the young woman at once forgets his name. Nothing should be easier to remember than these five syllables and they are forever on the tip of her tongue, but there is nothing she can do; the name escapes her, despite her most desperate efforts. She finally confides in her husband, who, in the name of their love, makes several journeys as far as hell itself, from whence he returns each time with the name and tells it to his wife. But she again forgets it.

The fateful hour of the devil's return inexorably approaches. But the story has a happy ending: at the very last moment, the name of the Evil One is pronounced, and he is defeated as he comes to find his prey. Such is not always the case in life, where the name that is locked away by the union of a couple can play evil tricks aplenty. The seduction of a satanic father sets up for the lovers a pleasure that ought not to be, in counterpoint to incest, in the parricidal forgetting of his name. The enjoyment is actualised not so much because it is forbidden as because it is carried out with a man other than the father and less as an occult 'transgression' than a kind of fantasmatic 'reverse shot' of the father, who is reduced to his spirit. Forgetting the name of such a father forges a dream of harmony for the couple, by internal exclusion of his ternarity. But is the name of the Evil One not always still present on the tip of the lovers' tongues when they kiss?[83]

Women enjoy ten times more than men . . . but at what cost?

'Women enjoy ten times more than men'. The unfortunate Tiresias barely had time to make this report than he was struck blind by Hera. But his words were hardly news to anyone, and we may wonder if the poor man deserved to keep his eyes when his clairvoyance in the matter was so limited. For how can one not see that this feminine enjoyment is what ignites the enjoyment experienced by her lover? And how can we fail to notice the price she pays for this apparent benefit because, if women enjoy more, there is a disparity working to their disadvantage in which their supposed privilege generates a measureless claim, despite their tenfold pleasure? If they enjoyed ten times more than men, they should be happy to make the most of it; two lovers should be even after lovemaking, able to take their leave and stay friends. But that is not what happens.[84] Nothing can assuage the feminine grievance; there is always 'something more' that has to be granted and which, moreover, never succeeds in compensating for the 'something less' of orgastic depersonalisation. This 'less' comes from a long way back; it is created by desire itself, from its hallucinatory and depersonalising origin. Desire carries this threat within itself right from its beginning.

When she is desired, a woman is outside herself. The attraction she exerts may please her, but at the same time, she rebels against it in her whole way of being. Desire sets a trap, and the risk of falling into it is so great that it often prompts a retreat. Although they might seek to please, many women experience men's desire as a burden.[85] Putting it bluntly: male desire splits women's bodies. Women are both at the place where they provoke an erection and at the place where they actually are. If 'having the phallus' depends on the partner's desire, this mode of appropriation is produced in a certain impersonality. The mere fact of walking the tightrope of this split induces giddiness, which forces a quickening of the step; women are here and they are elsewhere, in the creation of a space that may be quite vertiginous. They are pleasing because of what they provoke, because of the erection that displaces them outside themselves, to a place where they can only find themselves if they themselves also desire what makes them lose themselves. Is this not the vanishing point where the orgasm is situated?

When the time comes to give in to one's desire, the question of the name will matter in proportion to this alienation. The name anchors the subject. It is the lifeline that saves the subject from the tide of their own fantasy. As soon as the subject desires, they are at risk of being swept away by this force that emanates from the self but which is experienced as if it came from without. As soon as the subject begins to enjoy, this force threatens them even more, and if the orgasm finally prevails, they will fear an impersonal submersion. So this loss of control of the body is countered by the anchoring of the name.

Our own desire controls us, and we no longer know who we are in obeying it. Faced with the risk of this loss, the subject can still obtain an enjoyment thanks to the name, which subsists outside the body. This is why love – which demands a recognition of the person beyond qualities and beauty – is a condition of erotism for most people. Transgressive enjoyment can, of course, take on the same meaning by following a contrary path, which is also potentially orgasmic. To transgress any rule is (by displacement) to subvert a law of the father and thus to take shelter from his name. But this will be at the price of an anomic fall or even at the risk of a brief melancholic moment.

If sex remains anonymous, without any subjective anchoring, a chasm opens up after the enjoyment. On the one hand, excitement increases and pushes us to give in to it. But on the other hand, its outcome is distressing, and one must not give in to it, at least not without precautions. Women accumulate prerequisites and conditions, from love to recognition and giving, and do so much more than men (at least than those men whose relationship to the name does not subject them to the same danger).

Is the term 'depersonalisation' appropriate to describe this effect of orgasm? It certainly resonates with our relation to desire. When love is lacking and enjoyment divides them violently, some women experience fits of jealousy almost immediately after orgasm, as if another woman had enjoyed through them. What the woman is jealous of is this hallucinated part of herself. Nothing is more difficult to temper than this torment of otherness at the heart of what is most intimate. And, bizarrely, enjoyment taken to its culmination can also lead to a breakup if the woman does not feel sufficiently loved. If she can only achieve orgasm with a random man, separation follows close on the heels of orgasm.

This kind of division does not affect men but a man also impersonalises himself when he causes enjoyment and derives enjoyment from this. He is confronted with a father in the moment of a pleasure that exceeds him. A third 'person' participates in the event. So sexual passion exacerbates jealousy, even when nothing 'real' justifies such jealousy. Orgasm in itself actualises a primal scene. And yet the woman will have taken enjoyment in the impersonality of the man, while her lover will have seen in the woman his own division. And if this 'normal' jealousy finds some pretext in reality, one of the protagonists will draw from it a certainty, sometimes to the point of putting their very existence in danger. He or she will believe that they are playing the role of the dead – the party excluded from a couple. The dramatisation of these circumstances can go as far as actual death, which then functions as a kind of macabre substitute for the orgastic moment.[86]

Coming back now to Tiresias and his estimate, we could say that desire and enjoyment are shared by both men and women, albeit in different measures. The man's desire, to which the contradiction of 'activity with a passive goal' is foreign, can externalise itself twice as positively as the woman's desire. Enjoyment, for its part, is more or less equally distributed; each of the two sexes benefits from it. But orgasm is on the feminine side alone. It would appear, then, that the woman has an additional pleasure. The question immediately arises, though: by 'whom' was this pleasure of orgasm taken? Precisely by nobody since it is accompanied by a depersonalisation. It is not 'ten times more' because it is not susceptible to measurement since 'nobody' has taken it. For this infinite pleasure to be taken, it must be able to be given.

The so-called 'supplement' is a fool's bargain, and it is clear that if the orgasm opens up the risk of depersonalisation, its subject will demand something that immediately allows a kind of 're-personalisation'. The man must pay his debt! For he cannot leave just like that, immediately after lovemaking. The brevity of pleasure contrasts with the duration of this debt. You have to start by giving time and presence. And if the lover has to leave in the end, he must leave a *sign* of his presence. Just as the orgasm has relieved the incestuous dimension of the father's desire, a symbol of the father – for example, his name – can compensate for the 'minus' of the orgastic loss. Eroticism demands the singularity of a bond that becomes a sometimes unique condition of arousal – at least for a majority of women, for whom the question of the exclusivity of the bond takes precedence often over enjoyment itself.

'The desire to have the phallus' is certainly the compass that orients feminine sexual arousal. But it hardly ever happens that a woman enjoys an anonymous phallus with a stranger who has not shown some identity that harmonises in some respect with her fantasies. The penis of a casual encounter must have a name that is invoked at the crucial moment; it is the formative arch of enjoyment, from its beginning to its end. An anonymous love of the phallus may trigger enjoyment, but it does not set it free. Finding the phallus is easy enough. What is more difficult is for the name of the one who bears it to be pronounced and for this enunciation to correspond to a sexual fantasy.

Enjoyment, depending as it does on the enjoyment experienced by another body, threatens to depersonalise in proportion to its intensity. So it is better to have a name for protection at the moment of release. Sex remains anonymous and depersonalising when it lacks this legitimation. The depersonalisation, the loss of the name at the moment of orgasm, has as its counterpoint the giving and taking of the man's name. This is why most women refuse to sleep with random interchangeable lovers.

It is true that women enjoy more than men, but what they gain here threatens their identity. This is why the gift of a name has been a condition of enjoyment in almost all cultures before it was a sign of alliance. It is true that today, this gift of a name (which in France has only ever been a custom) sometimes seems outdated. But it will likely remain a paradigm because the name is the secret anchoring point of the subject to their body when it enjoys. What is at stake is not so much the legal act of marriage celebrated at the town hall as the feeling of belonging that follows from sexual love. Certainly, two lovers belong to each other in equal part, but what they give differs: orgasm on one side; a name on the other. A man can give other gifts as well – jewellery, clothes, furs, etc. – that recognise the priceless value of the person, dressing up their emptiness. But of all possible gifts, the gift of a name is the only one not subject to exchange. A woman cannot sell the name she has been given. No gift has the specificity of a proper name. An orgasm for two and a name for two: such is the equation of the sexual relationship.

This name certainly matters when gifts are given and exchange occurs, but it also has the effect, which no other gift has, of marking exogamy. Because the very fact of this name's difference from the father's name is an implicit parricide. Incest threatens and the refusal of the father opposes it; the crisis looms, ramifies and (at best) explodes. The orgasm is weighted by the name, and the exchange here with another subject is what creates the relationship itself. The loss implied by the enjoyment '*of* the woman' is exchanged for the name '*of* the father', where the genitives ('of') are to be read in both subjective and objective senses. They symbolise a relationship, where each enjoys the other in the ambiguity of the genitive, and the orgasm occurs at the point where the objective genitive turns into the subjective genitive. The 'sexual relationship' is this cross-exchange between two subjects where the name is the anchoring point of enjoyment at its point of passage to exogamy.

This exchange in itself does not imply a belonging, but insofar as the subjective genitive is exchanged for the objective genitive and vice-versa, each of the partners perhaps finds themselves alone, but they have found themselves! From the perspective of this final solitude, one might think that the sexual relationship did not occur; it is forgotten in its very result.[87]

Do sexual relations find an equilibrium in this cross exchange of orgasm and name? That would be too much to hope for because a man is not the owner of his name. He is only its tenant and must pay the rent from day to day, which he does through the acts that legitimise it. So it is with the sexual act, which first requires a raising of the tension between the masculine and the feminine and then the orgastic release of their contradiction. But if the name conditions such a resolution, to whom does it belong? It is given and taken in the act, but it also dates from before life, and at the same time, it is a vehicle of the death drive – Moira, the last of the Fates, present in each of our acts.

The division of the subject persists despite the sexual relationship. To enjoy the enjoyment of the other is not to make One, as the myths of mating would have it. Far from uniting two bodies, making love separates since it actualises the subjective division of each of us; we may be reconciled with ourselves thanks to the other, but we are no less alone. It is perhaps done gratefully but surely in solitude and in a solitude that distinguishes each of us from the rest of the human race, as if it happened only to us. Do others make love too? Is it the same for them? The solitude of this 'making' could almost make us doubt it. What is made in the act of love? A body is momentarily reconciled with itself, and one might take it for just another narcissistic illusion if, at the same moment, the name did not anchor and fasten the subject to this reconciled body. One might hope for lasting peace thereafter, but alas, the name is only legitimised during the limited time of the act.

Fantasy has only been relieved here by an intermediary, each of the protagonists having given to the other that which continues to be lacking in them. And desire then resumes its course. It relays a lack which relaunches it. Desire has no object, from its hallucinatory origin onwards. The subject is infinitely drawn out of him- or herself by this internal split. The relationship of the subject to their name, which they seek to stabilise in erotism, will never be resolved in the satisfaction of desire itself. The name is a strange grail; people are set in pursuit of that which they already have and which only appears and shines for so long as the pursuit continues. It fades as soon as they stop looking for it.

The relationship of each subject to his or her name poses a crucial question since the name taken from the father in the parricide fantasy symbolises the death drive, which is always at play in erotism. This function of the name is illustrated in

Kiyoshi Kurosawa's film *Cure* (1997), which shows something like the vampirisation of one subject by another when one of them loses their name. The principal character is a handsome young man with identity amnesia. He provokes love in those he meets, and this love, together with the forgetting of his name, creates a relentless transitivism, a certain transfusion of aggression from one body to another and its gradual contagion. The love he triggers has a hypnotic quality, as if by lacking a name, he is no longer confined to his body. Those who love him become like him – forgetting their own identity in turn. They are transformed by a dark force into murderers who at once forget their crimes.

Each of them has met this wanderer, this mysterious and involuntary instigator of their crimes, by chance, and the love of this fascinating young man, living in an eternal present, demolishes the house of cards of their dreams to the point at which they take the step to action. He is welcomed by a succession of people, with whom a hypnotic relationship is quickly established, and each of his hosts becomes immersed, first in the telling of their own story, then in the recounting of a memory that is as violent as it is repressed. Finally, an identification with this brutal desire leads the hypnotised person to a fatal act, turning them, in turn, into an amnesiac assassin.

What did the hero ask of his chance interlocutors? Almost nothing. He was lost, in need of help and of love. And their unconscious desires were made manifest through this anomalous love, which summoned up a repressed desire and pushed them to its realisation. The schoolteacher who is his first host kills his wife and throws himself out of a window. The model employee whom the young man meets next murders the prostitute he goes to see shortly afterwards. A series of tragedies follows, sparing none of the archetypal figures of society. And in the final sequence, we are given to understand that the police commissioner in charge of the investigation, whose profession should have led him, more than anyone, to repress the fascination of crime, is himself obsessed by murder. When we see the faces of those who become murderers in this way, their blank stares show us that they are no longer in control of their intimate madness, held in check until then. The love of the amnesiac has made them lose their identity, as if it had been pumped out of them, and they kill from the depth of their hypnosis.

What this reveals is the role of the name, thanks to which each person inhabits their own body without transfusing into the body of whoever dominates them at the height of their experience of love and whom they might kill were it not for the identity that restrains them. For to have assumed one's name is to have killed once and for all in the murder of the father, establishing a guilt that will from then on prevent further killing. The guilt of a first fantasmatic murder, linked to the taking of the name, holds in check the criminal that each of us conceals. And when this name is lacking, the transitivism of a void of identity shifts onto the succession of bodies that love seizes on. The amnesiac makes those who love him into agents of the death drive; he becomes a 'black hole' in the minds of his victims. As the hero of Kurosawa's film says: 'Everything I was passes into you. In exchange, I infiltrate minds and my own mind is full of emptiness'.

Women and children first! The gift, subjectivation of enjoyment

Soon after birth, the moment always comes when a child says 'no'. Instead of accepting everything out of love for the mother, the child refuses that excessive something which would have made them into an angel, into an ideal that is always already dead. What is rejected is a part of the child's own self with which they would have had to identity if they accepted being the mother's perfect object. So that, psychically, this ideal image that the child has expelled is outside them and threatens them with reprisals in proportion to their guilt.

This division is already at work when the child cries out from 'inside' through the mouth and hears the cry 'outside' through the ear. The return differs from the outward journey because the sounds that return from outside have been infused with maternal demand (in the form of how she interprets the cry). So the child's own cry demands something of the child without the child knowing what it is, and they are frightened by this. The 'double' of the self which the child hears already corresponds to their division by their own enjoyment. What is perceived outside could have the effect of annihilation because its sound returns to the child heavy with an objectifying commandment, which sets in motion the lasting relation of Being to Nothingness that is specific to subjectivity. Its two-stroke engine moves between a pleasure, which affirms Being, and an excess of pleasure, which threatens collapse into Nothingness. The child is desired, is called to be born as the mother's phallus (Being), but at the same time, this maternal phallus does not exist (Nothingness). To not be in the very event of birth – such is the contradiction that initiates the drama of narcissism and the aggressiveness that goes with it, forever verging on resolution in suicide or murder.

Gifts given to the child seek to appease this persecuting double. A teddy bear offers the child mastery of their own double that was outside them (it is a 'transitional subject' rather than a 'transitional object'). The teddy locates a rejected ideal half of the self, which, if it was not symbolised, would come back to persecute the child. It functions as a kind of *alter ego* – a confidant to whom the child speaks in the private language of the drive, before having mastery of words. This anthropomorphic present symbolises the enigma of the child's enjoyed being and the child subjectifies it. The bear, for example, is a first token of the animality of the body, rejected by subjectivity. A reconciliation takes place between the child and the bear. The child embraces this intimate part of themselves, put at their disposal by the Other, who might have snatched it away. It is a gift given by someone who recognises the child's division, which is why the cuddly toy calms the child and soothes their distress.

A fight to the death was underway between the child as subject and their 'ideal ego', which sought to impose its law in the name of an annihilating love by taking the child away from themself. The gift returns the child to their own self; it makes the distinction between subjectivity and ideality. So the gift builds a rampart against depersonalization; it allows the child to recognise themselves in their subjective division because it was given by another subject. This intersubjective recognition gives the child back their unity, reconciling them with themselves. This subject-to-subject connection has a significance greater than the market value of a gift, although it would not have been established without the giving of that gift.

This gift is all the more precious when given by the very person who was the original cause of subjective division. For the mother embodies both the Other and the subject who denies this Other, protecting from its own excess. She is at once 'nobody'[88] (the impersonal Other, source of a commandment that kills) and 'somebody'[89] (the subject of love). The maternal Other could have continued to enjoy the child's body, which, from a certain point of view, is itself a gift or even a symbol. But precisely, a child is not a gift; the child refuses this place, and the gift that the child receives is a recognition of this. So enjoyment shifts to the level of the gift itself, a priceless gem, a symbol. Each gift intervenes at the exact point of the subject's division. Embodying the child's ideal part, the soft toy reconciles the child with their own self because a fellow-being who saw their division offered it to them. The child loves this intimate and rediscovered part of themselves, which embodies ideality by not being useful, consumable or exchangeable.

By giving, the maternal Other loses her omnipotence and admits that she also is only a subject. The symbol signifies this alliance. Without this pact, the opposition of Being and Nothingness, the struggle of master and slave, would continue indefinitely. The subject-to- subject recognition pushes into the back-ground – represses – the phallic signification that the child's body has for the Other. A symbol that escapes exchange represses this mortal enjoyment. No 'counter-gift' would repay it, even if the subject who received the gift is keen to take their turn at giving. He or she will also want to offer a gift in order to legitimise their own subjective birth, but what they give is no longer their enjoying body but the recog-nition of this intersubjectivity. The superficial appearance is of a giver and a debtor who gives back. But what can a small child offer in return? The child will give by conforming with what is expected of them; all of the child's 'learnings' (starting with learning to talk) are its gifts.

Of course, one gift may respond to another, but each of them remains incom-mensurable, and their sequence legitimises their meaning. Each gift places two subjects on an equal footing, without one of them being strong and the other weak, because the party who receives may refuse the gift, and the alliance is legitimised by what they in turn may give. The gift creates, attests to and commemorates this alliance; it crystallises a performance (in Austin's sense) and establishes a duty of loyalty.[90]

But does a gift to a child really symbolise enjoyment? The child's body might certainly invite possession, but does it have this hyper-eroticised meaning which a gift will relieve? This dimension becomes clearer if we consider the consequences of the gift or of its absence: children without toys cry, they sleep badly, they stop eating. They slide into negativism and struggle against an annihilation that lacks mediation. The sexual meaning of all this becomes clearer later on. When the child who has grown up continues to be troubled by their past and relives it from the perspective of the adult in their own erotic experiences, the lack of a gift that they may have experienced in childhood will appear to them in retrospect as a sexual violation. They will sometimes feel certain of this (without having the slightest proof) and will construct fictions accordingly. It is as if children who had no toys were traumatised in the sense of a sexual trauma.

How is this to be explained? Through childhood the subject has to confront a succession of ordeals or traumas that are part of the process of growing up, the sexual meaning of which only appears retroactively. From birth onwards, the Other alienates the subject, whose psychical life develops through this confrontation. So the subject climbs a succession of steps and only escapes the initial alienation by the maternal Other through seeking salvation with the father. But then, for better or for worse, paternal seduction creates a trauma, the repetition of which will be the warp and weft of ordinary erotism. Even as it actualises the subject's desire, the seduction fantasy is accompanied by the idea of a deceit that calls for compensation. What happens in love affairs will echo what happened around the enjoyment offered by the infant's body, an enjoyment that was symbolised and dialecticised by the toys which the infant received. So we see the analogy between the infant's enjoyment and sexual seduction, symbolised by the dialectic of the gift. Retroactively, a fantasy of having been raped will follow from an absence of gifts in the first period of life. Just as in infancy, the toy symbolises retroactively an incestuous seizing of the body, enjoyment in adult erotism requires gifts that enable a threatened alienation to be avoided.

In this sense, intuition suggests an equation between the distress of the infant and a more specifically feminine anxiety concerning rejection and abandonment, perhaps after having been loved but with the feeling of having been abused. Is it not the fact of having been treated as an object of enjoyment that creates the connection between these two figures of dereliction? Both the child and the woman are offered to enjoyment in an objectification that calls for compensation. The gift has an obvious relationship to enjoyment in sexual relations: the woman gives herself. To make love all the way to its orgastic conclusion is to lose oneself. Compared to the abandonment of the infant, the self-giving of the orgasm certainly highlights other (sexualised)[91] invariants of the division of the subject, but the two are alike in engendering a momentary 'depersonalisation'.

The cry of sexual enjoyment expresses this loss of self; a woman gives herself at this moment, just as the cry of the child, mentioned earlier, signifies that the child's body is an object of enjoyment for the maternal Other. And if we consider the orgasm as a gift without measure, it, too, calls for an act of giving in return, or at least for its symbol. What it calls for is not a 'counter-gift'; any payment would inhibit it (prostitutes do not have orgasms). Men occasionally misunderstand the incommensurability of this gift and believe that they can pay for it – that they can buy themselves a woman. But if a man wants to buy pleasure, he is embarking on a quest that is doomed to be fruitless since to monetise it is to miss what is at stake here.[92]

We can now try to see what links the two questions which we have treated separately up to now: the enjoyment of the baby's body (compensated for by the gift of toys) and the gift of orgasm offered by a woman (to which gifts of various kinds can create an echo). The course of life would have it that the first of these enjoyments which call for a gift – the enjoyment of the child – precedes the enjoyment of sexual relations and the gift offered to a woman. However, this order is actually reversed because it is only because the child is the fruit of the parents' sexual desire that they will be taken as a body of enjoyment that requires a symbolisation.

The expression we sometimes use 'to give a child' (to someone) reflects a truth: love carries within it a lack that the child can mitigate. Wanting to give a child to the loved partner denotes lack (the fact that love always wants more) and a means of making this good. Naturally, a child is only a gift for as long as it is desired but yet to appear; as soon as it is born, its own existence creates a distance from this aura, although the aura hovers nearby. So the division of the subject is expressed in terms of debt and gift. As a gift, the child is objectified. Insofar as it resists this objectification, the child demands gifts (children consider that everything is owed to them in return for the 'everything' that they represent). So the child represents a gift but of a particular kind since the child's existence leads it to claim, in turn, a gift.

The child also represents a gift from another aspect. The story goes back further than love between a man and a woman since each of them is also a son and a daughter who owe something to their own parents, notably, in the form of a child. The child born of love is at the same time the child born of a debt owed by each of the lovers to their parents; their love conceals a transgenerational debt. From the debt to the gift of a child, a desire of the Other is actualised.[93] From the point of view of filiation, and depending on the specifics of neurosis, a child born of the love between two lovers is at the same time expected from the father or given to the mother of each of them. The love between the lovers obscures and represses this incestuous dimension of the desire for a child, which is transgenerational. This crucial position of the desire for a child situates it in such a way that exogamous love represses the incestuous endogamous dimension of filiation. The repression of this same incestuous dimension gives to desire its power and to orgasm its explosive force.

We can say that if orgasm resolves the contradiction of the seduction fantasy by actualising the parricide in enjoyment, this resolution calls for a child as the price of the debt. So that, logically, if not chronologically, orgasm precedes children understood as gifts and precedes the gifts made to children at their birth. Besides, lovemaking must occur before a child can be born. The child seems to be the most precious gift, but the desire for a child itself depends on a sexual relationship that precedes its birth. The child to be born will be born of the orgastic cry before it cries itself. Its cry extends the first cry; the orgasm precedes its birth and carries it forward.

Curiously enough, Freud writes in the *Project* that the child's cry recalls the cry that precedes it.[94] But who emits this cry that comes before the first cry? One may well answer that the first cry from the mouth immediately remembers itself through the ear. But more poetically perhaps, it can also be said that the first cry remembers the orgastic cry of its conception. If we consider orgasm as the Sovereign Good, its logic anticipates the temporality of life, which seems to begin at birth, but only begins somewhat later in the *post-partum* period. Our life always comes late to its own fullness because of this delay – this moment of limbo. In the fantasy, it seems as if we could only find ourselves in the unconsciousness of orgasm, and even if we never get there, this event haunts us. It counts for more than our divided birth, which it renews blindly. So that a sexual dream inhabits the psyche as an ever-present obsession.

Orgasm and the name

A person's name cannot be reduced to their surname, despite what our identity papers suggest. Rather, it is woven between a given name (the first name), the received name (the surname) and, possibly, an acquired name or nickname. Each of these has its own function, and while the surname is the most important for civil status, the first name is generally the most important in love.[95] That is because it is the given name. The gift of a name is an exception to the list of other things that are given. Even though it is not unique to the person, there is no more specific symbol of singularity. The bearer has received it, and yet it is completely his or her own. A child will not survive without the mutual recognition that the first name implies because the gift of the first name mediates enjoyment and saves the body from being a pure object of enjoyment. The calling of the first name by the mother signifies for the child a gap between 'being enjoyed' – the body of the drive – and the subject whom the child is. The name wards off excitement and dialectises the desire of the Other.

Like other gifts, the given name also has a function in alliance and separation. Calling a child by its name in order to ask it to do something generates a paradox: the imperatives of enjoyment are contradicted precisely as they are uttered. For example, a mother who pressures her child to eat, but calls the child by its first name as she does so, gives the child a means of resisting her at the same time as the order to eat seeks the opposite. The subject can oppose the injunctions by identifying with the given name. More than that, from the point of this nomination, the child can have the enjoyment of him- or herself, just as the Other seeks to enjoy the same! In short, the child can reap the benefit of 'being enjoyed'.

Calling by the first name signals a complete reversal of the relation to enjoyment. The first name is an exception in the series of gifts because it allows the enjoyment of oneself from the outside, from the perspective, as it were, of one's name. It makes it possible to take advantage of one's own drive body in the same way that the Other takes advantage of it. So the child can give him- or herself and enjoy their own objectification, which they are no longer obliged to reject, lock, stock and barrel, in order to exist. The mother, of course, enjoys her child; she mimics eating it up, caresses it, uses it as a prop to exorcise her own lack. But as soon as she calls the child by its name, the situation is reversed and the child enjoys the mother, using her and delighting in her. Now it is the child itself that benefits from having let her benefit! So at the moment of nomination, the child has the enjoyment of itself. The difference is palpable. Children who have barely been named are instrumentalised and devoured; they must struggle to resist and extract themselves. But children who are well armed with their name enjoy being enjoyed as objects, all the more so because it is their mother who now becomes the object. What she wanted to take, she has taken, but she is now what is taken.

This sheds light on a complex problem concerning primal repression. Repression results from the investment of the child's body by maternal demand. The child tolerates this erotisation up to a point but then represses it.[96] This rejection of an incestuous demand is clearly justified since the demand threatens annihilation. But it is more difficult to understand why it is accepted 'up to a point' because what objectifies the child should be unbearable. The difference is that erotisation of the body becomes bearable once it is permitted by a subjectivation through the name. Indeed, for children who are not called by their name, things tend to go badly. Negativism is their sole recourse.

The name plays an analogous role in the second round of the relation to enjoyment, which is the sexual act. In this central piece of 'adult' sexuality, calling the person by their name functions (again) as a symbol of the gift of enjoyment; it produces the orgastic reversal from being enjoyed into enjoying. To be taken solely as an object would inhibit pleasure, which would thus fall short of the moment of relief. The calling of the name in love opens up a new space. The person who is called by their name can have an enjoyment of themselves, can be taken as an object without being abused and is, therefore, able to give themselves. This turnaround moment of enjoyment liberates them; it gives them possession of the orgasm which would otherwise be depersonalising. As in early childhood, calling by the name has two sides:

> It is I who give it and you who take it, but at the same time, it is yours. I give to you what belongs to you. I identify myself with you, and the enjoyment is reversed so that you have the right to enjoy me.

This does not mean (unfortunately) that calling your lover by his or her name is enough to trigger orgasm. But it does at least suggest that anonymity might block this release. Calling someone by their first name in love – with this use of the name signifying a gift and not a demand – is to subjectify an otherwise impersonal enjoyment.

The first name is the key that opens the door, but what happens next? In this solitary moment of the subject being alone with their enjoyment, the surname in a way takes over from the first name, fixing the degree of the subject's attachment to their own psychical body. Because there is no guarantee that a subject has a firm hold on their body unless they have assumed its name. Despite appearances, 'he' or 'she' is not so firmly attached to their body, and 'he' or 'she' may evaporate every time they enjoy because enjoyment imposes itself initially from the outside. The person flits between 'he/she' and 'I'. We see here the function of the surname – the part of the name which is not given but transmitted. To say that this name is transmitted is not enough for it to be taken. This name remains the father's for a certain period of time, and it takes a struggle for the child to appropriate it so that it becomes not only received but also taken.

It is taken, first of all, in the Oedipal conflict. We might say that the first name is a 'pre-Oedipal' gift, whereas the surname must be taken in the battles of the Oedipus complex (which does not always happen). We should also note that the nature of these battles depends on the choice of psychical gender. Girls will fight less hard because, for them, taking the father's name will have the meaning of an erotic link proportional to their feminisation. Indeed, it is because the surname has this sexual overtone that they will be able to get rid of it quite easily. Boys, on the other hand, cannot compromise on this taking. To identify with the father through confrontation is to take his name. And since this confrontation forbids drive enjoyment, the name is the hook by which the subject remains attached to his body. The guilt of taking the name represses the incestuous wish.

A man takes on his name only to the extent of his actions. In the childish darkness of Oedipal confrontation, he first appropriated his father's name at the moment when he supplanted him in fantasy. In most cases, this name was passed on to him, but he did not necessarily take it. And he only began to bear the name in earnest when he won it through a fight. For in reality, a struggle has to occur between father and son before the latter can take the former's name, which he then has to honour in his later actions. Some names do not hold fast to their original bodies at this time of struggle. They evaporate. And one particular event in the succession of symbolic events that call for the name – the sexual act – deserves special mention.

No sooner activated, sexual arousal dispossesses the subject of their autonomy because arousal stems from fantasy, which another person has been made to embody. A greater force has taken control and imposes itself from outside in a tension that awaits its relief from the other body – in a situation that dictates its own law.[97] Desire under the sway of such dispossession is not exactly a pleasure. As on the first day of its life, the psychical body experiences the distress of being a body which is enjoyed even if consenting. The subject only survived this shipwreck of their first distress thanks to their name. In the same way, much later, at the moment of sexual arousal, the subject can only hold on to their body if their name keeps hold of them. Coming from the other, sexual enjoyment sucks the body outwards, and this reversal can only be managed if a name is given as happened so much earlier in life. Unless they have a form of reappropriation of themselves at the moment of enjoyment, she who enjoys – the feminine part of a subject – may well swear to themself that they will never let this happen again.

The taking of the name is tested in the sexual act, the second round of human sexuality, which stages a repetition of the Oedipal drama masked by a change of role since the son is now in a place that was that of a father, and the daughter is in the place of the one who meets a man who replaces the father. So the calling of the name takes on a particular meaning in the moment of enjoyment; a son is called by his name, and the woman who calls him thereby exorcises the name of her own father. When a woman calls her lover by his name, she gives the name to him, and he can only take it if he faces up to this renewed parricide. The sexual act is a new struggle and a new birth. It reiterates the taking of the name which occurred long before in the Oedipus complex.[98]

When in early childhood the subject took their name, this act gave a point of attachment to their speech so that they would not be lost in their own words when speaking. And this name is also that which metamorphoses the other body's enjoyment into their own during the sexual act, again preventing them from becoming lost at the high point of pleasure. The man appropriates his name once more through the sexual relation. A serious setback sometimes occurs at this moment, precisely when the name has not been taken, when it has only been stuck on like a label, without the legitimation of having been won. It may then be detached in the squall of a depersonalising enjoyment coming from another body. In some psychoses, the hallucinatory explosion coincides with the moment of orgasm (if it is not inhibited). The hallucinations will be all the more terrifying if the orgasm was triggered by a partner whose love is uncertain, a lover who gives nothing (neither the weight of the name nor the glitter of jewels) and is faithful only to passing, transitory loves. In contrast, the more secure the love is, the more generous its gift and the more it will compensate for the instability of the name.

Orgasm, like a sort of black hole, is the reverse side of the dead father, and although it operates for both lovers, its gift is made by the woman only, and in this, she risks depersonalisation. Men avoid this threat. Sex confronts them with a father with whom they identify at the moment of the act, which he forbade them in the past. They assume their name in this confrontation, so it is their way of ceasing to be children; they renew their identification. In this sense, when the sexual act legitimises their relationship to the name, it is reassuring rather than anxiety provoking. There is an obvious proof by the contrary: in the psychoses, where the assumption of the father's name was a problem, sex is sometimes the harbinger of a hallucinatory episode. With this exception (which proves the rule), men are confirmed of a name that women lose in proportion to their enjoyment.[99]

During lovemaking, the call of the name can trigger orgasm – the moment when a son takes on his name as a man. If he wants to leave childhood behind, the renewal of his name can occur through sex. This is why men are so obsessed with the act which, of all acts, attaches them to their body. Men are not aroused by hormones; the legitimisation of their name is what really sets them on fire. Human sexuality is so strange here because the fixed axis of its obsessions does not really belong to the body, which that axis may direct either well or badly (for better or for worse). So Eros opens one door after the other in this pursuit that runs from an autoerotic entry to an orgastic exit.

In love, women do not take men's names; they give them their name, and through this process, they have it too. The subjectivation of the name also applies to the man, who takes on his name when he gives it. It is a taking that gives, just as the one who gives the phallus owes it only to desire, in a comparable exchange. The degree of inhibition of orgasm depends on this attachment of the body to the name because, without this anchoring, orgasm will seem too risky. And the woman appropriates her enjoyment only on condition of receiving what she gives, i.e., what has the status of the name.

In the exchange of name and orgasm, the woman enjoys for two, and the man's name is good for two. This relationship becomes more visible when the woman bears a husband's name, so it seems to legitimise the patrilineal mode of filiation. But women have been making this choice for several centuries, in France and in many other countries, without being obliged to do so. That is not, of course, to say that this custom, which seems to allow exogamous pleasure and which is practised blindly, guarantees an orgastic result. In particular, it is not to be read as implying any sort of majesty to a father whose name would then be replaced by that of the husband.

In favourable fantasmatic circumstances, orgasm is triggered when somebody pronounces the name of his or her partner during sex or even merely in conditions of arousal when the bodies are at a distance from one another (it could be over the telephone). Does this situation border on pathology? Less than one might imagine, if we remember the mystics of all religions who fall into a swoon at the mention of God's name; if we are to believe the testimonies of their confessors, prayer could transport them to a seventh heaven. Indeed, what name could match that of the Eternal Father, at once dead and alive? It might seem a rare commodity, but it is within the reach of anyone who believes. Far from being sublimated, it is, on the contrary, an *Urvater*, a father of base alloy, the agent of the first incestuous enjoyment, who was promptly dispatched to the heavens for all the trauma he caused. As such, his name governs an enjoyment of the body, which remains in the order of carnal love. It is not a matter of spiritual onanism but of divine nuptials and not without at the same time taking enjoyment in the death of the man of flesh and blood – he who desires on this earth. Catherine of Siena once asked to be allowed to climb the scaffold to assist a condemned man in his last moments. When he was beheaded, she lingered with his head clasped to her bosom and then refused to change her blood-stained clothes.

In this sense, the religious ecstasy of the mystics appears as the paradigm of the 'sexual relation'. A paradoxical relationship since here, God is the protagonist. But the paradox precisely reveals the limit of the disappearance of the Father which orgasm requires. It releases a body that has been incarcerated since childhood in a parricidal fantasy. And true to the taboo on the dead father, the name that is pronounced has been definitively decapitated from the body. It is the breath of the Spirit, or even, it is nothing – nothing but an escape route that offers relief, the lowest level of tension, of which one might say that it is not written, if the zero were not written. But zero is written, not as a positional zero (repetition of an order in a numeration), not as a nothingness that would precede everything but as the zero that results from an equation. This mathematical vocabulary shows that orgasm serves an unconscious calculation (like the symptom, which inscribes its displaced writing) and that the zero of its algebra calls for a symbol (the name) that reconciles it with subjectivity in the same way that the zero of an equation calls for the quantification of an x or a y at the parity of the equals sign (the equalising lowering of tension of the death drive).

From pleasure to enjoyment and (perhaps) to orgasm

So far, various stages have been examined in chronological order. In reality, however, they are stacked vertically, so we need to present them diachronically in order to see what light this sheds on the orgastic event. Each level, from autoerotism to erotism and from the latter to orgasm, has its own specific psychic conditions. The drive has its own requirements: its likes and dislikes, an aesthetic, a facial feature, an arch of the back or large breasts, etc. But none of these attractions is sufficient to trigger arousal. In order for sexual desire to be triggered, the infinity of the active/passive movement of the drive must first be transposed into masculine/feminine in the seduction fantasy. There are key thresholds here: for example, being taken or possessed is actualised in the fantasy of the beaten child. In the sequence of events in love, this being taken is what appears first. Without the charms of appearance, nothing gets going. However, its connection with seduction is made via a fantasy train that was already in motion long before. 'One day, my prince will come' was being hummed long before the prince actually appeared. The song precedes the face. Moreover, the main ingredients of the love potion – the choice of one's psychical gender and that of the sexual object – were already predetermined by fantasy. Before a man can be seduced 'drive-wise' by a woman, he must be on the masculine side and be attracted by women, both of which are down to the fantasy. Cupid's arrow, fired from the bow of the drive, seems to be what comes first in the love story, but the arrow in fact comes from a specific direction, and it is fired by a specific Cupid. So the drive, even though it retains its own specificities, is appropriated retroactively by the fantasy.

Drive pleasure differs from enjoyment, which differs from orgasm. Each of these has its own characteristics and its own benefits. But a latent crisis at work in each of these pushes the subject upwards to the next and different step. Autoerotism gives erotism its strength by offering it a point of support. But this support represses what it draws its power from. A continuous exclusion is then established between the autoerotism of the drive, connected to the body, and purely fantasmatic erotism, which might be labelled 'out of body' if it was not constantly linked to another body. A discontinuity is created between pleasure, enjoyment and orgasm. 'Phallus envy' initiates sexual arousal and is at work in each of its stages, stacked vertically onto each other. The autoerotic discharge of the drive, dealing with excess, may be distinct from the erotic, but they are nevertheless threaded together by lack. The drive merely relieves its overflow and starts up again as soon as it can. It misses a partner only by their literal absence, as when one is hungry for bread or thirsty for wine. One certainly likes good bread and good wine. But what a difference between that and the lack of love, which is not lack of the person but their lack when they are present, a lack which they generate precisely as they fill it and do so without satisfying the appetites of the drive, which is always in excess. If a solitary autoerotism precedes an autoerotism for two, which in turn precedes erotism proper, how is the progress made from each of these steps to the next?

From the sexual games of childhood onwards, a latent love awaits liberation from lack by the good graces of the other. This will be what enables erotism to detach itself from autoerotism for two, which, however intense its pleasure, will still seek relief from its own nothingness. Although the drive just wants to seize another body, it is 'this particular person' of love, and no other, that creates a kind of beyond which works against the drive. This creationist combustion of erotism subsumes each stage of the body's erogeneity into a single lack. The different animistic powers – the gaze, the kiss, the skin, the voice, the smell – are converted into one single lack. And this new monotheism generates its own fantasmatic system. A kiss would be nothing, or even repulsive, if it were not framed by a fantasy. Sexual attraction varies between people, time and situations because it is predicated on fantasies. If their tension were to fall, the drive would lose its hold, unable to raise the stakes of desire on its own.

Lack is hollowed out in the beyond of the presence of the person who summons up fantasy and, with it, arousal. Its erotism differs from masturbation for two; it is launched thanks to another subject rather than another body. Can one enjoy making others enjoy? In this way, the quest for such enjoyment goes on ad infinitum, *without* orgasm. The hand that tries to grasp light grasps only shadow. Its relief recedes like a horizon that is never reached because lack triggers an arousal which seeks immediately to use the tactic of possession, as if to say, 'Give us back this excess that belongs to us!' The 'us' here exceeds the 'I'; there is an urge to reduce the 'us' to the 'I', to take ourselves back, to denounce this 'us' in the subjective intimacy of the fantasy.[100] The orgastic flash will fall from a planet, which is distinct from this uninterrupted crescendo. It will spring from the fantasies that its infinity summons up, and only their contradictions can short-circuit its infinite ascent.

The contradictions of fantasies transpose drive enjoyment into another system, the tensions of which can be released by orgasm.[101] For example, the death drive metamorphoses into a parricidal fantasy during the rivalries of love and then seeks release in orgasm. Each of these stages opens onto the next. When drive enjoyment tries to possess another body, it is relieved only for a moment – the time it takes to meet the resistance of the subject who inhabits this body. But its call for air summons up the fantasy. For example, the very violence of dissatisfaction invokes the fantasy of the beaten child, and with it, there comes a father, who is the master of liberating transgressions. Contrary to autoerotism and its onanism, erotism and, *a fortiori*, orgasm proceed from a staging that involves another human presence. Fantasies come onto the stage activated by the desire for a partner who could incarnate and sustain the tension that they involve. The contradiction of a certain fantasy appears or disappears, depending on what a certain person provokes, depending on what he or she brings forth of a part of us that sets desire in motion. This progress from enjoyment to desire, and then to its orgastic relief, can easily seize up or be inhibited by its own contradictions, showing the boundaries between pleasure, enjoyment and orgasm. This boundary is manifest, for example, when one body penetrates another. The 'making' of love then crosses a threshold beyond which one must take the place of the father or allow someone else to. Nothing is decided yet, and the game has barely begun because this moment can be accompanied by intense pleasure or by total rejection.

Desire carries within it a contradiction conducive to the orgastic internal short-circuit, a purely psychical event, which, moreover, can occur outside the body and not only in mystical experience. But it can also swing over to its opposite. Here again, such effects of the contradictions inherent to fantasy are unrelated to the physiology of the sex organs[102] and are based only on the stages previously passed through, the requirements of which remain present. Disgust at a physical trait may, for example, serve as a pretext for rejecting seduction. But this rejection itself may ultimately trigger orgasm. For reasons that stem from the drive (such as a certain physical characteristic), a particular person will trigger the urge to possess, creating a lack that serves as a projection screen for fantasies.

This effort to possess may or may not be reciprocal. On one or both sides, there may be love and no desire or rather love and a desire for non-desire. For example, love requited (love responded to by love) will not necessarily have an arousing, still less an orgastic outcome, which may, however, ensue where there is no such reciprocity (perhaps an orgasm triggered by rape). A beating fantasy is obviously best actualised with someone who delivers a beating, at least in a moral sense. This does not mean that each person's fantasies have to match – disharmony can also be orgasmic. Moreover, the fantasy machinery works unconsciously, with or without the consent of the lover, whose non-consent, real or simulated, may in itself be sufficient to trigger orgasm. The internal discordance of the fantasy will either inhibit or inflame desire as far as orgasm, depending on what a lover represents, or on the contrary, a sexual symptom may be created in its place. But a limit will thus be established to the infinite vertigo of drive enjoyment and then to the turmoil of a bisexuality that finds no ready solution but is constantly engaged in a war of the sexes that knows no respite.

The orgasm, return of the primally repressed

We must now examine a process that does not result from an incremental progression but from an interactive development, the modifications of which stack up, as it were, one on top of the other. The drive aimed to discharge itself by taking possession of another body. In this way, it actualised its destiny – a certain voracity hastening towards its own abolition. It sought to possess, and in doing so, its own subject was lost. It is against the background of this loss that fantasmatic machinery is set in motion, displacing drive annihilation onto sexual arousal. This means that for the human being, the actualisation of the fantasy becomes a matter of life and death. Born of the paternal spark, the fantasy is 'outside the body', and it takes over from the drive, which always remains 'of the body' but threatens to make the body implode. So the fantasy and the drive are both in action all the time, the one repressing the other. The drive is always working the body, pushing it forward without knowing what the push is towards, and the fantasy is always seeking release for this overflow. The repressed drive constantly underpins the fantasy like the back and front of the same surface. It is always ready to spill over and drown the fantasy, as indeed happens when a contradiction in the fantasy causes a break in its tension.

This emergence of drive enjoyment occurs, for example, in a slip of the tongue; there is a gap between what someone meant to say and what they actually say. Before this moment, the fantasy repressed the drive at the speed of speech until it went beyond its internal limit. All speech actualises something of the fantasy, and its very unfolding represses the drive energy of the body. We speak while forgetting our body and in order to forget it, and the body re-emerges whenever the speed slows down, which may allow the internal fracture to appear. Laughter is one manifestation of this overflow of enjoyment. This gain of pleasure of the body occurs when the anxiety provoking contradictions that may trap a subject are loosened. In the same way, during sleep, consciousness is no longer in a state of tension working to discriminate perceptions, and our fantasies, which locate us in space-time, become disjointed. Drive energy re-emerges in the dream thanks to this fracture. The formations of the unconscious appear in such fractures, and *the orgasm is a formation of the unconscious* like a slip of the tongue, laughter or a dream.

This can be seen if, in a sexual relationship, a creation of fantasmatic tension is followed by a breaking of the tension, entailing the return of drive enjoyment. Orgasm occurs when there is a disjunction of the polarised field of fantasy.[103] The drive energy of the 'body', the repressed excess of which has continued to insist, breaks through thanks to something 'outside the body', insofar as another body – that of the lover – has been invested by the fantasy. The fantasy is put into a state of tension because it is borne by the other (the partner) who is the space in which the contradictions of the fantasy are now played out. As soon as the contradictions appear, they release the repressed drive energy. Repression yields to the conditions of its own contradictions.

The variability of orgasm for each person, the fact that it is triggered or not triggered depending on the partner, the situation, the time of life, etc., shows that it does not depend on physiology but on the actualisation of the fantasy and whether the latter is inhibited or pushed to its orgastic consequence by the circumstances, the lover, psychical age, etc. Orgasm is the outcome of a relationship. Inhibition of the orgasm depends on fantasmatic discordances, and its realisation results from a resolution of the internal tension of fantasy. If, for example, the movement of the fantasy eliminates a father who was nevertheless loved, the drive enjoyment of the body returns in the fault line of this contradiction. The body rediscovers itself in its original strangeness, while the subject, regaining consciousness, divides itself again, split once more by the infinite circularity of desire.

But orgasm has a particularity that distinguishes it from other formations of the unconscious, for which the return of the repressed is actualised thanks to the drive *object* and the erogenous zone (for example, the symptom is characterised by pain in a certain part of the body, etc.). Orgasm, in contrast, involves less the means (the drive) but its *goal* – i.e., the phallic signification of the body – which is refound thanks to the phallus itself (the erect penis), displaced now into a relation with another body. In other words, what is externalised in the orgasm is what was at stake in primal repression itself. The subject undergoes this return of a primally repressed – the phallic goal of the body's drive energy, which corresponds to this orgastic eruption – as an event independent of their own self and which goes beyond the self. If at the moment of fracture of fantasmatic contradictions, it is not only the excess of the drive that returns – if it is not simply an object of the drive but its goal that is exteriorised – then the archaic identification with the phallus, that of primal repression, refinds itself in an extraordinary liberation of the body. It rejoins for an instant its own excess – that which was constantly pushed away for the benefit of the subject's existence. This amounts to an 'extraordinary' liberation because in order for the phallic signification, repressed from the time of primal repression, to be set free, there will have to have been an erection of the phallus thanks to another body, which actualised the hallucinatory dimension of desire. And then this other body, because it is depersonalised by an enjoyment that was momentarily incestuous, will have to summon up this same phallic signification. The distance between two bodies – we might call it a non-relation – produces the orgastic outcome of sexual relations.

What is the purpose of the drive? It is an identification of the body with the phallus, which can only occur in this transitivism with another body that maintains the fantasy at a distance. This phallus belongs to neither of the two bodies but results from desire, i.e., from the fantasy. We cannot obtain this liberation on our own; it needs to have an addressee, an otherness (just as we will never make a witticism or a slip of the tongue alone). We set ourselves free through someone else. It is necessary and, therefore, sufficient that we find the 'someone' who can evoke and carry this fantasy for us, which (even if not shared) puts the phallus into this common space. God, for example, probably does not share the fantasy of his creatures, even if they are mystics. And yet, without insisting on their enjoyment (so obviously orgastic), the figure of an eternalised father orients their desire, propelling it after having long inhibited it. To hallucinate the body of a divine revenant seems improbable, but the sustained contemplation of the divine can indeed produce orgasm.[104]

Orgasm is the return of the most profoundly repressed – a phallic signification that haunts the memory of the body like an eternal revenant in search of liberation. Separated from itself from the outset, it rediscovers itself in this new birth. The hallucinatory nature of primal repression is embodied: to be for a moment one's body, which is no longer 'one's own' in the Hegelian sense of the appropriation of a separate being. Contrary to the myth, sexual love is not resolved in a unity with the beloved but rather, by refinding one's own dream through such love. It is not a harmony, via the matching of the fantasies of each lover, but the fracture of their internal contradictions thanks to the other, which provokes this hallucinatory reunion of the psychical body and the real body (this flesh always already screened by the fantasy). It's a conjunctive disjunction.

The orgasm would be a formation of the unconscious like any other if it did not correspond precisely to the moment when its actual formation is abolished. Nothing shows this better than the sexual symptoms which arise from the failure of orgasm. They incarcerate the same fantasmatic contradiction that the orgasm sets free. But they are at the level of secondary repression; they miss the origin because they lack the exteriority of another person made into the bearer of the fantasy.

The equation of a return of the primally repressed and the orgasm is still more manifest if we notice the characteristics of the voice at this moment. The desire for the phallus and the desire to give the phallus 'transport' the subject to fever pitch – a dispossession of oneself destined to possess. The fantasy of seduction intensifies this contradiction which cannot be spoken and which leaves no room for anything but the voice, that voice which was the first to be able to signify the out-of-body enjoyment of this body. We may notice that, like music, this voice of sexual enjoyment has a rhythm and a syncopation, and it is this sonic dimension that enables the woman's enjoyment to become that of the man. The sonic impact, the permanent drive transfusion from outside and inside, makes the other partner experience what is happening to the first.

Music itself has other characteristics than the vocal rhythm of sexual love; it adds phrasing and meanings that evoke feelings in a more or less expressionistic way, depending on the culture and the time. But music and the sound score of love share a common feature, namely, the emotional relationship that unites musician with listener and the (orgastic) syncopation of the phrase, which tears the listener away from him- or herself, brings tears to their eyes or, in any case, procures for them the profound inner pleasure of an enigmatic rediscovery. Guy Rosolato uses the term 'hypnotic listening' to describe this sense of fusion.[105] The specificities of this transport are worthy of note, and the term 'transport' seems more appropriate than 'fusion', as shown by what separates each protagonist of such an event. The musician plays, as it were, the score of the listener so that, from the outside, the music seems to 'recognise' the listener.[106] How can it be understood that 'music' – an impersonal external entity – recognises its listener and draws them in? It does so by evoking the shared exile of several subjects who listen together, besides the composer and the musician. There is a multiplicity of subjects who share the same exile, and the subject who hears the music is thus recognised in this otherness, or more exactly, the subject's division is presented thanks to the musical score [partition].[107] On the side of the artist and on the side of the aesthete-listener, the work brings the two sides of a divided subject into contact.

What is at stake here is the same clash that occurs in sexual love, where repressed drive energy rejoins a body thanks to the otherness of its 'moiety'.[108] So this subjectivation of the repressed does not in any way abolish distance but enjoys its very exile. The effect is that which Julie de Lespinasse describes when she writes after hearing a famous passage from Gluck's Orpheus and Eurydice:

I would like to hear this aria, which tears me apart and gives me the enjoyment of what I miss, ten times a day. 'I have lost my Eurydice'. This music drives me mad, it carries me away, my soul is greedy for such pain.[109]

Here, desire, which is not a pleasure, shows its obscure side – that of a desire for pain.

But this parallel between musical pleasure and erotism would remain incomplete if it did not evoke the moment of fracture where enjoyment becomes orgastic – the syncopation which puts the subject out of step with another part of themselves. The melody must include this internal element of surprise; this shift that enables enjoyment to attain its resolutive moment. It occurs when something incongruous occurs with respect to a certain rhythm – a note that disagrees with what the harmony would have led us to expect, the 'blue note' described by Georges Sand hearing Chopin play the piano.[110] This syncopation expresses the contradictory face of desire, opening the breach to the overflow of the drive. Among all the drives, the voice is the one that betrays its companions. Words are forged from its sound material, folded into the meaning of sentences, the flow of which represses the drive energy of the body. It is through the voice that the return of the repressed makes itself heard, thanks to the point of syncopation of a harmony, whether melodic or fantasmatic.

Notes

1 The exception being Wilhelm Reich, who distanced himself from the psychoanalytical viewpoint by considering orgasm as a physiological potentiality. His work nevertheless highlighted a gap in analytic theory. Lacan only ever mentions orgasm in a few passing remarks.

2 For example, Marquis de Sade, *Three Complete Novels*. New York: Grove Press, 1965, pp. 205–206.

3 Writings that would hardly appear licentious today were forbidden from publication in France (a relatively liberal country) just a few decades ago. Nabokov's *Lolita* was banned for a year in 1955, and the Marquis de Sade only came out of the shadows at the end of the millennium, after several contretemps with the police.

4 I translate 'jouissance' as 'enjoyment'. It can connote orgasm (as, for example, in 'jouissance sexuelle'). But the author sometimes distinguishes between 'jouissance' and 'orgasme' (translator's note).

5 'Infracassable noyau de nuit' (André Breton, *Entretiens 1913–1952*. Paris: Gallimard, 1952, p. 141).

6 The literature of a particular era, and its art in general, illuminate problems that are often barely recognised and do so long before any theorist tries to describe them directly. This is because painting, writing and film are able to show opaque contradictions that are difficult to unravel and translate into ideas. The theorist is a clumsy latecomer compared to the writer who, in a few words, describes a scene that reveals to everyone their own obsession.

7 Yukio Mishima, *La Musique*. Paris: Gallimard, 2000. The novel has not been translated into English (translator's note).

8 *Ibid.*, p. 40.

9 Freud [1950, 1895], *Project for a Scientific Psychology* in *Standard Edition 1*, p. 331.

10 Mishima, *op. cit.*, pp. 52–53.

11 *Ibid.*, p. 93.

12 *Ibid.*, pp. 53–54.

13 Pierre Corneille [1636], 'Cid' in *Cid, Cinna, The Theatrical Illusion* (J. Cairncross, trans.). London: Penguin, 1975.

14 Mishima, *op. cit.*, p. 84.

15 *Ibid.*, p. 115.

16 *Ibid.*, p. 117.

17 *Ibid.*, p. 119.

18 *Ibid.*, p. 140.

19 In matrilineal filiations, the mother's brother takes the paternal function of educator (see: Claude Lévi-Strauss [1949], *The Elementary Structures of Kinship* (J. Bell, J. von Sturmer, trans.). Boston, MA: Beacon Press, 1969).

20 Mishima, *op. cit.*, pp. 256–257.

21 *Ibid.*, p. 262.

22 *Ibid.*, p. 235.

23 *Ibid.*, p. 236.

24 *Ibid.*, p. 238.

25 Euripides, *Medea* (D. Kovacs, trans.). Cambridge, MA: Harvard University Press, 1994, lines 408–409.

26 'What appeared normal yesterday is invisible and irrelevant today' (translated from: Charles Melman, *La nouvelle économie psychique*. Toulouse: Érès, 2009, p. 30).

27 As for laws (at least in France), they not only abstain from any moral viewpoint or from taking sides but follow the movement enthusiastically if they have not already gone on ahead of it, making minority claims into propositions that are valid for all.

28 'Sexual satisfaction appears as a requirement so justified, a dimension so natural, an end in itself so independent of the aims of procreation and the pacts of love that not only has it become the object of a discourse that is public – and no longer intimate – but it has also become the object of attention and care for an entire series of therapists and sexologists' (Colette Soler [2003], *What Lacan Said About Women* (J. Holland, trans.). New York: Other Press, 2006, p. 167).

29 One enjoys what one ought not to do. Some languages do not have these nuances. In German, 'Lust' connotes both pleasure and its culmination but without the transgressional flavour of the French 'jouissance' (or 'goce' in Spanish). In English, psychoanalysts who want to take advantage of the Latin complexity use the French word because it has no equivalent in the luxuriant language of Shakespeare.

30 Rather than in the signifier, which denotes neither passive nor active.

31 In the book of *Genesis,* we find the term 'Letzaheck' to describe what happens between Isaac and Rebecca, and the word is used a second time when Ishmael is sent away, but its translation is controversial. We would have to rely heavily on the commentary by Rashi (12th century) to make it mean 'orgasm'.

32 See: Hippocrates, *Aphorisms* (C. Adams, trans.). New York: Dover, 1868, section IV, parts 1and 10; section V, part 29. In these few lines, Hippocrates deals with pregnant women and acute illnesses.

33 One thinks of the fantasmatic excitement of the beaten child and the parricide who takes revenge for this violence.

34 The verb 'organ' derives from the root 'orgê', which means 'violent movement, passion, anger'. It relates to the Sanskrit 'urga', which is more focused on food and vigour. It is also used to refer to fertile land and, by analogy, to the overflow of desire.

35 The famous *Encylopedia* compiled by Denis Diderot and Jean le Rond d'Alembert in 1751–1752 uses the term 'orgasm attacks' to describe nervous episodes of a manifestly hysterical nature. Lamarck, in his *Zoological Philosophy* (published in 1806), used the word in the same sense as Hippocrates. In the 18th and 19th centuries, 'orgasm' was used to describe a physiological effervescence and tension and figuratively to describe a psychical ebullition with somatic manifestations.

36 See Rainier Lanselle, 'Les mots chinois de la psychanalyse' in *Essaim. Revue de psychanalyse 13, (Horizons asiatiques de la psychanalyse)*. Toulouse: Érès, 2004.

37 One finds apparently specific terms in Robert Van Gulik, *Sexual Life in Ancient China*. Leiden: E.L. Brill, 1961, but these are interpretative translations of words with other literal meanings (such as, for example, 'joy').
38 Similarly, in some parts of Asia, the name of Buddha is not to be uttered; it functions as a monotheistic paternal principle.
39 'Patients often tell one that they have had a pollution during sleep, although the accompanying dream content had no sensual character, nor indeed betrayed any sexual connection' (Sandor Ferenczi, 'Pollution without Dream Orgasm and Dream Orgasm without Pollution' in *Further Contributions to the Theory and Technique of Psycho-Analysis* (J. Suttie *et al.*, trans.). New York: Boni and Liveright, 1927, p. 297).
40 'passages à l'acte' (translator's note).
41 In other scenarios, some men ask their lover to insert some object into their anus to generate such a reminiscence. Outside sexual relationships, scratching of the anus often involves the same representations.
42 Karen Horney, in her 1924 article, 'On the Genesis of the Castration Complex in Women', takes up the conception that prevailed at the time: 'the castration complex in females is entirely centred in the "penis-envy" complex' (*International Journal of Psycho-Analysis*, 5(1924): 50–65, 51).
43 See Jules Glenn, Eugene Kaplan, 'Types of Orgasm in Women – A Critical Review and Redefinition' in *Journal of the American Psychoanalytic Association, 16* (1968): 549–564.
44 Helene Deutsch, 'Frigidity in Women' in *Neuroses and Character Types* (J. Sutherland, M. Masud R. Khan, eds.). London: Hogarth Press, 1965, p. 360. She also writes: 'I have seen very sick women, even psychotic women, who experienced an intense vaginal orgasm, and women relatively free of neurosis who had never had this experience. I have seen aggressive, masculine, demanding, and efficient women for whom the vaginal orgasm was an absolute condition of the sexual act, and loving, giving, maternal, and happy women, for whom the vaginal orgasm was *terra incognita*. Many women had not the slightest doubt that their sexual needs were fully gratified in intercourse; yet vaginal orgasm was not included in their conception of gratification' (*Ibid.*, p. 359).
45 One of my female patients confided to me that she had only experienced orgasm at the age of 60 and then only in a dream and only with me, her analyst, who had transgressed the rules of the analytic art during this dream scene. Perhaps she had forgotten her past as a woman, or perhaps the transgression played a large part in it, or perhaps she was trying to please me by giving a superlative turn to her narrative. In any case, I was still not entirely sure, despite her descriptions, what it was that she was calling 'orgasm'.
46 The Kinsey Report is the name under which the seminal works by Alfred Kinsey, Wardell Pomeroy, Clyde Martin, *Sexual Behaviour in the Human Male* and *Sexual Behaviour in the Human Female, Were Popularised.* Philadelphia, PA: W.B. Saunders, 1948 and 1953.
47 Kinsey, Pomeroy, Martin, *Sexual Behaviour in the Human Female, op. cit.*, p. 583.
48 William Masters, Virginia Johnson, *Human Sexual Response.* Boston, MA: Little, Brown & Company, 1966.
49 More demonstrative still: a homosexual woman might enjoy and make another enjoy thanks to an organ that she does not have. Clearly, just believing in it is enough.
50 Especially since the feminine orgasm is useless when it comes to procreation.
51 One can explain this ignorance by assuming that the 'scientific' obsession of these authors led them to seek objective criteria, which do not take subjectivity into account.
52 'in matters of human sexuality, anatomy teaches us little more than what fantasy adds to it' (translated from: Jacques André, *La sexualité féminine*. Paris: PUF, 2009, p. 297).
53 'the vagina comes to function in the genital relation through a mechanism that is strictly equivalent to all the other hysterical mechanisms. [. . .] Recognizing the necessity of the

empty place in a functional point of desire, and noticing that this is right where nature itself, right where physiology, has found its most favourable functional point, frees us of the weight of paradoxes that would lead us to devise so many mythical constructions around so-called vaginal jouissance [enjoyment], and also thereby puts us in a clearer position, though not of course without something being able to be indicated beyond this' (Jacques Lacan, *Seminar 9, Anxiety* (J.-A. Miller, ed., A. Price, trans.). Cambridge: Polity, 2014, p. 71).

54 These different processes will be discussed in more detail later.

55 See: Claude Lévi-Strauss [1962], *Totemism* (R. Needham, trans.). Boston, MA: Beacon Press, 1963.

56 'Sensual sucking involves a complete absorption of the attention and leads either to sleep or even to a motor reaction in the nature of an orgasm' (Freud [1905], *Three Essays on the Theory of Sexuality* in *Standard Edition 7*, p. 180).

57 But guilt immediately works on the body, pulling it back, sucking it into a field from where only fiction (play, busy activity) can move the question of taking and giving onto other fantasmatic terrains, for example, that of rivalries between boys or of having a baby for girls. This masturbatory guilt opens up the space for thought that is already ethical in nature, pitting good against evil, good guys against bad guys, cowboys against Indians, etc. Making war is a necessity, but war is not enough. Indeed, nothing will be enough ever again.

58 It would happen before the very birth of the subject because this act would put the child in the place of one of its parents. It would be dying before living.

59 In a recent study of 800 women, 21% of respondents said they did not experience orgasm before the age of 38, 18% not before 46, 13% not before 50 and 6% not before 54 (Marie-Christine Laznik, *L'impensable désir. Féminité et sexualité au prisme de la ménopause*. Paris: Denoel, 2003, p. 91).

60 Akin to a 'speech act' as described by John Austin, *How to Do Things with Words*. Oxford: Oxford University Press, 1962.

61 In a seemingly different register, believers are encouraged to make gestures of faith, to conform to the liturgy, to pronounce the name of God and to engage in silent prayer. By doing so, they experience the happiness of putting their destiny in the hands of a father who is really their own invention. Far from being gratuitous, this analogy between two semblances – religious ritual and the gestures of love – evokes in each case the duplicity of paternal seduction.

62 Translated from: Marie Darrieussecq, 'Simulatrix' in *Zoo*. Paris: P.O.L., 2003, p. 139.

63 If men claimed to have the phallus and that women are deprived of it, then feminist criticisms of this would be justified.

64 'The fact that the phallus is not to be found where it's expected, where it's demanded, namely, on the plane of genital mediation, is what explains how anxiety is the truth of sexuality, that is, what appears each time its ebb tide washes back and lets show the sand beneath. Castration is the price of this structure, it comes in the stead of this truth. But in actual fact, this is an illusory game. There is no castration because, at the locus at which it occurs, there is no object to castrate. The phallus would have to have been there for that, but it is only there so that there won't be anxiety' (Lacan, *Anxiety, op. cit.*, pp. 268–269 (translation modified)).

65 'In other words, the fact that male desire meets its downfall *before* entering the jouissance [enjoyment]of the female partner, and even the fact that the woman's jouissance is crushed, to take up a term borrowed from the phenomenology of breast and nursling, crushed under phallic longing, implies that woman is thenceforth required, and I would almost say condemned, to love the male Other only at a point situated beyond what halts her, her too, as desire, and which is the phallus' (*Ibid.*, p. 304).

66 Feminist criticisms here tend to overlook the fact that men do not have this phallus any more than women have it; the phallus is only erected between the two.

67 This remark does not imply symmetry. For in this joint possession, one has it on lease, the other on sublease. The first (who may be a woman) is masculine. The second (who may be a man) is feminine. Nothing shows this better than some female homosexual couples where one, the lease holder of the phallus, makes the other, her subtenant, enjoy. And yet there is no penis to be seen here.

68 This diminishes the importance of clitoral enjoyment for some women.

69 'everything can be attributed to a woman insofar as she represents the absolute Other in the phallocentric dialectic' (Lacan, *Écrits, op. cit.*, p. 616).

70 'Throughout his life man seeks to recover this part of his erotism, which constantly escapes him because it is outside him and which has no value for him except because it is external to him' (translated from: René Diatkine, 'Un colloque sur l'orgasme' in *Revue française de psychanalyse*, no. 4 (L'orgasme, 1977): 565).

71 'I am accustoming myself to regarding every sexual act as a process in which four individuals are involved', Freud wrote in a letter, referring to bisexuality (Freud, *Complete Letters to Wilhelm Fliess*, letter of August 1, 1899 (J.M. Masson, trans.). Cambridge, MA: Belknap Press, 1985, p. 364).

72 'Since man will never bring the leading edge of his desire this far, one is able to say that man's jouissance and woman's jouissance will never conjoin organically' (Lacan, *Anxiety, op. cit.*, p. 265).

73 Expanding Lacan's adage, 'Woman does not exist', at least not at the moment of orgasm.

74 This is the source of a banal male fantasy – that of seeing two women make love. This division assures the man of his own virility. By watching a woman make another woman enjoy, he breaks free of his own femininity and thus completes his own masculinity without having to do anything more than watch. So he is a voyeur of the act that he performs, while his partner is an exhibitionist of herself with another woman. The fantasy is actualised not so much by putting two women in the same bed as by making one of them suffer with the other and vice-versa. The eyes widen on what there is of the fantasy that cannot be seen. Stanley Kubrick's film *Eyes Wide Shut* (1999) is an example of this, as its title makes plain. Is this not the practice of many couples, who keep their eyes closed?

75 'The paradox of this statement is inescapable: whatever the pacts of love may be, no contractual relation is possible with the Other of jouissance! There have been cultures in which abduction was raised to a rite, but in which very real mutual agreements presided over marriage, and which required commitments on the part of many people other than just the husband and wife. Such commitments, however, were covered over by the ritualized violence of a fictive kidnapping of the bride, as if to symbolize the non-contractual part of the sexed relation between a man and a woman' (Soler, *What Lacan Said About Women, op. cit.*, p. 187).

76 'We perceive that for purposes of discharge the instinct of destruction is habitually brought into the service of Eros' (Freud [1923], *The Ego and the Id* in *Standard Edition 19*, p. 41). The death drive finds in the father someone to talk to.

77 'Death is the result of the sexual crisis only in exceptional cases, but the significance of these is admittedly striking, so much so that the exhaustion following the final paroxysm is thought of as a "little death"' (Georges Bataille [1957], *Erotism* (M. Dalwood, trans.). San Francisco: City Lights Books, 1986, p. 100).

78 For example, Don Juan or the Cid (in Pierre Corneille's play, *Cid, op. cit.*) 'kill the father', this being the exogamic condition for enjoyment.

79 'Let us specify: this appetite for death, this absolute taste for a violent dissolution of forms, whereby beings [les étants] are repudiated as unfit to take the place of Being [l'être]; hence Wagner's famous phrase: 'That ancient tune of anxious yearning sounded, [. . .] asking me then, and asking me now, for what fate was I then born? For what fate? The ancient tune tells me once more: to yearn – and to die!"' (translated from: Roland Gori, *Logique des passions*. Paris: Flammarion, 2005, p. 40. Quotation

from: Richard Wagner, *Tristran and Isolde*, Act 3, https://www.murashev.com/opera/Tristan_und_Isolde_libretto_English).

80 One could gather examples *ad infinitum* from literature or cinema that combine orgasm with scenes of murder. But that does not entail that their conjunction is necessary. The representation of violence is by itself sufficient to relieve a sexual overflow even if it does not involve any erotism.

81 It often happens that a woman's desire oscillates between an older and a younger man. These two positions are not symmetrical because what is generated by the desire for the father (the older man) is of a different order than the desire for a younger man, who is an *alter ego* but of the other sex.

82 Pascal Quignard, *Le nom sur le bout de la langue*. Paris: Éditions POL, 1993.

83 We will try to show in a future work that so-called matrilineal societies are built on an analogous forgetting of the name of the father.

84 Orgasm is presented as a free gift, in the sense that nothing can make equal measure with it.

85 To the extent that, in some cultures, they may accept the wearing of the veil as a lesser evil.

86 In Pascal Bonitzer's film *Je pense à vous* ('I Am Thinking of You') (2006), a series of triangular situations spawned by the burial of a man culminate in the suicide of a woman.

87 We have been careful in this book to avoid commentaries on the Lacanian aphorism 'There is no sexual relationship', which has tended to become a catch-all that stops us from thinking about the problems of sexuality. Naturally, there is no sexual relationship in the sexual theories of children; children's heroes (Tarzan, Spiderman, Lara Croft, etc.) never think about it, let alone get involved in it. Children's enjoyment is entirely based on the drive, just as, in Frazer's theories of totemic reproduction, children are descended from a totem that has been seen, dreamt of or ingested by the mother. The gap between this absence and the psychical reality of sexual trauma is what writes a sexual relationship. Not to take this gap into consideration as a prerequisite is one of the current ways of invalidating psychoanalysis, which was discovered by starting out from sexual trauma and a symptomatic writing of the sexual relationship.

88 'personne' (French for 'nobody') (translator's note).

89 'une personne' (French for 'a person') (translator's note).

90 All sorts of objects can also have a function of reconciliation; a piece of cloth, for example, can have a drive-based significance so that the infant becomes very attached to it. But because it has not been given, it will never be the kind of symbol that marks a separation and a union.

91 As we have said, the being and the nothingness of the first enjoyment have been transposed into the opposition of masculine and feminine.

92 One of the two partners in love can give without the other doing the same, and this disparity will have its own consequences. One might think that the person who has received without giving will judge him- or herself the winner. But the opposite usually happens: the one who does not give back will most often be the one who pays, as if the fact of having received alienated him or her and generated hatred.

93 And this may happen with or against love because lovers can also want a child against their parents in order to erase a bad memory of their own childhood.

94 Freud [1950, 1895], *Project for a Scientific Psychology* in *Standard Edition 1*, p. 331.

95 For the sake of clarity, we shall conform to general usage by distinguishing the first name and surname in the present discussion. It should be remembered, though, that the surname is no more the 'name of the father' than the first name, which is also given in the name of a particular father. Moreover, in France, the first name was considered to be the only name until the Edict of Villers-Cotterêts was issued by François I . . . who did not apply it to himself. His name remained 'François'.

96 Freud speaks of this process in terms of the repression of the drive in his papers on metapsychology written at the time of the First World War. He later uses the term 'Ausstossung' ('expulsion') in *Negation* [1925] (*Standard Edition 19*, p. 219).

97 It is as if the (always already external) power of desire was pulling the strings of a puppet towards its centre, where the puppet will be consumed. But is it not already consumed if it always knew that it would eventually submit?

98 In some civilisations, men change their names when they marry. In the same way, in our civilisation, men assume their name as a man, although this passes unnoticed.

99 So men avoid depersonalisation, if not a certain impersonalisation, when they are activated by their desire rather than activating it.

100 'The orgastic action becomes, as it were, ineluctable whenever the fantasmatic articulation (both individual and dual) as well as the articulation between fantasy and reality have been carried out in conditions which exceed the threshold of possible mentalisations in the direction of the conscious' (translated from: Jean Bergeret, 'Essai psychanalytique sur l'activité orgastique' in *Revue française de psychanalyse*, no. 4 (*L'orgasme*, 1977): 602).

101 'For each partner there is a coming together and then a mixing of an unconscious fantasy (filled energetically with desire for expansion and conflictualisation of this desire) with the perception of an object or conscious fantasy that exacerbates the same desire and conflictualisation' (*Ibid.*, 596).

102 They have weak innervation – very weak indeed on the feminine side and dependent on the drive on the masculine side. The surface area occupied by their cerebral projections is small compared to the disturbances they provoke, which are sufficient to trigger the pseudo epileptic seizure of orgasm that irradiates the brain in its entirety.

103 'From the *economic* point of view, any fantasy, whatever its variety, implies the presence (recognised or not) of the *subject* and of this subject included in a *conflictual*, archaic and repetitive situation that includes both the desire and the prohibitions that affect this desire' (*Ibid.*, 590).

104 The orgastic dimension of mystical transports leaves little doubt. Beatrice of Nazareth describes the 'fruition' (intimate union with God) thus: 'In this, love [. . .] becomes so immoderate and breaks out in such a way [. . .] that the chest scorches, and the throat dries up so that the face and all the limbs take part in the heat inside and participate in this primal rage of love' (Beatrice of Nazareth, *On Seven Ways of Holy Love* (Wim van den Dungen, trans.). Brasschaat: Taurus Press, 2016, p. 22.

105 Guy Rosolato, 'L'écoute musicale comme méditation' in *Psychanalyse et musique* (J.A. Caïn, ed.). Paris: Les Belles Lettres, 1985, pp. 144–148.

106 'You are recognised by the music' (translated from: Alain Didier-Weill, 'De quatre temps subjectivants' in *Ornicar 8*. Paris: Navarin, 1976, p. 49).

107 The French 'partition' mean both 'musical score' and 'division' or 'sharing' (translator's note).

108 This is what Theodor Reik describes when he evokes 'a time when the infant listened to his mother who sang or talked to him, [. . .] a phase in which what was said was scarcely understood', so a time when the child heard only the music (Theodor Reik, *The Haunting Melody. Psychoanalytic Experiences in Life and Music*. New York: Grove Press, 1953, p. 115). Similarly, Michel Poizat likens sexual enjoyment to music: 'the moment when the impossible rediscovery is experienced' (translated from: Michel Poizat, *L'opéra ou le cri de l'ange*. Paris: Métailié, 2001, p. 285).

109 *Lettres de Mademoiselle de Lespinasse*. Paris: Charpentier, 1876, pp. 105 and 134.

110 Georges Sand, *Impressions et Souvenirs*. Paris: Michel Lévy, 1873, p. 86. Catherine Clément, in her book *Syncope: The Philosophy of Rapture*, examines how phenomena as varied as a thunderbolt, a tango, an orgasm, anguish or a sneeze share this syncopated quality. For Clément, syncope is 'a surprise, a delay in relation to life, a violent anticipation, and a slow return to what one calls the "self"' (*Syncope. The Philosophy of Rapture* (S. O'Driscoll, D. Mahoney, trans.). Minneapolis, MN: University of Minnesota, 1994. p. 21).

Chapter 9

What the study of the orgasm brings to psychoanalytic theory

The links between the epileptic fit and orgasm

Freud did not write a specific text on orgasm, which he only mentioned in connection with other problems of sexual life or with the death drive. However, his text entitled *Dostoevsky and Parricide*[1] mentions orgasm, not so much as a problem but rather as if it was a question that had already been solved, specifically as if there was a self-evident equation between the parricide wish, orgasm and the hysterical version of the epileptic fit. Sexologists tend to forget that the principal organic location of the orgastic trigger is the brain. Orgasm begins as the equivalent of an epileptic fit, as neurophysiologists have long observed in noting how the hysterical epileptic seizure presents in the same way.

In *Dostoevsky and Parricide*, Freud draws a parallel between the epileptic fit and orgasm[2] and shows how they are linked with a parricidal wish.[3] During his childhood, Dostoevsky suffered frequent hysterical absences under the influence of a paternal seduction which, by making him wish for his father's death, had as a consequence the simulation of his own death. There is much to suggest that this 'little death' was raised to orgastic dignity by the anxiety of paternal incest. The 'fit' resulted both from guilt and from enjoyment of the fault, its spasmodicity purging this contradiction. At a first level, this hysterical epilepsy corresponded to an annulment of the father and, therefore, of the name, and since the subject must bear his name in order to be conscious, he fainted.[4] This brief loss of identity resolves the contradictions of the seduction fantasy. In this depersonalisation, consciousness fades in proportion to the murderous psychical act, which it prefers to ignore, while the positive and negative differentials of the meaning of perceptions in general are abolished.

Is such a hysterical epileptic seizure identical to the 'seizure' that ends the sexual act? This would be the case if the fantasies required in the sexual act seek their resolution through it. Neuroscientific studies corroborate such a homothety as the level of cortical excitation. The epileptic seizure is the result of equal and simultaneous excitation of neurons which, in the conscious state, are excited unevenly. This difference in level produces the flux of consciousness (like water in a river flowing downwards). Consciousness can be thought of as a movement that seeks to

DOI: 10.4324/9781003519287-9

understand a problem (at the top) by moving towards its solution (at the bottom). This current of consciousness stagnates when (for example, during sleep) there is no longer any need to respond to the demands of waking life. What causes the loss of consciousness in an epileptic seizure is not so much neuronal hyperactivity but rather, the equalling out of differences in potential between areas of the brain. A seizure may ensue when a lesion provokes hyperactivity that equalises top and bottom, leading to a loss of consciousness. But this flattening out can also occur as the opposite of what happens in consciousness. Such is the case in the other kind of epilepsy, so-called hysterical epilepsy, which can, in fact, occur in any psychical structure.[5]

Generally speaking, consciousness results from the act of a subject who, when examining a certain object (the top), discriminates the qualities of their internal or external perceptions (the bottom). But who is this conscious subject? For we must first know 'who' is conscious, i.e., what is the name of the conscious subject. The discriminated qualities relate to (denotative) drive sensations and conscious-ness orders them to the extent that the subject first bears his name (performance). From the *hapax* of the name, conscious thought is ordered in the form of an 'I think – I who call myself so-and-so [performance] – that "this is that" [denota-tion of a sensation by one of its qualities]'. If the performance does not frame the thought, the 'I think' is cancelled out in favour of an 'it thinks', as usually happens in daydreams, which are largely non-conscious. The difference in potential that is the mark of consciousness only arises from the moment when the person who thinks does so in their own name, i.e., consciously.

In a 'hysterical' epileptic seizure, some event occurs that invalidates the legiti-macy of the name of the father. As a result, the difference of potential – the slope on which conscious thought flows – is suddenly abolished. For example, a man who has some feature in common with her or his father has tried to seduce a hysteric.[6] So this seducer is no longer a father worthy of their name, and in this collapse of the father's name, the world is flattened out, provoking the seizure, which is marked by enjoyment, as shown by the blissful moment of the aura that precedes it. When the act of consciousness, as performance, is abolished, the denotation of sensations continues to function to the rhythm of a kind of equalisation of Being with the surrounding world, with 'everything'.[7] The denotation of the world creates analo-gies of colours, smells, sounds between some sensation and some quality of that sensation or between such and such a present or past association. Time is abolished, following the dynamics of an incest that precedes life. Hence, the aura: a moment of hypersensitivity where a universe of drive analogies and reminiscences shines forth in an iridescent grace that precedes the fall.

We can also speak of a moment of aura in sexual relations. The mere presence of another body, its vision, already makes our exteriority to ourselves acutely felt. Each presence is surrounded by a more or less intense aura which pulls us away from ourselves. 'More or less intense' in the sense that our body heats up to varying degrees, to the point at which we are able to forget ourselves as we look at the other person. The aura of their presence metamorphoses us, puts us outside ourselves in a state where we dream of rejoining ourselves in the foreignness of the other. This aura calls for an epileptic, orgastic resolution.

Epilepsy and orgasm are concordant[8] if the moment of depersonalisation in enjoyment also corresponds to a loss of the name of the father in favour of the man's name (which is often called out in these moments). The (epileptic) loss of consciousness corresponds to the parricide that desire involves. To give one's name at the time of this fall of the father's name is finally to possess it. This is probably why most men are so passionately taken up with their partner's pleasure that they set little store by their own. In orgasm, it is true, the loss of consciousness is only slight because the enjoyment impacts a body other than one's own. This is obvious for the man, who, in a way, enjoys through another person. But it is also true for the woman, who is caught up in the enjoyment as if it was that of another woman, with whom she can identify on the condition of love.

Does the capacity for orgasm depend on psychical structure?

Opening and closing of the orgasm

Men seem to take pride in their partners' orgasms. In any case, they often work hard to bring them about. Consciously, at least, it is rare for a man to react with anxiety when he provokes an orgasm in his partner. But he may be panicked by the indirect or implicit consequences – notably, by the call of his name and the demand for love, which can cause him to flee or even trigger an episode of madness. For women, however, even if they experience orgasm, it does not seem to be the upmost concern. Enjoyment and its conclusion are usually subsidiary to love, which is always preferred even when it offers little by way of pleasure. Women impose strict symbolic conditions on their erotism, universal precautions that stem from the risk of a loss of identity in the orgastic moment. Who is it that enjoys in this moment? The depersonalisation here may be so anxiety-provoking for some subjects that they shy away from any new erotic experience after having once experienced it.

They refuse not only the sexual dimension of their own desire, which may carry them away against their will, but also the simplest pleasures. Extreme asceticism is sometimes the last temptation because to battle against oneself, to make oneself suffer in a thousand ways, from anorexia to all kinds of physical torture, is still a temptation. For the person who follows this path, the crueller their masochism, the more they lock themselves in the clutches of the Other from whom they claim to flee. This may go so far that, from privations to drive-based auras, the subject attains mystical beatitude, experiencing the orgasms of paradise that spare the saints all commerce (at least all carnal commerce) with their fellow human beings.

These generalities about enjoyment leave an open question that needs to be addressed: is orgasm a potentiality in *all structures*, or is it reserved only for a certain psychical configuration? Which of the three – neurosis, psychosis, perversion – offers the best ground for orgasm? Neurotics, who like to think of themselves as the norm, often claim that they are the only ones to properly enjoy orgasm since they are the only truly mature subjects (or so they believe). But their inhibitions are often such that they do not reap the rewards from orgasm that they like to imagine. Most importantly, as the facts attest, it is simply false that love, orgasm and procreation are beyond the reach of psychotics. Passion drives them, whether they just suffer it or act on it, whether it saves them or ravages them (or more often both). To affirm that desire, love, sexuality and the wish to have children are absent in the psychoses is to totally ignore the lessons of the clinic and of everyday experience.

Capacity for orgasm does not depend on psychical structure or the capacity to love or a supposed genital maturity. It depends purely and simply on the resolution of sexual arousal, which is to say that it depends on the contradictions inherent to fantasy as a function of certain situations (which love sometimes prohibits). All the fantasies of neurosis exist in psychosis with the sole exception of parricide, which, therefore, seeks embodiment in various scenarios and passages to the act, especially in love life. Since parricide is the quilting point of secondary repression, fantasies in psychosis do not have the same presentation as in the neuroses, but it is easy to show their presence and that it is their presence that generates action.

The lack of the 'safety valve' which the parricide fantasy represents for the death drive shows the risk that orgasm poses in the psychoses. Parricide is equivalent to the taking of the father's name. The moment when enjoyment is triggered exteriorises the body from itself and locates it in the partner, so the lack of a firm anchor for the name results in depersonalisation. The consequences of enjoyment here are occasionally dramatic: a hallucination, then a delusional episode. This is often how adolescent schizophrenias begin at the start of sexual life. The fact that a hallucination can follow an orgasm is of great theoretical importance. On the one hand, we see the depersonalising impact of orgasm, and on the other, it offers proof (if such were needed) of the structural place that is occupied by the names of the father in sexual enjoyment.[9]

This 'foreclosure of the name of the father' results from the lack of the parricide fantasy, but it does not by any means signify a paternal absence. In psychosis, the invariants of the paternal complex are, to a certain extent, organised as in neurosis. A father is always there on a square of the chessboard of desire, stoking the fires of fantasy to the point where they risk becoming hallucinatory. Foreclosure is compatible with a paternal presence. It signifies the impossibility of symbolising the death of the father by his name. There is always at least one mythical father to be found in schizophrenia, a 'degree zero' of the paternal presence. This is a father who suffices to decide on the choice of gender, even if the choice is precarious.[10] A sexual father is incarnate and very present in paranoia. But this father never lets his child grow up (he does not let himself 'be killed') as we can observe by rereading Schreber's *Memoirs* and particularly what he calls the 'bellowing miracle', which is something like the enjoyment of copulation with a deified father.[11] Orgasm begins under the blows of the father. It could have ended with his murder. But this is precisely what the crushing authority of Schreber's real father never let him even hope for; there was no possibility that Schreber could in any way rival his father, so the former was left forever feminised. Hence, the hallucination that came to him one morning of 'how beautiful it would be to be a woman undergoing copulation' and that was followed by the delusion of his marriage with God. Finally, in melancholia, a parricide fantasy functions in relation to an incarnated father, but his murder resists symbolisation.[12]

Even when it is mythical, this paternal presence always has a sexual function in the psychoses: that of assisting the passage from 'Being the mother's phallus' to 'Having a penis or a clitoris', according to the rules of entry into organ enjoyment (as attested to, for example, by the long masturbations often found in schizophrenia). A simplification of psychoanalysis might suggest that since 'the father' forbids incest, he protects against the death drive. But this father only prohibits maternal enjoyment for as long as it takes to seduce; he saves in order to threaten in his turn, although this new violence changes the regime of enjoyment. When he comes onto the scene, the violating father also brings enjoyment, all the way to death by incest, unless his symbolic murder provides a name, which, later on, will be actualised at its internal orgastic limit. Without parricide, an indestructible paternal presence invites incest with a living father, a monster in league with the Other. Incestuous sexual enjoyment then has the effect of depersonalistion and causes the body to fall into the void of this Other.

In the second round of human sexuality, orgasm involves a terrible risk, returning the body to the edge of this hole, which it risks resembling unless passion holds it back. The enjoyment of the partner is sufficient to open the field of orgasm, but there is no guarantee that it will close it again (just as the father's grave does not close again), leaving the subject nameless, depersonalised and thus prey to the hallucination of his or her own division. Orgasm can be followed by hallucination, when the psychical body take flight and acquires a life of its own – grander, limitless, intoxicated, drugged, outside time. Hallucination represents this body from outside and delusional thoughts then seek to counter it. This moment of depersonalisation follows the failure to transmit the name which would have anchored the subject in their body.

We can be even more precise here since the name breaks down into several terms that do not have the same function in relation to enjoyment. The first name is in a way 'pre-Oedipal'. Giving it allows the subject to have the enjoyment of themselves as they are enjoyed by another, and it subjectifies a practice such as masturbation (which any subject can engage in). But even at this level, there is a necessary nuance because the first name is not always given. Some mothers do not call their child by their name, or they call him or her by other means – by insults, for example. In this case, autoerotic enjoyment is itself depersonalised, and its emergence submerges subjectivity (it may, for example, be accompanied by hallucinated insults). The first name more generally has the function of opening in relation to orgasm, whereas the surname has a function of closure.

These two functions of the name mark the entry to and exit from the orgastic moment; calling the person by their first name liberates the subjectivation of enjoyment, while the surname bounds and closes its (potentially hallucinatory) field of expansion. In the psychoses, the orgasm begins – with its depersonalising hallucinatory opening – but it does not end, leaving the subject in an infinity that a delusion may then attempt to make sense of. The hallucinatory consequence of the orgasmic opening, if it does not close, is quickly enmeshed in such delusional mazes.[13] Delusions may suddenly appear almost immediately after the experience of pleasure, often in the form of delusional jealousy directed against another woman or another man who were allegedly the real agents of the enjoyment. Everything happens as if the lightning strike of pleasure had fallen on another body, especially when the rampart of love or the whispered name are lacking. Sexual enjoyment becomes problematic when the struggle to supplant the father was unable to take place. The struggle is too unequal if the confrontation is with a purely mythical and, therefore, impregnable father.

Whatever the degree of psychosis, orgasm can occur during a sexual act. It opens but may not close, like a fall into the void: 'Father, are you there?' 'Yes!' 'But did you name me, and did I take your name?' The absence of an answer to this question leaves a yawning abyss. Autoerotism (alone or for two) will surely function, but desire meets a dramatic upper limit at the moment of orgasm. The relation of the psychoses to an excess of enjoyment that has not been dialectised by the name of the father is thus shown clearly.[14] The psychoses show the knotting of the orgasm to the parricide fantasy, and this link explains its briefly depersonalising dimension in the neuroses, as if the enjoyment happened to another, momentarily divided body.

In neurosis, each subject plays out his or her division in the field of bisexuality, transposing what opposes them to their own self into the games of seduction between men and women. In this way, the relief of anxiety is left to the good offices of a sexual relationship that is always yet to come – an ideal stitching together of subjective division and a moment when the body of psychical enjoyment will come to coincide with the organism. So sexual desire tries to cover sexual division by creating a state of temporal tension. This temporality is thus a result of sexual desire (as shown by the infinity of time, or 'out-of-time' experienced in acute moments of schizophrenia or melancholy). The division of the subject is temporarily made good thanks to desire, if the desire is sexualised – a condition without which its hallucinatory dimension becomes manifest.

In the psychoses, on the contrary, this same subjective division presents itself in sex in the form of a split between one part of the ego and another part, namely, that part which enjoys in the Other from the partner's enjoyment. This other part is situated 'outside'; it is hallucinatory and never repatriated to its body of origin. When this division of the self occurs, a chasm opens up, and the subject does not know what it represents. This rift does not close, as if an infinite orgasm had sucked everything into its wake.[15] This orgasmic opening up divides the psychical body and sends the ideal ego of the drive – the ego that always enjoys too much already and that requires constant repression – outwards. This same 'ideal ego' is also present in the neuroses but remains in harmony with the body of the lover immersed in his or her enjoyment. Psychosis unfolds as an infinity in linear time, which, in the neurotic orgasm, exists perpendicularly and triggers an infinity '*in situ*' that is vertical to the vital Eros.[16] Why in the psychoses does this exteriority of enjoyment fail to be repatriated to its body of origin? Because sexual enjoyment seeks to resolve the tensions of the fantasy, starting with that of seduction, which results from the sexual trauma of the father. In order for sexual enjoyment to be appropriated, the agent of seduction – i.e., the father – has to be removed. The orgasm always opens from the outside, but it can only close through the murder of its agent; it includes this extremity, so it gives a kind of goal to the death drive.

In certain psychoses, suicide puts an end to an endless incestuous orgasm or – what amounts to the same thing – to the hallucinatory command of an Other who enjoys unto death a body that has been reduced to being the object of insults. Suicide here aims to put an end to a life that cannot get started because, to paraphrase Nietzsche, 'one can die from being immortal'. Incest with the father is located in a time before birth and creates a certain impossibility of entering the time of one's own life so that the subject remains, as it were, behind glass, watching others go about their incomprehensible business on the other side. Only the thought of the murder of this father could close this timeless enjoyment. Such is the ever-present infinity of this opening of the orgasm, experienced in the dimension of a temporality before life.

In neurosis, the subject who is both actor and passive subject of this orgastic drama withstands enjoyment thanks to parricide. The symbolic conditions of the murderous Oedipal wish are able to set a limit to the infinite potentiality of the orgasm. The orgasm once opened can be closed again (just as a grave can be opened and closed). Though it lasts only a brief moment, the orgasm is nonetheless outside time, in an infinity that is neither in a linearity nor in a repetition but in this punctual temporal gap, allowing a glimpse of life torn asunder as a 'before-life', the unbearable vagina of origin.

Sexual love is certainly different from a psychosis since it adds a spatio-temporal closure of enjoyment. But like psychosis, it poses the question of the name, which shows its specific role at the moment of orgasm. The lesson to be learnt here is that erotism bears the burden of a certain madness since risking the legitimacy of one's identity with the dice of passion can generate an endless torment. It is not surprising, then, that sexuality in general, and enjoyment and orgasm in particular, are a constant obsession, even while provoking strong resistance. Sexual love stirs up the anxiety of a relationship tormented by the question of identity that has been left to the good offices of desire.

These issues loom too large in human life to be sidestepped. If orgasm represents a danger, it cannot always be avoided, psychosis or not; human beings must take the risk as a condition of their existence. But anxiety greatly complicates how we approach it. This is why, when it comes to erotism, many psychotic subjects prefer to use 'perverse' solutions[17] (masochism[18] or other transgressive practices), as if the perverse denial of maternal castration compensated for a lack of paternal prohibition. Various 'perverse' practices are nearly always necessary in latent psychoses. In manifest psychoses, they can become dangerous.[19]

Similarly, to achieve its ends, the erotism of psychosis often requires complex stagings that aim to replace parricide with transgression; the psychotic may, for example, need to construct scenarios between three people or make a loved woman jealous so that the guilt which is aroused can then enable sexuality to be actualised with some success.[20] Various identificatory scenarios may also seek to avoid the anxiety of orgasm. For example, an older man's psychosis can be stabilised at a certain age thanks to the love of a very young woman. The paternal signifier is thus both staged and abolished in sexuality. In one way or another, a 'murder' is always on the agenda.

In his short story *A Woman's Revenge*, Barbey d'Aurevilly describes a woman's unbridled enjoyment in these terms: 'There was something so animalistic, so fierce in it that she seemed to want to take her own life or that of the partner in her caresses'.[21] Her lover senses that he is but the agent of such transports: 'A voice from deep inside him called out to him, "It's not you she's making love to"'.[22] But the deeper truth of this common misunderstanding appears when it becomes clear that her quest for enjoyment is animated by a thirst for revenge – an insatiable vengeance that leads her straight to the madness of an orgasm that opens and never closes.

Beyond all these stratagems, the erotism of psychosis finds its most successful pathway thanks to the experience of passion.[23] No less blind than its neurotic counterpart, this 'passion' is nevertheless distinct from the love born of lack. It certainly has the same drive base, but the lack that it hollows out serves as a point of support for hallucinatory and then delusional projection. These projections (for example, in jealousy and erotomania) exteriorise features familiar from neurosis, except for the certainty that accompanies them in psychosis. What is it about love here that not only offers rescue from the abyss of psychosis but also liberates a perilous sexuality? Love re-stages the Oedipal triangle; for as long as it lasts, it establishes 'the law' over again and functions as a name of the father in many low-level psychoses. Being loved gives a name and allows closure of the orgasm that is opened up by enjoyment.

To declare one's love – as Juliet does to Romeo – is to lose even one's own name (symbol of the discord between Montagues and Capulets) in order to establish another. So love is initiated by a kind of parricide through the loss of the name. And the name of the dead father is the only 'name of the father' which by itself it is sufficient to replace. This is why love assumes such importance in the psychoses; its passion personalises depersonalisation.[24] This requirement is what distinguishes psychotic 'passion' from ordinary love. Neurotic love merely re-establishes a name that has already been taken. By contrast, psychotic passion seeks to establish through love the legitimacy of the name.

The passions of psychosis are resolved as far as possible (and despite the danger) in orgasm. It is true that this violence is liberated at less cost by the workings of the parricide fantasy; a symbolic father is always already dead, and the orgastic reiteration of his murder frees the drive from its murderous charge. So that, thanks to love, death travels from one edge of its empire to the other; it goes from maternal drive incest to its *pas de deux* around the totem, where it is blocked on its last frontier at the moment of orgasm, the extreme point of the liberation of a body finally rid of itself, but alive. The opening of the orgasm closes in a brief 'in-between' space, clinging, as it were, to the branches of love, which break its fall.

Salvador Dalí considered himself to be a paranoiac. He wanted his painting to bear witness to his hallucinatory relationship with reality. Running in a shaky equilibrium along the tightrope between his madness and his art, destabilised by stormy friendships and without the slightest erotic life beyond frenetic masturbations, he was saved overnight (as he wrote) by the love of Gala – his first partner. He seemed to sense that this encounter represented his last chance. 'I knew that I was approaching the "great trial" of my life, the trial of love',[25] he wrote. He confronted this experience abruptly and without the slightest preparation: 'Never in my life had I yet "made love"'.[26] His friends testified to his complete transformation; in one night, Dalí changed completely, and his speech became repetitions of what Gala said. He had lost and found himself, as if the event had involved a kind of identity amnesia. Such an absence – when the person who has lost themselves is still present and yet not present, suffering the harsh dispossession of love and its intoxicating alienation – comes at a price. Will a lover who no longer belongs to themself nevertheless seek to refind themself? So it was with Dalí; the transitivism of love having driven him out of himself, he then sought to eliminate this woman, whose love seemed to annihilate him. He was overwhelmed by an outpouring of bottomless aggression: 'She too had come to destroy and annihilate my solitude, and I began to overwhelm her with absolutely unjust reproaches: she prevented me from working, she insinuated herself surreptitiously into my brain, she "depersonalized" me'.[27]

Not only did Gala understand this seemingly hopeless conflict, but she resolved it by pushing it to the limit. The love of a woman accomplished much more here than an analysis could have achieved. Such, at least, was Dalí's certainty when he used the metaphor of Gradiva (dear to Freud) in order to describe Gala:

She was destined to be my Gradiva, 'she who advances', my victory, my wife. But for this she had to cure me, and she did cure me! Here now is the story of this cure, which was accomplished solely through the heterogeneous, indomitable and unfathomable power of the love of a woman, canalised with a biological clairvoyance so refined and miraculous, exceeding in depth of thought and in practical results the most ambitious outcome of psychoanalytical methods.[28]

How did Gala achieve such a dazzling result? Far from resisting Dalí's murderous aggression, she externalised it and took it upon herself and up to the hilt. By offering him as a gift the crime he would have liked to commit, she delivered him from it. 'What do you want me to do to you?' Dalí asked her one day. 'I want you to croak me',[29] she answered. By consenting to Dalí's fantasy, which she had brought to light, she saved him from it. 'Gala thus weaned me from my crime, and cured my madness. Thank you! I want to love you!'[30] Her answer may not have been the only answer possible, but it was the one that enabled him to commit to this love unto death.

She had saved him – and through him his painting – as shown by the number of his paintings that were signed 'Gala-Dalí'. This two-name signature has an exemplary dimension. The continuous orgasm of psychosis found its limit in the gift of the name, offered in this unique way by a woman, by Gala, who took on a role usually assigned to a man. She had been able to enjoy the terrible enjoyment of her Dalí, and in exchange, she had given him her name – a striking example of the name given in exchange for the orgasm, in a relationship that reverses its usual direction.

Would it be far-fetched to suggest that love saves from psychosis? Not only by offering it an anchoring point in the gift of the name but because this gift establishes a law that had not previously been legitimised. Correlatively, Dalí existed only in the presence of Gala and thanks to her. She was the 'visible woman' and he the 'invisible man', to borrow the titles of his paintings, which exemplify so well the transitivism of love and the depersonalisation of the enjoyment-bearer. The woman existed and he did not exist, unless because of her; 'Every good painter who aspires to create authentic masterpieces must before anything else marry my wife'.[31]

The link between speech and the sexual relationship

There is a secret connection between speech and sexuality. Freud's discoveries would not have brought much that was new if he had only shown that repression of sexual desire emerges from time to time in speech. In fact, desire structures the entire alchemy of speech. But what is the sexuality at stake here? The psychoanalytic clinic only illuminates a limited portion of sexual life, perhaps more inhibited or more symptomatic for its analysands than for the average population. In any case, most patients talk little or reluctantly about their erotic practices. This does not much matter because analysis is not sexology but deals with the subject's relationship to phallic signification and the name implied by speech and with the formations of the unconscious that follow from this.

From this point of view, what invariants do we find between the kind of relationship that is established by speech, on the one hand, and the sexual relationship, on the other? The answer is far from obvious. One wonders what it has to do with sex when someone says, 'Pass me the salt', or comments on a verse in the Bible or a page from Kant. And yet, however dry a statement may be, it is always the case that one person has addressed another person and has at the same time signified *something else* to him or her – 'I love you', 'I hate you', 'I find you attractive', etc. Whatever the message may be that underlies a statement, it is always present, and it means that I say something to you other than what I am talking about, and this by virtue of the torment that a body experiences as soon as it is confronted with another body.

Whenever someone speaks, this obligatory doubling of the message can be represented in space; as the sentences unfold, a fantasy unfolds. Two parallels unfold simultaneously: on the one hand, the statement of an explicit sentence, and on the other (in the same space-time), an implicit sexual fantasy. The act of speaking (whatever it says) is accompanied by an unspoken fantasmatic tension. All speech involves one of the fundamental fantasies. With the seduction fantasy or the fantasy of the beaten child, no proof is necessary; one just has to listen to people around us talking in order to be convinced that they are trying to seduce or that they are complaining. Is it not clear that every word spoken, regardless of its meaning, seeks to seduce, to complain, to display or to attack, depending on the discourse position of each speaker?[32] You only have to listen to someone speak in order to hear this simultaneity. Some of their words seek to seduce, following the mysteries of the seduction fantasy. Others are an endless lament – the exhibition of a beaten child. Still, others attack, vituperating against politicians, a boss, even God or the devil or against some scapegoat. Others, finally, ratiocinate, displace their reasons, doubt them, oppose someone to someone else, grant one thing to its opposite or make two metonymic elements copulate rather like a primal scene. The fantasy unfolds at the same time as speech – 'unconsciously', as we might say. But it would be better to say that this fantasy is 'non-conscious' rather than 'unconscious', the latter being a quality which concerns that which is repressed and can return in the gaps of consciousness: slips of the tongue, dreams, symptoms, repetitions . . . and orgasm. The fantasy is 'non-conscious' because it is the immediate concomitant of an utterance that is conscious. It sticks to it and yet we don't see it.

The parricide fantasy requires more explanation because it is profoundly implied by the act of saying 'I' in one's name. No one can say his or her name at the same time as they frame a sentence. If they thought it useful to state their identity, they would not say, for example, 'Smith thinks the weather is fine'. If they did, they would speak like a very young child, who often expresses itself in the third person. In order to abandon the 'he/she' and begin sentences by saying 'I', the name of the father must be suppressed, and this name is what is always implicit in an utterance. This grammatical twist makes desire explicit; speaking in his name implies parricide. Every act of speech that begins with 'I' represses the primary sexual trauma of a father, with whom, if the seduction had succeeded, incest would have signified death. So the grammatical structure of the simplest speech is 'sexual' from the moment it says 'I' and thereby evokes the erotism of an initial murder.

But that is not all because afterwards, words must be forged with the musicality of sounds, i.e., by repressing their drive aspect. Under the feet of the subject who, from the height of their name, thinks as fast as they can, the impersonal underworld of enjoyment opens up – that of the mother tongue – with its taste for prohibition and perdition that commemorates this moment of distancing, the unbreakable obsession of erotism. The speed of thought flees from the drive energy that precedes and pursues it – a drive energy that knows no relation, no exile, no progress, that is always already there in excess, without any past or future.

So speech is underpinned by a sexual fantasmatic tension. Men, according to a statistic, think about sex once every three minutes. The regularity of such thoughts for women is unknown. But these statistics are surely false because anyone, whenever they are thinking about it. The cause of desire pushes them into its emptiness, imposing its regime before it says what it wants. Its dissatisfaction might evoke the myth of Sisyphus, but Sisyphus knows what he is after: the fruit that slips away. The indeterminacy of the object of desire could also bring to mind the chain of signifiers, each of which calls for another in an indefinite succession. But why should thought and speech ever stop? Why do words sail out to sea in this way, if not because someone is trying to understand what they desire, a questioning that keeps thought going? The concatenation of signifiers does not cause this desire because each of them refers indefinitely to the next. On the contrary, the subject thinks because it does not know what it desires. Moreover, it always thinks about something else and, therefore, endlessly. Thought sets out on its journey without understanding what sets it in motion. It ratiocinates and invents unrelated explanations as it goes along.[33] So the subject thinks; it frames sentences, explains things to itself and tries to find itself in its ratiocinations.

But we must measure the import of the magic blow of speech; its grammar alone brings to life what its ideational content does not. As we have said, the subject assumes their name each time they complete a sentence. This name is that of their father, and this act of parricide at once stirs up the well of fantasy from which sexual arousal results. Human erotism is thus hardly 'natural' but is predicated on the flow of language, which gives it an incessant quality. The subject who desires to the extent that they speak navigates with the compass of an objectless desire. And without ever understanding what causes it, this desire sails forth following the map of the signifying metonymy that punctuates the drive energy involved in speech. So the subject of speech is identified with that of sex. If we wanted to sum it up in an image, without meaning to shock Descartes (who, after all, was in the military for quite some time), every speaking subject is in erection, admittedly more or less inhibited (for the sake of propriety): 'I have a hard-on, therefore, I am', '*Coito, ergo sum*'.[34] As soon as thought signs itself with a name, that is to say as soon as it is conscious, the cycle of sexual fantasies that underpin this thought (however ethereal) opens up at the same time. Thought presupposes the existence of some subject who, in order to appropriate their own content – i.e., to think consciously – must produce it in their name. The name is the reflexive condition for the appropriation of conscious thought. This appropriation of a name that was initially that of the father constantly underpins every thought with sexual fantasy.

In the relationship to our addressee in both speech and in the sexual relationship, a fantasmatic dimension generates a tension that seeks to be discharged and that is continually repeated. The expression 'to make love' meant 'to court with words' long before it meant the sexual act. On the other side of speech, fantasy repeats itself but without remembering what it repeats.[35] This joint deployment of the fantasy and of speech suggests the symbolic figure of the meeting of two interlocutors . . . or of two lovers since the tension of the fantasy between two bodies depends on these symbolic conditions. However, the analogy seems to stop there because this tension between two lovers can only be released by orgasm.

But perhaps the particularities of the amorous encounter reveal a permanent potentiality of speech, which was initially at the service of love and enjoyment before it began to communicate messages. Originally, there was a consubstantial relationship between vocal drive enjoyment (crying out) and the formation of sentences. The infant begins by babbling with sounds made from its cries, and words are then fashioned from the material of this vocal music. Each word is chiselled out from drive sound, and the linking of words with one another then forms sentences appropriated by maternal demand, itself oriented by phallic signification. To frame a sentence is to define a sound by another sound, uniting a noun with a qualifier. A sentence is constructed by making one word copulate with another; it makes a relation. In this way, by starting to speak, the child is no longer in the same relation with its mother; the subject displaces the drive energy in its body, translating it thanks to the drive energy of sounds to the different dimension of sentences. So talking frees the child from its identification with the phallus, and each sentence, whatever it says, therefore, carries phallic signification.

In speaking, the sonic drive enjoyment of the cry is transferred into the maze of words, each of which crystallises a particle of pleasure and carries it away. This 'particle' is the musicality of each sound, which was initially the cry, the drive energy of which was part of the enjoyment of the Other. Speech functions as the standard 'shield against excitation', defending against an excess of enjoyment because, from sonic drive material, deflected from its goal by the articulation of words with each other, it creates speech, and the meaning of this speech represses musical enjoyment. The child, through its babble, copulates with its mother rather than being copulated with. More generally, the linkage of words and the meaning of words depends on a message being addressed to someone and thus involves a form of love. This shows the relationship of vocal drive energy to the phallic signification of sentences. It is homologous to the relationship of drive energy to 'genitality'. This 'relationship' is what is always at stake in both speech and the sexual act.

But evoking the passage from the enjoyment of the Other to phallic enjoyment tells us nothing about a possible homology between the orgastic conclusion of love and the quilting point that concludes a sentence. Is there a homology between sexual orgasm and the full stop that quilts a sentence? Yes, if we notice, for example, that in certain ways of speaking, speech can unravel into multiple associations, moving forward without ever coming to a conclusion (as, for example, in schizophrenic word play or manic episodes). Similarly, certain copulations never attain their orgastic goal.

The subject's relationship to their name is implicitly at stake in the sexual relationship. Is the same not true of the act of speaking? The 'performance' of speech makes the relation to one's own name more obvious.[36] If we consider the act of speaking from the point of view of its performance rather than what it says (the denotation), we realise that in most conversations, the dimension of 'I am talking to you' counts for more than the information which is transmitted. We talk about almost anything – rain, sunshine, fashionable topics, shows, etc. – mainly in order to create links and recognition. 'I am talking to you' is implicit in every message. When a subject makes an utterance, he or she speaks in their own name, i.e., the name that they have taken from their father. So they actualise a parricide fantasy.

This act of speaking, like the sexual act, is centred on a quilting point. Whether speaking or making love, the subject is concerned with the legitimation of their name, which they have taken by force. Whoever speaks 'takes the floor',[37] as one might take another body. Modelled on the defused sonic drive, each act of speech creates an ersatz of the sexual relationship between two people, where the parricidal endpoint is like an orgasm, however diluted by the way that the drive's sonorous musicality has been damped down. Similar to what happens in sex, the disarmed enjoyment of speech inscribes a relationship between the subject and their name, legitimised by the interlocutor and the impersonal love that made the interlocutor into the addressee. In the same way, the orgastic infinite of the sexual relation is limited by the name in a way that is homothetic to the relation of the subject to language; the subject is also anchored to his or her sentences by their proper name. The sexual relationship, like speech, cannot happen without the person who is its protagonist. The name is pinned down thanks to this interlocutor who has given their name to the subject who asked them for the same legitimation. So speaking establishes between its two actors a relationship of each of them to their own self, independently of the content of their messages. As in sexual love, the address made to the other in speech enables a refinding of oneself, an affirmation of one's identity, a reconciliation of a subjectivity that was always divided between itself and some other in the field of love.

We can now see the difference between the relationship of speech and the sexual relationship. Putting it briefly, we could say that in speech the drive is repressed, whereas in sex, the drive returns. If the relationship is one and the same in the two cases, what we witness are its two different sides. Each sentence creates an equivalent of the sexual relation, albeit disarmed of its drive charge by the passage from sound to meaning. The sonic drive energy of each word is damped down as soon as it is associated with another word to signify (denote) something, and the violence of the death drive is defused by the same token. Distanced from the body, each word of an utterance ejaculates the death drive, drip by drip. It is discharged through the act of enunciation and the naming that this implies, generating aggression or love towards the interlocutor.

So the death drive is sapped along these two axes: the assumption of the name (parricide) and aggression towards a fellow-being (narcissism). In this journey towards speech, each word disarms the drive aspects of the voice; then the signification of the message damps down the violence of the demand for love; and, finally, the act of utterance puts the aggressiveness of speaking at its service. In this way, the enjoyment of speech is masked, diffused in the successive waves of what is said. Although it contains the same invariants as the sexual act, speech almost completely de-eroticises the enjoyment that animates it to the point that linguists have treated it as if it was an instrument of communication (which, by default, it becomes).

Speech seeks to establish a relationship that is as risky as the sexual act, in the anxiety of the subject's relationship to their name. This relationship concerns the interlocutor who embodies something like a 'half' of the subject in the same way as a lover can evoke that half. The person we address does not merely receive our speech; he or she gives it back to us. We discover our own thought by speaking to someone who is in the place of an 'ideal double'. In reality, our conscious speech returns to us from the place to which we speak.[38] In this sense, the person we speak to holds half of our subjectivity, which would otherwise remain unconscious. We say sometimes that an 'electric current' passes between two people. When we speak, half of what we say comes back to us from our interlocutor; we think thanks to him or her in a transference that is really the motor of speech and the effector of consciousness. This creative role of the interlocutor escapes us because once we have completed a sentence, we have the impression that we were its sole author, owing nothing to anyone, failing to realise that even this feeling of autonomy owes something to love. The presence of the other electrifies us and makes us speak,[39] suturing the division of the subject, at least when what is said is signed with a name. In this way, the enjoyment of speaking is pinned down at the end of each sentence, which, like orgasm, frees subjectivity and reconciles us with ourselves.

Numerous clinical facts – even the entire psychoanalytical clinic – confirm this displaced homothety of speech and the sexual act. Symptoms do not only have a sexual origin but they also possess in themselves a sexual meaning, to which the act of speaking can be made equivalent. Certainly, yacking has less effect than ejaculating. The first only shakes the body of our sentences to their own rhythm and does not stir the physical body to any great extent. We say that speech does not trigger an event similar to an orgasm. But can we be so sure of that? After all, there are moments in hysteria when speech provokes an epileptic seizure. Is that not an orgasmic equivalent? Epileptic seizures are certainly exceptional, but is it not the same when a symptom is formed? There are countless examples of frozen orgasms: a lady has a sudden migraine when she is about to go to bed with her partner, a man is paralysed by a cramp when he is about to do the honours with a new conquest, etc. And even without looking as far as the formation of symptoms, are witticisms and laughter not a displaced orgasm? And could sexual fantasies ever be formed without an act of speech that precedes them and then reiterates them? Once the machine is up and running, however, there seems to be a huge difference between making love and speaking. Speech simmers our fantasies for so long before erotism actualises them that their affinity is forgotten!

Notes

1 Freud [1928], *Dostoevsky and Parricide* in *Standard Edition 21*, pp. 173–194.
2 'The "epileptic reaction", as this common element may be called, is also undoubtedly at the disposal of the neurosis. [. . .] Thus the epileptic attack becomes a symptom of

hysteria and is adapted and modified by it just as it is by the normal sexual process of discharge. It is therefore quite right to distinguish between an organic and an "affective" epilepsy. [. . .] It is extremely probable that Dostoevsky's epilepsy was of the second kind' (*Ibid.*, p. 181).

3 'We have one certain starting point. We know the meaning of the first attacks from which Dostoevsky suffered in his early years, long before the incidence of the "epilepsy". These attacks had the significance of death. [. . .] They signify an identification with a dead person, either with someone who is really dead or with someone who is still alive and whom the subject wishes dead. [. . .] The attack then has the value of a punishment. One has wished another person dead, and now one *is* this other person and is dead oneself. [. . .] For a boy this other person is usually his father and the attack (which is termed hysterical) is thus a self-punishment for a death-wish against a hated father' (*Ibid.*, pp. 182–183).

4 In 1923, Freud noted the idea that epilepsy corresponds to increased motor excitability and excessive rage. He writes: 'We perceive that for purposes of discharge the instinct of destruction is habitually brought into the service of Eros' (*The Ego and the Id* in *Standard Edition 19*, p. 41). See also *Beyond the Pleasure Principle* in *Standard Edition 18*, pp. 1–84.

5 Freud finds it impossible to maintain the unity of the clinical entity 'epilepsy'. There is a similarity of symptoms 'both in the case of disturbances of cerebral activity due to severe histolytic or toxic affections, and also in the case of inadequate control over the mental economy. [. . .] Behind this dichotomy we have a glimpse of the identity of the underlying mechanism of instinctual discharge. [. . .] Nor can that mechanism stand remote from the sexual processes, which are fundamentally of toxic origin: the earliest physicians described coition as a minor epilepsy, and thus recognized in the sexual act a mitigation and adaptation of the epileptic method of discharging stimuli' (Freud, *Dostoevsky and Parricide, op. cit.*, pp. 180–181).

6 'we can trace back the fact of his extraordinary sense of guilt and of his masochistic conduct of life to a specially strong feminine component. Thus the formula for Dostoevsky is as follows: a person with a specially strong innate bisexual disposition, who can defend himself with special intensity against dependence on a specially severe father' (*ibid.*, p. 185).

7 'One thing is remarkable: in the aura of the epileptic attack, one moment of supreme bliss is experienced. This may very well be a record of the triumph and sense of liberation felt on hearing the news of the death, to be followed immediately by an all the more cruel punishment. We have divined just such a sequence of triumph and mourning, of festive joy and mourning, in the brothers of the primal horde who murdered their father, and we find it repeated in the ceremony of the totem meal' (*Ibid.*, p. 186).

8 Freud reverses the proposal of Galen, for whom coitus is comparable to a minor epileptic attack: 'If all neuroses go back to similar complexes, what then is the source of the different forms of neurosis, whose determinants must be specific? No doubt, a certain violence of the motor apparatus plays an important role in this respect. The motor components that otherwise spend their aggressive force in coition fuel the [epileptoid hysterical] attack, which is the purest equivalent of coition. This ancient saying by Galen is confirmed: intercourse is a minor epileptic attack; only we would say it the other way around' (*Minutes of the Vienna Psychoanalytic Society, Volume II, 1908–1910* (M. Nunberg, trans.). New York: International Universities Press Inc., 1967, pp. 20–21).

9 That orgasm occurs in the psychoses is a proof of the existence of desire in this structure. Desire is not a late, post-Oedipal event in subjective structuring. It follows from the infant's first hallucination, which is repressed from the outset and which animates the dream.

10 The transsexual wish is situated at the limit of this precariousness.

11 Daniel Paul Schreber, *Memoirs of My Nervous Illness* (I. Macalpine, R. Hunter, trans.). New York: New York Review of Books, 2000, pp. 189, 358; Freud, *Psycho-Analytic Notes on an Autobiographical Account of a Case of Paranoia* in *Standard Edition* 12, pp. 1–82.
12 See: Gérard Pommier, *La mélancolie. Vie et oeuvre d'Althusser*. Paris: Flammarion, 2009.
13 We could even go so far as to define manifest psychosis as an open orgasm (or a semi-orgasm, which has not been closed).
14 This is surely why most anti-hallucinatory drugs are anti-dopaminergic, dopamine being the neuro-mediator of pleasure.
15 See Jean Cournut, 'L'orgasme infini' in *L'ordinaire de la passion. Névroses du trop, névrose du vide*. Paris: PUF, 2002.
16 In the sense that it is opposed to the death drive.
17 Perverse activity operates in all structures. Perversion proper is a further structure in addition to the others.
18 See the spanking mentioned by Jean-Jacques Rousseau at the beginning of his *Confessions*.
19 They sometimes pose a problem for differential diagnosis, if a case is hard to distinguish from perversion proper.
20 See Pommier, *La Mélancolie, op. cit.*
21 Jules Barbey d'Aurevilly, *Diaboliques. Six Tales of Decadence* (R. MacKenzie, trans.). Minneapolis, MN: University of Minnesota Press, 2015, p. 237.
22 *Ibid.*, p. 238.
23 'The paradox of passion makes it appear as a pain suffered from the outside, as an unfortunate event that happens (this is the meaning of "pathos"), contrary to nature and reason, though really it is the initial condition that makes them possible. Passion imposes its harsh necessity and its logic so that subjectivity can come about, while presenting itself as the most serious threat to subjectivity' (translated from: Roland Gori, *Logique des passions*. Paris: Flammarion, 2005, p. 28).
24 A young man thought he had lost the love of his girlfriend, of whom he had had no news for several days. To the feeling that a part of himself had been torn away from him was added the idea that he would have preferred for his father to die. And on top of this obsession came the certainty that her father was responsible for her disappearance. Both fathers were present at the place of absence.
25 Salvador Dalí, *The Secret Life of Salvador Dali* (H.M. Chevalier, trans.). New York: Dial Press, 1942, p. 241.
26 *Ibid.*, p. 242.
27 *Ibid.*, p. 233.
28 *Ibid.*, p. 233.
29 *Ibid.*, p. 244. The literal meaning of the original French is 'I want you to make me die' (translator's note).
30 *Ibid.*, p. 248
31 Salvador Dali, *Fifty Secrets of Magic Craftsmanship* (H.M. Chevalier, trans.). New York: Dial Press, 1948, p. 79.
32 This fantasmatic doubling is what gives speech its specific style. Each culture has its particular way of speaking. Brazilian speech, for example, is often plaintive and inflected as an interrogative request, whereas the same language in Portugal asserts without complaint and without question, although not without stiffness. It is as if, between the masters who colonised and those who were colonised, the prevailing fantasy had changed so that the new flexions imposed on language almost make it into another idiom and each group has trouble understanding the other, even although the vocabulary remains more or less identical.
33 Thought is unrelated to an object that it does not know. There is no relation between thought and what it takes to be its cause.

34 This applies to both men and women. It perhaps explains why some women may at times try to give the impression that they are less smart than they really are, perhaps half thinking that this may have a seductive effect on men.

35 This is the oddity of repetition; it transits from passive (seduction undergone) to active (seducing, possessing a body similar to that which was once the seducer's body), but once this change of place has occurred, the repetition has already forgotten what it meant to be rid of, which it only catches sight of in a flash in the orgasm. The orgasm is this flash: a light that is too bright for it to be possible to see a past that is immediately plunged back into darkness.

36 'Performance' here in the sense of Austin's 'speech acts' (John Austin, *How to Do Things with Words*. Oxford: Oxford University Press, 1962).

37 In French, 'prend la parole', the literal meaning of which is 'takes the word' (translator's note).

38 This is the 'transference' that is at work in analytic treatment.

39 It is perhaps by following this intuition that the telephone was invented. In 1848, Antonio Meucci, an Italian-American emigrant and inventor of genius, experimented in Cuba with the use of electricity to treat various illnesses. He adjusted the strength of the current by applying electrodes to himself as well as to his patients, and on one occasion, having connected all the wires to administer treatment to a migraine sufferer and having clamped a shunt electrode on his tongue, he heard his patient talk into his (Meucci's) mouth. A few years later, Meucci invented an early version of the telephone. The incident is a fine metaphor for how speech comes back to us from others and is externalised through our own mouth!

Chapter 10

What never ends

Freud believed that 'actual neurosis' (which he also called 'sexual neurosis', or 'simple neurosis') was a cause of neurasthenia, a term that today would be included in the catch-all category of depression.[1] He initially attributed this neurosis to *coitus interruptus*, a widespread sexual practice of his time that was recommended as a means of avoiding pregnancy. A particular kind of anxiety results from this deferred pleasure, which (in most cases) would be an orgasm that had not been allowed to reach its culmination. This retention would be followed by a stasis of the libido, a lack of pressure, a 'depression' (if we insist on using this vague term). For want of a psychical orgasm, the stasis of drive power pushes the subject into a neurasthenic hole. *Coitus interruptus* shows the gap that exists between physiological discharge (as it occurs when the penis is withdrawn prior to ejaculation) and the orgastic electroshock, which, in this case, would not occur or would at any rate be diminished. This theorisation is appropriate not only to *coitus interruptus* but also to the avoidance, not of sexual intercourse but of orgasm (to the extent that orgasm is felt to be frightening and disorienting). The fantasmatic tension thus remains unassuaged, even if love, which has no need of either sex or beauty, may be present.

These few remarks suggest a distinction between several kinds of *coitus interruptus* which do not have the same consequences. If what is meant is only the manoeuvre which avoids orgasm out of anxiety, it would be better to say *orgasmus interruptus*. In this sense, such an interruption also occurs when sexual intercourse is, to outward appearance, absolutely 'normal' but is practised as masturbation until discharge, without regard for the feminine orgasm. If, on the other hand, a sexual practice remains attentive to this orgasm, making it (and not physiological discharge) the objective of the procedure, then the fantasmatic electroshock will occur; in this case, if *coitus* occurs without respect for the laws of nature, it is not so much *interruptus* as *deviatus* (displaced).

The first perspective on *coitus interruptus* in Freud's study of the actual neuroses is important for measuring the effects of avoiding orgasm. Enjoyment, which is both pleasure and an excess of pleasure, is distinguished from orgasm, which releases this contradiction. Enjoyment is characterised by a continuum which does not always lead to orgasm since orgasm can be voluntarily or involuntarily avoided.

DOI: 10.4324/9781003519287-10

242 What never ends

Some men, who hold back their own orgasm as long as possible, nevertheless enjoy their partner's orgasm. On the other hand, an orgasm can occur in a state of anxiety and without pleasure (as in premature ejaculation).

By emphasising the neurasthenic quality of 'actual neurosis', Freud focuses on only one aspect – the anxiety of going all the way to orgasm – which leaves desire unable to free itself. Yet orgasm is an intense psychical ordeal; it is both desired and feared for the risk of depersonalisation that it brings and the engagement with the name that it demands. To discharge before orgasm and as quickly as possible is, therefore, a temptation. Or even not to discharge at all, not to reach an endpoint, either physiologically or fantasmatically. In reality, and whatever the sexual practice, we can say, as a first approximation, that Freud's actual neurosis results from a failure of orgasm.[2]

Could this be an argument in favour of Wilhelm Reich, who founded an entire psychopathology, psychosomatics and sociopolitics on orgasm, which, according to him, is a natural given that has been repressed by the Oedipus complex and by society? This idea led him away from psychoanalysis and, ultimately, towards neurophysiology. In *The Function of Orgasm*,[3] Reich continued to rely on the Freudian concept of 'actual neuroses', as if the latter resulted from the frustration of a natural orgasm (whereas, in fact, orgasm depends on fantasmatic tension). Yet Freud had spelt out the place of psychoneurotic symptoms in relation to these actual neuroses (the concept of which he never renounced) in his *Introductory Lectures on Psychoanalysis* (1916): 'In such cases they play the part of the grain of sand which a mollusc coats with layers of mother-of-pearl'.

Reich then suggested that for a successful orgasm, unconscious fantasies must remain mute; 'It cannot be easily determined whether unconscious fantasy activity is also at rest. Certain factors would indicate that it is'.[4] The solution which Reich came to was that 'the elimination of the actual neurosis, the somatic core, also erodes the groundwork of the psychoneurotic superstructure'.[5] For Reich, the 'somatic core' of orgasm became a totalitarian concept, unifying theory and practice, neurosis being reduced to a disorder of genitality. 'Gradually, it became clear', he writes in *The Function of the Orgasm*, 'that it was fundamentally incorrect to try to give the experience in the sexual act a psychological interpretation'.[6] From here, it is not far to bioenergetics and the catch-all of neuroscience. This error made by Reich is nonetheless useful to put actual neurosis in perspective, foregrounding the question of what there is in desire that orgasm fails to resolve.

One might think that when orgasms are indefinitely withheld, either symptomatically or voluntarily, infantile autoeroticism has replaced them, sometimes with all kinds of justifications and without the pretext of contraception. Thus, in courtly love (*fine amor*), tantric practices, safe-sex-made-in-the-USA or even for apparently erotic reasons, some men (and some women)[7] prefer to give enjoyment rather than letting themselves go. But this is not a simple return to childhood neurosis. In 'actual neurosis', a man and a woman can be attracted to each other and love each other without their fantasies letting either or both of them go as far as the orgastic moment. Their desires are oriented differently even though love is present.

The 'making' of love shares out passive and active proportionately in the guise of masculine and feminine, resonating with the seduction fantasy. As the clinic (or ordinary experience) shows, when this proportion is not established, the difference is a ground for sexual symptoms: impotence, frigidity, premature ejaculation, etc., to which we can rightly add neurasthenia. So reflecting on actual neurosis invites us to distinguish *sexual symptoms*, of which neurasthenia and *orgasmus interruptus* form a part. The sexual symptom displaces the inscription of a relationship that cannot be proportionate. The sexual symptoms themselves realise desire; they inscribe a *displaced orgasm*. Frigidity, premature ejaculation, impotence, etc., actualise a dream of enjoyment and its punishment at one and the same time. If, for example, an active man meets an active woman, they will take great pleasure and exhaust themselves trying out positions and situations. But orgasm may not be forthcoming. Or a man who is a premature ejaculator with his tender wife will, on the contrary, accomplish feats of sexual prowess with a woman considered unattractive, mean, etc. Or again, a man who is on the side of passive seduction will remain impotent when he is with an active woman, etc. The fantasmatic ratio that conditions the culmination of enjoyment proves evasive. A symptom is created where the sexual relation fails; it remembers what went wrong. When fantasy enjoyment endures without any relief, a sexual symptom marks this gap.

Sexual symptoms that may be experienced as involuntary (cystitis, premature ejaculation, frigidity, impotence, etc.) are not 'after-effect' or 'retroactive' symptoms, as we might use that epithet to describe what is found in the neuroses. Rather, they are symptoms that can be related to actual neurosis since what is lacking here is psychical orgasm. 'Actual' means that the neurosis results from the eternity of the fantasy. The neurosis is not a retroactive effect of the infantile in the present but results from the fantasy movement alone – from a sort of '*in situ*' repetition that misses its fulfilment in its very process. The equivalents of an unfulfilled orgasm that are inscribed in sexual symptoms are displaced ciphers of the sexual relationship, echoed also in the auras of epilepsy. These symptoms are the diplopic projection of a relief that is sought but becomes enmired in its own contradictions.[8] The symptom is created by a present situation and not by the past. For example, a man is impotent with a certain woman and not with another, etc. Such symptoms of actual neurosis are consequences of the inadequacy of fantasies and are not the after-effect of a childhood trauma.[9]

Sexual symptoms – displaced ciphers of the sexual relationship – are a sort of 'freezing' of the orgasm, inhibiting drive energy. Such a coquettish definition of the symptom as a 'frozen orgasm' signifies that an enjoyment has become entangled in its prohibition, just as the 'yes' of orgasm depends on the 'no' to incest, or exogamy to endogamy. The 'freeze' denotes the endogamous regression of enjoyment to the place of the offence; a body desired as much as desiring which, as a result, is immobilised. The symptom, however, gives no pleasure but rather, pain – an excess of enjoyment gone awry, confronted with an exogamous body which it does not dare to access. Regressing then to an endogamous body, it avoids the exogamous body of the other. This suffering pays the incestuous price of endogamy and yet falls short of the hallucinatory split of orgasm. The symptom of actual neurosis is the endogamous double of the exogamous sexual orgasm. If the pain of the former pays the for the required guilt, the orgasm offers liberation from guilt but at the cost of a splitting.

'Actual' sexual symptoms represent a mismatch of the lover's fantasy to that of their beloved, a mismatch, at least, as regards the ability to go as far as the fantasies' resolution, overriding considerations of love, aesthetics, esteem, etc. Such symptoms may crystallise from the very first encounter in the form, for example, of a migraine, cramp, angina or a bout of cystitis on the following day. But they may also be triggered later on, when fantasies that had previously been workable cease to be workable. For example, when a couple has had a child, the child may draw such investment from them that fantasies, which had been active up until then, become inoperative. Or 'actual' sexual symptoms may ensue when the 'war of the sexes' is interrupted as the problems of bisexuality no longer activate desire. When the torments of bisexuality in the intimacy of a couple are suspended, this cessation of the dispute may have the 'normal' outcome of a kind of love that puts sexual desire to sleep. Such is the fate of many couples, particularly when they have had children. The family space becomes conducive to a more or less marked de-erotisation. What is the future of a love without sexual desire? It may be a neurosis, or an accommodation may be found by separating love from desire, each playing its part on different stages. But it also happens that desire for the loved one persists but cannot be acted on. In this case, it often leads to illness, without the erotism being consciously connected to the symptoms. To coin a somewhat sugary formula, it is 'the disease of happiness'.[10]

'Actual' sexual symptoms are not the result of neurosis since they are not about the superimposition of a childhood memory on a present situation. And yet to the extent that the orgastic defect can cause a regression to childhood sexuality, it acts as a sort of point of attraction for neurosis, surrounded by the traumatic offcuts of the person's history (which are, properly speaking, neurotic). This 'vacuole', this nucleus of dissatisfaction, forms a potential nucleus of the neurosis itself; it evokes the major figures of infantile lack. This past world threatens to come alive again on the pretext of an occasional reminiscence or of a new situation that could entail a regression and the formation of symptoms, just when everything was going so well. So neurosis can be given a new impetus by the dissatisfaction occasioned by actual neurosis. In this sense, any failure in erotic life can have an immediate symptomatic consequence: a migraine, a cramp, etc.

One might question the use of the term 'neurosis' in 'actual neurosis' when the latter is a state so different from 'retroactive' neurosis. But the use is justified because 'actual neurosis' highlights a feature of normal erotism which is manifest in the rhythm of fantasy as such. Orgasm reveals that which it has not been able to satisfy and which repeats indefinitely a dissatisfaction linked to enjoyment. Desire is endlessly exacerbated in this situation, even though desire may be otherwise in good working order, propelled along by fantasies that are in the best of health and travelling under full sail with no pathological flaw other than that of wanting to endure for their own sake. The enjoyment of the contradictoriness of fantasies, which is relaunched by their own resolution, is, therefore, an enjoyment of desire. Neurosis proper adds the impurities of past history to the same scenario. These leftovers of the infantile are still there, but they evaporate to a certain extent when love asserts its power in the present. As soon as its power wanes, the leftovers of the neurosis assert their rights once again, presenting credentials that may have a distant origin (when, for example, a disappointment in love is followed by anorexia, bulimia, etc.).

This application of the concept of neurosis to two apparently distinct phenomena is so well justified that Freud coined another term, that of 'mixed neurosis', to express the interactivity of the present and the infantile. Actual neurosis, which is latent in a functioning erotism, remains constantly connected to neurosis proper; the fireworks are present and ready to explode at the first opportunity in hysteria, obsessions and phobias.[11] This potential revival of neurosis forms a kind of pulsating core of the present because what does not work still always beats at the heart of what does work, lending the cadences of childhood to every moment of the adult present. On August 3, 1938, Freud wrote of this lack that is the motor of the libido from childhood onwards:

> The ultimate ground of all intellectual inhibitions and all inhibitions of work seems to be the inhibition of masturbation in childhood. But perhaps it goes deeper; perhaps it is not its inhibition by external influences but its unsatisfying nature in itself. There is always something lacking for complete discharge and satisfaction – always waiting for something that never came – and this missing part, the reaction of orgasm, manifests itself in equivalents in other spheres, in absences, outbreaks of laughing, weeping, and perhaps other ways.[12]

What went wrong a long time ago was the drama of childhood, which every later problem risks reanimating. This beating heart of the present endlessly revives desire, making it go round in circles or become more intense, pushing it towards a history that will often repeat in reverse what was its own history (the former child becomes an adolescent, who wants to become a father, etc.). The crisis moment of actual neurosis pushes towards such transitions. This expanded repetition, which can only occur at the risk of neurosis proper, is the engine of our love lives, which are living things.

There is no avoiding the conclusion that this 'vacuole', this impurity that jams the erotic machine, is none other than its very motor or rather, its detonator – the power of activity seeking to relieve itself of its passivity through repetition but not able to do so. It is enough to have changed place, from passive to active, for the risk of failure to be immediately present. A never-ending reaction orients the compass of desire towards the vacuole. This risk is inherent to human sexuality, so much so that a significant number of men and women prefer to renounce erotism sooner or later in their lives, whether permanently or in order to take a break – a psychical andropause or menopause.

In this respect, the actual neuroses invite us to question the generality of erotism. If orgastic relief itself relaunches a dissatisfaction that continues afterwards,
the actual neuroses manifest a characteristic of the usual functioning of normal,
healthy erotism, which only becomes pathological (in the sense of the neurasthenia
described by Freud) in specific circumstances. The non-pathological form of actual
neurosis is the 'madness' of a desire that nothing can satisfy, the dissatisfaction of
which risks sending us back to the starting point of neurosis proper.

Even if orgastic pleasure in sex is exchanged thanks to the body of one partner
and anchored thanks to the name of the other, a dissatisfaction remains at the heart
of love, a thorn that can certainly trigger desire but can also make it seem hopeless,
inhibit it or drive it away. How then are we to understand this 'actuality', if not as
an internal difficulty of sexual life? Even when it responds to the lover's desire, the
actualisation of fantasies remains unfulfilled – from the point of view of repetition,
on the one hand, and from the point of view of love, on the other. Love – even when
shared – takes its toll. It creates a lack that sexual satisfaction cannot fill. The lack
inherent to love precedes orgasm but also follows it because the orgasm itself is not
a union but a *separation*. This blow will always remain unrecognised, especially
when everything else seems to be going so well. It is a blow that strikes the lover
even when they are fulfilled. And this invisible punishment revives the fantasy of
the beaten child and of an excitation yet to come. This potentiality of neurosis is a
result precisely of consummation rather than of its impossibility. Consummation
relaunches a repetition. Actualised desire revives desire and seeks orgastic relief
from the contradictions of fantasy. But it depends on the sexual relation which
(anticipated in the future perfect tense) both creates and proves it. *Endlich und
Unendlich*. What can have an end is the ciphering of the sexual relation in the
symptom. What does not have an end is the type of sexual relation that forgets itself
in the orgastic moment and that then has to be created yet again.

Notes

1 Lacan noted Freud's interest in the actual neuroses but without developing the question:
   'At the origin of the actual neuroses, a problem which has been too neglected, but that
   is of great interest to us' (Lacan, *Ethics, Seminar 7* (J.-A. Miller, ed., D. Porter, trans.).
   New York: Norton, 1992, p. 41, (translation modified)).
2 'In fact, Freud's first intuition leads him to locate a particular source of anxiety in *coitus
   interruptus* where, through the very nature of the operations under way, the instrument is
   brought to light in its function, which is suddenly stripped away, of being an accompaniment to orgasm in so far as orgasm is supposed to signify a common satisfaction. [. . .]
   The subject may well be reaching ejaculation, but it's an ejaculation on the outside
   and anxiety is provoked by the side-lining of the instrument in jouissance [enjoyment].
   Subjectivity is focalized in the falling-away of the phallus' (Lacan, *Anxiety, Seminar 10*
   (J.-A. Miller, ed., A. Price, trans.). Cambridge: Polity, 2014, p. 168).
3 Wilhelm Reich [1927], *The Function of the Orgasm* (V. Carfagno, trans.). New York:
   Farrar, Straus and Giroux, 1973.
4 *Ibid.*, p. 109.
5 Wilhelm Reich, *Character Analysis*. New York: Simon & Schuster, 1972, p. 15.
6 Reich, *The Function of the Orgasm, op. cit.*, p. 131.

 7 'The theory of orgasm as Reich expressed it from the beginning of his work has tended and still tends to erase the Freudian scandal: the discovery of infantile sexuality' (Janine Chasseguet-Smirgel, 'La théorie de l'orgasme chez Freud' in *Revue française de psychanalyse*, no. 4 (L'orgasme, 1977): 640–641).

 8 They might be called 'actual symptoms'.

 9 Freud writes of the actual neuroses that 'their symptoms, unlike psychoneurotic ones, cannot be analysed. That is to say, the constipation, headaches and fatigue of the so-called neurasthenic do not admit of being traced back historically or symbolically to operative experiences and cannot be understood as substitutes for sexual satisfaction or as compromises between opposing instinctual impulses, as is the case with psycho-neurotic symptoms' (Freud [1912], *Contributions to a Discussion on Masturbation* in *Standard Edition 12*, p. 249).

10 Going against this model, there are the 'abnormal' cases of people who can continue to profit from this situation by bringing their desire back to the crisis state.

11 Freud writes, for example: 'A noteworthy relation between the symptoms of the "actual neuroses" and of the psychoneuroses makes a further important contribution to our knowledge of the formation of symptoms in the latter. For a symptom of an "actual" neurosis is often the nucleus and first stage of a psychoneurotic symptom' (Freud [1916–1917], *Introductory Lectures on Psycho-Analysis* in *Standard Edition 16*, p. 390).

12 Freud [1941, 1938], *Findings, Ideas, Problems* in *Standard Edition 23*, p. 300.

Chapter 11

In search of the Sovereign Good

Orgasm is a kind of Sovereign Good because it re-establishes the name, without which the appropriation of any other good is problematic. So it constitutes a keystone of subjectivity in the same way as the name itself. But its advent presupposes an immeasurable gift on the part of the woman – all the more immeasurable in not being obvious. It immediately entails a claim on her part – the demand for a 'counter-gift' that could symbolise it. The importance of such symmetries in the relations between men and women can be seen in all societies, but they seem to be relegated to the sphere of private life. What is less visible is how they organise exchanges far beyond what binds a man and a woman. This social function of the symbols of the Sovereign Good remains clear in certain so-called 'primitive' societies, where symbols circulate which, without being comparable to currencies, are invested with a high value. Anthropologists have shown that certain gifts of precious objects seal alliances between clans and require counter-gifts, although they serve no practical purpose and are not marketable. This circulation of objects, which never enters directly into commercial exchange, forms circuits that are parallel to commercial exchange. In fact, they may well have preceded commercial exchange. Wouldn't alliances on the basis of symbols of enjoyment have had to be made before trade, as we understand it, could emerge? The circulation of symbols concerning sexual life must have preceded other exchanges.

When symbols of enjoyment form a social bond

In some cultures, these symbols are gendered, male or female, which is not the case for financial currency. George Turner, for example, studied practices similar to the *potlatch* among the Polynesian tribes of Samoa,[1] involving the exchange of masculine and feminine gifts. Some of these prestigious and prized ornaments were originally intended for women.

More specifically, Bronislaw Malinowski described the *kula* ceremonies in the Trobriand Islands, which involved the exchange of gifts (*vaygu'a*) of two types: necklaces (*sulava*) intended only for women and bracelets worn by both sexes (*mwali*). Malinowski writes:

DOI: 10.4324/9781003519287-11

It [the *Kula*] only consists of an exchange, interminably repeated, of two articles intended for ornamentation, but not even used for that to any extent. Yet this simple action – this passing from hand to hand of two meaningless and quite useless objects – has somehow succeeded in becoming the foundation of a big inter-tribal institution, in being associated with ever so many other activities.[2]

Malinowski writes that men and not women preside over these ceremonies, so we may wonder why the symbols, which they exchange, are not purely and simply symbols of virility or even why they have a sexual reference at all. But these special, purely male ceremonies involve symbols of both genders, with an assumption of 'the smaller value of the female principle'.[3] The sexual meaning of this circulation of offerings is undeniable: 'When two of the opposite valuables in the *kula* are exchanged, it is said that these two have married. The armshells are conceived as a female principle, and the necklaces as the male'.[4] The circulation starts from a first gift, *vaga* (opening gift), which commits the person who receives it to make another gift in return, *kudu*, translated by Malinowski as 'the clinching gift', but the polysemy of meaning is wider: 'Kudu means "tooth", and is a good name for a gift which clinches or bites'.[5] These practices of the *kula* are part of broad circuits of exchange, gifts and obligatory trade that pervade the entire economic and ethical life of the Trobriand Islands.

The key to the system lies in the 'opening gift', an ornament of primarily aesthetic value, which, again, is gendered.[6] These prestigious ornaments are hoarded and are not used for trade. When they cease to circulate, the offerings testify to the authority and prestige of their keepers. They become 'prestige goods', testifying that the word of their guardian has been successfully upheld many times and may be upheld again. The weight of speech and, therefore, the authority of the name that utters it increases as the precious objects accumulate.

The *kula* system of exchange is based on a circular movement between the islands. The *mwali* items, which are bisexual, travel from west to east and the *sulava* items (feminine) from east to west. Their 'gender' determines their direction of travel. The opposite directions of travel seem to indicate a heterogeneity linked to sexuality, and the circulation of the one type conditions that of the other. The circulation of these ornaments must not be interrupted, and it is inappropriate to hoard them for too long. Only privileged partners can retain them for a time, provided that they live on the route along which the necklaces or bracelets are passed. Their possession is at once a temporary property, a pledge, a lease, a fideicommissum, 'implying a novel type of ownership, temporary, intermittent, and cumulative'.[7] It is imperative that these gifts be passed on to a third party, a 'distant partner' (*muri muri*). It is because each owner has to part with the precious item that the *kula* practice is equivalent to the *potlatch*.[8] These objects have a value like money, although they are not money. What makes them akin to money is only their highly ritualised circulation and they have a feature – intense personalisation – the absence of which is definitive of money. Each of the *kula* objects has its own name and story. Some people even borrow the names of the objects, and they consider their temporary possession as a comfort that offers relief and healing. But these living symbols must move on to their next owner. Their temporary possessor must part with them, always continuing to give and receive.

From family symbols to society-building symbols

It happens that major discoveries sometimes attract criticism that merely serves to reinforce them. Such was and is the case of psychoanalysis, and it is interesting to note that Malinowski's studies were used to buttress anti-Freudian speculations, casting doubt on the universality of the Oedipus complex.[9] The *kula* gave too much privilege to men. Several Trobriand customs that were studied after Malinowski's observations involved an obligation to give based on sexual premises but ones that were specifically female. This referred primarily to the distribution of food. A man does not harvest yams – the staple food in the Trobriand Islands – for his own family but must give them to his sister's family (children belong to the mother's clan and are under the authority of their maternal uncle). When a woman marries, her family undertakes to feed the couple, and a brother (real or classificatory, a cousin, for example) offers his crop to them. The husband does the same for his sister, etc. So an obligation to give sets in motion a circulation which is itself the result of a sexual linkage. The propagation through women of gifts that are not market exchanges (in the parity sense) is based on marriage, which involves sexual enjoyment before it involves procreation.

A study by Annette Weiner[10] shows an even more active role played by women in Trobriand rituals, and she argued that the discovery of a female counterpart of the *kula* cast doubt on Malinowski's deductions. She noted that the same wives who feed their own families using their brothers' crops are responsible for organising the funeral rites that accompany a deceased man to his final resting place. They have to distribute special items: skirts or banana tree leaves, which are precious symbols of fertility, although they have no commercial value. In addition to their role in the funeral rites, these female ceremonial goods are exhibited and offered at special occasions in social life. According to Weiner, the set of services and protocols associated with them represent a counterpart to the *kula* system among men.

However, far from contradicting Malinowski's observations, these customs demonstrate a return to the origin of value (women's adornments at key moments of funeral rites), as there is an important difference between the (male) *kula* and its female counterpart. The latter is limited to the family space or, at most, to the endogamous clan of matrilineal filiations. The *kula*, however, is patently exogamous; its procedures encompass vast inter-clan geographical spaces, and its rituals are the prerequisite for multiple activities. The evidence suggests that the endogamous feminine counterpart, based on ornaments given to women and funeral offerings, was only the preliminary of the *kula*. The female rituals remain in the family (at the time of a wedding and at the time of the homage paid to the dead). They are, in a way, relayed by the symbols of exogamous exchanges in the rites of the *kula*, which then become only masculine. Between the endogamous and exogamous spaces, the crux is the gendered nature of the 'opening gift' (a feminine symbol), which serves as a sort of valve (a first passage) between these two spaces. There is a necessity to exit from the family starting from the opening gift (female jewellery). The sexual nature of the opening gift is then displaced onto the seemingly non-sexual scene of men's relationship with each other. What is the magic of the opening gift if not the sexual power of its primary female aura?

The foundational meaning of the gift made to women

We could pause this description of the data discussed by anthropologists to recall the meaning of the gift made to a woman. As we already discussed, it might appear that once the sexual act has been consummated, the man and the woman who have enjoyed it equally would have no further claims on each other. But this is not correct; the woman asks for something more.[11] A mismatch unbalances the exchange – a 'surplus value' reflected in the form of a supernumerary female demand which may be for presence, marriage, a name, a gift, money, a child or an outing but basically something more and occasionally something manifestly impossible. A woman demands a gift because she gives herself and, therefore, loses herself, and nothing will ever be valuable enough to compensate for this loss. The relation between the man's sexual satisfaction and the woman's enjoyment seems inequitable. There is a disparity here which calls for a supplementary value. Such is the ever-excessive character of the orgasm that makes its gift the only true gift, to which no 'counter-gift' can do justice, except through the trust granted to its symbol. No kind of payment can compensate for this debt, although it may well be claimed.

This sometimes inextinguishable claim, exacerbated by what was meant to quench it, precedes what is actually claimed, and it is this 'nothing' that is materialised in jewellery, a garment, an aesthetic object, a fetish, the name, a child, etc. This investment of a 'nothing' gives a symbolic dimension to what is given. A thing (res) gives form to this 'nothing'.[12] So gifts are really ornaments of nothingness, and this is the secret of what makes them so precious and distinct from other expensive objects. A jewel that is gifted leaves the commercial realm, and it sparkles with the singularity of the name; a certain person has offered a jewel that is now unique.

Linguistic note on the nature of the true gift

In his article 'Gift and Exchange in the Indo-European Vocabulary',[13] the linguist Émile Benveniste noted that the syllable 'do', the root of the French verb 'donner' ('to give'), is employed by most Indo-European languages in the same web of meanings around the concept of gifts and giving. Ancient Greek had five distinct terms to render what we translate today as 'donation' or 'gift'. Most of these five words are symmetrical with counter-gifts; they entail compensations and, therefore, do not fall within the scope of a gift given with no expectation of recompense.

But there are some exceptions where the same root means not only 'give' but also its opposite, 'take'.[14] The same peculiarity exists in the Antipodes; in Fiji, teeth of the sperm whale are used as a currency called 'tambua', and each tooth is completed by a stone called 'mother of the tooth'. The ensemble is treated with affection, similarly to how a girl treats a doll, and it has two implications: to present the tambua is implicitly to make a request, and to accept them is also to commit oneself.[15] So they index both gift and counter-gift; the giver receives something when they give, even if nothing is actually given in return. When used in commercial exchanges, the tambua continues to carry this double meaning; the same word means both buying and selling, both lending and borrowing.

The conjunction of 'take' and 'give' has a particular meaning when erotism is concerned. Who takes and who gives the phallus? A woman gives the phallus to a man when she is desired by him since she provokes his erection. She takes what she gives, which is, in a way, her property. This dual aspect of the gift appears in the subjective or objective genitive of desire; when we use the expression 'the desire of so-and-so' to describe a desiring relationship between man a woman, there is ambiguity as to who is desirer and who desired. Far from being a linguistic exception, this form of giving, which is also a way of taking, delimits what is at stake in a sexual relationship.

As we noted earlier, what is given in orgasm corresponds to an inextinguishable debt – to damages [dommage] linked to the enjoyment of the giving of oneself. These damages stretch way back; they originate in the young child's fantasy of seduction by the father, to which the child cannot submit without falling victim to death by incest. This conflict gives rise to a parricide wish proportional to the father's desire. Damages, like that of the sexual trauma of childhood, are reproduced precisely as they are compensated for in symptoms and then in orgasm. In this sense, the Indo-European root of the gift, 'do', has the same etymology as 'dommage'[16] (found in the Latin 'damnum'). The dommage of sexual trauma is consubstantial with sexual enjoyment, which imposes a gratuitous gift since nothing can compensate for it in equal measure. The disparity of sexual trauma beats at the heart of erotism and generates an emptiness, the product of the contradiction between the damages and their enjoyment. How is enjoyment to be symbolised? Can it be done by gold, by ornaments offered to women, by the name, by the conception of a child? However significant such gifts may be, the damages that this same enjoyment entail will never be covered over. The creation of fiduciary values is always unequal to the absolute value that was initially claimed by the woman as compensation for an enjoyment from which she perhaps draws advantage but which has also wronged her.

How the gratuitous gift becomes fetishised in relations between men

A gift has been made to a woman, echoing the priceless enjoyment which she gives. Its aura originates in this gift, which symbolises orgasm. The specificity of a gift made by a man to a woman – a sulava jewel (a 'clinching gift'), for example – symbolises the depersonalising gift made by a woman to a man (her orgasm). The man offers his gift, as the other side of the orgasm (the 'opening gift'). This gift then enters a circuit of forced exchange because – between men – it is always unequal to its function. We could suppose that the same issue is at stake when it is men who give each other such gifts. The men put their femininity into play in a sacrificial ceremony that saves them from going to war. The bisexuality of men is the 'valve' that enables communication between the private exchange of male-female sexual relations and generalised exchanges between men. What was at first a jewel offered to a woman subsequently circulates between men in search of its own value, a journey that is certainly longer than a destruction – an infinite journey.

In alliances between men, the overwhelming moment of orgasm is not replaced by a ceremony as obvious as the *potlatch* but by the obligation to part with the given object. So the function of alliance is combined with that of a separation rather than a destruction, a separation which, moreover, leads to an extension from one person to another of the social bond established thanks to the symbolisation of a sexual relationship and the mutual recognition that each gift-giving ceremony implies. In a nutshell, the opening gift has the same value on the male side as a sexual relation, the orgasm being mimicked by a destruction. By virtue of this opening gift, the circulation of a symbol, which still carries its feminine character, plays the same role as a *potlatch* or, indeed, as a war because war is inevitable in a relationship between men when they deny their femininity in order to be men.

In the sexual relationship of woman to man, the gift of oneself is certainly incommensurable with a gift that would claim to reciprocate. In the relationship between men, on the other hand, and even more so when they are struggling against their feminisation, the gift calls for a counter-gift, an equivalence that would cancel out this potential feminisation, a neutralisation that is never better implemented than through the abstraction of money. Nevertheless, if we consider orgasm as the Sovereign Good, it remains the implicit model of these exchanges (just as gold remains the standard for money). Strengthened by the trust established by alliances, an asexual currency of exchange takes over from the first sexual jewels, opening the way to monetary equivalents, and so moving, as it were, from an erotic meaning to desexualised exchanges. In ordinary trade, gifts are annulled by counter-gifts in the movement of exchange, not without a constant process of inflation, a pale reflection of the incommensurability that remains the latent motor of this process.

The desacralisation of the original jewel – i.e., the repression of its orgastic aura into gold – continues in the commercial universe, which, by dint of exchange, loses its original erotic resonance. At this second level – the trade of useful objects – parity exchanges completely abolish any notion of a gratuitous gift. Supposedly without any 'scent', money certainly no longer retains any of the value characteristics of the Sovereign Good.[17]

An infinite but circular journey

Malinowski could not find anything in common law or in novels that would illustrate the practice of offerings or explain the necessity of the circulation of objects. But does their obligatory movement not arise simply from a necessity that is internal to the offering? If it initially symbolises an overwhelming enjoyment (the orgasm), it must, therefore, circulate (or be destroyed). To the extent that men cannot achieve in their exchanges what the object was meant to symbolise (sexual relations), it will be passed on to another who will then do the same. The relative feminisation of every man, his bisexuality (*mwali*), must travel, while at the same time being measured by the yardstick of the Sovereign Good.

The adornment intended for a woman served to seal alliances between men. The jewel diverts an enjoyment towards the circuits of exchange; it acts as fiduciary against its original sexual meaning, just as the 'masculine' (or rather bisexual) offerings travel around the Trobriand Islands in a contrary direction to the 'feminine' offerings. A masculine-feminine relationship, a kind of contrary enmeshment, keeps exchanges moving in search of symbolisation. Ornaments, the fetishism of which denies castration, are first given to women and form the matrix of value. By exchanging them, men engage in a struggle against their mutual feminisation, a competition to not be 'the woman'. Their violence, whether warlike, sacrificial or commercial, is prolonged in proportion to an impossible orgasm. When they avoid destruction, they exchange the symbols of the enjoyment they repress. If the offerings preliminary to the recognition of an alliance and, then of trade, derive their fiduciary (trust) value from ornaments – fetishes – which served initially as jewels for women, it is thanks to these adornments of castration that trust is placed in commodity prices. Still today, gold, the most useless standard of all, dreams of its orgastic filiation in the coffers of central banks.

So from fetish to fiduciary, money no longer has any scent – not that of embraces nor that of the effort made by a man to lose himself in making in order to ultimately refind himself. By anxiety, deception, betrayal, the sons divert a Sovereign Good from its sexual meaning, and multiple goods are born and proliferate from this duplicity.

The incommensurable symbol of orgasm in its exchange between men

Why is the Sovereign Good, and then its symbol, degraded to the level of commercial circuits? The Sovereign Good, born of sexual relations, seems to be strictly private: why should it serve as the secret standard of money, which is a public thing? We could certainly conjecture that the repression of homosexuality will make the symbol of orgasm into the displaced standard of exchange. But homosexuality is not always repressed, even if its warlike consequences are universal; in a society of men (even homosexuals), violence decides who is on the masculine side and who is on the feminine side. We could argue that war, the gift or the *potlatch* symbolise this confrontation. But this hypothesis is insufficient to explain the forced circulation of symbols, which is not located at the moment of a sacrificial ceremony but exerts a constant pressure on us.

We should recognise here that the symbol of enjoyment evokes the question of the name and the identity of each subject and brings it into focus at every moment of the day as a condition of any of the subject's thoughts and actions. Whoever enjoys gives themselves, even when they are content merely to think of such enjoyment; they risk losing themselves and need the name to anchor themselves and the acts and works which they sign. The name, on which mutual recognition in society depends, is invoked at the most extreme moment of enjoyment. So the social bond itself is invoked at the very heart of what is most intimate. At the same time, this subject who assumes their name fulfils a fantasy of parricide, which once again places them in a relationship of debt. And how will the subject pay for this guilt if not in a currency legitimised in the second degree by the Sovereign Good? The subject who has assumed their name falls into the world of guilt and debt and begins the interminable pursuit of its payment. A forced hierarchy is thus established, which is transferred from the Sovereign Good (the private orgasm) to the circulation of goods (in the social, public bond).

This is how the name and the circulation of the symbol are soldered together. It is striking that some of the Trobriand gifts of jewellery that are passed from hand to hand bear a name which their temporary owners can borrow. So if the writing of the sexual relationship is the proper name, legitimised in lovemaking, the gift that symbolises the orgastic gift also bears a name.[18]

Fortified with a name legitimised by love, men nonetheless reject the feminine, i.e., their own castration. They do so even when they have the jewel at their disposal, using it in a way opposed to its immeasurable value, in a trade that they maintain between themselves. So in the denial of castration (i.e., in perversion), they divert the jewel from its primary erotic function. Is it not on this account that a fetishised value, a fetishism of the commodity, dominates the circuits of exchange between men? We can ask this question when reading Malinowski and Mauss, provided that we turn our attention to a gift that really is a gift – namely, to what is at stake in the sexual relationship. If what is at stake there claims its symbol, it will generate a series of consequences:

The psychical conflict internal to fantasy seeks its solution in orgasm. This psychical fact is incommensurable and has no counterpoint.

The orgasm depersonalises and yet demands an identificatory counterpoint (the name, the totem) at the same time as the loss of value seeks compensation (fetishes). This loss governs the gift economy – that of a symbol, which is always unequal to its object and which, therefore, always keep going.

The gifts given to women, starting with jewellery, gold and fetishes, symbolise this Sovereign Good.

Gifts circulate similarly between men on this model and on the basis of a latent feminisation, but because feminisation is repressed, they are either destroyed (*potlatch*) or the egalitarianism of parity exchanges obscures their 'surplus value'. The goods of the commodity relationship circulate in a direction opposite to the sexual relationship that is repressed in this exchange.

This is exemplified in the societies of the Trobriand Islands; gifts that have been made to women circulate in one direction, while those given to men circulate in the other. One particular good cannot be exchanged, namely, that which can be obtained on occasion in sexual enjoyment. Given unwillingly or perhaps given in abandonment, it is the only 'free' gift but one that nonetheless also seeks its counterpoint, its symbol that will always be unequal to the original Sovereign Good. It is the vertigo of a relationship in search of its inscription, forgotten as soon as it is traced.

Notes

1　George Turner [1884], *Samoa. A Hundred Years Ago and Long Before*. Suva: University of the South Pacific, 1989, p. 52.
2　Bronislaw Malinowski, *Argonauts of the Western Pacific*. London: Routledge, 1922, p. 86.
3　*Ibid.*, p. 356.
4　*Ibid.*
5　*Ibid.*
6　See: Marcel Mauss [1925], 'Essay on the Gift' in *The Gift* (J. Guyer, trans.). Chicago: Hau Books, 2016, p. 98.
7　*Ibid.*, p. 514.
8　The analogy between the potlatch and the Trobriand gift ceremony is clear from the fact that, in the latter, one must part with what has been given. The homothety appears in this separation, which at the same time underscores the role of sacrifice in social bonds.
9　The children of the Trobriand Islands are not raised by their father but by their uncle, their mother's brother, who exercises the equivalent of paternal power. But what this shows is that the father is not a person but a complex of functions. In the Trobriand Islands, the father-educator is embodied by the uncle, while the father as progenitor is excluded from this role; he is always already dead, as is required by another paternal function. This seems at first sight to be quite foreign to our own culture, but perhaps it is not. Consider a play as prestigious as *Hamlet*, whose hero is raised by his uncle, murderer in his place (and following Hamlet's own desire) of a father reduced to the role of a ghost! So the criticism of Freud based on Malinowski's work is unjust.
10　Annette Weiner, *Women of Value, Men of Renown: New Perspectives in Trobriand Exchange*. Austin, TX: University of Texas, 1976.
11　She does so even if she may appear to have received the best she could have hoped for and when her pleasure is considered the more important.
12　French 'rien' ('nothing') derives from Latin 'res' ('thing') (translator's note).
13　Émile Benveniste, *Problems in General Linguistics* (M.E. Meek, trans.). Coral Gables, FL: University of Miami Press, 1971, pp. 271–280.
14　This is also the case for other verbs concerning exchange, such as 'buy' and 'sell' in Germanic languages ('kaufen') or 'lend' and 'borrow', which also have the same root.
15　Mauss, *op. cit.*, pp. 105–106.
16　French for 'damage', 'detriment' (translator's note).
17　And yet money conveys, albeit invisibly, a certain spirit of value, which is always in some way personalised, since whoever produces a good puts his or her soul into it, a part of themselves that personalises the objects more or less visibly, all the way to their monetary abstraction. Every object, however far its meanings extend, is somehow invested with the *mana* of its maker.
18　Similarly, although only as a remarkable exception, Maurice Leenhardt has observed 'that often its name [the name of the coin] is given to the girl as a proper name, but not necessarily to the elder daughter' (translated from: Maurice Leenhardt [1930], *Notes d'ethnologie néo-calédonienne*. Paris: Institut de l'ethnologie, 1980, p. 48).

Index

For Product Safety Concerns and Information please contact our EU
representative GPSR@taylorandfrancis.com
Taylor & Francis Verlag GmbH, Kaufingerstraße 24, 80331 München, Germany

www.ingramcontent.com/pod-product-compliance
Lightning Source LLC
Chambersburg PA
CBHW050634280326
41932CB00015B/2645

* 9 7 8 1 0 3 2 8 5 6 5 8 2 *